REASSESSING THREATS TO CANADA'S NATIONAL SECURITY

In *Stand on Guard*, Stephanie Carvin sets out to explain the range of activities considered national security threats by Canadian security services today. As new forms of terrorism and extremism appear, especially online, we need a responsibly widened view of such threats and how they manifest in the contemporary world. Canadians should not be more fearful, Carvin explains, but a more sophisticated understanding among security services personnel and the general public is needed if we are to anticipate and ameliorate threats to national security.

As a former security analyst tasked with providing threat assessments to high levels of government, Carvin writes with both authority and urgency. Her book presents an insider's look at the issues facing the Canadian security and intelligence community. Timely and accessible, *Stand on Guard* will be required reading for scholars, practitioners, and any Canadian concerned about national security in the twenty-first century.

STEPHANIE CARVIN is an associate professor at the Norman Paterson School of International Affairs at Carleton University in Ottawa.

THE MUNK SERIES ON GLOBAL AFFAIRS

Books in the Munk Series explore issues that transcend borders and are critical to understanding contemporary global affairs. Their concise narratives will appeal to anyone seeking an informed perspective and a deeper understanding of the world.

Published to date:

Innovating for the Global South: Towards an Inclusive Innovation Agenda / Edited by Dilip Soman, Janice Gross Stein, and Joseph Wong (2014)

Making a Global City: How One Toronto School Embraced Diversity / By Robert Vipond (2017)

Quebec in a Global Light: Reaching for the Common Ground / By Robert Calderisi (2019)

Making and Remaking the Balkans: Nations and States since 1878 / By Robert C. Austin (2019)

Stand on Guard: Reassessing Threats to Canada's National Security / By Stephanie Carvin (2021)

STAND ON GUARD

REASSESSING THREATS TO CANADA'S NATIONAL SECURITY

STEPHANIE CARVIN

UNIVERSITY OF TORONTO PRESS
Toronto Buffalo London

© University of Toronto Press 2021
Toronto Buffalo London
utorontopress.com
Printed in Canada

ISBN 978-1-4875-0672-8 (cloth)   ISBN 978-1-4875-3472-1 (PDF)
ISBN 978-1-4875-2451-7 (paper)   ISBN 978-1-4875-3473-8 (EPUB)

Munk Series on Global Affairs

Library and Archives Canada Cataloguing in Publication

Title: Stand on guard : reassessing threats to Canada's national security / Stephanie Carvin
Names: Carvin, Stephanie, 1978– author.
Series: Munk series on global affairs.
Description: Series statement: The Munk series on global affairs | Includes bibliographical references and index.
Identifiers: Canadiana (print) 20200345362 | Canadiana (ebook) 20200345400 | ISBN 9781487506728 (cloth) | ISBN 9781487524517 (paper) | ISBN 9781487534721 (PDF) | ISBN 9781487534738 (EPUB)
Subjects: LCSH: National security – Canada.
Classification: LCC UA600 .C375 2021 | DDC 355/.033071 – dc23

University of Toronto Press acknowledges the financial assistance to its publishing program of the Canada Council for the Arts and the Ontario Arts Council, an agency of the Government of Ontario.

   Canada Council   Conseil des Arts
                      for the Arts   du Canada

Funded by the   Financé par le
Government   gouvernement | Canadä
of Canada   du Canada

Contents

Preface vii

Acknowledgments xvii

Introduction 3

1 Violent Extremism: The Canadian Context 17

2 Violent Extremist Threats in Canada Today 55

3 Espionage 87

4 The Economy and National Security 115

5 Cybersecurity 147

6 Clandestine Foreign Influence 183

7 Disinformation and Threats to Democratic Institutions 221

Conclusion 261

Appendix: The Canadian National Security and Intelligence Community 281

Notes 289

Select Bibliography 375

Index 385

Preface

When I began researching for this book in the fall of 2016, I could not have envisioned that I would finish editing it in the spring of 2021, in my fourth week of lockdown as a pandemic ravaged the world. My intention has always been to write a book that explained to Canadians many of the national security threats they heard about in the news. Today, however, the COVID-19 pandemic will have a more far-reaching impact on the lives of everyday Canadians than any of the threats in this book.

This reality raises interesting questions: Have we paid too much attention to threats such as violent extremism in recent years at the expense of preparing for events like pandemics? Should pandemics be considered a national security threat? If pandemics have such a great impact on society, was the failure to prepare an intelligence failure? Might the same be said for issues such as climate change?

Before answering, I think it is important to state my position clearly: pandemics are not national security threats – they are public health emergencies with national security elements in them. We are not at "war" with the pandemic.[1] We have developed public health models to deal with pandemics and disasters, and although emergency laws may be necessary to cope with the strain on our health systems, a war/security framework is unhelpful. For years scholars have warned about the pitfalls of approaches that "securitize" pandemics (such as AIDS) that have stigmatized victims and, in some cases, justified human rights violations or "biosurveillance" that disproportionately targets marginalized persons.[2]

There is no "enemy," there will be no ceasefire or peace agreement. This is not politics by other means – it is saving lives for their own sake.

However, just because the pandemic is not a national security threat does not mean there is an absence of national security issues *in* the pandemic. Indeed, almost all the threats discussed in this book (violent extremism, cyberattacks, and foreign influence operations) have, unfortunately, been part of the global reaction to COVID-19. A quick survey of the national security-related events of March–April 2020 reveals the extent to which governments and national security agencies have quickly had to adjust to a new normal.

Violent extremism: While a pandemic can disrupt the plans of violent extremist groups, in other cases it may simply change the target of an attack. Within a month of the pandemic taking hold in North America, there were two serious terrorist incidents in the United States by individuals espousing rhetoric consistent with far-right extremism. First, in March 2020 a man was shot and killed as the FBI attempted to arrest him for reportedly planning to attack a hospital treating COVID-19 patients in Kansas City, Missouri. Later that month, a man believing a conspiracy theory about the pandemic being cover for a U.S. government takeover crashed the train he was driving near a medical ship in California. Media reporting indicates that the man did so to "wake people up" to the conspiracy he saw in his mind.[3] Moreover, while much of the talk between extremists online may not amount to more than "chatter" or perverse fantasy, there have been concerns that violent extremists may be using the global pandemic to encourage each other to mobilize.[4]

Within Canada, there have been a series of hate crimes linked to COVID-19, with an individual calling a restaurant and threatening to kill all Chinese people and a second incident involving a threat to visit Indigenous persons with a view to spreading the virus to them. While police in Alberta have said there is no information to connect the attacks to far-right or extremist groups in Canada, threats of this nature are consistent with far-right extremist ideas. A 2021 report to Vancouver's police board indicated that hate crimes in the city were up 97% and anti-Asian hate crimes increased by 717% in 2020.[5]

Cyber-threats and espionage: Another major area of threat-related activity is a significant increase in cyber-threats to Canadian institutions and individuals as a result of COVID-19. In the first instance, criminals have tried to take advantage of the understandable panic about the pandemic to create malware and ransomware, often delivered through malicious apps, "drive-by-downloads" on websites, bad links, or infected attachments. Individuals working from home are without tech support and are, therefore, easier targets. Disturbingly, reports indicate that many of these cyber-criminals are increasingly targeting hospitals, already under great stress from a surge of COVID-19 patients, with ransomware – attempting to lock up electronic health systems at a time they are needed most.[6]

There are also indicators that some threat actors may be trying to target national and international institutions. The U.S. Department of Homeland Security (DHS) was targeted by a distributed denial of service (DDos) attack[7] by an unknown actor (although very little disruption is said to have occurred).[8] Similarly, in March 2020 it was reported that the World Health Organization (WHO) saw a surge of cyberattacks.[9] This is an unfortunate and needless distraction at a time when the WHO is expected to be coordinating the global response to the pandemic.

It is also possible that hostile state actors may be working towards using the chaos created by the pandemic to further their espionage operations. In April 2020, the Cybersecurity and Infrastructure Security Agency (CISA) within the U.S. DHS, and United Kingdom's National Cyber Security Centre (NCSC) issued a joint statement indicating that there was a growing use of COVID-19 in state-sponsored malicious cyber threats, which they assessed was likely to increase in both severity and number as the pandemic continued. In particular, they noted that these state actors were looking to engage in both espionage and "hack-and-leak" operations.[10] In July 2020, Canada, the UK and U.S. issued a joint statement attributing hacking attempts targeting organizations working on COVID-19 vaccine research to Russia.

All of these cyber-threats have prompted the Canadian Centre for Cyber Security (housed within Canada's national cryptologic agency, the Communications Security Establishment, or CSE) to warn of cyber-threats to Canada's health organizations and cyber-attackers seeking to take advantage of high-profile events.[11] Moreover, for the first time in the CSE's history, it announced that it was taking part in government-wide efforts to take down websites that "spoofed" the Public Health Agency of Canada (PHAC), the Canada Revenue Agency (CRA), and most recently, Canada Border Services Agency (CBSA).[12]

Foreign influence and targeted disinformation: Finally, with the spread of the pandemic has come a surge of conspiracy theories and disinformation shared across social media and messaging apps. This includes everything from false information about treatments or preventative measures to arguments that the virus is either overblown or entirely fake, to conspiracy theories about the origins of the virus, linking it to either state actors or the roll-out of 5G networks across the world. While these theories may seem far-fetched, they have had real world results, such as the sabotage of 5G towers in Europe.[13]

Not all information is shared for malicious purposes: some may be passed on by scared or nervous individuals looking for answers in a confusing time, or well-meaning individuals hoping to help their friends and loved ones. However, some waves of disinformation are being propagated by groups with ties to extremism and potentially to state actors.[14] Even before the pandemic began, Russia was linked to efforts to spread disinformation about the relationship between 5G and health.[15] Media reports suggest that suspected Russian government online "trolls" have been pushing COVID-19 conspiracy theories as a way to discredit the United States and trigger tensions with its allies.[16] The information environment has also been targeted by these Chinese government efforts to shift blame for the pandemic, with its diplomats and foreign ministry claiming the United States was lying about what it knew about the origins of COVID-19, possibly to deflect attention from China's own flawed response to the pandemic.[17] (Of course, none of this was helped by the outlandish claims on U.S. President Donald Trump's Twitter feed.)

All of this suggests that while COVID-19 or pandemics may not be a national security issue upon which the intelligence community traditionally would gather large amounts of intelligence, key national security issues are affected by pandemics. Therefore, we should not be surprised that national security departments and agencies are inevitably part of the government's response. However, we should not mistake these necessary actions for leadership of the pandemic response or a case for securitization.

The Spy Who Came in from the Lab?

The survey of issues discussed above shows that national security agencies will probably have to be involved in responding to pandemics. But what form should this response take? Some have argued that it should go much further on a broader range of issues. In the early stages of the pandemic, this has come out in two ways: tactical/technical support, typically in the form of surveillance,[18] and expanding the mandate of national security departments and agencies to include pandemics.[19]

In terms of tactical/technical support, calls have been made for national security agencies to develop, manage, and run a biosurveillance architecture for federal, provincial, and municipal governments. This surveillance would help monitor and prevent the spread of the pandemic earlier, by helping the government to trace contacts (to find individuals who may have been in proximity to a person known to be infected with COVID-19) or even to enforce the strict physical-distancing measures enacted by cities and provinces.

Canadians worry about the security of their personal data, but in a crisis they just might be more willing to be flexible about privacy – if mass surveillance can end the lockdown, then Canadians could believe the trade-off is worth it. For example, a poll conducted in April 2020 found that up to 65 per cent of Canadians supported using cell phone data to track individuals who should be self-isolating.[20]

However, immediate practical and ethical issues demonstrate how complex a shift towards health intelligence would be for the national security and intelligence community. First, where are the data that would feed these programs coming from? Would they be anonymized? How would we know that they were accurate? Programs often require years to be verified and tested before they are used by intelligence agencies. What about individuals who have few technological devices (such as the homeless or senior citizens) who may be among the most vulnerable groups in a public health emergency? And would we want our intelligence and national security services to collect, organize, search, and store these data? What would be done with the information when the pandemic was over? Would such efforts necessitate a public/private partnership – and what would the expectations of the private partner be? While these questions may sound academic or philosophical, a pandemic does not negate the Canadian Charter of Rights and Freedoms. The right to be free from unreasonable search and seizure – something Canada's courts have increasingly interpreted as applying in the digital realm – will still apply in some way during an emergency.

As noted above, there is no shortage of threats in a pandemic – would we want to draw national security specialists away from countering these threats to monitor individuals who may be going to the corner store one too many times in a week? It is true that states have powerful abilities to survey many aspects of people's lives if they feel they need to, and if they are able to obtain the proper legal authorization. However, that form of intense surveillance is time-consuming and resource-intensive, much harder than it looks in the movies or on television.

Ramping up advanced surveillance programs would be a massive undertaking and require a significant shift of resources away from traditional national security threats. Nevertheless, while the feasibility of establishing mass targeted surveillance in Canada is now uncertain, it may not always be.[21] And there are significant concerns that "temporary" measures may be hard to remove once established.[22]

A second broader question is the relationship between national security and major issues with global consequences. Should intelligence agencies collect information on pandemics or, on another crucial planetary issue, climate change? These issues have the potential to affect almost every aspect of our way of life. The year 2020 demonstrated the social and economic devastation that a pandemic in our globalized world can wreak. And scientists and activists have argued for decades that climate change will cause havoc through an increase in severe weather, flooding of coasts and coastal cities, and desertification of farmland worldwide. Scientists and social scientists predict that this will lead to increased competition for resources, such as fresh water, in some areas and create waves of migration across the world as individuals are forced to leave their homes. Moreover, a less hostile and more accessible Arctic may be the scene of future global rivalry and competition.[23] Given the disruption caused by COVID-19 and the anticipated turmoil of climate change, some might argue that these are the real national security threats.

Yet it is not clear that intelligence agencies such as CSIS or CSE should be major leads on these large global challenge files for three reasons. First, these intelligence agencies have tools to collect and assess information and to advise the government on it. However, it is questionable if the tools used for intelligence gathering can be used to collect information on pandemics, the environment, or climate change. This relates to a second point: it would not be a good thing if security agencies attempted to duplicate key research already being done by other government departments with developed expertise. This includes the work of researchers and scientists at the PHAC, the Department of Environment, and Climate Change Canada (ECCC), and even assessment bodies closer to the centre of government with a wider mandate, like the Privy Council Office's Intelligence Assessment Secretariat (PCO IAS). The Department of National Defence (DND) has a small unit within the Canadian Forces Intelligence Command (CFINTCOM) with a medical intelligence (MEDINT) unit. But this information is gathered largely in relation to force readiness and deployment, not necessarily providing warnings to the government. It may be possible to expand the mandate of the unit, but this might come at the cost of helping the Canadian Armed Forces (CAF) deploy to places like Mali or Ukraine where there are complex health preparations required.

Third, as noted above, we are not at "war" with pandemics or climate change. Yet something about the profound risks that these issues present to our society and way of life often creates a sense that they must be treated as security issues. Perhaps it is that in the years since 9/11 Western states have been building large security apparatuses and we are therefore inclined to use these agencies for a wider set of issues. Yet the solution to these problems depends on international cooperation, developed through formal and informal political and diplomatic channels. Security and intelligence analysis that inevitably views medical patients or migrants as "threats" or securitizes vast swaths of Canada, like the Arctic, may hinder the international community's ability to find political solutions to these challenges rather than help them. As pandemics and disasters tend to affect the most marginalized groups first, the surveillance required will disproportionately affect those groups that may already have the lowest levels of trust in government. And they will have little to no say over the algorithms that will be used to monitor their lives and behaviours, and little control over how those data are searched, stored, and collected by their own or other governments. And echoing the point above, this is another reason why the approaches intelligence services use to monitor the threat posed by the Islamic State, for example, does not neatly transpose to other areas of concern.

So if national security and intelligence agencies like CSIS and CSE have an important but secondary role in dealing with climate change, what does this look like? Generally, this will entail doing the kinds of things that the Canadian national security and intelligence community are already doing: responding to violent extremism, cyber threats, and disinformation in a fluid threat environment. They may join other government departments to exchange information in order to build their knowledge of the threat of climate change or pandemic response into their own assessments while providing advice on potential security implications. This will especially be the case if the pandemic response necessitates a lengthy shutdown or heightens global tensions. Or if, as predicted, climate change leads to more violent conflict, global instability, heightened tensions between countries, and competition for resources.

The thesis of this book is that we need to *responsibly* widen our understanding of national security threats in order to better empathize with those who are ultimately affected by them. Empathy, not fear, will help us counter the strategies of malicious actors who seek to benefit from our fear or sense of helplessness. This is not, however, a case to widen what we consider a national security threat to be. Chasing viruses is best left to medical professionals. Keeping those professionals safe is the responsibility of the Canadian national security and intelligence community – and Canada will be better off if we try to keep it that way.

April 2021

Acknowledgments

I have wanted to write a book about threats to Canadian national security since working as an intelligence analyst between 2012 and 2015. I am grateful that my job at the Norman Paterson School of International Affairs (NPSIA) at Carleton University has provided me the opportunity to do so. Indeed, my colleagues have been brilliant in providing advice and support as I restarted my academic career in Ottawa. In particular, Steve Saideman provided excellent guidance in helping me formulate my book proposal and as Directors of NPISA Dane Rowlands and Yiagadeesen (Teddy) Samy have helped me navigate the early part of my third career. Jean Daudelin, Fen Hampson, Philippe Lagassé, Meredith Lilly, and Jez Littlewood have also offered fantastic advice in helping me frame my research and career path. The Faculty of Public Affairs under Dean André Plourde provided collegial and financial support in assisting me to finish this work. And importantly, my MA students at NPSIA and the Infrastructure Protection and International Security Program at Carleton have been a delight to work with. I am inspired by their questions, hard work, and excellent presentations. Three of these students helped me compile information for chapter 5: Lucas Brydges, James Murray, and Mireille Seguin.

I am grateful for the friends to whom I could turn for assistance in constructing this book. My *Intrepid Podcast* co-host, Craig Forcese, has been an outstanding mentor and patient guide through the world of national security law. Working with Craig on the podcast helped me think through many of the issues raised in this book, which in turn assisted with the writing. Throughout he has been happy to help answer my (many) questions and provided advice on several chapters. While all errors remain my own, this book is unquestionably better because of our conversations and his excellent feedback.

In addition, I am grateful to Amarnath Amarasingam, Jessica Davis, Thomas Juneau, and Leah West for reading sections of the book and providing feedback and amazing moral support. In addition, Tim Oliver provided me a chance to get over some writer's block by generously opening his doors in Florence, Italy, in 2018. Brett Kubicek and Katherine Burke took the time to help me talk through my ideas, often as passengers in my 2003 Tracker. Likewise, Laura Payton and Laurie-Anne Kempton provided a lot of cheerleading and moral support. Margaret McCuaig-Johnston provided extremely useful feedback on China and Chinese foreign investment, and the Public Policy Forum gave me the opportunity to present my ideas on economic national security to a forum of scholars, as well as current and former government officials.

There are many individuals serving in the Canadian intelligence and national security community to whom I owe thanks but cannot name. During my time working as an intelligence analyst they took the time to teach me about making assessments, explaining how the community works and how to translate my academic writing into putting the "bottom line up front." The job could be very frustrating at times, but there was a lot of patience shown to me. I am grateful for the opportunity to have worked with so many smart, dedicated, and wonderful people who continue to work to protect Canada.

As the notes of this book will show, I am in debt to the national security reporters who cover this often poorly understood and complex world.

I am also grateful to Daniel Quinlan of University of Toronto Press who helped me navigate my way through to publication, even in a pandemic. His advice and support have been excellent, and the book reads much better for his efforts. In addition, the manuscript has benefitted from the helpful comments of two anonymous reviewers who took the time to send thoughtful feedback, much of which I could incorporate into the project.

Finally, I would like to thank my family, Tom, Darcy, and Chris Carvin and Malaika Babb for their love and support over the years. My parents have provided me a space for the last two summers to help me focus my efforts and complete the manuscript for this book. It would have been a much harder task without them.

STAND ON GUARD

REASSESSING THREATS TO CANADA'S NATIONAL SECURITY

Introduction

Just watch me.

So said Canada's Prime Minister when asked by journalists Tim Ralfe and Peter Reilly just how far he would go to combat the Front de Libération du Québec (FLQ) in 1970. Pierre Trudeau had invoked the *War Measures Act* in response to the kidnapping of British Trade Commissioner James Cross and, five days later, Quebec Labour Minister Pierre Laporte (who was later killed).

The moment, filmed on the steps of Parliament Hill, is iconic in Canadian history – Trudeau dismissing the "bleeding hearts" who are concerned about civil liberties while he tries to find a way to deal with the extremist group.

But it is unlikely that we'd see such a scene today – Canadians have expectations beyond "just watch me." In an era of "WikiLeaked" revelations, declining trust in institutions, and increasing expectations of privacy, the sudden introduction of far-reaching executive powers to constrain civil liberties without review or oversight is no longer acceptable. Indeed, improving review of Canada's national security apparatus was a major issue in the 2015 election, even as the Islamic State[1] dominated the headlines.

And yet it is often said that the first and most important duty of any government is to protect its citizens from harm. Canadians expect that their society will be free from terrorist attacks, that their online systems are secure, and that they will have free and fair elections without foreign interference. All of this requires a robust national security apparatus that has the power to investigate threats. This means interacting with communities, and the use of surveillance powers to monitor and prosecute those involved in threat-related activity is and will remain necessary.

Therefore the key security puzzle for Canada is how to balance the growing demands Canadians have for privacy and transparency in government actions with the need to counter ever-evolving and increasingly sophisticated threats.

This book aims to contribute to this necessary conversation by discussing what national security threats are, with a view to helping to generate discussion about how we, as a society, should respond. My answer is that Canadians need to *responsibly* widen their understanding of what constitutes a national security threat. This does not mean Canadians need to be more afraid. Rather, we need to be more empathetic to those most affected by these threats, whether they be marginalized communities or small to medium-sized business enterprises. Empathy is the basis of greater communication, trust, and cooperation that is fundamental to addressing the national security challenges of the twenty-first century.

What Is National Security?

National security is arguably one of the most important concepts any democracy needs to address – especially as matters of "national security" often provide justification for deviation from regular application of the law. Yet, frustratingly, "national security" is seldom defined, especially in the Canadian context. As law professor Craig Forcese notes, the term "national security" appears in at least thirty-three Canadian laws but is undefined in most of them.[2]

A search of Termium, the "Government of Canada's terminology and linguistic data bank," defines "national security" as "the condition achieved through the implementation of measures that ensure the defence and maintenance of the social, political and economic stability of a country."[3] It is important to note that we are not just talking about safe borders here. The definition includes "the social, political, and economic stability of a country," suggesting a broad view of what security actually means to Canadians. It is all fine and well that we are invasion-free, but if our economy is at risk from extremist attacks, whether foreign or domestic, or if social stability is destroyed as a result of job losses following the closure of plants that have had their intellectual property stolen, Canadians can hardly be said to be secure.

At the same time, this definition is too broad to be useful. Economic stability can be wrecked by a stock-market crash based on "bubbles" and bad investments, and Canadians might not like it, but it cannot be said to be a true national security risk. Short of criminality, there are other branches of government that can deal with these risks other than the RCMP.

Instead, to reasonably limit what constitutes "national security" for the purpose of this book, we can turn to the mandates of our key national security agencies – in this case, the Canadian Security Intelligence Service (or CSIS/"the Service"). According to the *CSIS Act*, the Service has the mandate to investigate:

(a) espionage or sabotage that is against Canada or is detrimental to the interests of Canada or activities directed toward or in support of such espionage or sabotage,
(b) foreign influenced activities within or relating to Canada that are detrimental to the interests of Canada and are clandestine or deceptive or involve a threat to any person,
(c) activities within or relating to Canada directed toward or in support of the threat or use of acts of serious violence against persons or property for the purpose of achieving a political, religious, or ideological objective within Canada or a foreign state, and
(d) activities directed toward undermining, by covert unlawful acts, or directed toward or intended ultimately to lead to the destruction or overthrow by violence of, the constitutionally established system of government in Canada but does not include lawful advocacy, protest, or dissent, unless carried on in conjunction with any of the activities referred to in paragraphs (a) to (d).

In other words: espionage, foreign influence, violent extremism (or terrorism), and subversion. This gives us a good start in thinking about national security threats – albeit one in need of some modification. In the first instance, CSIS has not had a unit to investigate subversion since the mid-1980s.[4] Additionally, while the *CSIS Act* provides a useful scope of national security concerns in Canada, we still lack a useful definition. Therefore, for the purpose of this book, national security will be considered *the condition achieved when a country is able to protect its social, economic, and political stability from internal and external clandestine threats as well as the overt threat of political violence.* This condition is achieved through intelligence-led activities used to monitor these threats and the use of criminal investigations to counter them.[5]

Why This Book?

There are a number of reasons why a book on Canadian national security is important. First, for most of its history, including the Second World War, Canadians have never had to think hard about security problems. Canada, often described as "The Peaceable Kingdom"[6] or even "America's Hat"[7] reflects our relative security in the world. Surrounded by three oceans and with a (mostly) benevolent neighbour to our south, Canada has not faced a realistic threat of imminent invasion since the mid-nineteenth century. Indeed, the eminent social and political theorist Karl Deutsch described the relationship between Canada and the United States as a "security community" – that is, a region in which the large-scale use of violence (such as war) has become very unlikely or even unthinkable.[8] While Canada is certainly vulnerable to nuclear weapons, this puts us in the same category as virtually every other nation on earth. For the last seventy years our "security dilemma" (to use the language of social science) is exceptional in that there is not much of a dilemma; at worst, our situation (a shrinking military affected by relentless cuts and our difficulties in procuring military equipment) is self-inflicted.[9]

Second, what writing there is on Canadian security largely reflects traditional defence issues: the Canadian military generally,[10] relations with allies and organizations,[11] our procurement problems,[12] peacekeeping/peace-enforcement,[13] and recent missions (especially Afghanistan).[14] These are all important books and they provide the context for understanding the current state of Canada's global commitments and ability to keep them. However, for the most part, they do not address the role of security at home. Even books that describe themselves as Canadian "national security" tend to focus almost exclusively on defence issues.[15]

To be fair, the lines are not always clear. The Department of National Defence has a role in many aspects of national security as defined here. Although unknown to most Canadians, it has the greatest number of personnel working in intelligence out of any government department or agency, and it is also the lead ministry of the civilian Communications Security Establishment (CSE). DND intelligence personnel play a role in detecting and deterring espionage and foreign influence, and its special operations forces have a role in responding to serious terrorism incidents domestically. However, other than the CSE, which as of 2019 has its own statute, DND is not the lead agency for investigating most national security threats as outlined in the *CSIS Act*.[16]

There are a number of other explanations for this lack of literature. First, the Canadian national security community is relatively small: we do not have legions of former national security officials who have written books or public commentary – especially relative to the United States. Relatedly, as most national security officials in Canada are life-long civil servants and not political appointees (as in the United States), there are few who cycle in and out of a university or think-tank system who can teach or spread knowledge about the Canadian national security community. In this sense, there are few individuals with experience who have chosen to write or speak publicly about national security.[17]

This means that work on national security in Canada tends to be historical,[18] critical,[19] or both.[20] This is not to downplay the importance of much of this work. Let's state the obvious: the landscape of Canada's national security community is littered with the casualties of wrongly targeted individuals and communities, over-reaction, and missed opportunities. Many of these cases will be discussed in this book. Canada's national security community is not and should not be immune to criticism. However, it does matter that few of the books on Canada's national security agencies are written by those with at least some experience in government. But even when that is the case, the authors often tend to be former employees with serious grievances.[21]

Fortunately, dedicated reporters cover these issues in Canada, many of whom have written books on national security, particularly terrorism.[22] Coverage of national security by journalists, however, has been hurt by the shrinking of newsrooms across Canada, with fewer and fewer reporters dedicated to these topics. In-depth coverage is being replaced by wire stories or reporting by young journalists with multiple files who do not have the opportunity to develop knowledge and sources.

The result is a distorted and sometimes superficial view of Canadian national security agencies, the people who work for them, and the issues they address. Terrorism and violent extremism tend to disproportionately dominate coverage in the news while issues like cybersecurity come down to false choices between creating a surveillance state and a free-for-all space for criminals online.

Significantly, part of the blame for this state of affairs rests with the national security agencies themselves, who have constantly refused to tell their own stories in the way other allied agencies have. For example, the UK government has commissioned "official histories" curated by qualified and cleared academics and writers.[23] While most national security services in Canada have taken steps to improve their public outreach, a key argument of this book is that more needs to be done to further public understanding and trust.

The Peaceable Kingdom in a Changing World

The most important reason for writing a book on Canada's national security threat is that Canada finds itself in the most complex threat environment since the Second World War. Global leadership appears to be in flux, and the international order that defends the rules and norms under which Canada has prospered are no longer guaranteed. While this means that Canada may have to step up its international presence, it also means that threats are challenging Canada's national security at home in unique ways, necessitating new policy responses.

There are difficult questions we must confront. First, how should we manage the evolving threat of terrorism/violent extremism? When I began commenting publicly on national security in 2016, the Islamic State, and its so-called caliphate, which drew tens of thousands to Syria, was the pre-eminent national security threat. Since then, the Islamic State has gone from a terrorist proto-state to having lost its territory. At the time of publication, the movement's next steps are not clear. It may gradually disappear, be absorbed into other groups, or make a comeback as previous iterations of the group have done. Further, other terrorist groups continue to plot attacks globally. Despite counterterrorism pressure, Al Qaida remains a threat and is determined to carry out attacks against the West while some splinter groups with a foggy relationship to it continue to adhere to a hard-line extremist view and a commitment to violence.[24]

Moreover, trends in international terrorism have a clear impact at home. Over two hundred Canadians were inspired to go overseas to support extremist groups in places like Afghanistan, Pakistan, Syria, and Yemen. Many have engaged in killing and violence, or actions that support extremist groups such as recruitment and facilitation. A key concern for Canadian security officials is that these individuals may have developed links to terrorist networks, received training in extremist violence, and then leave conflict zones to facilitate or carry out violent attacks at home. Additionally, those who are unable to go overseas (thwarted travellers) may be motivated to conduct attacks within Canada.

Yet although much of the emphasis on terrorism in the last two decades has been on Al Qaida and Islamic State–inspired extremism, it is essential to recognize that terrorism comes in many different forms and that the nature of the threat is always evolving. Since 2014, at least nineteen people have been killed in attacks by individuals subscribing to far-right and/or anti-government ideologies.[25] We are seeing the rise of single-issue extremism and far-right, militia-style groups that seem determined to take the law into their own hands to "defend" Canada from what they see as an existential threat from immigration.[26] Although these attackers may differ in their specific grievances, a worrying trend is that some see themselves a part of a larger movement, increasingly referencing each other in their manifestos; the perpetrator of the 2019 Christchurch massacre had the name of Canada's Alexandre Bissonnette (who attacked a mosque in 2017, killing six and injuring scores of others) on his weapon in a perverse tribute. Even CSIS has increasingly spoken about the challenge of a rising far right. In the spring of 2019, Director David Vigneault told a Canadian Senate committee that the Service is "more and more preoccupied" with the threat of violent right-wing extremism and white supremacists.[27] In this sense the Service has had to "increase its posture" on far-right extremist threats, including groups focused on gender, race, religion, sexual orientation, and immigration.[28]

How should the government manage the constantly evolving threat of violent extremism? Some movements, like "incels," are already challenging conventional notions of what terrorism is under Canadian law.[29] And importantly, this comes at a time when the government is experiencing problems with terrorism prosecutions. For example, few foreign fighters have been charged or convicted with a terrorism offence.[30] And despite the severity and violence of their actions, people like Alexandre Bissonnette and Abdulahi Sharif have not been charged with committing acts of terror. Although this may make sense from a practical standpoint (as will be discussed in chapter 1), it can be confusing to the average person and a source of grievance to affected communities.

On the other hand, although Canadians remain largely concerned about the threat of terrorism, it is worth asking whether the billions of dollars Canada spends on this particular threat are actually proportionate to the real risks that terrorism poses. While much has been made of the threat of returnees, only a handful have come back from Syria – with open source information indicating that perhaps three had any kind of fighting role.[31] There have been few, if any, internationally driven plots against Canada – indeed, most successful plots have been carried out by lone actors who can hardly be described as masterminds. Might other national security threats be overshadowed by this serious but limited threat? Or do we need a wider understanding of the social harms of a wide array of violent extremist activity to better understand the problem?

The changing threat environment is increasing the prominence of issues such as cybersecurity and economic espionage. In particular, both speak to a neglected question in Canadian security: what is the relationship between our economy and our national security? Since the 1980s, the market mantra has been to get governments out of the economy. Yet the manifestation of threats from other countries increasingly targets the engine of our economy: the theft of intellectual property, the ability of large, state-owned enterprises to enter into an industry and skew its landscape with uncompetitive practices, and the ability to increasingly manipulate information in real time.

Of course, while wider social trends are having an impact on our democracy, they are having a subtle effect on national security as well: the decline of trust, the shrinking of newsrooms and the gradual death of local media, and the rise of populist movements in an age of uncertainty all have implications for democracy.[32] Adversarial countries that have no interest in seeing a successful or prosperous West can take advantage of these trends and clandestinely work to amplify information that suits their interests and supress what does not. The 2016 U.S. presidential campaign was not an anomaly, but rather the continuation of a trend by Russia to interfere in the elections of other states. Unfortunately, other states and entities are learning from this experience, and we can expect more actors to at least attempt to engage in similar activities. Canada will not be immune to such efforts.[33]

But the decline of trust has not been driven by foreign entities alone. Online "WikiLeaks" campaigns in the early 2010s showed that Western spy agencies are engaged in activities that many felt crossed the line in targeting and surveillance. These agencies use a number of techniques, including exploiting vulnerabilities in popular mobile web applications, tracking individuals using free airport Wi-Fi, and searching thousands of documents and videos uploaded to online file sharing services, among other activities.[34] Further, through recent Federal Court rulings, Canadians learned that CSIS had not been entirely forthcoming with judges when seeking warrants or the kinds of information it was storing.[35]

It is a problem if Canadians believe that our national security services are not being reasonably transparent in explaining how they monitor threat-related activities. A report on the findings of national security legislation consultations conducted between September and December 2016 found that a majority of (self-selecting) participants did not believe that challenges by investigators in the digital world justified circumventing rules protecting privacy. Indeed, a clear majority of respondents were found "to have an expectation of privacy in the digital world that is the same or higher than in the physical world."[36] Somehow our national security agencies must navigate the waters between a robust investigation of threat-related activity and meeting the high expectations of Canadians.

Structure of the Book

Although no single work can solve these dilemmas and challenges, this book aims to promote a better understanding of national security issues in Canada. As such it is anchored in the main areas of threat-related activity: violent extremism, espionage, cyber and clandestine foreign influence.

There are limits to how far such a book can go in describing the national security threat environment. First, the book is obviously limited to open-source information; it works on the assumption that there are more cases out there that remain classified. Second, and relatedly, there are few cases to draw upon for detailed statistical analysis. While the book does draw upon the few quantitative approaches by others examining the threat of violent extremism, especially travel for extremist purposes, in other areas such as espionage there is little to draw upon to build a quantitative study.

Therefore, the chapters in this book proceed by first providing a description of how national security threats (as understood by the *CSIS Act*) work in Canada, and second presenting historical and contemporary case studies to illustrate this further. The book does not claim to speak to the frequency of these threats, as it is not possible to say how often they occur. The examples simply provide an idea of what has happened in the past in order to suggest what could happen in the future. The chapters end by highlighting "big-picture" questions that national security departments and agencies are dealing with.

This is an appropriate method, given that a key claim of this book is that certain threats, especially violent extremism, can change quickly. As noted above, within three years the Islamic State changed its strategy from inviting its followers to join it in Syria and Iraq to encouraging violent attacks abroad by homegrown extremists. With such rapid change, it is useful to understand the range of activities and the kinds of actors that engage in them through a historically grounded approach.

In adopting this method, this book seeks to provide an accessible guide for Canadians to the nature of national security threats in Canada; a resource for the national security and intelligence community and policymakers; and a place for students of national security issues to begin their studies and research.

Chapter 1 sets the stage for a better understanding of the current threat of violent extremism by exploring the historical and contemporary contexts for threat-related activity. While much of our current focus is on Al Qaida/Islamic State–inspired extremism, violence carried out for religious, ideological, or political reasons has a long and diverse past in Canada. The threat has evolved and will continue to do so. Chapter 2 then highlights five ways the threat of violent extremism manifests in Canada: attack planning, travel for extremist purposes, facilitation, financing, and radicalization. While many may think of "terrorism" as bombs exploding in the streets, this chapter will make the argument that actually a wide range of activities support violent extremism and they can have an even greater, yet unseen, impact.

Chapter 3 examines the history of espionage in Canada, how it has changed since the Cold War, and how the motivation of individuals who engage in such activities has changed. While few Canadians may see our country as an espionage target, our close ties with the United States and NATO countries and our defence arrangements have been key targets for hostile countries. Building on this, chapter 4 examines the current major threat of spying in Canada: economic espionage and national security threats. By the end of the Cold War, hostile foreign intelligence services increasingly moved to steal intellectual property with a view to overtaking Canada and the West in manufacturing. Today the challenge of "economic security" has only grown more complex, especially with the national security risks of certain state-owned enterprises and their impact on the landscape of the free market in Canada. All signs point to the need to have a serious conversation about the relationship between national security and the economy.

Chapter 5 examines how malicious cyber-activities have helped national security threats to evolve in the form of attacks, espionage, and crime. States and malicious groups can use cyber techniques to not just steal information, but to compromise it, deny access to it, and even destroy it. These threats have serious implications for how we address terrorism, espionage, and clandestine foreign influence in the future.

Chapters 6 and 7 focus on clandestine foreign influence, one of the hardest national security threats to define. All states engage in foreign influence (this is why we have embassies), but when these activities become *clandestine* (that is, when they are done in secret and for the purpose of engaging in an illegal activity), a national security nexus emerges. We now associate clandestine foreign influence with the 2016 U.S. presidential election, but it is best understood as a range of activities with a long history in Canada, one that has manifested through the setting up or support of advocacy groups, the clandestine influence of elected and non-elected officials, pressure on expatriates and expatriate groups to support the position of a government or violent extremist entity, and now digital interference in domestic politics. Once a low-priority issue for security services, especially in the post–Cold War era, clandestine foreign influence has become one of the most pressing threats Canada faces. As such, chapter 6 will focus on how "traditional" clandestine foreign influence threats continue to affect Canadian national security. Chapter 7 will trace how the threat is evolving in its challenges to democratic institutions.

The book concludes by looking at themes that emerge throughout the chapters, including the complexity of the threat environment and the need for greater trust and openness on all sides. As security challenges become increasingly complex, the need to balance civil liberties and an effective national security apparatus is a challenging prospect, one all Canadians should be concerned about. This includes a more empathetic approach to affected communities and entities, a debate over the future of the relationship between national security and the economy, and strategies to improve communication between citizens and governments on our national security.

Finally, while the goal of this book is to provide an overview of threats rather than national security agencies, a brief overview of the architecture of Canadian national security is provided in an appendix.

Conclusion

To describe something as a national security threat or, as international relations scholars put it, to *securitize* an issue, is an inherently political act. It is to describe a phenomenon as an urgent priority requiring the immediate resources of the state. We see this when politicians describe something as a "crisis," whether it is drugs, disease, or migration. Too often, though, to securitize something is to stigmatize someone or some group. Drugs become a matter for police rather than public health agencies. Those suffering from AIDS are seen as a societal risk, and migrants are seen as "illegals," threatening public order. The result is that an issue may be successfully prioritized and resources may be given to an issue, but very often those who may be the most in need of help are seen as threats. Rather than coming forward, they may shun the attention of authorities, even where those authorities require the assistance and cooperation of the communities that exclude or vilify them. In the end, we are all worse off in such a scenario.

As noted above, the argument underpinning this book is that, if we are to properly counter national security threats, Canadians need to *responsibly* widen their understanding of what these threats are. To be sure, the issues here under discussion have already been securitized. However, in presenting this book, I hope it can achieve two further goals. First, to produce empathy for those who are most affected by the threats discussed. After all, the impact of these activities is not abstract; the harm done to Canadians is real. Families are devastated in the aftermath of a loved one's decision to join the Islamic State, mistrust grows in communities where known radicalizers are targeting youth, there are job losses at companies that have had their intellectual property stolen, and fear, anger, and suspicion are generated through vicious intimidation campaigns in real life and online. Empathy – being aware of, understanding, and appreciating the ordeal of others as they experience the impact of threat-related activity – highlights the need to robustly tackle these challenges, but to do so in a way that minimizes distrust.

Second, the goal of this book is to inform. As the international environment in which Canada has thrived is rapidly evolving, it is important for citizens to understand key national security threats so they can better answer the questions about the security challenges of the twenty-first century:

- How should we prioritize rapidly evolving threats in a world of finite resources? While violent extremism remains a real threat to Canadians, other threats (especially cyber) are growing in prominence.
- What should the relationship between the economy and national security be?
- Is the rise of populism a national security threat?
- Who is responsible for cybersecurity – the state, the private sector, or individuals?
- What are the major challenges and opportunities of new technologies on national security?

There are no easy answers to these questions, but getting acquainted with national security threats at least gives us a place to start and a useful departure point in contemplating a stronger, more resilient Canada.

1

Violent Extremism: The Canadian Context

We will never know the full story of Michael Zehaf-Bibeau or understand why he mobilized to violence on 22 October 2014. After choosing targets that represented the Canadian military and government, he charged the War Memorial with a rare, single-shot .30-30 Winchester rifle, killing Corporal Nathan Cirillo who had been standing guard. From there, Zehaf-Bibeau proceeded to storm the Parliament Buildings, where he was killed in a hail of bullets.

Despite many lingering questions, media outlets have pieced together elements of Zehaf-Bibeau's life. He appears to have been a troubled individual who cycled between stints working in Alberta's oil fields, to drug and sex-fuelled binges in Vancouver, to repentant phases in which he re-embraced his faith as he recovered in homeless shelters. We know he was asked to leave a mosque in Vancouver for his extremist views and drug-addled behaviour.[1] Perhaps seeking a way out of this cycle, Zehaf-Bibeau sought a passport to travel abroad. His first attempt to obtain a Canadian passport was denied when it was sent to the RCMP for a criminal background check. He then travelled west to Ottawa to apply for a Libyan passport in person, but again was denied after exhibiting bizarre behaviour and told it would take at least three weeks to process his request. Within weeks of these incidents, Zehaf-Bibeau began to mobilize.[2]

Yet, in the video he left behind, Zehaf-Bibeau mentions none of this. Instead, his actions are framed through the prism of Al Qaeda's ideas about struggling against the West and revenge for Canada's military mission in Afghanistan. Just how Zehaf-Bibeau came to adopt an extremist view and why he conducted his deadly attacks in Ottawa on that day is still not publicly known. Indeed, it is still unclear if his views were instilled by a radicalizer, influential group or consumption of AQ/Islamic State propaganda on the internet (or some combination of all the above).

The case of Zehaf-Bibeau is a good example of the hurdles that security services in Canada face in combating the threat of extremist violence. It combines the challenges of stopping lone actors, the influence of a global terrorist propaganda campaign, the pull of conflicts abroad, and ways to balance the protection of our critical infrastructure and democratic institutions with the freedoms we cherish as Canadians.

In order to understand the threat of violent extremism in Canada, the next two chapters provide an overview of threat-related activity in this area, as well as the context in which it has occurred. This chapter specifically examines the history of violent extremism in Canada, focusing mostly on the later twentieth and early twenty-first centuries, highlighting the diversity of the threats. Next, it discusses the major contemporary violent extremist challenges: Al Qaida and Islamic State–inspired extremism, far-right extremism, state-sponsored extremism, and far-left extremism. It concludes by highlighting the major challenges in confronting this threat as the nature of violent extremism evolves.

What Is Violent Extremism?

There is no agreed upon definition of terrorism. It is now a cliché to note that "one man's terrorist is another man's freedom fighter" – a phrase that captures the idea that political meaning, context, and (perhaps) success play a role in whether or not the violent actions of a group or individuals is perceived as legitimate. However, since 9/11 the term has become even more contentious. It is not unusual to see commentators point to the inconsistency in which the term "terrorism" is used: when Muslims are involved in incidents, terrorism is often suspected (even when the motivation is unknown), but white males who commit similar acts are often deemed "mentally ill" or engaging in lesser crimes.[3]

Already, readers may have noticed this book tends to use the term "violent extremism" more frequently than "terrorism." This is a deliberate attempt to avoid the "terrorism" trap – there are acts of political violence that fall short of our legal definition of terrorism that may still meet the threshold for being a national security concern. For example, the 2014 attack by Justin Bourque against RCMP officers in Moncton, New Brunswick, is not typically described as terrorism, but Bourque appears to have subscribed to conspiracy theories and anti-government ideologies. The use of the term "violent extremism" captures this, where terrorism does not. Moreover, in the public imagination, terrorism tends to refer to specific acts of violence, whereas this book is concerned with the wide spectrum of activities that can go into supporting it, including facilitation, financing, and radicalization. These individuals might not actually engage in acts of terrorist violence but they support an extremist view generally and the idea of using violence to bring about a particular vision of how life should be. Here too, the term "violent extremism" is more appropriate.

Canada did not have an actual terrorism criminal offence until 2001 when, in the aftermath of 9/11, the government of Jean Chrétien passed legislation creating a number of such crimes. Of course, Canada was already party to international treaties banning terrorist activities prior to 9/11, and had enacted criminal code offences to implement these treaties. They include the 1970 Convention for the Suppression of Unlawful Seizure of Aircraft, 1971 Convention for the Suppression of Unlawful Acts against the Safety of Civil Aviation, and the 1979 International Convention against the Taking of Hostages, as well as several financial treaties.[4] Yet even in the aftermath of several prominent and deadly attacks, there was no legal definition of terrorism: violent extremists were charged with murder or attempted murder or the crimes listed in the treaties Canada had signed and implemented, such as hijacking.

In the aftermath of 9/11, however, new international legal instruments emerged with which Canada needed to comply. The government's response in late 2001 – Bill C-36, the *Anti-Terrorism Act* – went a long way in doing so, creating a definition of terrorism in Canadian law, terrorism and terrorism financing offences, as well as new statutory authorities to investigate it.[5]

Today the legal definition of terrorism in Canada is found in section 83.01 of the Criminal Code and has four parts. First, it includes any act or omission that includes counterterrorism offences within the international treaties that Canada is party to. Second, it outlines the motivation required, stipulating that the act must be conducted for a "political, religious or ideological purpose, objective or cause" (although these are not required for offences that implemented treaty obligations, discussed above). This is key – it means the perpetrator have not just perpetrated or facilitated the act, they have done so for a purpose that the prosecution *must* prove in Court. (That this has been the source of recent controversy will be discussed below.)

Third, it lists the actual terrorism acts: any act or omission that intentionally:

(a) causes death or serious bodily harm to a person by the use of violence,
(b) endangers a person's life,
(c) causes a serious risk to the health or safety of the public or any segment of the public,
(d) causes substantial property damage, whether to public or private property, if causing such damage is likely to result in the conduct or harm referred to in any of clauses (A) to (C), or
(e) causes serious interference with or serious disruption of an essential service, facility or system, whether public or private, other than as a result of advocacy, protest, dissent or stoppage of work that is not intended to result in the conduct or harm referred to in any of clauses (A) to (C).

Additionally, it lists conspiracy, attempt, threat, or being an accessory to or counselling in relation to any of the acts listed above.

Finally, section 83.01 defines a terrorist group as either "an entity that has as one of its purposes or activities facilitating or carrying out any terrorist activity" or any "listed entity" – basically any group listed engaged as determined by the process in section 83.05.[6]

In addition, this section of the Criminal Code includes financing (83.02), facilitation (83.03, 83.19), participating in a terrorist group (83.18), travel to join a terrorist group to participate (83.181), facilitate terrorist activity (83.191), or commission of an offence for a terrorist group (83.201) or terrorist activity (83.202), and instructing someone to engage in a terrorist act (83.22). These activities will be discussed in further detail in chapter 2.

Sources of Violent Extremism in Canada

Despite the lack of a terrorism crime until after 9/11, Canada is no stranger to violent extremism. Throughout its history, a diverse number of violent movements have operated within Canada or used our country as a base from which to export terrorism. The first threats were from groups that sought to use Canada as a platform from which to strike the British Empire. This includes the Irish Fenians, who sought to attack Canada from the United States in order to free Ireland from British control between 1866 and 1871. There was also concern about anti-imperial sentiment within the South Asian immigrant communities in British Columbia in the 1920s.[7] The Sons of Freedom – a splinter group of the Doukhobors (a Russian religious sect) engaged in arson and bombings in the 1920s through to the 1960s.[8]

By the middle of the twentieth century, Canada began to experience terrorism influenced by different trends: nationalism/separatism, proxy conflicts of the Cold War, and state-sponsored terrorism. Moreover, terrorist groups began to take advantage of modern technologies, targeting mass-transportation and utilizing mass-media to spread their messages.[9]

Canada's first truly domestic act of terrorism exhibited all these influences. Inspired by revolutionary actions in Cuba and Algeria and European violent extremists: the Front de Libération du Québec (FLQ), a violent extremist separatist group that was responsible for hundreds of acts of terrorism, including a series of bombings against a range of targets, including the federal government, armed forces, RCMP, media, railways, and economic targets. At least six individuals died as a result of FLQ operations.[10] The most infamous incident occurred in October 1970 when the group organized the kidnapping of British Trade Commissioner James Cross and Quebec's Labour Minister, Pierre Laporte, the latter murdered a few days into the crisis. As a result of these actions, public support for the FLQ plummeted. Although the movement continued to engage in bombings throughout Quebec, the movement was largely infiltrated by 1973 and dispersed.

Transnational/Spillover Terrorism

Much of the violent extremism experienced within Canada in the latter half of the twentieth century was driven by what is often described as transnational or "spillover" terrorism. Essentially, transnational terrorism is the internationalization of a primarily domestic dispute.[11] Frequently this term is used to describe cases of violent extremism in which the citizens or interests of a country are targeted when they are seen by an extremist group as a sponsor and/or ally of regimes and states that are fighting against insurgent movements. It also refers to situations in which violent extremists, typically operating within a diaspora, use a country as a base from which to orchestrate violent extremism in another country. This includes fundraising, facilitation, arranging for extremist travel, creating propaganda, and (as discussed in chapter 6) clandestine influence.

Between the 1960s and the 1990s, Canada's experience of "spillover" violent extremism was mostly in the realm of facilitation and financing groups abroad. Entities such as the Irish Republican Army (IRA), for example, used Canada as a platform for fundraising.[12] Nevertheless, there were serious acts of violence. In the 1960s, anti-Castro Cubans in the United States and Canada engaged in twelve attacks within Canada between the 1960s and 1980s, resulting in one death and several persons injured as well as serious property damage.[13]

In the 1970s some Armenians turned to extremist violence in order to bring about a homeland. Between 1982 and 1985, there were five attacks on Turkish targets in Canada associated with Armenian groups. The more left-leaning Armenian Secret Army for the Liberation of Armenia (ASALA) aimed to have Turkey cede territory for an Armenian homeland as well as admit responsibility for the deaths of Armenians in 1915. In 1982 they tried to assassinate a Turkish commercial attaché, who was seriously wounded. Also in 1982 a group called the Justice Commandos of the Armenian Genocide (JCAG) assassinated the Turkish military attaché, Colonel Atilla Altikat, in Ottawa while his car was stopped at a red light.[14] The same group (which changed its name to the Armenian Revolutionary Army) attacked the Turkish embassy in Ottawa by ramming a van with explosives into the building, killing a security guard. Eleven hostages were taken, but the attacker surrendered after four hours.[15] Today, neither of these groups is thought to be active.

As noted above, there was concern about South Asian and Sikh separatism in Canada as early as the 1920s. By the 1960s and 1970s, a very small minority within the Canadian Sikh diaspora began to plot against Indian interests. Sikh grievances within India included demands for more autonomy, decentralization of resources and power, as well as certain economic imbalances.[16] However, two events in 1984 had a radicalizing effect on a minority within this movement: the storming of the Golden Temple at Amritsar, the most important shrine in Sikhism, by the Indian army in October, as well as the aftermath of the anti-Sikh riots in India following the assassination of Prime Minister Indira Gandhi by her Sikh bodyguards in November that left at least three thousand dead.[17]

On 23 June 1985 Sikh separatists planted two bombs targeting Air India planes. The first exploded in Japan as luggage was transferred from a Canadian Pacific flight to an Air India flight, killing two baggage handlers and injuring four others. Less than an hour later, a second bomb detonated on Air India Flight 182 over the Atlantic, killing all 331 persons on board, including 268 Canadian citizens.[18] This attack had the dubious distinction of being the world's worst violent extremist attack on aviation until the 9/11. Although the level of Sikh separatist activity in Canada is believed to have dropped since the 1980s, supporters of Sikh separatism are believed to still fundraise and facilitate violent extremism against India within Canada, a frequent complaint of the Indian security services.[19]

Of note, both Public Safety Canada's 2018 *Public Report on the Terrorist Threat to Canada* and the CSIS 2018 *Public Report* observed that there was an "increase in observed threat activity, wherein Canada is being used as a base to support this view as well as attacks targeting India."[20] However, the initial description of this activity in the Public Safety report as "Sikh extremism" was met with outrage from the Sikh community. Given that no public report had discussed Sikh separatism in well over a decade, the government's assertion was met with incredulity and shock. The resulting political controversy resulted in a change of wording from "Sikh extremism" to "extremists who support violent means to establish an independent state within India."[21]

Finally, by the 1980s, tens of thousands of Tamils began to flee the civil war in Sri Lanka for countries in the West, including Europe, Australia, and Canada. The conflict, where the Liberation Tigers of Tamil Eelam (LTTE) – commonly known as the "Tamil Tigers" – fought for independence from the Sinhalese, has killed tens of thousands of people and led to the assassination of India's Rajiv Gandhi, Sri Lankan President Ranasinge Premadasa, and over 100 other politicians. Further, the group is infamous for perfecting the use of suicide bombers, including pioneering the use of women bombers, as well as the use of suicide belts. The "Black Tigers" within the LTTE were world leaders in suicide terrorism between 1980 and 2003.[22] Many of these suicide operations targeted civilian targets, such as religious temples and transportation hubs.[23]

Despite this bloodshed, the conflict in Sri Lanka remained relatively obscure in the West. This allowed LTTE operatives to take advantage of the Tamil diaspora in Canada, often resorting to extortion to raise funds that were channelled into supporting violent extremism overseas. Much of this activity was done through the creation of a front organization called the World Tamil Movement (WTM), which attempted to infiltrate other Tamil organizations to control the diaspora community. When individuals or groups criticized the LTTE or refused to pay the WTM money, they were sometimes subject to violent attacks such as arson and intimidation.[24] However, some willingly handed over valuable possessions and hard-earned money to the cause.[25] Eventually the LTTE was listed as a terrorist organization in 2006, and the WTM in 2008. (The clandestine foreign influence of the Tamil Tigers is discussed as a case study in chapter 6.)

Lessons from the Past

Although the threat of violent extremism from these groups has lessened (although it has not vanished) there are at least two lessons here for thinking about terrorism-related activity in Canada. First, "spillover" terrorism is a misnomer: the effects of such activities have a very real impact on individuals in Canada. This includes diaspora who are intimidated into silence or handing over money and resources to extremist causes, assassinations on Canadian territory, and – in the case of Air India Flight 182 – the murder of innocent individuals. And yet not only is the wider impact of these attacks not truly appreciated, many such incidents are not understood as attacks against Canadians or as a Canadian problem. Part of this may have to do with the complexity of the conflicts from which these extremist groups sprang, but so long as most of those affected were overseas or recent immigrants, many Canadians simply do not care. Indeed, up until the early 2000s, Canadian politicians often attended the events of organizations of groups that soon would be listed as terrorist entities or bought into their propaganda while downplaying the harm that civilians might face at the hands of these groups abroad.[26]

Second, many of the individual perpetrators were locals – either born in Canada or had spent much of their lives here (perhaps with the exception of the LTTE/WTM).[27] While the origins of the conflicts may have been overseas, the idea that the terrorism was entirely imported to Canada's shores is misleading. Indeed, the idea of "spillover" terrorism has allowed Canada to ignore the fact that terrorism has been a Canadian problem for a longer period than is generally recognized.

Al Qaida and Islamic State–Inspired Extremism

Since 9/11, the main focus of Western intelligence services has been "Al Qaida/Islamic State–inspired extremism." This term is often shorthand used by governments and security agencies to describe the beliefs of groups that adhere to violent extremism motivated by what is called the "single narrative" or "common narrative." In brief, the "single narrative" is a series of erroneous ideas that the West is at war with Islam, Muslims have a duty to resist, and, therefore, they must engage in violent jihad.[28] Although often attributed to Al Qaida and, more recently, the Islamic State, this world view dates back to the writings of extremists in the 1960s and 1970s, especially Sayyid Qutb. Moreover, it has inspired extremist groups across the world such Lashkar-e-Taiba (LeT) Jaish-e-Muhammad (JeM), and Harakat-ul-Mujahideen (HuM).[29]

In the late 1980s, national security agencies began to see the emergence of individuals with ties to violent extremist networks on Canadian soil such as Hamas and Hizballah. In the beginning of this period, the threat-related activities of these individuals reflected other "spillover" terrorism groups: they raised funds for the mujahideen in Afghanistan and Bosnia under the guise of charitable activities.[30] Two prominent cases are noteworthy here. First, that of Fateh Kamel, an Algerian who gained Canadian citizenship through marriage. Following travels in support of extremists in Afghanistan and Bosnia, Kamel was arrested in Jordan and deported to France in 1999. There he was convicted of being part of a criminal terrorist conspiracy as well as providing false documents to terrorists linked to a series of bombings and armed robberies.[31] Second, the case of Ahmed Said Khadr, who came to Canada in 1975, gained citizenship, and began to fundraise for the Afghan mujahideen, disguising his activities as a humanitarian aid worker. He was eventually arrested in Pakistan in 1995 for his role in facilitating a bomb attack against the Egyptian embassy in Islamabad but was released after intervention from Canadian officials. In January 2001 Khadr was designated as a terrorism financier by the United Nations and was killed in a shootout in 2003. At that time, he was described as "a very high-ranking member" of Al Qaida.[32] Khadr is, of course, the patriarch of the Khadr family that has been at the forefront of several violent extremist-related controversies in recent years.

The tenor of cases began to change by the late 1990s as foiled plots and arrests of Canadian citizens or those with ties to Canada made it clear that many extremists were beginning to use this country as a platform from which to mobilize to violence against targets in the West. In particular, the case of Ahmed Ressam, the "millennium bomber," served as a wake-up call. Ressam was caught entering the United States from Canada with explosives in the trunk of his car for the purpose of attacking the Los Angeles Airport in December 1999.

A study of terrorism between 1980 through to the first decade following the 9/11 attacks reveals that most violent extremists in Canada may have wished to attack the West, but they did not yet see harm to their fellow citizens as a primary objective.[33] These extremists had a generally outwards and overseas focus in their aims and targets. Mohammed Mansour Jabarah, who moved to Canada with his family at the age of twelve, was arrested in Oman in 2002 for planning to bomb Western embassies in Southeast Asia.[34] Additionally, the first individual to be tried and convicted under the 2001 *Anti-Terrorism Act*, Mohammad Momin Khawaja, was found guilty of trying to facilitate a terrorist act in the United Kingdom. After travelling to Pakistan, where he spent a short time in a training camp with other British extremists, Khawaja returned to Canada, where he began to develop remote detonators. He was arrested in 2004 and convicted in 2007.[35]

A second trend is that, violent extremists increasingly turned to the internet to conduct their activities. In 2009 Said Namouh, a member of the online Global Islamic Media Front – an online network of extremists, was convicted of facilitation. Namouh had been distributing propaganda, as well as facilitating a bomb plot in Austria by individuals in his network.[36] Also, in 2018 Faruq Khalil Muhammad 'Isa pled guilty in a U.S. court to providing money and long-distance support to Tunisian jihadists responsible for a 2009 suicide attack that killed five U.S. soldiers in Iraq.[37] Much of this activity was coordinated online. More recently, Islamic State operators not only recruited but also facilitated the travel of individuals to Syria over the internet, through social media and encrypted apps.[38] Further, there is evidence to suggest they have also provided online logistical support for attacks against the West, especially as the group shifted tactics.[39]

It was not until halfway through the 2000s that Al Qaida–inspired violent extremists who sought to plan attacks against Canadian targets began to emerge. The most prominent case is that of the "Toronto Eighteen," a cell of young men who were discovered planning attacks against the Toronto Stock Exchange and security- and defence-related targets.[40] Here, a cell of radicalized individuals, although fractious, sought to train and mobilize to create a "Battle of Toronto," an attack involving three fertilizer bombs: two in the downtown core and one against a military base. CSIS and the RCMP learned of the plot and intervened to ensure the bomb components the cell received were inert.[41]

In 2010 three individuals were arrested in Ottawa on terrorist facilitation charges, of whom two were later convicted. Hiva Mohammad Alizadeh was charged with conspiracy to knowingly facilitate a terrorist activity after it was discovered that he had smuggled fifty-six circuit boards to be used as detonators in explosive devices from a training camp in Afghanistan.[42] He pled guilty in 2014. Misbahuddin Ahmed was found guilty of similar charges for his role in the plot.[43]

In sum, in the decades before and after 9/11, Al Qaida–inspired extremists in Canada generally went from a "spillover" model to more of a homegrown one that increasingly targeted Canadians. The concern that a small cell directed, facilitated, or inspired by Al Qaida would carry out an attack in Canada, or use Canada as a base to attack another country (especially the United States) soon became the paramount national security concern for national security agencies, which sets up the context for terrorism concerns today.

Violent Extremism in Canada Today

An overview of the context in which violent extremism has existed in Canada demonstrates the rise and fall of movements, as well as the fact that they have come from a wide variety of political, ideological, and religious sources. In this way, it is hard to predict where the next significant threat may come from or which movement may fade away in the short-to-medium term. Nevertheless, the following movements are likely to remain for the foreseeable future and will continue to pose challenges for national security agencies.

Al Qaida and the Islamic State

At the time of writing, the "ecosystem" of violent extremism driven by the "single narrative," which continues to affect Canada is in flux. It can be described as having four overlapping parts. First, two large rival organizations: Al Qaida and the Islamic State; second, a network of affiliates – some with more formal links than others to two larger entities; third, independent groups such as the Afghan and Pakistani Taliban, Lashkar-e-Taiba (Let), etc.; and finally, a broader community of extremist sympathizers, some who may try to mobilize to violence in small cells or as lone actors.[44]

Al Qaida and the Islamic State have come under significant counterterrorism pressure – in the case of the former, since 2001, and in the case of the latter, since 2014. Nevertheless, experts and security services note that these groups still remain a serious threat: they maintain the intent and capacity (albeit somewhat reduced) to attack within their local surroundings as well as the West, including Canada.

Of the two, the Islamic State has received the most attention since 2014 after shocking the world with its dramatic split from Al Qaida, successful takeover of wide swaths of Iraq and Syria, and declaration of its then leader, Abu Bakr Al Baghdadi, of a so-called caliphate. Inspired by this call to arms and its apocalyptic vision, former Al Qaida affiliates, independent groups, and individuals flocked to the new group, creating a global schism in the jihadist movement.[45] At its peak, it is estimated that the Islamic State controlled a territory the size of Great Britain with eight million people and forty thousand fighters from all over the world.[46] (Some of the "hybrid" tactics of the Islamic State are discussed further in chapter 7.)

Today, after years of fighting, the Islamic State has lost the territory it once controlled. But this raises two key questions over what is next for the terrorist entity, especially in the fate of its foreign fighters as well as its strategy. First, there has been considerable concern that Western Islamic State members would return home as the group took on losses. In Canada, media reports indicate that the RCMP prepared for a "flood of foreign fighters" as the conflict dynamics in Syria and Iraq changed and evolved.[47]

However, it seems clear that the vast majority of Canadian foreign fighters are not returning. In 2018 Public Safety estimated that there were "approximately 190 individuals with a nexus to Canada, and close to 60 who have returned."[48] These numbers have held steady for several years, implying that few individuals have been able to travel or return. Public Safety attributes this to government strategies to prevent these individuals travelling on planes, fear of arrest upon return, capture and detainment within the region, or their (unverified) death overseas.[49] Importantly, researchers believe there are at least forty Canadians, twenty-five of whom are children of extremist travellers, detained in Kurdish prison camps as of April 2020. However, only two to five of these forty are believed to be former fighters, although some of the women may have played supportive roles.[50]

Nevertheless, extremist travellers may have fled to other zones of conflict such as the Philippines, Yemen, and especially Libya.[51] However, none of these conflicts seem to have achieved the same level of interest and attention as Syria. Other ISIS fighters and supporters may be lying low in Turkey or Iraq, hoping to stage a comeback.[52] And, despite the scale of ISIS's recent setbacks, this is a real possibility. The group has faced serious counterterrorism pressure before: it survived the killing of several of its leaders, including the notorious Abu Mus'ab al-Zarqawi, and U.S. counter-insurgency in Iraq between 2006 and 2010 by managing to lie low and gradually rebuild its networks of disaffected Sunni groups in Iraq. Since 2007 a rallying cry for the Islamic State has been that it "will remain" (*baqiya*).[53]

There may also be a shift in the Islamic State's strategy. In April 2018 a spokesperson for the Islamic State called for attacks on neighbouring Arab nations as a priority, possibly to return to its roots as a regional insurgency.[54] However, all violent extremist groups are opportunistic and there is no reason to think that the group would hesitate to organize, support, or claim an attack in the West, should the chance arise. Significantly, the Islamic State continues to have a global presence online, particularly through encrypted apps, which it uses to inspire small cells and individuals to carry out attacks in the West. For example, in February 2020 Saad Akhtar allegedly murdered a woman with a knife in Toronto in what police believe was a violent extremist attack motivated by the Islamic State, although much remains unknown about the case.[55] If confirmed, it is evidence that years after the Islamic State has lost its so-called caliphate, it continues to inspire individuals in Canada to commit violence on its behalf.

Al Qaida experienced high-profile blows between 2011 and 2012 involving the targeted killing of its leadership, including Osama bin Laden, its most effective propagandist Anwar al-Awlaki, and Abu Yahya al-Libi, considered to be the group's deputy leader. This prompted some speculation that Al Qaida as a major terrorism threat to the West was largely finished.[56]

It is far too soon to pronounce Al Qaida over as a threat, and there are signs that its leadership might be quietly rebuilding while most media attention and counterterrorism pressure has shifted to the Islamic State.[57] Al Qaida continues to maintain a global network of affiliates that pledge allegiance to its head, Ayman al Zawahiri, including Al Qaida in the Arabian Peninsula (AQAP), the group usually assessed as the most capable of attacking the West.[58] Notably, an AQAP sleeper cell was responsible for the deadly attack on the Paris offices of the satirical magazine *Charlie Hebdo* in January 2015, demonstrating that the group still has capacity abroad.[59] It continues to have affiliates in West Africa, Somalia, Yemen, and Afghanistan. These still pose a threat to Canadian interests through their recruitment of foreign fighters, targeting Canadians and Canadian assets abroad, and attacking Canada's allies.

Additionally, although the Islamic State has dominated the headlines in Syria, Al Qaida has tried to maintain a presence in the region since 2003. At that time, it accepted the allegiance of Jama'at al-Tawhid wal-Jihad (Group of Monotheism and Jihad) led by Abu Musab al-Zarqawi, which established Al Qaida in Iraq (AQI), later the Islamic State of Iraq (ISI). In order to capitalize on the emerging Syrian civil war, the group sent an operative, Abu Mohammad al-Julani, to set up a franchise that would become known as Jabhat al-Nusra (JN). JN has had a tumultuous history, including its dramatic break with the Islamic State of Iraq (which by this time was calling itself the Islamic State of Iraq and the Levant, later the Islamic State) and its decision to stay with Al Qaida. More recently, it has gone through several name changes and merged with several other groups between 2016 and 2017. Today the organization is known as Hayat Tahrir al-Sham (HTS) and is believed to have a strong network of between 10,000 and 20,000 fighters deeply imbedded in Syria.[60] However, tensions between HTS and Al Qaida resulted in a public break in early 2018. While analysts differ on the strength of the relationship, even loose connections between the two organizations is cause for concern, as HTS may provide Al Qaida with an additional base of operations from which to plot regional and international attacks.[61] Additionally, in the aftermath of this split, a group calling itself Hurras al-Din (Guardians of Religion Organization) has emerged as the Al Qaida affiliate ensuring that the group still has a presence in the region and is widely viewed as posing a threat to Western interests.[62]

Finally, Al Qaida's relatively low profile in recent years should not be mistaken for its fading away. By staying quiet the group may be trying to avoid counterterrorism pressures that are being directed towards the Islamic State. Unlike the Islamic State, Zawahiri has advocated a strategy that avoids mass civilian casualties, especially those that might kill Muslims, in order to appear (strangely) more moderate than its rivals and to avoid outraging the audiences it is trying to reach. Al Qaida has largely taken the view that building a caliphate is a long-term project that requires grass-roots support in the region, which cannot be achieved by killing and brutalizing Muslims. In addition, Al Qaida has always distinguished between a "near enemy" (states ruled by corrupt leaders within the Middle East) and a "far enemy" (the West) with a view that attacking the latter would result in ending its sponsorship of the former. There is no indication that Al Qaida has given up its more global ambitions and, as such, it is likely that it may be regrouping to attempt attacks later. In a March 2018 speech titled "America Is the First Enemy of the Muslims," Zawahiri argued just this – that the priority for Al Qaida remained attacking the West.[63]

The main implication is that while both Al Qaida and the Islamic State are weaker than they once were, both have the capacity to rebuild. In their attempt to regain support, both have an incentive to attack the West and will likely continue to do so, whether through directed, facilitated, approved attacks, or claiming those who act in their name as their own. In this sense, Canadian national security agencies must continue to work with their partners globally, regionally, and locally for the near future and likely into the long term.[64]

State-Linked and State-Sponsored Violent Extremism

State-sponsored terrorism is "the active and often clandestine support, encouragement and assistance provided by a government to a terrorist group."[65] Although the idea of supporting the violent extremist groups that oppose your enemy has a lengthy history, state-sponsored terrorism became a tool of certain regimes to achieve foreign policy goals. In the 1970s the governments of Iran, Iraq, Libya, and Syria began to sponsor or commission terrorist acts against Western, especially American, diplomatic and military targets in the Middle East. These actions became a cost-effective means of waging war against a larger foe.[66] However, the way in which states sponsor terrorism can vary greatly. Daniel Byman suggests that state sponsorship of terrorism should be considered along a spectrum. He differentiates between "active" sponsorship (the provision of direct assistance) and "passive support" (turning a blind eye to the activities of violent extremists, but not providing direct aid).[67]

In more recent times, one of the most notorious cases of this is the Lashkar-e-Taiba (LeT), a Pakistan-based violent extremist group that seeks to force the accession of Indian-administered Kashmir to Pakistan and to create states run on hard-line religious principles. The group has also been linked to Al Qaida and engages in suicide attacks as well as armed attacks on government targets and civilians. The most infamous of these is the 2006 bombing of commuter trains in Mumbai that killed 209 people and injured more than 700, as well as the 2008 attack against buildings in Mumbai that lasted almost three days and killed 164 people.[68] The group is supported by Pakistan's Inter-Services Intelligence (ISI) to effectively pursue a covert war against India.[69]

Although the group is focused primarily on India, the LeT is a good example of how such groups can pose a threat to Canada. In 2005 one member of the Toronto Eighteen cell, Jahmaal James, travelled to Pakistan to get training that would benefit the group. (It seems that James was unsuccessful in his efforts after becoming sick in the training camp early in his stay.)[70] Had he been successful, the Toronto Eighteen could have been far more capable. James's facilitator, Aabid Khan (a British citizen also known as Abu Umar) travelled to Toronto to meet with some of the cell members and reportedly hoped to set up a facilitation network and/or a terror cell in Canada.[71]

Another example of a group with close links to a state (Iran) is Hizballah, a Shiite Muslim political party and militant group considered to be a terrorist organization by most Western governments. Hizballah emerged during Lebanon's fifteen-year long civil war following Israel's invasion and occupation in 1982.[72] The group's ultimate goals are to "obliterate" Israel and consolidate its position as a dominant actor in Lebanon where politically it has become increasingly important.[73]

From its beginnings, Hizballah has been sponsored by Iran and Syria and is seen as a useful foreign policy tool. As such, Iran helped to transform the group from a disorganized and ragtag collection of fighters to one of the most formidable guerrilla and terrorist groups in history.[74] During the Lebanese Civil War, the organization was responsible for the bombing of the U.S. embassy and U.S. Marine barracks in 1983, which left a combined 258 Americans and 58 French service personnel dead.[75] The group is also responsible for the hijacking of TWA Flight 847 which, over a period of seventeen days, saw passengers beaten and the murder of a U.S. Navy diver.[76] Today, despite its political wing, the group continues to engage in violent extremism and has been active in the ongoing civil war in Syria. It is well funded, well organized, and extremely capable.

Hizballah has been the subject of considerable political attention in Canada for well over a decade. As a result of the group's social services network (sometimes described as a "state within a state" in parts of Lebanon), the group sometimes receives money via the

Lebanese government intended for Palestinians. Concern was raised in the early 2000s that humanitarian aid money going to the Lebanese government was funding Hizballah's violent extremism. After a storm of controversy, the Liberal government listed the group as a terrorist entity in 2002.[77]

For the most part, Hizballah's activities in Canada have been in financing, facilitation, and extremist travel. In the late 1990s Mohammed Dbouk was indicted in a U.S. federal court for his role in a Hizballah fundraising and procurement network. According to the FBI, Dbouk's network procured night vision goggles, cameras, scopes, surveying equipment, global positioning systems, mine and metal detection equipment, video equipment, advanced aircraft analysis and design software, laptop computers, stun guns, radios, mining, drilling, and blasting equipment, radars, ultrasonic dog repellers, and laser rangefinders.[78] Dbouk's network also engaged in crime and fraud to fundraise and assist the organization, including passport fraud, credit card fraud, immigration fraud, use of counterfeit currency, etc.[79]

What is most concerning for national security organizations is the fact that Hizballah has used Canadians to engage in extremist travel and terror attacks abroad. In 2002 Israeli authorities arrested Fauzi Ayub, who fought in the Lebanese civil war and joined Hizballah in 1983. Ayub immigrated to Canada in 1988 and appears to have led a normal life before moving back to Lebanon in 2000. He was reportedly re-recruited by Hizballah around this time and tried to infiltrate Israel in order to train other violent extremists and to engage in intelligence-gathering operations and possibly an assassination plot but was caught and arrested in 2002. Ayub was released as a part of a prisoner exchange in 2004.[80]

More recently, in July 2012, Canadian Hassan el Hajj Hassan was one of two individuals who conducted a Hizballah attack against Israeli tourists at the airport in Burgas, Bulgaria, killing six.[81] Hassan is believed to have immigrated to Canada when he was eight, but to have left when he was twelve when his parents divorced. Hassan reportedly travelled back to Canada in order to collect $100,000 in Canadian and Australian bank accounts prior to the attack. It is likely that Hassan travelled on his Canadian passport as well as fake identification.[82]

Even if state-sponsored groups are focused elsewhere, these two cases demonstrate that it is possible for them to threaten Canadian interests and national security. Further, having cultivated networks in Canada, they could turn their attention to attacking our country should they find it advantageous to do so. Nevertheless, it seems that the main threat continues to be financing, facilitation, and extremist travel. As will be discussed in chapter 2, though, even if this does not immediately put Canadians in danger, it may result in the deaths of innocent civilians abroad through the clandestine use of Canadian institutions and infrastructure. It does, therefore, constitute a national security problem.

Far-Right and Single-Issue Violent Extremism

Unlike the groups discussed above, describing the far-right ecosystem is much more difficult. There is no "single narrative" that effectively describes the ideology behind groups. And yet, while there may not be coherence, there is a shared framework of beliefs, ideas, concepts, and literature that cuts across the groups in order that they may be designated "far-right extremism." For the purpose of this book, the definition used by Barbara Perry and Ryan Scrivens will be adopted: "A loose movement, animated by a racially, ethnically, and sexually defined nationalism. This nationalism is typically framed in terms of White power, and is grounded in xenophobic and exclusionary understandings of the perceived threats posed by such groups as non-Whites, Jews, immigrants, homosexuals and feminists."[83] In support of these beliefs, far-right extremist groups are willing to assume both an offensive and defensive stance "in the interests of 'preserving' their heritage and their 'homeland.'"[84]

Scholars have identified several waves of far-right extremist activity in Canada in the wake of the Second World War. In the 1960s, the Toronto-based Edmund Burke Society, an anti-Left/anti-Communist group that called for "militant conservative activism," attacked Vietnam War protestors and gatherings of labour groups and Marxists.[85] This group later became the more overtly racist and anti-Semitic "Western Guard," but its membership declined by the late 1970s. The Ku Klux Klan, a racist, nativist, and anti-Semitic group came to Canada via the United states in the 1920s. There was a resurgence in the group's activities in the 1970s and 1980s, but this was forestalled by the conviction and imprisonment of much of its leadership.[86] However, there are signs that the Klan and people sympathetic to its aims exist in Canada today; in 2017, flyers claiming to be from the organization were distributed in British Columbia.[87]

The skinhead movement came to Canada in the 1980s. Importantly, this "movement" is unstructured and deeply divided; many skinheads do not adhere to far-right extremism. There are non-racist and anti-racist skinheads such as Skinheads against Racial Prejudice (SHARPs), far-left skinheads and anarchist skinheads.[88] It is clear, however, that there are neo-Nazi skinheads in Canada who subscribe to anti-immigrant, anti-LGBTQ2, and racist beliefs. Today the group continues to target youth through music, websites, and internet forums.[89]

In the 1970s Ben Klassen, a Canadian living in the United States, established the "Church of the Creator," an ethnically based religion to advance the white race.[90] Today, "Creativity" is an anti-Semitic group that claims to be "non-violent," although its members have engaged in violence. The movement developed the concept of "RAHOWA" or "racial holy war," a term now in use by many far-right extremists of all types. This message was spread by Canadian band RAHOWA, which was influenced by the British skinhead band Skrewdriver.[91] These were distributed by a Canadian far-right extremist record label, Resistance Records.

RISE IN FAR-RIGHT GROUPS
In recent years there has been a new wave of far-right extremism driven by anti-immigrant/anti-Islam groups coinciding with a number of issues, including the massive displacement of refugees into Europe following the Syrian civil war, a perceived failure to deal with immigration issues in several countries, and the rise of the Islamic State. Also, important has been the campaigning and presidency of Donald Trump, who frequently utilizes racist, anti-immigrant terminology in his speeches and social media posts, downplays concerns over ethno-nationalism, and was elected with a promise to ban Muslims from travelling to the United States. Researchers note that

his campaign appears to have galvanized Canadian-based white supremacist ideologies, identities, movements, and practices.[92]

The results of these trends are jarring. Scholars of far-right extremism believe that the number of active groups in Canada nearly doubled between 2015 and 2019 – from 150 to almost 300.[93] Moreover, during this time the deadliest violent extremist attacks in Canada have come from far-right extremists, not Al Qaida or Islamic State–inspired individuals. While it is not possible to document every far-right group in Canada in this chapter, it is important to note that these new groups are focused on a wide range of issues creating a far-right ecosystem that often overlaps and feeds off each other. This includes cultural chauvinists and misogynist groups such as the Proud Boys who are known to contribute to violence at political rallies and target Indigenous groups,[94] through to violent neo-Nazi gangs. The following overview provides some insight into the far-right in Canada.[95]

First, it is important to note that many of the currently active far-right groups have been around for decades, such as the KKK and racist skinhead groups mentioned above. Of these groups, researchers have assessed Blood and Honour, a transnational neo-Nazi network as among the most active.[96] Several members of this group have been involved in violent hate incidents in Canada, including one in 2011 where a Filipino man was set on fire in Vancouver, BC. In 2019, Blood and Honour, along with it its "armed branch" Combat-18, were the two first far-right/white supremacist groups to be listed as terrorist entities by Public Safety Canada.[97]

More recent are groups like the Quebec-based anti-Islam/anti-immigration group La Meute (the wolf pack) whose anti-immigrant views align it with others in this category.[98] The group has held protests at government sites as well as border checkpoints. The bulk of its activity, however, takes place online, which will be discussed further below.[99] In late 2018 media reports indicated that Le Meute was suffering from "petty interpersonal drama and infighting," leaving the future of the group in question.[100]

Canada has imported far-right movements as well. A group called Patriotic Europeans against the Islamization of the West (PEGIDA) has held rallies in the streets of several Canadian cities, including

Montreal and Toronto, sometimes leading to violence.[101] This German-based neo-Nazi, nationalist, and anti-Islam group also has a robust social media presence with 33,000 members "liking" its Facebook page.

The Soldiers of Odin (SOO), an anti-Islam/anti-migrant vigilante-style group that began in Finland, set up chapters in Canada at the end of 2015 and beginning of 2016. Although the group often portrays itself as a volunteer and community-oriented organization, members of the group frequently show up at anti-migration protests and engage in "street patrols" to protect Canadians from what they wrongly see as a threat from Islam but are really part of an intimidation strategy against immigrants and non-white Canadians.[102] SOO are also known to target institutions they believe are allied with anti-fascist groups (Antifa) and mosques.[103]

SOO attempts to normalize itself politically and socially through strategies such as being photographed with politicians[104] and trying to establish links with Canadian Royal Legion chapters.[105] The resulting controversies have forced some SOO chapters to disband, but many have re-formed under different names such as the "Canadian Infidels," and "Wolves of Odin."[106] Some groups have splintered off from the SOO and formed new but ideologically similar groups such as "Northern Guard" and "Storm Alliance."[107]

In late 2018 far-right extremists hijacked the Canadian manifestation of the "Yellow Vest" movement that began in France. While the French protests originally focused on the cost of living and rising fuel prices, in Canada the movement was quickly co-opted as a platform to protest migration/refugees, promote conspiracy theories about the United Nations, and espouse anti-Muslim views. Rather than a centrally organized movement, the Canadian Yellow Vests often serves as a banner for individuals who hold far-right views to mix with far-right and conspiracy-driven hate groups, especially at small but frequent protests around Canada.[108]

In addition to these groups, there are concerns that new movements are emerging in Canada that are more actively committed to extremist forms of violence in the name of racist ideology. In 2015 an American far-right, pro-gun, anti-Islam/anti-immigrant group called III% (Three Percenters) emerged online and began to set up chapters in Canada. As well as their online activities, the group is reportedly monitoring mosques, conducting live fire paramilitary-style training, claiming to buy land, and plans for creating smoke and flash bombs.[109] Similarly, it was reported in the spring of 2019 that there were members of the American neo-Nazi group "Atomwaffen" in the Canadian military, possibly to seek military training and experience.[110] However, a November 2018 Department of National Defence assessment indicated that the group's footprint in Canada is believed to be small.[111] In March 2020, in the aftermath of arrests of five members of the group in the United States, and amidst media reporting that the U.S. State Department was on the cusp of declaring Atomwaffen a foreign terrorist organization, one of the chief influencers of the movement declared the group was disbanding, although at time of publication it was not clear if this was the case.[112] (In April 2020 the State Department designated the Russian Imperial Movement and several of its members as a "specially designated global terrorist," reflecting concerns about the transnational links between white supremacist organizations.[113])

In the summer of 2019 Patrik Mathews, a Canadian Armed Forces reservist, was outed as a recruiter for a neo-Nazi terror network called "The Base" (a deliberate English translation of "Al Qaida"[114]) by the *Winnipeg Free Press*.[115] The group, which has ties to Atomwaffen, is dedicated to unifying fascists in order to begin a race war in the West.[116] It is often described as subscribing to an "accelerationist" ideology, which believes that acts of violence are necessary for the collapse of liberal democracy, civil war, and the emergence of a white ethno-state.[117] To prepare members, it encourages them to engage in paramilitary training, preaches survivalism, and encourages hate crimes such as targeting synagogues.[118]

After reporting about his affiliation with the Base, Mathews illegally crossed into the United States and was arrested by the FBI in January 2020 and charged with weapons offences. It is believed that he was involved in a plot to trigger a race war. Prosecutors allege that Mathews videotaped himself advocating for murder, poisoning water supplies, and derailing trains.[119]

USE OF THE INTERNET

As will be discussed in chapter 2, the role of the internet in radicalization is complex. Nevertheless, it is hard to separate the rise of the far-right in the West without understanding how individuals and groups have been using the internet to share their ideas as well as bring their beliefs to the mainstream. Indeed, far-right extremists and white supremacists seem to have grasped the importance of the internet very early. Stormfront, one of the oldest white supremacist websites, was established in 1995 and, despite several takedowns, remains one of the most important online spaces for hate groups internationally. Today the relationship between the far-right and collections of like-minded "alt-right" individuals is steeped in online "trolling culture." While this will be discussed further in chapter 7, for now it is worth noting two ways in which the internet has been key to the far-right's rise since the mid-2010s.

The first important trend is the recent marrying of far-right ideas with the internet culture, largely created by user-created message boards, such as (but not exclusively) 4Chan and 8Chan/8kun. Researchers describe this culture as having four characteristics: (1) the use of deliberately offensive speech; (2) antipathy toward sensationalism in the mainstream media; (3) the desire to create emotional impact in targets of action; and (4) the preservation of ambiguity, "where racist speech and content is bandied around in such a way that it can be read either as the trolling of political correctness or as genuine racism."[120]

Whereas far-right extremists had long-used the internet to share their ideas, they had typically done so using dense, text-based blogs. The adoption of these ideas on image-based message boards, where users could participate in creating their own (often deliberately poor-quality) version of the notion being conveyed, allowed these ideas to spread more quickly and farther using loosely organized networks than ever before.[121]

A 2019 investigation in the *Globe and Mail* analysed 150,000 messages by 180 far-right extremists posted in chatrooms on the Discord app (a voice and digital distribution platform originally designed for gamers to coordinate with one another), between February 2017 and early 2018. It found discussions that glorified the alleged racist, sexist, and homophobic behaviour of the participants of the chat, and discussions that joked about the Holocaust and championed Nazism. The report noted, "Many of the in-jokes and memes the members share resemble those propagated by the far right in the United States and Europe."[122] Worryingly, the group appears to do more than chat, reportedly meeting in real life, to share ideas and find ways to bring down Canada's multicultural approach to integration.

A second trend has been the number of groups and individuals that have emerged who capitalize on the ease and popularity of social media, podcasts, YouTube videos, etc. Canadians have been at the forefront of some of these efforts to promote virulently anti-immigrant and white nationalist sentiment. One example is Faith Goldy, a far-right activist and former candidate for mayor of Toronto, who has appeared on neo-Nazi podcasts, and Laura Southern, who has been banned from the United Kingdom and was delayed entry into Australia over concern about the impact of her extremist views.[123] (While these individuals may not be violent, they have aligned themselves with groups that encourage violence against visible minorities and others.) *This Hour Has 88 Minutes*, a play on the Canadian TV series, *This Hour Has 22 Minutes*, has been described as Canada's most popular far-right podcast and lasted ninety episodes before it was outed by Vice Magazine in May 2018.[124]

This alternative far-right online media ecosystem helps to launder many of the ideas of the far-right into more mainstream platforms, where they may be picked up by other publishers and broadcasters, or shared by thousands on Facebook and Twitter. These groups have been able to take advantage of lax user "terms and conditions" by the major social media companies that have not only allowed their content to exist, but to earn money while doing it.

In the wake of a number of far-right terror attacks in 2018–19, the major social media companies, crowd-funding sites, and web-hosting companies have begun to remove (often described as being "deplatformed") far-right publishers, broadcasters, and certain groups online such as the Proud Boys and SOO, as well as far-right activists such as Faith Goldy.[125] However, most of these groups have turned to other less-regulated (but also less-well-known) outlets such as Gab and Mind to continue to broadcast their views and services such as Bitcoin to fund them.

ANTI-GOVERNMENT AND SINGLE-ISSUE EXTREMISTS

An imperfect fit within this ecosystem are anti-government and single-issue extremists. Anti-government and single-issue movements are even more decentralized than most far-right extremist groups.[126] They exist through virtual communities on web forums and videos. This is true of the Freeman-on-the Land (a Canadian version of the American Sovereign Citizens Movement), which began to appear in Canada during the 1990s.

Many of the individuals who subscribe to anti-government ideologies do not subscribe to all views of the far-right extremist groups listed above – they may be preoccupied more with their personal grievances than with racist ideology. Instead, what unites these individuals (and where there is overlap with some far-right extremists) is the belief that government is illegitimate. In this sense, they do not believe they are required to pay taxes, and some practise squatters' rights by occupying vacant properties and ignoring the authority of those sent to evict them. This is where trouble can emerge, as subscribers to the Sovereign Citizen/Freeman-on-the-Land Movements have been known to attack and sometimes kill police officers, judges, and government employees in defence of what they see as their rights.[127] For example, in 2015 Norman Walter Raddatz killed a police officer and wounded another while they were serving a warrant for failure to appear in court in Edmonton. He fired over fifty bullets from his home before turning the gun on himself.[128] While there is no evidence that Raddatz was a part of the Freeman-on-the-Land Movement, he espoused their anti-government views online, was known to make homophobic comments, and had been investigated for anti-Semitic harassment for over a year.[129]

Justin Bourque's attack on RCMP officers in Moncton, New Brunswick, appears to have been inspired by anti-authoritarian and pro-gun beliefs, and his views fit within the spectrum of the Freeman-on-the-Land movement.[130] Bourque has been described as increasingly anxious and paranoid in the months leading up to the attack, subscribing to anti-government conspiracy theories, obsessing over the right to bear arms and a looming apocalypse. Two months before shooting and killing three RCMP officers, he wrote on his Facebook page, "We're already losing the silent war you don't wanna believe is happening."[131]

Single-issue extremists are fixated on a particular ideological issue such as taxes or abortion.[132] Like anti-government extremists, they do not necessarily subscribe to all views of far-right extremists, but there is often some overlap. For example, prior to his alleged Toronto van attack in April 2018, Alek Minassian posed a Facebook message that may give clues to his motivation: "Private (Recruit) Minassian Infantry 00010, wishing to speak to Sgt 4chan please. C23249161. The Incel Rebellion has already begun! We will overthrow all the Chads and Stacys! All hail the Supreme Gentleman Elliot Rodger!"[133] It may seem nonsensical, but the message appears to be Minassian's self-identification with the "Incel" (involuntary celibate) online internet subculture. Those who identify with this subculture believe that the "system" is rigged against men in favour of women, and that it is responsible for their inability to find a sexual partner. It is an extreme form of misogyny and anti-feminism – an area where there is a connection with most far-right extremist ideologies. Elliot Rodger, referenced in Minassian's Facebook message, held a similar world view and murdered six people in California in 2014 in response to his inability to find a sexual partner. Rodger is held up as a hero by many within the Incel movement.[134] It seems likely that in Rodger's actions, Minassian found something to emulate. In an interview conducted by police immediately after his attack (released to the media in September 2019), Minassian indicates that he felt "radicalized" after Rodger's attack and daydreamed about doing something similar. Having attacked so many, Minassian tells the police that he feels that he "accomplished his mission."[135] In January 2020, Alexander Stavropoulos pled guilty to randomly selecting and stabbing a woman multiple times and injuring her baby in Sudbury, Ontario, in June 2019. Stavropoulous indicated that his desire to kill was grounded in his sexual frustration and he was inspired by Minassian.[136]

FAR-RIGHT CHALLENGE FOR NATIONAL SECURITY

A number of challenges make far-right extremism difficult to fight. In the first case, the groups themselves walk a fine line between free speech and counselling violence. Most groups promote hatred, racism, white supremacy, anti-Semitism, and anti-government views. For the most part, though, groups have not traditionally engaged in organized violence in the way that Al Qaida, the Islamic State, or groups inspired by them do.

Instead, there are generally three ways that individuals in far-right extremist groups mobilize to violence. First, individuals often engage in spontaneous violence against visible minorities and LGBT2Q persons. Indeed, this is the predominant manifestation of right-wing extremist violence. A survey of such violent extremism identified hundreds of incidents between 1980 and 2015. Sometimes this activity becomes "berserking," in which far-right extremists become inebriated and then target random individuals and/or property associated with minority groups.[137] As researchers note, this violence often erupts among themselves or at anyone who may be perceived as having looked at the group the wrong way.[138] Second, this violence can become more organized and develop into campaigns of violence against particular communities. As these attacks tend to be planned, they often involve weapons such as baseball bats, eggs, and fireworks.[139] In June 2019 a number of anti-LGBTQ2 and suspected Yellow Vest Canada protestors disrupted Hamilton's Pride event, resulting in fighting.[140] A few days later, members of PEGIDA, the Yellow Vests, and the "Canadian Nationalist Party" were involved in a fight at the Toronto Eaton Centre after targeting the city's Dyke March.[141]

Third, far-right extremists are more likely to engage in lone-actor attacks. As will be discussed in chapter 2, lone-actor attacks are one of the most difficult forms of violent extremism to counter, given the low number of participants and opportunities for intervention. The 2011 attack by Anders Breivik that left seventy-seven people dead in Norway demonstrate just how deadly an attack by a disciplined and determined extremist can be.

Nevertheless, it seems clear that these lone actors do not see themselves as such. Many attackers in recent years have seen themselves as a part of a larger movement or informal network centred upon the themes discussed at the beginning of this section: racially, ethnically, and sexually defined nationalism targeting immigrants, LGBTQ2 individuals, non-whites, Jews, and feminists. Alexandre Bissonnette voraciously consumed anti-immigrant and far-right propaganda online as well as information about firearms and mass killings, especially Dylann Roof, who murdered nine Black parishioners in a South Carolina church in 2015. An investigation of his computer revealed an obsession with Nazis, Donald Trump, and the American alt-right social media sphere. In the lead up to his attack, Bissonnette researched the interior and exterior of the Quebec City mosque he would attack as well as its Facebook page, which suggests his decision to mobilize may have been quick, but it was not instantaneous.[142]

Unfortunately, Bissonnette's actions can be contextualized as part of a disturbing trend in far-right attacks where individuals appear to be inspired by and/or specifically reference other killers as motivation. As noted above, Bissonnette appears to have been inspired by Roof. In March 2019 the perpetrator of attacks against two Christchurch, New Zealand, mosques that left fifty-one individuals dead, referenced Bissonnette's name on one of his gun cartridges, along with other far-right murderers, in an apparent dedication, which was visible in the live-streamed video of his rampage.[143] A study by the *New York Times* found that up to a third of far-right extremists "since 2011 were inspired by others who perpetrated similar attacks, professed a reverence for them or showed an interest in their tactics."[144]

Worse than merely referencing, some violent far-right extremists appear to be challenging each other to increase the lethality of their attacks. Researchers at the open-source investigative journalism site Bellingcat refer to this phenomenon as the "gamification" of terrorism:

> Ever since the Christchurch shooting spree, 8chan users have commented regularly on [the attacker's] high bodycount, and made references to their desire to "beat his high score"…
>
> This is the way far right terrorism works: it is foolish, bordering on suicidal, to attribute attacks like the El Paso shooting or the Gilroy Garlic

Festival shooting to "lone wolves." Both shooters were radicalized in an ecosystem of right-wing terror that deliberately seeks to inspire such massacres.[145]

There are two challenges here for national security agencies and law enforcement. The first is that the style of far-right attacks that tend to be done by individuals or small groups are difficult to disrupt (as discussed in chapter 2). The second issue is that it is not clear who should have the lead in monitoring these groups. As is apparent from the overview above, far-right extremist violence in Canada tends to be characterized by weak leadership, infighting, and transience of members, making these groups highly fractious and unstable.[146] Some far-right violent extremist groups tend to drift towards focusing on crime (especially drugs and illegal markets) rather than extremism.[147] This makes them very difficult to follow from a national security perspective; organizations such as CSIS are not well placed to investigate barroom brawls, assaults, and random acts of violence. These are seen as threats to *public order* (law enforcement) rather than *national security*. As such, far-right extremist groups are often better investigated and prosecuted by local and provincial police forces, who are closer to the ground and communities in which these gangs operate. Indeed, for decades local and provincial forces have had the lead in far-right violence cases. It could be disruptive for national security and intelligence agencies to take over the mandate of these investigations.

Nevertheless, from a practical standpoint, there is a place for national security agencies in this space, particularly as far-right extremism becomes more lethal and as transnational links grow between movements. In 2016 CSIS shut down its far-right extremism investigations, noting that the activities of these movements "were 'near to,' lawful protest, advocacy, and dissent." It added that the public order concerns were being adequately addressed by law enforcement and questioned if their efforts added any value – especially at a time when the organization was occupied by the threat of Islamic State returnees.[148]

However, in the aftermath of the Quebec mosque shooting, CSIS reopened its far-right investigations. The challenge today, as noted above, is determining where it fits in, given the work that is being done at local and provincial levels.[149] In its 2018 public report, the Service noted that it was working with "government and law enforcement partners on the right-wing extremism landscape" and "has increased its posture to gain a better understanding of the landscape in Canada, gain insight into the key players and assess the nature of the current threat environment."[150] Given that groups such as "the Base" (or whatever may follow it) may represent a transition to more organized and transnational form of extremist violence on the far-right, national security organizations will likely play a greater role in countering this threat. By 2019, CSIS overhauled its vocabulary, using the term "violent extremists and terrorists" in its annual public report, and breaking the traditional concept of terrorism into three distinct categories: "religiously motivated violent extremism" (such as AQ/IS), "politically motivated" (violent separatist groups) and "ideological extremism" (far-right and grievance-based extremism).[151]

Already we have seen the Federal Bureau of Investigation (FBI) move in this direction in the United States. In the wake of several violent shootings by far-right and anti-Semitic extremists, the Bureau stated to a House of Representatives committee in February 2020, "The top threat we face from [domestic violent extremists] stems from those we identify as racially/ethnically motivated violent extremists. Racially/ethnically motivated violent extremists were the primary source of all ideologically-motivated lethal incidents and violence in 2018 and 2019 and have been considered the most lethal of all domestic violent extremists since 2001. We assess the threat posed by racially/ethnically motivated violent extremists in the homeland and will remain persistent going forward."[152]

There is no reason to believe that Canada is immune to these trends.

Far-Left Violent Extremism

The analysis of far-left violent extremism in Canada suffers from many of the same problems as far-right extremism: such groups are fractious and small, and the threats they pose often amount to issues of public order rather than national security. They are also focused on a wide range of issues that do not fit into one category. What has constituted far-left politics has evolved, from late nineteenth-century anarchism to radical environmentalism today.[153]

Generally, scholars note that while far-left violent extremist groups may have little in common, there are "major identifying characteristics": a similar ideology and belief about human nature; views on economics and the distribution of wealth; base of operations (urban environments); tactics (use of small cells with emphasis on operational security); and targets – which prioritize symbolic targets (government, military, symbols of capitalism). This last point is especially important – far-left violent extremist groups are far less likely to target persons than far-right groups, which engage in spontaneous violence aimed at minorities.[154]

But further complications make this a sensitive subject. First, it is well established that the RCMP monitored far-left groups as a counter-subversion threat during the Cold War and did so on the basis of questionable evidence. Some critical scholars maintain that the RCMP is now seeing the same movements through the lens of terrorism.[155] Second, there have been concerns that attempts to monitor such threats are really just attempts by the state to monitor, for example, Indigenous activists and their allies in order to advance an agenda of "colonial structural violence."[156] Third, in hyper-partisan times, the issue of "whataboutism" arises – if there is a far-right violent extremist threat, surely there *must* be a far-left violent extremist threat too?

All of this can distort the reality of the threat of far-left violent extremism in Canada. The answer is that there *is* a threat from far-left violent extremism, but it is extremely small and has been far less deadly than other forms of extremist violence. As noted above, one hallmark of such violent extremism is that it tends to avoid directly attacking people.

Canada's history of far-left violent extremism is fragmented. While far-left European groups such as the Italian Red Brigades and German Red Army Faction engaged in deadly campaigns of violence in the 1960s and 1970s, the closest Canada came to such a phenomenon was the FLQ crises described above. Even the United States had far more far-left violent groups with a series of revolutionary, anti-war, and anti-establishment attacks beginning in the late 1960s.[157]

In the early 1980s, a group called "Direct Action" targeted what it saw as symbols of capitalism: pollution, the defence industry, and pornography. One of its attacks on a BC power substation in May 1982 caused five million dollars in damage.[158] In October of that year, the group drove a stolen pick-up truck filled with 250 kilograms of stolen dynamite from Vancouver to Toronto, where they bombed Litton Industries, a company producing components for American Cruise missiles. Although members of Direct Action called to warn of the attack, ten individuals were injured in the explosion. The next month, the members of Direct Action, having returned to British Columbia and calling themselves the "Wimmins Fire Brigade," firebombed three franchises of a chain of video pornography stores.[159] The members of Direct Action were arrested in 1983 and became known as the "Squamish Five" for the city in which they were captured.[160]

In 1986 there were terrorism hoaxes in Canada directed against the apartheid regime in South Africa. While these incidents caused no physical damage, they resulted in financial losses as companies were forced to destroy produce and wine from South Africa that the groups claimed to have poisoned.[161]

However, since the mid-1980s, violent extremist groups motivated by revolutionary ideology have largely disappeared – one might say they have ceded ground to the far-right.[162] While there have been far-left anti-globalization and anti-capitalist movements, their activities have been in the realm of public order threats (such as violent protests at global summits) rather than national security ones.

Nevertheless, there have been some sporadic attacks coming from the radical left. Between 2004 and 2014, every bomb that went off in Canada can be seen as a far-left or hybrid far-left/single-issue case. From 2004 to 2010, the Initiative de Résistance Internationaliste (IRI) (later Résistance Internationaliste or RI) claimed three bombings in Canada: a hydroelectric tower near the Quebec-U.S. border, the bombing of an oil executive's car in Montreal, and a Canadian Forces recruitment centre in Trois-Rivières.[163] Despite extensive criminal investigation, no one has been charged for these acts.[164] In 2010 a retired civil servant firebombed a Royal Bank branch in Ottawa, allegedly for the institution's sponsorship of the 2010 Vancouver Olympics, a major source of protest for left-wing groups at the time.[165] Finally, a series of attacks were carried out against natural gas pipelines and infrastructure in Trickle Creek, Alberta, during the late 1990s and 2000s. Police arrested Wiebo Ludwig, a former pastor, farmer, and outspoken activist against the natural gas facilities, and he served a short prison sentence for his actions. It has been alleged that Ludwig may have been involved in several other violent incidents during this period.[166]

Unlike far-right violent extremism, which has been driven by heightened tensions over race and immigration, it is not clear what the drivers of far-left violent extremism will be in the future. Some scholars note that far-left violence has become increasingly intertwined with "single issue" violent extremism, such as radical environmentalism and animal liberation movements.[167] So far such movements in Canada have been limited, mostly because there are non-violent channels available for dissent. In this sense, it is likely that far-left violent extremism linked to radical environmentalism will remain more of a threat to property than to people.[168]

Nevertheless, there are two possibilities here that would raise the likelihood of further violence. First, as radical environmentalism is characterized by "leaderless resistance" and small cells, it lends itself to lone-actor violence.[169] Second, with fierce debates over oil pipelines once again becoming a contested political issue, some activists could resort to violence in order to make their views known. Given that the Canadian environmental movement has been mainly peaceful, even if engaged in disruptive civil disobedience, it is very far from certain that this will be the case.

Conclusion

As this survey of violent extremism in Canada shows, it is a diverse and constantly evolving threat that is not likely to go away. Even within the same ideologies, we can see rapid strategic change: as discussed in chapter 2, the Islamic State's call for its supporters to join them in Syria and Iraq dramatically and suddenly changed the nature of the threat to Canada. A key national security challenge is to identify when these evolutions and shifts are taking place and to assess the implications for the country.

Additionally, violent extremism in Canada today presents a number of difficult policy questions but also ethical and moral challenges. In the wake of the April 2018 Toronto van attack, one of the most important questions to be asked is why some incidents are considered terrorism while others are not. As noted at the beginning of this chapter, terrorism charges have fallen almost exclusively on Al Qaida/Islamic State–inspired extremism. Violent extremists from the far-right have not been charged with terrorism. If "terrorism" charges are seen as targeting only one religion, can we say these laws are fair?

Addressing this issue is difficult, and structural stumbling blocks may require a re-think of our terrorism legislation. For example, our terrorism laws were created largely as a way to prosecute prospective terrorists who seek to engage in violence. In this way, terrorism charges help to augment the sentences of those who engaged in violent extremism but were foiled along the way. Once a crime has been committed, though, proving the intent of the perpetrator simply becomes extra work at a time when police and law enforcement already have evidence of a crime. The terrorism charge does not really accomplish very much in terms of sentencing, especially where murder and attempted murder charges are in play. Further, such charges may be a substantial risk for the prosecution to take because of the burden of proof required to demonstrate the perpetrator's mentality at the time. This is why there have been charges laid against individuals such as Alizadeh, Sher, and others who were not yet successful, but not those who have actually committed an offence, such as Bissonnette. The issue comes down to practicalities rather than morality.

A second issue already discussed above is that of the fragmented ideology of certain movements. Our terrorism laws require that prosecutors demonstrate that someone conducted an attack for political, ideological, or religious reasons, which presupposes that a coherent system of beliefs that can be pointed to. A gibberish-laden blog post or confusing statement on Facebook may provide some guidance on the motivation of a violent extremist, but it is not evidence of a coherent system of belief.

This creates a problematic impression. How can we point to similar acts and come up with different results? Unfortunately, it seems that the drafters of the 2001 *Anti-Terrorism Act* did not envision that an assortment of grievances and fears, driven by conspiracy theories in a leaderless collection of internet sub-forums, might constitute an ideology for conducting a terrorist act. But a lot has changed since 2001.[170]

Fixing this problem is easier said than done and taking a wider view of what constitutes a terrorist threat may simply produce further challenges. For example, it might be possible to remove the motivation clause from the terrorism offence. In this way, "terrorism" would simply constitute an act "in whole or in part with the intention of intimidating the public, or a segment of the public" – dropping the requirement for it to be attached to a "political, religious, or ideological" cause. This would seriously broaden the terrorism definition and include the actions of individuals such as Bissonnette and Minassian more easily. At the same time, it could conceivably sweep many of the non-terrorist crimes listed in the Criminal Code into this area, since almost all offences involve some kind of intimidation of a segment of the public – even if it is just one person. It is difficult to see this as a desirable outcome.

Yet even if we limit the discussion here to violent-extremist activity, such a widening of the definition might also capture actions and groups that some would be less comfortable including under this umbrella. For example, certain actions by environmental groups, such as blocking trains and roads and staging large protests, might more easily be seen as "intimidating the public." Lawful advocacy is protected, but would it be easier to see these actions as something more sinister? Counselling individuals to disrupt pipelines or teaching them how to do so might also fall under such acts. Given that some Canadian politicians were publicly questioning if Indigenous groups and their supporters were "terrorists" during the widespread anti-pipeline civil disobedience protests in early 2020, it is clear that widening the definition of terrorism carries significant risk.[171]

A second approach might be to list more groups as terrorist entities. Traditionally this option has presented something of a paradox: in order to be listed as a terrorist entity, it has to be proven that a group engages in terrorist activity. The Canadian Charter of Rights and Freedoms makes it clear that individuals are free to hold truly terrible and noxious opinions; but a security threat emerges only when individuals begin to act violently on these beliefs. In this sense, it has not been a useful preventative tool. However, as noted above, Blood and Honour and Combat-18 were added to the terrorist entity list in June 2019 and four more entities were listed in 2021, suggesting that this is an approach the government is adopting.[172]

Finally, it might be possible to require our national security institutions to take a greater role in monitoring these fringe and scattered groups like the "Incels." Considering that the largest mass killings in Canada (the 1989 École Polytechnique massacre, the 2013 Moncton shootings, the 2017 Quebec mosque shooting, and the 2018 Toronto attack) were carried out by individuals who appear to have held far-right extremist and/or bigoted or misogynistic views, there is merit to this argument.

And yet it is not clear how a greater role for national security agencies would work. Expanding the terrorism mandate would require more resources, but when individuals who engage in these actions are typically lone actors, how are agencies supposed to find them? Do we want CSIS trolling internet forums in search of offensive memes? There is another paradox here: there is increased attention to internet forums like 4Chan and 8Chan/8kun, but there is also widespread anxiety about government surveillance. The government will have to make difficult decisions about how it wishes Canadian national security agencies to proceed in this online space, given its significance in far-right violence while at the same time considering the implications of civil liberties and resources.

All this suggests that our understanding of violent extremism should be broadened beyond what is currently encompassed by the law. However, this widening of our understanding of violent extremism must be accomplished in a way that is grounded in empathy rather than fear. Politicians and the public should support communities that suffer attacks and feel free to call such events "terrorism" to show their support. Indeed, it is essential that we validate the suffering of those who experience violent extremism, whatever the motivation – but not just in the form of attacks. It is important to stand with communities who also suffer from the siphoning off of funds from community institutions, intimidating threats, or the presence of radicalizers targeting youth. How these actions affect communities and create the threat of violent extremism in Canada is the subject of the next chapter.

2

Violent Extremist Threats in Canada Today

On the evening of 13 November, 2015, eleven individuals, laden with guns and explosives, set out across six locations in Paris to conduct a sophisticated and well-coordinated attack. Fear and panic spread throughout the city as the national stadium, a concert hall, bars, and restaurants were targeted. One hundred and thirty lives were lost and hundreds more were injured. The Islamic State quickly took credit for the tragedy, and investigators soon learned that the attack was planned in Syria, organized by a cell of violent extremists based in Belgium.[1]

The fear in France quickly spread throughout the West – could this happen in other countries? Could this happen in Canada? Is this what will happen when foreign fighters return from Syria? How can we prevent such an attack from happening at home?

As we established in chapter 1, national security agencies in Canada focus on five kinds of threat-related activities: attack planning, foreign fighters/travel, facilitation, financing, and radicalization. While these five areas of threat-related activity remain relatively constant, violent extremists are adept at adopting new technologies (such as encrypted apps) and techniques (taking propaganda online) that make it very difficult for those in charge of investigating and prosecuting threats to detect, deter, and/or deny such actions. The main argument in this chapter is that the threat of terrorism goes far beyond the threat of violent attacks and includes activities meant to undermine economic, political, and social security. On the basis of this understanding, I argue that empathy with affected communities is a key element in addressing violent extremism.

Here we will look at the range of violent extremist actions that these groups engage in to illustrate the kinds of activities national security agencies investigate. It concludes by highlighting some of the key findings, as well as some issues and challenges that lie ahead, including mental health and technology.

Attack Planning

As mentioned, the risk of violent extremism and terrorist attacks is by far the biggest concern when anticipating threat-related activities in Canada, especially since 9/11.[2] But while the image in the popular imagination is that of a bomb going off in a major Canadian city, there are many different kinds of attacks with different implications for national security agencies. For the sake of convenience, these will be broken into four categories in this chapter: foreign-directed plots, foreign-approved plots, domestic plots, and lone actors. Although all these attacks may be deadly, each requires a different set of tools and techniques and entails unique forms of collaboration between national security agencies.

Foreign-Directed Attacks

Since 9/11, an overriding fear driving counterterrorism policy has been the idea that there are groups like Al Qaida plotting terror attacks against the West, or Western targets. Such attacks involve terrorist groups abroad developing the intent and capability to create such a plan and select targets in another country. It may require reconnaissance in the form of sending advance teams to collect information about potential targets and/or weapons or flight training.

At the time of writing, there are few publicly known, foreign-directed plots that targeted Canada specifically in the post-9/11 period. The most prominent is the 2006 transatlantic airline plot in which a UK-based network sought to detonate bombs on board planes travelling from Heathrow to North America. At least two Air Canada flights were among the possible targets.³ The network that plotted the attack has been described by U.S. intelligence authorities as an Al Qaida cell, directed by Al Qaida leadership in Pakistan. While it remains possible that the group authorized rather than directed the plot, it seems likely that the British plotters received training from members of the terrorist group and that much of the support for the plot came from Al Qaida.⁴

Despite this small number of direct threats, there are a number of reasons counterterrorism officials remain concerned. First, and most important, terrorist groups throughout the world have identified Canada as a legitimate target for attacks, including AQ and ISIS, and their affiliates.⁵ Although terrorist groups change their strategies and priorities over time, there is no reason to believe that either group has changed its mind over what it sees as the "legitimacy" of targeting Canada. Second, these groups are opportunistic: if it is perceived that carrying out an attack on a target in the United States or Europe is too hard, they may very well seek to attack an American target in Canada, or simply against a Canadian target.

A third reason for concern is that Canada and Canadians may be the victims of collateral damage of foreign-directed plots against other states. In 2009 Umar Farouk Abdulmutallab (more commonly known as the "Underwear Bomber") failed to detonate a bomb he was wearing as his flight approached Detroit. Had Abdulmutallab been successful, the attack could have occurred over Southwest Ontario, endangering Canadians on the ground. Likewise, many Canadians have been killed in overseas terror attacks that originated elsewhere. According to the Canadian Incident Database, between 2002 and 2015, there were forty-four incidents in which Canadians were the victims of violent extremist attacks.⁶

While foreign-directed plots have not been the major source of terrorist activity against Canada, there are important reasons to be concerned about this threat. It also suggests the importance of counterterrorism cooperation between states: working to keep our allies safe helps to keep Canadians safe in return.

Foreign-Approved Plots

Unlike foreign-directed plots, foreign-approved plots are those where individuals, typically already set in a particular country or location, seek the approval of a foreign-based terrorist group before carrying out an attack. Such individuals may travel to a certain location to seek approval, training, and guidance, or they may seek online approval through radicalizers and facilitators. The most notable cases of foreign-assisted plots are the 7/7 attacks in London (in which three of the perpetrators travelled to Pakistan to seek training and guidance in carrying out their attack[7]) and the failed attack on Times Square in 2009 (in that case, Najibullah Zazi had also travelled to Pakistan to receive training).[8]

There has been at least one possible foreign-approved attack in Canada: the 2013 Via Rail plot. Although it is still not clear what exactly took place, it is alleged that one of the plot's perpetrators, Chiheb Esseghaier, a Tunisian citizen doing doctoral research in Montreal, travelled to Iran, where he may have sought guidance from Al Qaida–linked cells.[9] However, the extent to which Esseghaier may have coordinated his activities with any terror group is not publicly known. (This highlights the problems analysts can have trying to differentiate between these modes of attack.) Other incidents of foreign-approved plots (for example, by Said Namough and Hiva Alizadeh discussed in chapter 1) focused their attacks on Europe. (Of note, at time of writing this case continues to be appealed through the courts.)

Another type of foreign-approved plot is one in which an individual or group seeks guidance and approval for such attacks online. Infamously, Anwar Al-Awlaki is said to have given individuals in the West "permission" and guidance in carrying out attacks.[10] This style of plot has been described as "remote controlled" – that is "violence conceived and guided by operatives in areas controlled by the violent extremist groups whose only connection to the would-be attacker is the internet."[11]

This kind of recruitment/attack planning seems to be of the sort that targeted Abdulrahman El Bahnasawy, a Canadian convicted of plotting a terror attack in New York City in 2018. Said to be suffering from serious mental health issues and drug addiction, El Bahnasawy eventually discovered radical, violent, extremist movements online. He was targeted by ISIS-linked recruiters and connected with other online individuals committed to carrying out a bomb plot. El Bahnasawy eventually procured bomb-making materials in Ontario, crossed the U.S. border (his unknowing family in tow) in the summer of 2016, and was eventually apprehended by the FBI.[12]

Domestic Attacks

The vast majority of terror plots in Canada fit into this category – that is, individuals or small cells of radicalized individuals who are inspired by ideologies and attempt to conduct attacks in the name of it. The most prominent of these is the 2006 Toronto-Eighteen case discussed in the previous chapter. Additionally, even though there may have been foreign connections to the Via Rail plot, it seems that almost all planning and preparation took place within North America.

Lone Actors

The deadliest attacks on Canadian soil since 9/11 have been carried out by "lone actors."[13] There is considerable debate within the counterterrorism literature over the appropriateness of the term "lone actor." As noted in chapter 1 (and discussed below), radicalization is often seen as a social activity – it is rare for someone to become radicalized without having some sort of interaction with others. But does this interaction need to be in person? What about online activity? And if "lone actors" see themselves as part of an online community, can it really be said they were "lone" in their radicalization and mobilization to violence?

Several leading terrorism scholars suggest that for lone actors, it is best to think about their connections to others as existing on a spectrum. In the digital age, online connections are rampant, and the key question for counterterrorism investigators must be how significant these connections were in the aftermath of an attack. At the lower end of the spectrum are those who consume large amounts of extremist propaganda and have limited contact with other conspirators, but decide to mobilize on their own. Further down the spectrum are those who may receive direct encouragement to conduct and attack but again formulate their own plans and decide when and where to act. Nearer the other end of the spectrum are those who are directly recruited online and groomed to conduct an attack by terror groups. Finally, there are those who choose to go overseas themselves in order to join a terrorist group, seek training, and return to carry out an attack by themselves.[14]

On the basis of publicly available information, Canadian lone actors can be seen to fall within the lower end of the networked spectrum. All seem to have interacted with other individuals at some point, frequently (but not exclusively) online, but to have made the decision to mobilize themselves. They seem to have formulated their own plans, even if their actions appear to be spontaneous. A survey of mobilized terrorist plots in Canada since 2014 shows this trend.

Martin Couture-Rouleau suffered from poor mental health and drug addiction. After his business failed, he reportedly became obsessed with conspiracy theories in 2013. Spending time in his father's basement, he became fascinated with ISIS and twice attempted to travel abroad, first to Pakistan and then to Syria, but was prevented from doing so by police. A few weeks later, in October 2014, after spending nearly two hours in a parking lot outside a Canadian Armed Forces recruitment centre, Couture-Rouleau attacked three individuals with his car, killing Warrant Officer Patrice Vincent. Following a nine-minute car chase, Couture-Rouleau was stopped and killed when he came out of his car and confronted police officers with knives.[15]

Only two days later, Michael Zehaf-Bibeau shot and killed Corporal Nathan Cirillo at the War Memorial in Ottawa before going on a shooting spree at Parliament Hill. Like Couture-Rouleau, Zehaf-Bibeau suffered from drug addiction and possibly mental health issues.[16] He had been living in a homeless shelter prior to his mobilization. Also, like Couture-Rouleau, Zehaf-Bibeau appears to have been a thwarted traveller – he was likely in Ottawa to attempt to get a Libyan passport to travel abroad. Zehaf-Bibeau is known to have been in contact with people with extremist views while he was living in British Columbia. However, the significance of these contacts is unknown: his decision to mobilize came years later and apparently very quickly after he was unable to secure a passport.[17]

Aaron Driver's father argues that his son converted to Islam as the result of a tumultuous childhood. Having spent much of his time online, he became involved with a group of mostly British jihadis fighting for ISIS on the ground or through social media. After posting messages online that supported violent extremism, Driver was arrested in 2015, and the police applied for a peace bond, which required him to abide by certain conditions, including wearing a GPS monitor, staying off the internet, and avoiding contact with all individuals with connections to ISIS. Driver was also required to attend religious counselling, but his lawyer appealed and won. Eventually other conditions were lifted. Several assessments concluded that Driver was not a sociopath and did not suffer from psychiatric illnesses but was consumed by an overriding religious conviction. Despite his peace bond conditions, Driver was able to build two bombs and set out to detonate them against an unknown target in August 2016. The FBI discovered a video that had been uploaded online in which Driver stated his intention to conduct an attack in Canada on behalf of ISIS and immediately informed the RCMP, who were able to stop Driver as he was getting into a taxi. Driver attempted to detonate his bombs, which failed, and was shot and killed by police.[18]

In September 2017 Abdulahi Hasan Sharif is alleged to have tried to kill an Edmonton police constable before running down four pedestrians in a rented truck he had decorated with an Islamic State flag.[19] Sharif was a legally admitted refugee to Canada with a history of mental health issues.[20] While he had no criminal past, he had been on police radar since 2015 for espousing "extremist ideologies," but the RCMP found that there was insufficient evidence to lay charges or to get a peace bond prior to the attack.[21]

Although these cases have been prominent for their association (albeit some very tenuously) with Al Qaida or ISIS-inspired extremism, other individuals who have mobilized to violence have been linked to far-right, anti-government, or single-issue ideologies. Justin Bourque, Alek Minassian, and Alexander Stavropoulos, all discussed in chapter 1, are examples of this phenomenon. Also, as noted in chapter 1, Alexandre Bissonnette voraciously consumed anti-immigrant and far-right propaganda online as well as information about firearms and mass killings, especially Dylann Roof, who murdered nine Black parishioners in a South Carolina church in 2015. An investigation of his computer revealed an obsession with Nazis, Donald Trump, and the American alt-right social media sphere. In the lead up to his attack, Bissonnette researched the interior and exterior of the Quebec City mosque he would attack, as well as its Facebook page, which suggests his decision to mobilize may have been quick, but it was not instantaneous.[22]

Upon review of available information, it seems that in none of these cases were individuals directly instructed to mobilize.[23] Some seem to have consumed more propaganda and interacted more extensively online than others, but all appear to have made the decision to mobilize by themselves. They then formulated their own plans, although in some cases they may have modelled their attacks on what others had done in the past.

This survey of violent extremist attacks in Canada raises three key points. First, violent extremism in Canada is an almost exclusively homegrown phenomenon: the threat is increasingly not from abroad, but typically comes from Canadian citizens who were either born here or immigrated at an early stage of their lives. Second, although there are more known plots that originate with Al Qaida– and ISIS-inspired extremism, attacks from far-right and single-issue extremism have been more successful and lethal.

Third, given the nature of the threat in Canada, it should not come as a surprise that most successful attacks have been by lone actors (broadly defined). With fewer people involved, there are less opportunities for national security agencies to detect any such plot.[24] Also significant is the fact that these individuals mobilized very quickly, making it difficult for authorities to recognize suspicious activity. Yet, as will be discussed below, studies of the behaviour of lone actors reveal that these individuals are more social than anticipated and there may be space for intervention by law enforcement.

This is not to say that terrorist attacks from abroad are not a legitimate risk. As noted above, groups such as Al Qaida and ISIS have continuously identified Canada as a target in their announcements and their propaganda. They may seek to send individuals to Canada to conduct a plot, use Canada as a platform to engage in threat-related activities elsewhere, or choose to strike at Canadian targets (such as companies and embassies) abroad. Groups may turn to Canadian foreign fighters in executing these attacks.

Travel for Extremist Purposes and Foreign Fighters

While the term "foreign fighter" is often used to describe the activity of those who leave their home countries to engage in threat-related activities abroad, these individuals engage in far more than fighting. When abroad, they are involved in recruitment, creation of propaganda, administrative support, and "law enforcement." For example, much of the ISIS propaganda encouraging travel to its so-called caliphate was aimed at encouraging doctors and engineers who could contribute to the foundation of a new society based on their extremist interpretation of Islam. To capture the breadth of activities, national security agencies sometimes refer to such cases as "Canadian extremist travellers" (CETS) or individuals engaging in "travel for extremist purposes," thus avoiding a narrow focus on combat. Whatever the motivation, the issue of extremist travel and foreign fighters is one of the most difficult counterterrorism challenges that Canada has faced in recent years.

It is important to recognize that this phenomenon is not new. Canadians have travelled to engage in foreign conflicts for decades. During the 1930s, over 1,600 Canadians travelled to fight in the Spanish Civil War.[25] More recently, Canadians have travelled to engage in activities with such groups as Hizballah, Mojahedin-e Khalq (MEK), the Tamil Tigers, and Sikh separatist groups.[26]

The issue of extremist travel began to attract attention following 9/11. There was concern that Canadians might travel to join Al Qaida (as was the case with the Khadr family), and it was believed that a number of Somali youth had left Canada to join Al Shabaab, including six who left Toronto in 2009. Four of the six are now believed to be dead. Tragically, one is believed to have led an attack on a court in Mogadishu that left at least thirty-five individuals dead and dozens more injured.[27]

By early 2013 it was apparent that Canada's foreign fighter issue was much more serious than previously thought and that the nature of terrorist activity with a Canadian-nexus was rapidly evolving. As noted in chapter 1, Canadian-Lebanese citizen Hassan el Hajj Hassan was one of two individuals who conducted a Hizballah-sponsored attack against Israeli tourists at the airport in Burgas, Bulgaria, killing six in July 2012.[28] It was later discovered that two teenagers from London, Ontario, Xristos Katsiroubas and Ali Medlej, had participated in an attack on an oil refinery in Amenas, Algeria. This incident killed approximately forty individuals and both men were killed in an ensuring fight with Algerian forces.[29]

The period between 2012 and 2015 saw the first mass mobilization of Canadian extremists, with most going Syria. In 2018 Public Safety Canada estimated that there were 190 extremist travellers "with a nexus to Canada" abroad, with slightly over half in Iraq, Syria, or Turkey.[30] While some may have been motivated by humanitarian or even nationalist reasons, most of the individuals travelling to this region are believed to have held extremist views. Realizing they had a problem on their hands, the Stephen Harper government moved to start tracking and preventing individuals from leaving Canada.

Though widely publicized, the number 190 presented by Public Safety Canada is vague: it offers no time frame for its scope (190 travellers since when?). Furthermore, as it is impossible to confirm if an individual has died, these people remain on the list even if they are reported killed. A substantial percentage of the individuals currently listed as "abroad" may be dead. Finally, the government lists include only fully identified individuals. There may be rumoured or partly identified individuals who are not on the list. It is important, then, to take this figure as an indicator and not an exact measurement of the problem.

What is clear, however, is that during the Syrian civil war there was an increase in the numbers of people engaging in extremist travel. One explanation has been the location of the Syrian conflict. Because the country is connected to Europe through Turkey, it is much easier for individuals to travel to Syria than to other areas where terrorist activity is rampant, such as Afghanistan, Iraq, Pakistan, or Somalia. As noted above, individuals from Canada could travel to Europe and then take a second plane, train, or other vehicle to Turkey, where they could make their way to the Syrian border.[31]

The symbolic nature of the conflict as a "push" factor cannot be ignored either. In the first instance, the brutality of the Syrian regime served as an important recruiting tool for extremist groups in the region. At least one study based on interviews with foreign fighters highlights their perception that there was a need to do something about the injustices faced by Muslims in Syria.[32] The religious significance of the location made this all the more urgent in the minds of foreign fighters. As William McCants notes, the Islamic State's writings and propaganda are full of apocalyptic prophesies and visions combining the idea of the return of an Islamic empire with the end of the world. Selectively drawing upon these prophecies, the Islamic State was able to convince its followers that they could take part in a fateful battle that would mark the end of days.[33] The desire to become a martyr in such a battle seems to be at the forefront of the minds of many surveyed fighters.[34]

Another explanation for the surge in extremist travel is that the Islamic State made it much easier for aspiring fighters to participate. This was a major innovation and drastically changed the nature of the terrorist threat to the West in 2012. While groups such as Al Qaeda are viewed as a global movement, they are also self-consciously elitist. In other words, they have traditionally recruited individuals who are smart, educated, capable, and seldom engaged in criminal activity that could draw the attention of authorities. These individuals may have been targeted at young ages and put through layers of recruitment over a lengthy period of time. This cautious approach did not result in large numbers of recruits, at least not initially.

Al Qaida began to "franchise" in the mid-2000s, turning the elitist group into more of a movement, choosing local groups in the Middle

East and Africa to bolster their brand. This was a significant shift in strategy, turning away from the group's historic focus on attacking the United States (the far enemy) towards attacking local regimes deemed to be corrupt and apostate (the near enemy).[35] While these groups may be focused on local and regional grievances, they continue to pose a threat to the West and serve as links, providing funds, fighters, training, and equipment to Al Qaida, a group with a far more committed international agenda.

ISIS's innovation beginning in 2012 was to effectively lower the barrier to entry for joining terrorist groups. It instructed its sympathizers to migrate to their so-called caliphate, regardless of their capabilities, education, or background. While groups such as Hay'at Tahrir al-Sham (HTS) were cautious about recruitment, ISIS conducted little to no vetting of prospective members. With the traditional barriers gone, thousands of individuals from all over the globe were able to join a violent extremist movement, creating a vast pool of fighters and potential terrorists to send back to their home countries. This approach effectively turned the Al Qaida model on its head.

It remains to be seen if other groups will adopt this model. Despite tens of thousands of recruits, the Islamic State was not been able to hold onto its territory. It no longer encourages individuals to join it in Syria but has, since 2016, ramped up calls for its followers to unleash attacks abroad and/or in their home countries. The transformation of more violent extremist groups into further mass movements is a frightening prospect.

Ultimately, the West did not anticipate the impact of the Syrian conflict and the way it would change the nature of the terrorist threat. It seems clear, however, that the number of individuals travelling abroad has diminished since its peak in 2014. This is likely due to the Islamic State's loss of territory, attempts by social media companies to prevent the spread of propaganda, as well as the efforts of national security agencies, including Canadian agencies, to recognize the signs of mobilization and prevent individuals from leaving the country.

Before moving on, it is worth considering why the government makes such efforts to keep people from leaving Canada. After all, some might say it is better for radicalized violent extremists to conduct their activities elsewhere, outside of the country. Do we really want to keep such people within our borders? Should we care if they want to kill themselves?

There are a number of national security reasons why it is important for states, including Canada, to prevent foreign fighters from leaving to engage in violence. The first problem is just that – these individuals want to support the killing and injuring of people overseas. If Canada knew of another country that permitted its citizens to come to our shores to conduct or support an attack, Canadians would be rightfully upset. Why should other countries feel differently? Even for countries with which we may disagree, we have a duty to prevent our citizens and residents from hurting innocent people. Second, and relatedly, when we allow our citizens and residents to go abroad to engage in these activities, they are ultimately supporting violent extremist ends. Canada has no interest in allowing its citizens to support the ends of terror groups that one day may choose to target Canadian interests or our country directly.

A third reason is that many assume that those who go overseas will be killed. This is not certain, of course. A major concern of counterterrorism officials is that those who go overseas will receive training in how to conduct deadly attacks. While the terror group may choose to use the individual in-theatre, they may also send that person to another country or back to Canada in order to engage in threat-related activity. This has major implications, as studies have suggested that "returnees" who re-engage in violence once they have gone elsewhere or back to their own country tend to produce attacks that are far more deadly than their domestic counterparts. A study of fifty-one "jihadist-inspired attacks" between 2014 and 2017 found that the average death toll in attacks carried out by returnees was thirty-five people versus seven for those carried out by individuals who had not travelled to conflict zones.[36] A second study of sixty-nine plots in the West between 2011 and 2015 found that the ratio was 7.3 deaths per attack when carried out by returnees, as opposed to 1.2 deaths per attack conducted by homegrown violent extremists.[37] In this sense, returnees are statistically less likely to conduct attacks, but when they do, they are far more deadly. The attacks on Paris in November 2015 is a clear example. Canada, therefore, has an incentive to keep individuals from acquiring and honing extremist skillsets while abroad.

Finally, extremist travellers hurt Canada's international standing. If it is known that extremist travellers can easily use Canadian travel documents to engage in threat-related activity, the reputation of our passport suffers, and it will become harder for Canadians to travel and do business abroad.

There is always a risk that individuals who are determined to act and are prevented from travelling ("thwarted travellers") will simply shift their focus to Canada itself. These is evidence that this was the case for Couture-Rouleau and Zehaf-Bibeau. Still, the moral requirement to be a good member of the international community, and the problems returnees can pose when they come back to their home countries suggest that prevention is still the more prudent path.

Challenges in Confronting Extremist Travel

Having established why it is important to counter the threat of extremist travel and prevent would-be foreign fighters from leaving Canada, it is also worth examining why this is so difficult for the government and national security agencies to do.

DETECTING
It is difficult to detect individuals who wish to engage in violent extremism abroad. While authorities have become increasingly successful at pulling down online information, there are guides available to the aspiring extremist traveller.[38] As such, many Canadians have managed to leave the country without raising the suspicion of family members or the authorities, and have done so using their legitimate passport. These individuals frequently engage in "broken" travel to avoid suspicion – that is, they disguise their final destination by taking separate flights or spending several days in an intermediate country. They may also fly to one area of the world and then simply take a different mode of transportation that is harder to detect.

PREVENTING

Once it is known that individuals wish to travel, Canadian authorities can cancel or strip them of their passports. Alternatively, concerned relatives and loved ones may attempt to confiscate the passport if they are concerned that someone may leave to join a terrorist group. While there were extremists like Ahmed Ressam who travelled on forged documents in the 1990s, modern advances in passport technology make this increasingly harder to do.[39]

But determined travellers still have a few options. They may travel on the passport of another nationality. If they are dual citizens, they can apply to that country for a legitimate travel document. Individuals may try to steal a passport of someone with whom they share a resemblance and try to pass for them. This worked for Ali Mohammed Dirie, a member of the Toronto Eighteen who, within a year of his release, used a passport that was not his own to get to Syria.[40] Hasibullah Yusufzai, the first Canadian charged under Canadian law for extremist travel in 2014 (after he had departed) was also able to leave Canada by using a passport that did not belong to him.[41]

That the numbers of Canadian travellers have remained largely static in recent years suggests that this issue may be subsiding at least temporarily as a national security threat. This may be the result of two factors. First, as the Islamic State has lost its territory, other conflicts, such as those in Afghanistan, Libya, Somalia, and Pakistan, are harder to get to and may not have the same appeal for would-be extremist travellers. Second, after years of trying to prevent violent extremists from travelling, governments have learned to cope with the threat.[42] In this sense, violent extremists may be looking to attack where they are or to support violent extremism in other ways.

At the same time, the threat of foreign fighters might be evolving in the West. There are growing concerns that far-right extremists are seeking to travel to Eastern Ukraine and Russia in order to get paramilitary training in order to engage in attacks.[43] It is not clear how many Canadians have made this journey, but in September 2019 the Soufan Group estimated that it could be up to 14 of the 49 travellers from North America estimated to have travelled there between 2014 and 2019.[44] To the author's knowledge, these individuals are not counted among the official extremist traveller number (190) provided in public reports. However, it is likely these fighters are seeking essentially the same benefits of extremist travel that ISIS fighters have sought – and that they pose a similar threat to Canadian national security.

Facilitation

Facilitation of a terrorist act is defined in section 83.3 of the Canadian Criminal Code as "every one who, directly or indirectly, collects property, provides or invites a person to provide, or makes available property or financial or other related services" intending or knowing that they will be used to facilitate a person or group.[45] Practically, this could include providing weapons or advice on how to obtain them, transporting goods, money, or services, or, most recently, information and guidance on travelling for extremist purposes (discussed above).

Traditionally, facilitation networks formed through friendships and relationships developed over time or through family ties. Aside from actually providing available information and resources related to the logistics of engaging in a terrorist act, these relationships often serve a particular purpose: facilitators can play a role in protecting terrorist organizations, groups or plots through getting to know potential recruits and vetting them.[46] Facilitators can also serve as a bridge between local networks to other groups and conflicts abroad.[47] Local facilitators can help feed individuals into more internationally focused entities. As discussed in chapter 1, Mohammad Momin Khawaja was found guilty of trying to facilitate a terrorist act in the United Kingdom after furthering his contacts with British extremists in a training camp in Pakistan.

Today, while facilitation still occurs in person, much of this activity takes place online. As noted in chapter 1, Said Namouh and Faruq Khalil Muhammad 'Isa were both arrested and convicted of facilitating extremist networks online. More recently, within Canada, ISIS has targeted individuals for recruitment and likely facilitated their travel overseas. For example, in April 2015 three girls from Toronto were intercepted in Egypt on their way to join the Islamic State.[48] It is likely that the girls had an online facilitator to meet them at the Turkish-Syrian border.

Finance

There is a long history of terrorist financing on Canadian soil; none of the activities discussed so far can take place without money. From the millions of dollars required to support large terrorist groups abroad, to a few hundred dollars for a plane ticket to Syria, violent extremists need money in order to conduct their plans. It is no surprise then that those who wish to engage in threat-related activities have become creative and strategic in raising funds and that Canadians have engaged in such efforts, often while inside the country itself.

Part of the problem is that for years Canada did not have a law against terrorist financing. In this sense, violent extremist Republican Irish, Iranian, Sikh, Tamil, and other extremist groups were able to fundraise with a certain degree of impunity. The only way to prosecute an individual was to link the money to a specific terrorist act. Sending cash to a group was not enough: how could it be proven the money was used for bombs and not medicine for a hospital?[49]

Of course, prior to 9/11, Canada was subject to international conventions that prevent money laundering the profits of drugs and serious crime.[50] Canada was also a founding member of the Financial Action Task Force (FATF), an intergovernmental body founded in July 1989 to counter money laundering. While it does not make law, it makes recommendations that have global implications.[51]

The first treaty to specifically target the financing of terrorism was the 1999 International Convention for the Suppression of the Financing of Terrorism.[52] Additionally, while Canada sat on the Security Council in 1999–2000, two significant counterterrorism resolutions were passed under chapter VII of the UN Charter with measures to prevent terrorism financing. First, in October 1999, resolution 1267 passed, requiring states to freeze the financial assets of the Taliban and report on their progress in doing so. This was expanded to include Osama bin Laden and Al Qaida in UNSCR 1333 in October

2000 following the attack on the USS *Cole*. All these measures remain in force today.

After 9/11, the most important international regulation was found in UNSCR 1373, which contained four counterterrorism financing measures: it (1) requires states to thwart and control the financing of terrorism; (2) criminalizes the collection of terrorist funds in states' territory; (3) freezes the funds, financial assets, and economic resources of people who commit or try to commit acts of terrorism; and (4) prevents individuals within their territory from providing funds, financial assets, or economic resources to people who seek to engage in or facilitate terrorist acts.[53] Additionally, the mandate of the FATF was expanded to include eight "special recommendations" for countering terrorist financing (expanded to nine in 2012).[54]

Canada met these post-9/11 obligations through the 2001 *Anti-Terrorism Act*, which created two new terrorism financing offences: 83.02, which incorporates the definition of terrorism in the International Convention for the Suppression of the Financing of Terrorism into Canadian law, and 83.03 which creates a financing offence tied to Canada's (broader) concept of terrorism in the Criminal Code. The 2001 *Anti-Terrorism Act* also created the *Charities Registration (Security Information) Act*, which allowed the Ministers of Public Safety and National Revenue to strip an organization of its charitable status.[55]

Unfortunately, when it comes to prevention and prosecution, Canada lags behind its allies. There has been only one conviction in Canada on strictly terrorism finance grounds that resulted in a six-month sentence for a man who provided $3,000 to the Tamil Tigers. International bodies such as the United Nation's Counter-Terrorism Committee and FATF have noted this poor track record and made recommendations for improvement in Canada's international obligations.[56]

Why Canada is behind its allies in prosecuting terrorism financing is not clear. One answer is that the RCMP may simply lack the capacity or expertise to deal with the information it is given from Canada's financial intelligence unit, the Financial Transactions and Reports Analysis Centre of Canada (FINTRAC). Multiple experts testified to the House of Common's Standing Committee on Finance in 2015 that the RCMP lacks the capacity and specialization to conduct complex terrorism financial investigations.[57] Second, in recent years the emphasis in counterterrorism has been on the prevention of foreign fighters from travelling abroad rather than countering threat-finance activities. In this sense, preventing terrorism financing may simply be seen as a lesser priority for governments and national security agencies in Canada.

To be fair, the small numbers of charges do not tell the entire story – in several cases, terrorism financing was part of a larger suite of facilitation charges under section 83.03 of the Criminal Code, including Khawaja and Namouh. In the absence of a systematic study of terrorism financing in Canada, the cases described here are intended to provide an overview of the ways this threat manifests within our borders.

Legitimate Means

The easiest way to avoid the attention of authorities is to use legitimate means to finance illegal ends. Legitimate means can be any way a person normally obtains money: working a job, government payouts (student grants, welfare), selling goods and services, selling property, including real estate, and obtaining a mortgage or loan. All of these are normal financial activities to get cash that can then be put towards a violent extremist end. As CSIS noted in its study of those who mobilize to violence, one of the first steps an individual will take is financial: maxing out a credit card and selling personal belongings.[58] While this may raise enough money to get someone to Syria, for example, more ambitious plotters need other means if they wish to generate larger amounts of funds.

Targeting Charity

Another way to avoid the attention of authorities is to use charities. This threat can manifest in two ways. First, individuals can take legitimate funds and redirect them towards violent extremist ends. It has been alleged that Ahmed Said Khadr used his position with Human Concern International (HCI) to siphon funds to violent extremist organizations in Pakistan and Afghanistan in the 1980s and early 1990s.[59] Second, violent extremists may set up fake charities, deliberately created to channel funds to support terrorist groups overseas. The Canadian branch of the Babar Khalsa, a violent extremist group, was able to register as a charity.[60] And prior to its listing as a terrorist entity in 2002, Hizballah was eligible to receive charitable donations.[61]

As discussed in chapter 1, the LTTE created the World Tamil Movement (WTM), which was banned in 2008. Disguised as a humanitarian organization, the WTM raised money for the Tigers (as well as keeping the sentiment of Tamil nationalism alive in the diaspora).[62] Immediately after it was established, the LTTE attempted to encroach on other Tamil organizations in Canada. In April 2007 an RCMP raid on the WTM found lists of ethnic Tamils living in Canada alongside how much they had donated as well as cheques from Tamil business owners, many in excess of $10,000 that had possibly been extorted.[63]

Other Criminal Means

A third way to raise funds is through criminal means, including the sale of counterfeit goods, fraud, robbery, and narcotics trafficking. For years, governments and experts have warned that terrorist networks use fake goods to raise money; infamously the attack on the French satirical magazine *Charlie Hebdo* was financed through the sale of counterfeit goods on the streets of Paris.[64] Yet, despite a reputation for being a relative haven for the production and selling of counterfeit goods, Canada has few open-source cases linking the practice to terrorism, and few attempts at prosecution.[65] Nevertheless Canadians have found themselves charged in the United States for these activities. In 1992 two Canadians were arrested in the United States on terrorism finance charges, including trafficking stolen bonds and selling counterfeit animal vaccines to farmers to benefit the Irish Republican Army.[66]

For years there have been allegations that violent extremist groups are involved in more serious crimes. Certainly, some listed terrorism entities such as the Armed Revolutionary Forces of Columbia (FARC) have used narcotics to fund their activities, including drugs that end up on the streets of North American cities. In the late 1990s the RCMP, Canada Customs, and the Sûreté du Québec investigated a Lebanese auto theft ring whose profits were linked to Hizballah.[67] Hizballah engages in other kinds of smuggling as well; the Dbouk network discussed in chapter 1 is an example. Additionally, in 2006 several Canadians from Windsor and Montreal were indicted in the United States for their participation in a counterfeit ring, the profits from which went to Hizballah. The ring smuggled in everything from cigarettes, to counterfeit Viagra and rolling papers, socks, toilet paper, and baby formula.[68]

Violent extremists based in Canada have been known to use petty crime to fund their livelihoods, if not terrorist groups and activities. Before his failed attempt to bomb the Los Angeles Airport in 1999, Ahmed Ressam and the group of Algerian-Canadians with whom he networked engaged in the theft and sale of forged or stolen documents.[69] One of these individuals in particular, Mokhtar Haouari, is believed to have engaged in bank fraud that supported Ressam.[70] Aspiring foreign fighters have also turned to theft to fund their travel abroad. In 2015 a teenager in Quebec was arrested for robbing a convenience store of $2,000 to fund threat-related activities. He had also tried to steal his parents' credit cards twice.[71] Similarly, when Ismael Habib was arrested for attempting to travel to Syria, the RCMP said he was carrying a machine to clone credit cards.[72]

Kidnapping for Ransom

A major fundraising activity for terrorism internationally has been kidnapping for ransom (KFR). Canadians have been taken hostage all over the world, and while Canada takes a strong stance against paying ransom to terrorists, other private individuals, companies, or local authorities may pay to get individuals back or to avoid public embarrassment. While their choice may be understandable, it tends to confound the problem. First, the payment is essentially a reward for kidnapping, and the success of the operation will encourage the same group or others to participate in further kidnapping. Second, the money that is raised is often put towards furthering terrorist ends and operations. For example, the UK government estimates that, between September 2013 and September 2014, the Islamic State raised U.S.$35–45 million from kidnapping. Similarly, between 2009 and 2014, Al Qaida and its affiliates raised an estimated U.S.$145 million. During this time, the average ransom payment was U.S.$2.7–2.9 million per Western hostage.[73] KFR operations are lucrative and it is very likely extremist groups will continue to engage in them.

Radicalization

Of all the areas of threat-related activity under discussion, by far the most problematic and difficult to define with any precision is "radicalization." This is because there is little about it upon which experts agree, and nearly two decades after the 9/11 attacks, neither social scientists, psychologists, medical professionals, nor national security professionals know what causes an individual to hold extremist views and then act upon them in a violent way.[74]

Within the national security space, the word "radical" relates to the idea of "coming from the root" or origin. Radicals seek to get back to what they perceive as the very basic core of a belief or way of being. In this way, the term relates to an all-encompassing fundamentalism – radicals do not seek compromise but, rather, to transform society with what they see as their own untainted version of the truth. It is important to note that not all radicals are violent: many believe that society should undergo transformative revolution but are not prepared to engage in violence to bring it about. On the other hand, by definition, violent extremists have radicalized: they have carried out, facilitated, or in some way counselled an act to further political, ideological, or religious ends.

Yet how an individual comes to hold this view and why, and what drives her or him to act upon such beliefs appears to be highly variable. There is no reliable terrorist profile to which one can turn in Canada. Violent extremists are diverse: they come from all races, religions, and socio-economic and educational backgrounds. In this sense, demographic information is not useful in trying to determine who radicalizes and mobilizes to violence.

In recent years, researchers have increasingly turned to other psychological, social, and/or behavioural factors for answers.[75] An important 2018 study that interviewed the family and friends of thirty Western foreign fighters (twenty-seven men and three women) found that these individuals experienced "an acute emerging adult identity struggle," maintained a "moralistic problem-solving mindset" conditioned by "an inordinate quest for significance" to make a difference in the world. They also found that these problems were "resolved" by these individuals through belief in an ideology and "participating in a fantasy (literally) of world change," and that this belief was consolidated by the psychological impact of intense small group dynamics, if not charismatic leaders. In the view of the researchers, for the foreign fighters these factors had fused "their personality with a new group identity and cause."[76]

In Canada, individuals and groups have mobilized to violence in a variety of ways. A brief typology of radicalization to violence based on Canadian cases developed for this book follows.

In Person: Hierarchal/Charismatic Leader

Many of the prominent terrorism cases in Canada have been those of individuals involved in groups (small dedicated cells or more loose networks) who eventually mobilize to violence. This has happened largely in two ways: First, cells can form around a charismatic leader who guides and encourages followers towards radicalization and then violent extremism.[77] Importantly (as discussed below), this radicalizing individual will often know how to stay within the boundaries of the law while walking followers right up to that line. In the case of Mohammed Mansour Jabarah (discussed in chapter 1), he appears to have been targeted, radicalized, and recruited by an Al Qaida sympathizer and religious teacher in Kuwait, Abu Gaith – who later turned out to be a major figure in the terrorist organization.[78]

In Person: Group Polarization

Friends who discover they share extreme views may come together to share their beliefs and increasingly encourage each other in their pursuit of their goals and mobilization. This has also been described in academic literature as a "lone wolf pack,"[79] or, more bluntly, "a bunch of guys."[80] This scenario has sometimes been described as an "echo chamber" to describe how the group cuts itself off from outside voices. A more apt description is "group polarization," or the tendency of a group to make decisions that are more extreme than the initial inclination of its members.[81] While much remains unknown about what exactly happened, it seems as though this describes the radicalization dynamics of a cluster of individuals in Calgary who left Canada for Syria between 2012 and 2013. This group lived in the same building, prayed, played sports and hiked together – and apparently also engaged in secret meetings. Without a charismatic leader per se, it appears the members were likely able to convince each other to engage in violent extremism.[82]

Online

As noted in chapter 1, the role of the internet in radicalization has been controversial, but the idea that the internet plays an important role in this process is increasingly accepted.[83] Indeed, radicalizers and terrorist groups seeking to spread their propaganda have utilized online networks since the early days of the internet, and their tactics continue to evolve. This has spread from websites to internet forums through to social media and, most recently, encrypted apps. These interactions create what has been described as "criminogenic environments," where "deviant and extreme behaviors are learned and absorbed and in which extreme ideas come to seem normal because of constant interaction with people who hold similar – and similarly extreme – views."[84] As such, they serve as spaces where group polarization can occur. Rather than expose themselves to different world views, the internet has made it easier for groups to isolate themselves from views that conflict with their own.[85] It seems clear that both Bissonnette and Minassian developed their extreme views online. At very least, their ideas were nurtured through such online interactions. Moreover, their actions are often held up on certain message boards as achievements to be replicated and surpassed.

Hybrid

These types of radicalization are not mutually exclusive. It is likely that individuals might originally encounter extremist ideas online before seeking out like-minded individuals. Additionally, radicalizers may show online extremist materials to their followers in order to promote their ideas. Those who seek to send individuals abroad to engage in extremist violence may also use contacts they have met online or in person to help individuals travel. In this sense, online tools serve as a kind of facilitator for eventual mobilization. Recent research into lone actors reveals that, in many cases, "lone" actors were far more social than anticipated. As one study of 111 "lone actors" found, there is plenty of evidence to suggest that many had interacted with co-ideologues during their radicalization and attack-planning. While 41 per cent had face-to-face interactions with members of a wider network of political activists, 30 per cent did so virtually.[86] For example, while the internet has played a significant role in discussions about how the Christchurch attacker radicalized, it has been reported that he also met with far-right activists in person during his travels to Europe in 2017.[87]

Radicalization and the Free-Speech Grey Zone

There is another, broader challenge for national security agencies operating in this space: to what extent is radicalization – essentially a state of mind – a *national security* threat? The answer may seem obvious: if people believe that all other races are inferior, that they have an obligation to defend their real or perceived homeland at all costs, that their religion or ideology is superior, or that voting is effectively a sham – and then seek to spread those views – there must be some kind of threat.

Extremist views present governments (if not Western democracies) with challenges in maintaining social cohesion and stability. However, until these individuals become violent or start encouraging others to do so, the national security nexus is not clear. The Canadian Charter of Rights and Freedoms is unequivocal on this point: individuals are free to hold odious opinions. Short of violence, it is not clear that national security agencies such as CSIS and the RCMP are either well equipped or well placed to deal with what is effectively a mindset. For these issues there are broader programs at Public Safety Canada and Heritage Canada, as well as locally based counter-violent extremism programs in several major Canadian cities.[88]

This points to a thornier issue – at what point can it be said that an individual's extremist beliefs have crossed over to promoting or even supporting violence? Is praising the actions of a violent extremist group the same as saying their acts should be emulated? Canada has been grappling with this issue since 2001 with the introduction of new terrorism offences. According to the counselling provision in the Criminal Code, anyone actively inducing such an offence is also participating in a crime.[89] Further, the *Anti-Terrorism Act* created an offence in terms of instructing someone to carry out a terrorist activity in section 83.22.

Following the October 2014 attacks, the Harper government introduced a new terrorism speech offence that made it illegal to communicate statements, knowingly advocate, or promote the commission of terrorism offences in general. Critics worried that the crime was too broad and risked undermining free speech and lawful dissent as protected by the Charter. They argued that elements of the new crime (such as "advocating" and "promoting") were not defined in law and that "terrorism offenses in general" was arguably far broader than the already listed "terrorist activities" outlined in the Criminal Code.[90] There was also a correspondingly broad definition of "terrorist propaganda," though this was changed by Bill C-59, introduced by the Liberal government in 2017, that rendered the definition closer to the counselling offence found in Canadian criminal law.[91]

This "speech crime" tale is more than just history – it illustrates the core problem of radicalization in democracies: in extremism, there is a spectrum where protected opinion lies at one end and crimes related to threat-related activity lie at the other. Somewhere along that spectrum there is an area where there is speech that is clearly problematic from a national security perspective, but may not be considered illegal. And this is where most radicalizers exist. Effective radicalizers know how to get a message across without crossing into the criminal space. For example, rather than saying, "You should bomb that building," they may say, "Isn't it great someone is bombing that building!" or "It is imperative that someone bombs that building!" A seed is planted without committing an offence. The key challenge for national security agencies, then, is to navigate between the right to hold odious opinions and their concern over how these opinions are being used, if at all, towards violent extremist ends.

Conclusion

As this chapter shows, the five main areas of violent extremist threat-related activity cover a wide range of behaviours and undertakings that national security agencies must deal with. This broad survey gives us the opportunity to highlight some key findings and challenges ahead.

First, as noted above, most violent extremism in Canada is homegrown. For decades terrorism was seen as the product of external influences and spillover conflicts. However, most attacks in Canada, especially since 9/11, have been by those born in Canada or individuals who have spent the vast majority of their lives here. Despite this change, Canada (like other Western countries) has spent increasing amounts of time, money, and energy on securitizing immigration and the border than ever before. As legal scholar Kent Roach notes, "Border security and immigration laws dominated the Canadian response in the mediate aftermath of 9/11. In the initial years after 9/11, Canada relied on immigration law as antiterrorism law as opposed to criminal prosecutions."[92]

Initially, after 9/11 this approach made up for a lack of domestic counterterrorism tools. Security certificates – which allowed the Ministers of Immigration and Public Safety to declare a permanent resident or foreign national to be inadmissible on security grounds based on secret intelligence an accused cannot see – are an example.[93] More important for our argument here, this view is consistent with the understanding of terrorism as an outside threat as opposed to one created within Canada.

Of course there are important reasons to secure the border: transnational crime, narcotics, weapons, and human trafficking are all key criminal issues in which a strong border plays a role. However, it does suggest that a substantial part of our counterterrorism policies is not aimed at where the risk is coming from, or that we are deluding ourselves if we think we can stop terrorist activity by curbing migration.

Second, all of these activities suggest we need to cautiously widen our understanding of what a terrorism threat entails. In violent extremism, we often focus on the act and not the ripple effect it can have in a community. Attacks undermine confidence and security for years, and radicalizers operating in communities or online seek to tear families apart as they guide individuals away from their loved ones and towards extremist ends. Financing channels money to those who would engage in these threat-related activities. Worse, this money may come from stolen or skimmed donations from well-wishing Canadians who think they are supporting humanitarian aid. We often lose this bigger picture when we think about terrorism – we look at the perpetrator and not the victims, or the torn community left behind. Moreover, all of these activities undermine trust and compassion in society.

So why is mistrust a problem for national security agencies? Trust is the basis of effective counterterrorism cooperation. A survey of 111 lone actors in the United Kingdom and United States found that 51 per cent had made verbal statements about their intent or belief to at least one friend or family member.[94] Confirming this finding, a 2016 CSIS Intelligence Assessment found that "in all of these cases of failed mobilization, family members ... played a key role in alerting the authorities. This statistic demonstrates the importance of families' role in countering mobilization." As such, "the vigilance of family members or friends plays a key role in preventing the mobilization of minors and young adults."[95] While we might not prevent all acts of violent extremism, many more acts may be stopped if those harbouring knowledge about people's intentions or suspicion about their actions are encouraged and feel safe to come forward.

Of course there are distinct disincentives that would keep a person from doing this. First, calling the authorities on a loved one is difficult under any circumstances. However, individuals coming from parts of the world where law enforcement is just as likely to blame and blacklist the family for the actions of a relative may make it hard for new Canadians who are afraid to come forward. Second, individuals may not even believe they come from an affected community. Individuals who espouse far-right threats are seldom associated with the same social stigma as Al Qaida– and Islamic State–inspired extremism and therefore family members may not come forward to authorities. Third, there is the concern over a loss of face within a community if the actions of a loved one become known. Finally, if communities feel they are being disproportionately surveyed as a result of the act of an individual or small cell, they may lack the confidence and trust to come forward if they believe doing so will simply make life harder for them. There is no perfect solution to these dilemmas, but it does suggest that a widened understanding of the impact of threat-related activity on communities can be the first stepping stone to building a necessary trust. It is an approach that puts the community first and offers to partner with them rather than making them feel isolated and or disproportionately surveyed.

Finally, the overview of violent-extremist activities in this chapter suggests certain issues that will be of importance. Here we will briefly focus on two: mental health and technology.

Mental Health

Nearly two decades after 9/11, we still do not have a good understanding of the relationship between mental health and violent extremism. Speculation about this relationship has varied widely over recent decades: in the 1970s terrorists were considered sociopaths who came from dysfunctional families or else were malignant narcissists. During the 1990s–2000s it was argued that group dynamics played a more important role than individual psychology. Indeed, it was proposed that there was very little mental illness among violent extremists – terrorist groups wanted agents who were capable of carrying out acts, not problematic individuals.[96] As one researcher notes, "Over the space of 40 years of research on terrorist motivation the literature has jumped from one extreme position ('they are all mentally ill') to the exact opposite ('by definition, a terrorist cannot be mentally ill').[97]

Today, research based on datasets is challenging the conventional wisdom once again, and the idea that all violent extremists are mentally ill or that none are mentally ill is seen as a false dichotomy.[98] Instead, scholars note that many violent extremists, particularly lone actors, show signs of poor mental health. In the study of 111 lone-actor terrorists noted above, 41 per cent had some kind of mental illness (although this finding should not be applied to group-actors who engage in violent extremism differently). Rather than being seen as a cause of violent extremism, though, poor mental health is seen as one of a number of factors that may cause an individual (especially lone actors) to engage in terrorist activity, such as social isolation or other "stressors" like a traumatic event or accident.[99] Ultimately, we will not end violent extremism through better mental health outreach. Nevertheless, this is an area in which further research is required. More importantly, it is important to avoid using mental health as an excuse for violent extremism, especially in cases of far-right extremism, as is often the case.

Emerging Technologies

One of the biggest challenges that governments face is emerging technologies. Violent extremist groups are utilizing encrypted apps and crypto-currencies in order to engage in threat-related activities. The issue of encryption in particular has been vexing for national security communities throughout Western countries. On the one hand, these governments depend on strong encryption to protect privacy, data, and intelligence. On the other, the inability to see what known violent extremists are plotting and planning is a huge security challenge. While some countries such as the United Kingdom and United States are much more eager to create "back doors" in encrypted apps in order to prevent violent extremism, Canada has not taken a strong stance on the issue. This is largely because there is no consensus in government. Some agencies, such as the Communications Security Establishment (our national signals intelligence and cryptological agency) work hard to keep data safe; weakened encryption will be used by nefarious actors to gain access to information, thus making their job harder. On the other hand, the RCMP worries that violent extremists (among other criminals) "going dark" means they will be unable to protect Canadians. CSIS has also expressed similar worries in its public report.[100] Comparable problems surround the use of crypto-currencies – anonymous transactions that allow actors to finance threats across national borders without raising suspicion.[101]

Beyond the trade-offs noted above, there challenges in regulating new technologies in relation to violent extremism. Significantly, the government wants to encourage technological innovation – clamping down on technological developments or weakening the product for security reasons may hamper these goals. Moreover, the technology behind these innovations (abstract math and blockchain) can be difficult for lawmakers to get their heads around. It requires expertise and advice that may be in short supply in the public sector, compared to the more lucrative private sector. Finally, while it can take months or years to set up new regulations, violent extremists can instantly begin to use the technologies on offer. In this sense, those who are engaging in threat-related activity may have a significant head start before governments can get new rules, regulations, or legislation on the books.

The Path Ahead

Predicting the future of violent extremism is something of a fool's errand: few saw the problems that the Arab Spring would create in extremist travel or in the form of a new wave of deadly directed and inspired attacks. Today many of the factors that allowed for the rise of the Islamic State have disappeared: governments have slowly figured out better ways to track and prevent extremist travel and to work with tech companies on suppressing their messages on social media. If there is a positive lesson here, it is that terrorism is challenging, but governments learn and adapt – albeit slowly. If the information presented in chapter 1 and the actions described in this one are any indication, we can confidently say that the threat of violent extremism in Canada will continue and is likely to evolve whether through the (re)emergence of an ideology or the harnessing of new technologies.

In the end, this chapter presents a contradiction: terrorism is a serious threat to Canada, yet very few people die as a result of it, certainly when compared to other crimes or even health issues, as seen with the COVID-19 pandemic. So is it worth all the time, energy, and money that goes into countering it? The answer here is a qualified yes; to measure the magnitude of the threat by looking at the numbers of dead or injured citizens fails to capture the broad range of activities and the variety of actors that encompass violent extremism.

The key issue will be to act out of empathy for those affected and not fear, and to find ways to partner with affected communities to counter the threat. Widening our understanding of threat-activity does not mean we have to be more fearful, but it suggests that we should look at how to strengthen communities by working with them, building trust, and avoiding language that separates them from the rest of society. Such a strategy means ensuring local actors, first-responders, public health agencies, community mental health programs, and schools have the resources they need to combat extremism. If we act out of fear, we inevitably fail, and that is what violent extremists want. We must counter this tendency in favour of empathy and resilience.

Another important step is to "right-size" the amount of attention we dedicate to terrorism as a national security issue. This chapter highlights the reasons why policymakers and national security agencies must continue to pay attention to terrorism as a major threat. At the same time, we can recognize the extent to which it dominates the national security political and media discourses at the expense of other issues. Importantly, in the shadow of these conversations, other threats to Canadian security have not gone away. The case can be made that they have been able to flourish on the sidelines as the West has focused its attention on the threat of violent extremism, and away from the threats of espionage, cybersecurity, and clandestine foreign influence. And it is to these issues that this book now turns.

3

Espionage

> Jim. I've been so dead. So dead inside.[1]

With these words came the confession of what seemed to be Canada's most notorious spy since the end of the Cold War, Sub-Lieutenant Jeffrey Paul Delisle, who transferred hundreds of highly classified Canadian and allied intelligence documents from a naval base in Halifax to Russian spies.

There were a number of reasons the case of Delisle shocked Canadians. The Russian connection played into memories of geopolitical rivalries between the West and the Soviet Bloc. But Delisle himself was no James Bond – there were no fast cars, tuxedos, or martinis in his story. Instead, Delisle was a depressed, diabetic, video game addict who blamed many of his problems on his ex-wife.

More troubling was the hit to Canada's reputation in the eyes of its allies. The Delisle case made public the extent to which Canada shares highly classified intelligence with its "Five Eyes" partners – that is, an alliance with Australia, New Zealand, the United Kingdom, and the United States. For years Canada had failed to detect the transfer of this information to one of the main targets of this joint intelligence collection. Could Canada be trusted? Just how much spying was happening in Canada anyway? Were there other Delisles?

In September 2019 Canadians learned that the answer to this last question could be yes: a high-level RCMP intelligence official was arrested and charged with sharing operational information in 2015 and preparing to share sensitive information with a foreign entity or terrorist organization, among other charges. At time of writing this book, much remains unknown about this case. However, given that he worked as the Director General of the RCMP's National Intelligence Coordination Centre, we do know that Ortis would have had a unique position within that organization in his access to intelligence. Unlike the carefully compartmentalized intelligence- and evidence-gathering units, his unit had access to a wide range of operational information and domestic as well as foreign intelligence used to brief senior officials to provide strategic guidance in decision making. If he is found guilty, this case would represent a second very serious Canadian espionage case within a decade.[2]

Despite these two cases, two factors complicate the discussion of espionage in the Canadian context. First, there is very little public information about how espionage works in Canada, and what we do know has come largely from scandals or failures. In this sense, the public understanding of espionage in Canada may be skewed towards the most sensational rather than the most typical cases, which are less dramatic and may play out quietly over decades.

Second, in recent decades, hostile intelligence services are just as likely to engage in "economic espionage," targeting private companies as much as (if not more than) governments. In doing so, they seek to steal intellectual property, company plans, and any information that may give them a competitive advantage in a bidding war or merger and acquisition. Importantly, when private companies are targets of espionage, there are several reasons they do not go public with this information. In the first instance, without active threat-monitoring they may not know it is happening or has taken place. Second, companies may wish to keep the fact they have been targeted quiet – hiding it from rivals, shareholders, potential investors, and consumers alike.

Yet, although much is unknown, the threat of hostile intelligence services targeting our public and private institutions is very serious and poses a major threat to the overall security and well-being of the country. To explain why this is the case, the next two chapters will focus on what is publicly known about espionage in Canada, looking first at what might be described as "traditional espionage" (the theft of information from governments and militaries), followed by a chapter on "economic espionage" (when adversaries target private sector companies in a bid to undermine the security of Canada).

Here the immediate focus will be on the former. This chapter will outline the origins and history of espionage in Canada, with a view to highlighting the continuity in methods and goals today. Next, it examines recent cases in order to understand the threats that traditional espionage continues to impose on Canadian national security. The final part of the chapter will examine the dark side of counter-intelligence, paranoia, which can also cause societal harm. Indeed, the human toll of a more subtle but still robust Canadian "Red Scare" during the Cold War highlights the need for strong and robust intelligence review and clear legislation guiding these activities.

What Is Espionage and Counter-intelligence?

As a starting point, espionage is typically understood as activities geared toward acquiring information through clandestine means and proscribed by the laws of the country in which it is committed.[3] This may include information from human sources (HUMINT), or signals intelligence (SIGINT) – the interception and analysis of communications and other electronic signals.[4] The clandestine and legal elements are important here. It is perfectly normal that states seek information about each other through legitimate means, whether media reporting, diplomatic channels, or conversations with citizens and business leaders, etc. However, a national security dimension emerges when states seek to obtain information that governments want to keep secret and do so through clandestine means that involve breaking the law.

To mitigate the threat of espionage, states engage in counter-intelligence (CI), the "information gathered and activities conducted to identify, deceive, exploit, disrupt or protect against espionage and other activities carried out by foreign states or non-state actors."[5] Mark Lowenthal, a former U.S. intelligence official, argues that counter-intelligence should not be understood as a merely defensive activity. Instead, there are several kinds of CI activity governments engage in. This includes the collection of an opponent's intelligence activities that may be aimed at one's own country, efforts to thwart hostile intelligence service to penetrate one's own intelligence service or sensitive government positions, and, finally, on the basis of information collected, trying to turn an opponent's agents against their own governments or feeding them false information.[6] To this may be added the protection of intelligence collection operations and the vetting of sources.[7] Counter-espionage and counter-intelligence are sometimes used interchangeably, but for the purpose of this book "espionage" will be used to discuss threat-related activity and "counter-intelligence" will be used to discuss the broad range of activities used to counter this threat and collect information on it.

The Canadian Context

Canada is unique among most of its major Western allies in that it does not have an external human source collections service. There is no Canadian equivalent of the Central Intelligence Agency (CIA) in the United States, the Secret Intelligence Service (SIS, also known as MI6) in the United Kingdom, or the Australian Secret Intelligence Service (ASIS). This has partly to do with Canada's colonial origins. Between the founding of the Dominion of Canada in 1867 and the First World War, the government's pre-eminent security concerns were individuals operating on Canadian soil whose real enemy was the British Empire and/or the United Kingdom itself. This included Irish and South Asian radicals who sought to spread their revolutionary and anti-colonial ideologies among ethnic diaspora in Canada. Rather than create their own foreign intelligence service to deal with this threat, Canada relied heavily upon Britain's extensive diplomatic and clandestine networks in its efforts to support the security of the empire.[8] Indeed, although Canada would engage in foreign intelligence activities in partnership with its allies during the Second World War, for the most part the Canadian government was happy to enter into intelligence-sharing relations where it was largely a consumer, first with Britain, then, by the 1920s, with the American Federal Bureau of Investigation (FBI).[9] Instead, Canada focused its efforts on threats within its own borders and posed by its own citizens via the Royal Canadian Mounted Police's Security Service, until the creation of CSIS in 1984.[10]

Whether or not Canada should have a clandestine service that could collect foreign intelligence has been a matter of some debate.[11] It is clear, though, that Canada has dabbled in the practice. "Diplomat-spies" are known to have collected information and intelligence and shared it with Canadian allies, especially the United States and United Kingdom.[12] This was certainly the case during the early 1960s through to the 1970s in Cuba, for example. CSIS has officers posted abroad in "foreign stations," although their primary responsibilities tend to be in liaison and cooperation with other intelligence agencies. The 2006 Conservative Party platform suggested that, if elected, it would create a new "Canadian Foreign Intelligence Agency." Once in office, however, it did not do so, most likely as the result of the tremendous cost of such an undertaking.[13] The Conservatives did take steps to formally widening the mandate of CSIS in Bill C-51, which made it clear that the Service could perform its duties "within or outside of Canada." These changes were kept in the subsequent overhaul of national security legislation undertaken by the Liberal government between 2017 and 2019.

Domestically, CSIS has been the lead agency investigating espionage threats since it was established in 1984. It is authorized to do so under section 2(a) of the *CSIS Act*, which states the Service has the mandate to collect intelligence on "espionage or sabotage that is against Canada or is detrimental to the interests of Canada or activities directed toward or in support of such espionage or sabotage." It took over these responsibilities (as well as that of "subversion," discussed below) from the RCMP, which now typically becomes involved only when a criminal case can be brought forward and a parallel investigation is opened up for the purpose of leading to prosecution.

Provisions that govern CSIS's intelligence-gathering are listed in section 12 of the *CSIS Act*, which states that the Service may collect, analyse, and retain information on threats to the security of Canada. (Legally, this collection is not "foreign intelligence" but "security intelligence" as it relates to the CSIS mandate outlined in the *Act*.)

In addition, "in relation to the defence of Canada, or the conduct of international affairs," section 16 of the *Act* allows the Minister of National Defence or the Minister of Foreign Affairs to request the Service to collect "information or intelligence relating to the capabilities, intentions or activities of:

(a) any foreign state or group of foreign states; or
(b) any person other than
    (i) a Canadian citizen,
    (ii) a permanent resident within the meaning of subsection 2(1) of the Immigration and Refugee Protection Act, or
    (iii) a corporation incorporated by or under an Act of Parliament or of the legislature of a province.

Nevertheless, for the most part, CSIS's counter-intelligence efforts have been internally focused and generally limited by its mandate and its resources. Indeed, there have been concerns raised that, in the wake of the 2014 terrorist attacks, CSIS has had to redirect resources away from counter-intelligence investigations towards counterterrorism.[14]

As such, Canadian foreign intelligence collection is mostly (but not exclusively) in the realm of signals intelligence carried out by the Communications Security Establishment (CSE) and certain intelligence-gathering activities conducted by the Department of Defence (DND).[15] For most of its history, the CSE's mandate has been somewhat ambiguous. However, under Bill C-59, the Liberal government created a new statute for the CSE in law (the *CSE Act*), clarifying its role in Canadian national security in five areas: foreign intelligence, cybersecurity and information assurance, defensive cyber operations, active cyber operations, and technical and operational assistance. Of particular relevance here, the foreign intelligence mandate under Section 16 is to "acquire, covertly or otherwise, information from or through the global information infrastructure, including by engaging or interacting with foreign entities located outside Canada or by using any other method of acquiring information, and to use, analyse and disseminate the information for the purpose of providing foreign intelligence, in accordance with the Government of Canada's intelligence priorities."

More important for the discussion of espionage threats to Canada is CSE's information assurance mandate. Information assurance aims to guarantee the integrity, confidentiality, and availability of information. It means that government officials and employees can be confident they will have access to the information they need when it is required, that it is accurate and it is protected. Section 17 of the *CSE Act* states,

> The cybersecurity and information assurance aspect of the Establishment's mandate is to
>
> (a) provide advice, guidance and services to help protect
>   (i) federal institutions' electronic information and information infrastructures, and
>   (ii) electronic information and information infrastructures designated under subsection 22(1) as being of importance to the Government of Canada; and
> (b) acquire, use and analyse information from the global information infrastructure or from other sources in order to provide such advice, guidance and services.

DND is one of the largest intelligence agencies in Canada and engages in a wide range of activities in this space in line with its defence mandate. The Joint Doctrine Branch Canadian forces Warfare Centre describes "defence intelligence" as encompassing "all intelligence activity conducted by or within the DND and the [Canadian Armed Forces (CAF)], and [including] joint, maritime, land, air, space, and cyber intelligence, from the tactical to the strategic level (as well as geopolitical economic, scientific, technical and security intelligence [level]) where such intelligence supports the defence mission and the government of Canada's broader responsibilities as it relates to national defence, national security and foreign affairs."[16]

In line with this definition, DND engages in foreign intelligence gathering using its signals, imagery, geospatial, and human intelligence capabilities and assets. What differentiates "defence intelligence" from the Canadian national security organizations discussed in this book is that all activities support military objectives and planning (international and domestic). Therefore, while there may be some overlap in national security, the focus on its defence mission upon foreign intelligence collection differentiates it from a typical Western, *civilian* foreign human intelligence agency (such as the CIA and MI6).[17]

Traditional Espionage Threats in Canada

"Traditional" espionage focuses on the theft of information that typically (but not exclusively) relates to government plans and strategies, military affairs and technology. For example, it has been well established that, during the Cold War, states on both sides of the Iron Curtain looked for information on a wide variety of military strategies and innovations. A "wish list" given to an agent within the Soviet military working for the CIA during the late Cold War included "future or present weapons systems ... aviation and radars, materials that airplanes were built from, design of airplanes and rockets, lasers, directed-energy research, aerosols, alloys and special metals, air strike tactics, electro-optics, tactics of forward air control and close air support."[18] Additionally, the agent was requested to purloin electronic components and photograph any documents related to the above information or any other military matter.[19]

At this point, it is worth briefly examining the history of espionage threats in Canada during the Cold War. Not only are these stories interesting, they are also revealing. As will be discussed below, in espionage, much remains the same in Canada, even though some of the actors may have changed. Indeed, there is a strong continuity in methods and overarching goals of traditional espionage from the 1940s to the present.

The first major defection of the Cold War on 5 September 1945 made it clear the Soviet Union was engaged in threat activities in Canada. On that night Igor Gouzenko, who had been posted as a cipher clerk at the Soviet embassy in Ottawa, left his post with an armful of classified documents. Once Canadian authorities had their hands on Gouzenko's papers, it did not take long for them to realize they had definitive proof of considerable, coordinated Soviet espionage directed against Canada, the United States, and the United Kingdom (although it famously took hours and several attempts for the Gouzenkos to convince Canadian authorities to take them seriously during their attempt to defect).[20] In particular, the documents revealed the presence of a spy ring that used civil servants as sources of classified information on political discussions as well as atomic and weapons research in Canada. Moreover, Gouzenko's documents revealed that the Soviets had sources of information in the National Research Council (NRC), the Wartime Information Board, and the Department of External Affairs (now known as Global Affairs Canada).[21] Even more shocking, the documents showed that at least two prominent Canadian Communists, Member of Parliament Fred Rose and Labour-Progressive Party organizer Sam Carr, were also participating in espionage on behalf of the Soviet Union. Further, the Gouzenko papers revealed that Alan Nunn May, a British nuclear scientist, had passed along atomic secrets to the Soviet Union while working in Canada at the Chalk River nuclear power plant. Upon his arrest in Britain in 1946, May confessed and was sentenced to ten years hard labour, serving six.[22]

For Love and Money

Moscow continued its efforts to obtain information, despite the discovery of its networks in the West. While Canada was probably never a main target of Soviet espionage, its links to atomic and nuclear research programs and its development of commercial technologies gave the USSR good reason to be interested in developments north of the U.S. border. The Soviet Union tasked its spies with gathering information related to the Avro Arrow airplane as well as research being conducted at atomic and other scientific institutions.[23] The real value of targeting Canada, however, was that it played an important role in the Western alliance. Canada was a member of NATO, NORAD, and the Five Eyes, and had access to many important secrets of the Cold War period.[24]

In the first decade after 1945, many of those engaging in espionage were ideologically motivated. These were people who had become Communists in the 1930s out of a belief that the world as they knew it was crashing around them and the only way forward was through socialist revolution. In their eyes, only communism could protect civilization from the Great Depression as well as the rise of fascism. Inspired by a socialist vision, these individuals were willing to give clandestine service to Moscow over a long period of time.[25] This was certainly the case of the spy ring unveiled by Gouzenko, including the aforementioned Alan Nunn May, who became a devout Communist while studying at Cambridge. In 1950 it was discovered that another nuclear scientist who had worked at Chalk River, the Italian Bruno Pontecorvo, probably passed on information to the Soviets. Pontecorvo, who had left Canada for the United Kingdom, turned up in the Soviet Union after both the RCMP and UK security services failed to conduct a proper screening.[26]

Many of those recruited by the Soviets were senior officials of the Communist Party of Canada who could "talent spot" or offer to become "live letter boxes," relaying instructions to other agents on behalf of the KGB.[27] In 1966 George Victor Spencer, a low-level postal worker motivated by a combination of ideology and personal grievance, was caught trying to pass information to the Soviets. Spencer was never convicted of espionage, given that the information he tried to provide was mostly open-source and he was dying of cancer at the time.[28] Nevertheless, the open-source information he was gathering could have been used to facilitate Russian "illegals" (discussed below) to enter the country, even if it was not exactly stealing classified information.[29]

Hugh Hambleton, a professor of economics at Laval University in Quebec City who spied for the Soviet Union from 1950 to 1979, seems to have had mixed motivations. There is speculation that Hambleton may have engaged in these activities as a way to bolster his sense of self-importance and "a craving for excitement" rather than ideological convictions.[30] Hambleton was recruited while studying in Paris in the 1950s and was convinced to apply for a job with NATO. Once employed there, Hambleton copied thousands of documents over a period of five years.[31] Hambleton cut off his activities in 1961 and returned to Canada but was persuaded to resume assisting the KGB in 1967. For the next twelve years, he continued to funnel information to the Soviet Union while serving as a consultant around the world.[32] Finally discovered by the RCMP, he arranged for Canadian immunity in exchange for confessing his activities in 1979. However, in 1982 Hambleton travelled to the United Kingdom, where he was arrested and convicted of espionage.

Not all spies were motivated by ideology or a sense of adventure. Many of those who aided Soviet intelligence did so for financial reasons. Bower Featherstone, a civil servant, sold classified maps of the ocean floor off Newfoundland for money to fund his gambling addiction.[33] He was discovered when an RCMP surveillance team trailed a Soviet diplomat across Ottawa and saw him meet Featherstone at a desolate shopping centre in February 1966. Later in the 1960s, RCMP officer Gilles Brunet told Soviet embassy staff about listening devices in their Ottawa building, disrupted surveillance operations of Soviet activities, and outed a Canadian military attaché in Moscow as a spy (although Brunet's wife actually raised suspicions about him, he was able to stay in the RCMP for another five years, and the extent of his actions was not known until they were revealed by a Soviet defector in 1985).[34]

Within the limited literature on espionage in Canada during the Cold War, there is no consensus on what motivated Canadians to turn against their own government. Former RCMP and CSIS Intelligence Officer Donald G. Mahar argues that most who spied against Canada were ideologically motivated with some ties to the Communist Party of Canada.[35] However, Whitaker et al. maintain that by the 1960s, this view was outdated: "While the Mounties, like their American and British counterparts, were chasing alluring spectres of ideological traitors from the long dead past, the real treason under their very noses wore the very contemporary, but disappointingly sleazy face of commonplace greed and self-indulgence."[36]

As noted in the beginning of the chapter, the fact that only sensational cases and public failures tend to attract attention makes it difficult to appreciate the actual extent of the issue or comprehensively know the motivations behind all those who engage in espionage. The survey of the most well-known, post-Gouzenko cases presented here suggests that spies engaged in their activities for a variety of reasons, and this remains true to the present day.

Legals and Illegals

Who actually recruited Canadian citizens to engage in espionage? The answer is "legal" and "illegal" Soviet spies. "Legals" refers to KGB/GRU intelligence officers who arrived in Canada as diplomatic staff to be posted to the embassies and consulates of the USSR. Although their real purpose was to run espionage networks, they could hide behind their legal status and diplomatic ties. According to a former Soviet diplomat, while spies often represented somewhere between 30 and 40 per cent of diplomatic personnel, from the 1960s through the 1980s this percentage sometimes exceeded 50 per cent in Canada (although after the Gouzenko Affair, much of the responsibilities of these officers appears to have been monitoring the normal diplomatic staff to ensure they did not defect).[37]

Whether through bugging, following, or analysing the movement of the Soviet embassy staff (or perhaps because KGB/GRU[38] officers seldom took part in normal diplomatic activities), spies could be spotted by the RCMP, who could then follow them to see what activities they were engaging in and whom they were talking to.[39] (This was the method by which Spencer and Featherstone were caught.) Alternatively, if they were deemed to be too much of a risk, the "legals" could be expelled by being declared persona non grata – or PNG'ed. While expulsions could temporarily disrupt spy networks, they also caused headaches, as there would inevitably be tit-for-tat retaliation against Canadian diplomats in Moscow, who would also be expelled. Moreover, after a few months, new KGB/GRU officers would be posted to Canada.[40]

The USSR also employed "illegals" in their espionage. "Illegals" refer to agents of a foreign power who come to Canada under false identities for the express purpose of engaging in deep-cover espionage. During the Cold War, Soviet intelligence officials searched newspapers, looking for the names of children who had died in infancy. As Whitaker et al. note, "Canada was a country of mass post-war immigration, which lacked any national, centralized record-keeping system for identifying individuals. This made it a particularly attractive country for such operations. For instance, there was no central matching of birth and death certificates, making it very easy for illegals to assume the identities of deceased Canadians, acquire social insurance and Medicare numbers, establish work records, pay taxes ... thus gradually filling out a profile that would be very hard to detect as false. And, of course, 'Canadians' could freely enter and leave the United States undetected, which was very useful."[41]

Using these names, illegals built legends (or backstories) before arriving in Canada, often through another country. They would then spend years further developing their "Canadian" credentials, starting businesses and familiarizing themselves with the places they claimed to be from. Having become credibly Canadian, the illegals would typically move to another country – often but not always the United States, although some were kept in Canada to manage espionage networks, and collect and pass on information.

One of the most famous cases is that of Konon Molody, a Soviet spy who appears to have been spotted as a child as a potential future illegal. Sent to live with an aunt in California to learn American English, Molody returned to the Soviet Union in 1938, where he served in in the Second World War. Eventually Molody was trained to infiltrate the West by the KGB. In 1954 he was sent to Vancouver to assume the identity of a Canadian businessman. Documents smuggled out of Russia in the famous "Mitrokhin Archive" suggest that Molody was able to enter Canada on the passport of a member of the Central Committee of the Canadian Communist Party who had never used it for foreign travel and willingly handed it over to Soviet agents in Ottawa.[42] Once he arrived, Molody took the name Gordon Arnold Lonsdale, a man who had immigrated to the Soviet Union with his mother as a child but perished in 1943.[43] From there, Molody moved to London to run Soviet agents and was eventually arrested for espionage, convicted, and traded for a British spy.[44]

There were numerous other cases. Yevgeni Vladimirovich Brik became "David Soboloff" – the name of a young Russian immigrant who returned to the USSR in the 1930s. Brik, a womanizing alcoholic, proved to be a bad spy for the Soviets. Having fallen in love with the wife of a Canadian soldier, he revealed his true identity to the RCMP, which planned to turn Brik into a double agent. Brik himself was then betrayed by a member of the RCMP, James Morrison, who was heavily in debt and sold secrets to the Soviets.[45] Rudolf Kneschke, a German who came to Canada via Brazil, received short-wave transmissions from Moscow while running a small radio-TV repair store in Vancouver. After starting an investigation in 1959, the RCMP appear to have established that he was almost certainly an agent of Soviet intelligence. Unfortunately for them, Kneschke was able to leave the country before he could be arrested.[46]

Although Czechs Ludek Zemenek[47] and Inga Jurman first assumed West German identities (Rudolf Adolf Herrmann and Inga-lore Moerke), they came to Toronto to build up their legends and credentials in the early 1960s. While there, Zemenek wrote political analyses and received messages on his short-wave radio. Called to Moscow in 1964, he was told his mission was to prepare himself to take over the network of Canadian spies, should the Soviet embassy ever be shut down, and to search for Canadian "progressives" who could be useful to the Soviet cause, including journalists and politicians. Upon obtaining citizenship in 1967, Zemenek was immediately told to move to the United States, where he maintained cover as a film-maker on contract with IBM. There he ran a spy network until his arrest by the FBI in 1977.[48] (Zemenek is also alleged to have eventually revealed his true identity to his son, who agreed to join the KGB and recruit through universities. His first year was spent at McGill University before moving to Georgetown one year later.[49]) Similarly, Gennadiy Petrovich (aka Peter Fischer) and his wife, Inge-borg Ziegler, came to Canada after having assumed West German identities in the early 1960s. From there they moved to the United States in 1965, where they coordinated intelligence dead-drops with an insider from the National Security Agency (NSA) before disappearing in 1968.[50]

In their book based upon smuggled intelligence from the Soviet Union, Christopher Andrew and Vasili Mitrokhin argue that, for all of the effort the Soviet Union put into "illegals," most missions were ultimately failures.[51] Indeed, other than Rudolf Abel (aka Vilyam Willie Fisher), who ran a network of spies for a number of years in the United States that smuggled atomic secrets to the Soviet Union, most seem to have accomplished little. Successful or not, it was clear that Soviet spies were operating in and through Canada.

The situation was such that, by 1969, the Royal Commission on Security (also known as the Mackenzie Commission) noted, "Canada has acquired a dubious reputation with regards to her passports, and there is evidence that hostile intelligence services have concentrated on the acquisition of Canadian documentation because of this relative ease of procurement. In her own self-interest Canada should exercise considerably more stringent control in this area, and in addition there is the consideration that a Canadian passport acquired by hostile authorities will in many cases not be used in Canada. As a member of the western alliance, Canada has an obligation to implement an adequate system of passport control, and not to represent a vulnerable link."[52] But even as Canada strengthened its rules for obtaining passports, the Soviet Union – and now the Russian government – has continued to use Canadian status as a clandestine cover for its espionage operations.

Traditional Espionage Threats in Canada Today

Although the Cold War has been over for decades, many of the same activities that took place during those years persist. Indeed, states seek the same information they did then: government and military secrets, research, and intelligence. Still, it is extremely rare for Canadian officials to identify espionage threats. In 2010, CSIS Director Richard Fadden told reporters that the intelligence services of at least five countries, including China, were involved in covert actions in Canada. Coinciding with a visit from Chinese officials, Fadden's statement created a media storm.[53] Rather than accept the story, Members of Parliament forced Fadden to testify in front of a committee and then publicly condemned him in an official report, this despite the fact that what he said was almost certainly true.[54] Therefore, until recently, statements about Canada's espionage threats have been few and far between. Occasionally, for example, under questioning, CSIS officials sometimes acknowledged China as a counter-intelligence target in Canada.[55]

This reluctance to publicly identify Canada's espionages challenges, however, has evolved in recent times with an increasing number of reports and speeches by intelligence officials naming Russia and China as having engaged in threat related activities in Canada and around the world.[56] In addition, Canada has publicly attributed cyberattacks and cyber-espionage to both countries (as well as Iran and North Korea) in recent years, often with its allies (as will be discussed in chapter 5). However, there is also a range of countries who spy on Canada to fill "intelligence gaps" that will serve their interests and ends who go officially unnamed, although reports in the media can provide some insight: in January 2020 a Canadian aerospace company was barred from national security work after it was alleged they had "consistent contact" with Indian intelligence.[57]

In their methods, the spy services of foreign countries continue to employ a combination of tactics that have their origins in the Cold War, including the use of legals and illegals who seek to recruit Canadians or run sources and intelligence networks. In 1996 two individuals working for the Russian Foreign Intelligence Service (Sluzhba Vneshney Razvedki or SVR) were discovered living in Toronto for at least six years. Yelena/Elena Olshanskaya and Dmitriy Olshanskiy adopted the names of two babies that had perished in 1965 and posed as Ian and Laurie Lambert. It was alleged that the "Lamberts" may have been developing their legends and met with Russian intelligence officials during their time in Canada, although it is not clear they had engaged in any espionage by the time they were caught.[58]

Of note, there has been a variation of the "illegals" method wherein individuals, at least in the United States, use their real identities in order to apply for visa status in which to conduct clandestine activities. For example, in July 2018 the FBI arrested Maria Butina for espionage. Butina engaged in networking through political organizations but also maintained her legal status in the United States through entering into a graduate program at American University. It is possible such tactics could be used in Canada.

Importantly, foreign spies attempt to recruit individuals through ideology, bribery, and even blackmail. Two post–Cold War cases highlight the ongoing threat of espionage in Canada.

"The Canadians"

Don Heathfield and his wife, Tracey Foley, were average émigrés from Canada to the United States. After selling a successful business in Toronto, the couple moved with their young sons, Alex and Tim, to Boston. From there they were able to establish a comfortable life in the United States; their sons attended private school and they travelled extensively. It was, however, a facade that was decades in the making.

The elaborate ruse came crashing down when the FBI arrested "Don" and "Tracey" – really Andrey Bezrukov and Elena Vavilova – Russians who had come to Canada as Soviet spies in the latter years of the Cold War on the identities of two infants that had died years before. Like the other illegals discussed in this chapter, Bezrukov and Vavilova trained extensively in the Soviet Union. They were able to build their legends and begin to move towards obtaining sensitive information for the SVR, a successor to the KGB. While Bezrukov seems to have prospered in business, the family was successful in leading a relatively normal life that did not come to the attention of national security authorities for years.[59]

The story of Bezrukov and Vavilov has become notorious for a number of reasons. In the first instance, it reportedly became the basis for the hit TV show, *The Americans* – although it is clear that the life the family led was not nearly as full of action and violence as what is portrayed on the screen. Another reason is that the family's children, Alex and Tim, appealed the stripping of their citizenship by the Canadian government in a lengthy legal battle. For its part, the Canadian government argued that Tim learned of his parents' real identity and agreed to go to Russia for training. How the government knows this has never been made clear; the house the family was staying in, however, had been bugged by the FBI.[60] In December 2019 the Supreme Court in Canada found in favour of the Vavilov children in a complex legal decision grounded in its interpretation of how the *Citizenship Act* applied to people born in Canada — even if those people's parents were in Canada illegally, pretending to be Canadians while working for the intelligence services of a foreign government.[61]

Most importantly for the argument being made here, the story confirms that Russia continues to utilize illegals to conduct espionage and clandestine activities. Indeed, Bezrukov and Vavilova were not the first to be found with ties to Canada in the post–Cold War era. An individual known as "Paul William Hampel" was arrested at Montreal Airport in 2006. At the time, he was carrying a fraudulent Ontario birth certificate, a Canadian passport, and the equivalent of $7,800 in five currencies. While it is believed that Hampel also worked for the SVR, the full extent of his activities in Canada are still not publicly known.[62] The government forced his removal back to Moscow using an immigration order to detain and deport foreign nationals and all other non-citizens, called a security certificate.[63] Canada should expect that the Russians, and perhaps other countries, will continue to use illegals.

Jeffrey Delisle

Perhaps the most famous incident of espionage in Canada in recent years is the case of former Sub-Lieutenant Jeffrey Delisle, discussed in the introduction to this chapter. Having gone through a variety of personal crises, including a divorce and video game addiction, Delisle appears to have come to a personal breaking point and made the decision to commit "professional suicide" and start passing information to the Russian government.[64] Delisle walked into the Russian embassy in Ottawa in 2007 dressed as a civilian. He flashed his military identification and asked to meet with someone from the military intelligence GRU.[65] From that point onwards, he was coached on what information to provide and how.

Suffering from diabetes, Delisle was unable to deploy abroad on a ship. Instead, he was posted to Trinity, the Royal Canadian Navy's intelligence centre at Halifax, which had access to information from Canadian security and intelligence agencies, as well as information from Five Eyes countries.[66] This, unfortunately, gave him access to large amounts of data that he was able to provide to his handlers. Worse, stealing the information appears to have been an incredibly simple task. Delisle transferred classified information from a secure computer to a floppy disk, which was then put into an open computer, from where he transferred the files to a USB key. After work Delisle logged on to an email account on a server based in Egypt and left the files there as a draft document. From there, Russian spies, who shared the password for the account, could download the files.[67]

Delisle has said little since his arrest. However, his publicly released confession to the RCMP provides evidence of what the current Russian intelligence agencies operating in Canada are looking for. Delisle was tasked with providing information on foreign agents targeting Russia, information related to the energy sector, and what information Canada had on Russian organized crime and links to their political leadership (given widely reported links between the Russian mafia and organized crime, this last task should not come as a surprise[68]). Interestingly, Delisle indicates the GRU was not interested in scientific or technical information. This either indicates a shift in collection priorities from the Cold War, or the fact that such information is more likely to be obtained through other means, such as cyber-espionage.

The Delisle case is an unfortunate reminder that espionage remains a serious threat to Canadian national security. (Delisle himself was surprised at the number of Russian spies working in Ottawa, remarking in his confession, "Ottawa is crawling [with] GRU."[69]) Beyond Delisle's motivation, it is important to consider the harm that he did to Canadian national security and interests. In a lengthy assessment, CSIS noted that the damage level of Delisle's actions was "high." First, the information passed on could identify a Service source to the Russians, damaging the ability to gather information (while not mentioned in the report, exposing a CSIS source could put the life of an individual cooperating with the Service at grave risk). Second, as the CSIS intelligence reports (CIRs) passed to the Russians by Delisle contained the names of individuals responsible for their content, Delisle exposed the names of an unknown number of CSIS employees.

Third, the information that was passed on to the Russians, especially at the Secret and Top Secret levels, would have enabled them to fill intelligence gaps on what was known about them by their adversaries and take countermeasures. As the Service itself noted,

> A security agency cannot operate effectively if the subjects of its investigation or other parties, such as a hostile agency, are able to ascertain

the state of the security agency's operational knowledge at a particular point in time, the specific operational assessment made by the agency, or the fact that the agency is in a position to draw conclusions on a subject. Efficacy is also compromised if the subject of investigation or other unauthorized parties are able to ascertain what is already known about them, the methods of operation being used against them or the extent of coverage they are being afforded at various points in time. The disclosure of this information may put the subject of investigation or other unauthorized parties in a position where false or misleading information can be inserted into the investigative process to the detriment of the security agency. As a result, the scope and reliability of information available would be severely affected. The subject of investigation or other unauthorized parties, would be in a position to take countermeasures against continuing or future investigations.[70]

Finally, the assessment notes that, in stealing classified information from allies, Delisle hurt Canada's reputation among Canada's top intelligence partners. If Canada's key partners believe that the information they share with Canada is at risk, they will quickly cut it out of intelligence-sharing arrangements. As Canada is predominantly an intelligence consumer, such an outcome is extremely detrimental to our national security (indeed, Canada's reputation may have been restored only after the significant intelligence leaks by former CIA contractor Edward Snowden in June 2013, which were much more consequential and make Delisle's leaks look small in comparison).

Delisle was sentenced to twenty years in prison and fined nearly $112,000. He was also the first Canadian sentenced under the *Security of Information Act*.[71] Additionally, in true Cold War fashion, the Conservative government expelled Russians from Canada in the wake of Delisle's arrest, including two diplomats (one a defence attaché) and two members of their "administrative and technical staff."[72]

The Dark Side of Counter-Intelligence and Subversion

Given the legitimate threat that espionage presents, counter-espionage remains a vital national security activity. It has also resulted in major controversies. In some cases, the fear of espionage has led to security measures that can be seen as perfectly appropriate, such as improving controls over access to information and the way sensitive information is stored. On the other hand, a fear of spies or subversives can create panic, sending national security agencies on years-long, panicked searches for moles and infiltrators. Fear of this kind of subversion has led to the surveillance of communities and citizens, and such monitoring activities have become prevalent enough to cause many to speak of a "surveillance state."

Here it is worth spending a moment discussing the tricky issue of subversion – a national security threat that has never truly been defined under any Canadian law. Generally speaking, the Canadian government follows the definition used by NATO: subversion is understood to be an "action or a coordinated set of actions of any nature intended to weaken the military, economic or political strength of an established authority by undermining the morale, loyalty or reliability of its members."[73] But this definition is broad. Indeed, it is not at all clear that the RCMP had a workable set of guidelines on what constituted "subversion" during the Cold War, despite the fact that they were running a series of programs designed to counter this threat. The closest one might come are the sedition laws in sections 59–62 of the Criminal Code. As these were written well before the 1982 Charter of Rights and Freedoms, however, it is hard to see how any prosecution would survive a legal challenge that invoked the rights of freedom of speech, conscience, assembly, association, etc.

We normally associate espionage and subversion hysteria with the "Red Scare" and "McCarthyism" in 1950s America. During this time, hundreds of Americans were erroneously accused of being secret Communists and posing a threat to the United States. Canada was not immune to this fear, but rather than take the American approach of publicly weeding out Communists in sensitive positions inside and outside government, the Canadian approach was more subtle. Authorities began to investigate civil servants for Communist ties or sympathies and quietly removed those deemed to be compromised. Individuals who were denied a security clearance were not be told that the grounds for denial were related to national security.[74] The entire process was secret, leaving no grounds for appeal.

By the end of the 1950s, however, the RCMP had ramped up its efforts to determine whether anything like the spy scandals that revealed Communist moles in the American and British governments had occurred in Canada. Project Feather Bed produced a list of suspected or known Communist sympathizers from 1957 through to the mid-1970s. Historians note that there is no evidence that Feather Bed "ever turned up a single case of espionage that could be acted upon," but the RCMP generated approximately a thousand files on individuals in the government without their knowledge.[75]

RCMP surveillance included politicians. In 2006 it was discovered they had a voluminous file on Tommy Douglas, who had served as premier of Saskatchewan and the leader of the federal New Democratic Party. Over three decades, Douglas's speeches were scrutinized for evidence of subversion, and his private conversations were closely monitored.[76] An RCMP source secretly taped a federal Cabinet Minister.[77] In Quebec the RCMP monitored the separatist but peaceful Parti Québécois (though there is some debate as to whether this was of their own initiative or passed down from the government or some other federal institution).[78]

It was not just civil servants and politicians the RCMP kept tabs on. During the Cold War, the RCMP maintained files on hundreds of thousands of Canadians who they believed could be potential subversives. While such fears had at one time centred upon individuals of certain ethnic backgrounds (especially Indian, Finnish, Ukrainian, German, Italian, and Japanese residents) and those involved in Communist movements backed by Moscow, by the 1960s and 1970s suspicions were being cast upon individuals in "New Left" and radical movements that had less to do with international Communism and more to do with changing Canadian society. The 1977 MacDonald Commission discovered that the RCMP Security Service maintained a subversive name index with 1.3 million entries, representing 800,000 files on individuals. As Whitaker et al. note, this might have been as much as 7–8 per cent of the Canadian population at the time.[79] In addition, the Mounties bugged the offices of politicians, monitored university campuses, and, in 1967, launched a "Key Sectors" program to determine the extent of penetration into "vital sectors" of societies, assess the threat of any penetration, and attempt to counter it.[80]

While most of the individuals surveilled were unaware of it, when the state made its interest in someone known, the results could be tragic. Canadian civil servants in sensitive positions were dismissed from their jobs if it was discovered they were homosexual, out of a fear they could be blackmailed by hostile security services. Canada's ambassador to Moscow, David Johnson, lost his job for this reason. Further, his retired predecessor, John Watkins, interrogated by the RCMP after they learned that he twice had slept with Soviet nationals, collapsed and died immediately following questioning.[81]

Perhaps the most public case was that of scholar and diplomat E. Herbert Norman who, after being publicly named as a potential Communist within the Canadian government by a U.S. Senate Internal Security Subcommittee, took his own life in 1957. Norman, it turned out, had crossed U.S. intelligence officials during the Second World War and the Suez Crisis. He had also studied at Cambridge in the 1930s, was a peer of other prominent Soviet moles, and had expressed Communist sympathies during that time. In their everyday cooperation with the FBI, the RCMP had handed over a flawed security report about Norman that fuelled much of the misinformation about him. Norman had already been investigated – and cleared – by the Canadian government in the early 1950s, but the public accusations coming from the United States proved to be too much for him.[82]

These Cold War cases remind us of the balance our government and security services must strike in their screening programs. As this chapter and the next show, the threat of espionage is real, and hostile intelligence services continue their efforts to obtain classified information. But in all Western countries, concerns about large, subversive movements have led to policies and programs of mass surveillance that citizens have objected to. Moreover, as research has shown, there is little public evidence to suggest that these programs weeded out any threats. (As it turned out, there was a mole in the government – RCMP Officer Gilles Brunet, discussed above.) This suggests that the large counter-subversion programs were either unnecessary or seriously disproportionate to their mission. At best, they appear to have diverted resources from new and emerging threats, such as the rise of new forms of violent extremism. After more information about the surveillance programs came to light, CSIS disbanded its counter-subversion section in 1986. (Successive governments have chosen, however, to maintain "subversion" as a threat to the security of Canada under 2(d) of the *CSIS Act*.)

Conclusion

The history and recent case studies of espionage in Canada have important implications for citizens. The first is that the threat did not end with the Cold War. There are still states (including, but not limited to, Russia) who continue to use many of the same methods and pursue the same goals as they did between 1945 and 1991. This includes exploiting "walk-ins," sympathizers, and illegals, as well as blackmail and theft. We can expect espionage to be a national security threat for the foreseeable future.

Canada's history of monitoring subversion and our own moderate but not inconsequential "Red Scare" reminds us that the need to protect Canada and prevent threat-related activity must be balanced. It is unacceptable that fears over Communist "moles" led to the monitoring of nearly a million Canadians, many of whom had done little more than join a union or express support for a left-wing cause. Worse, politicians seem to have avoided any responsibility for the actions of the security services in this area during the Cold War. When questioned about the monitoring activities of the RCMP, Prime Minister Pierre Trudeau insisted that he could not oversee or review national security matters, as doing so would violate the principle of "police independence." Trudeau argued that governments of any political party should be kept in ignorance of the day-to-day affairs of both the police and security service. "It is a matter of stating as a principle that the particular minister of the day should not have a right to know what the police are doing constantly in their investigative practices, what they are looking at, and what they are looking for, and the way in which they are doing it." For Trudeau, this was not pleading ignorance, but an important democratic principle not to interfere in criminal or security investigations.[83] It also conveniently shielded him from accountability.

Although it is unlikely that our security services would launch large-scale subversion monitoring programs as existed during the Cold War today, our past experiences demonstrate the need to ensure that the kinds of abuses we saw then do not happen again. This is, of course, easier said than done, but this chapter has shown that any such balance between accountability for and national security independence from rests on three things: laws, review, and institutional culture.

In matters of law, the experiences of the RCMP in the Cold War discussed in this chapter are enlightening. Part of the RCMP's problems with its monitoring of subversion was that the term was never actually defined in statute. As such, the default position of what actually constituted subversion became very broad. Similarly, in more recent times this is where some activists and scholars expressed concern over the way in which the Harper government gave CSIS "disruption" powers under Bill C-51 in 2015; the powers were not defined in any way except that the Service could not cause death or bodily harm, obstruct, pervert, or defeat the course of justice, or violate the sexual integrity of a person.[84] CSIS would even be permitted to breach constitutional law – the Charter of Rights and Freedoms – if it obtained a warrant to do so. The exceptionally broad nature of this law was seen as a huge risk that CSIS could commit some of the very actions that the RCMP were criticized for in the 1970s (and that, ironically, led to the creation of CSIS in the first place).

The second area is the review of intelligence activities. Pierre Trudeau was correct when he emphasized the need for governments to remain at arm's length from national security investigations: politicians directing spies to investigate individuals or institutions is fraught with moral hazards and risks. For decades, though, Canada was an outlier in its lack of review of intelligence activities. It was one of the few Western countries (and the only member of the Five Eyes) not to have any real form of review by legislators in this area. When difficult questions or controversies arose, there was no democratic review body capable of conducting a full investigation of classified and unclassified information. Instead, as in the case of Richard Fadden, the issue was played out in public, under full partisan glare.

Finally, there is institutional culture, which is understood here to be the values and behaviours of national security organizations as they go about their mandate. Practically, this means robust policies and procedures that are followed in decision-making. However, as no set of rules will be able to encompass all aspects of fast-paced investigations, good judgment is also required. In a thorough history of national security agencies in Canada, Whitaker et al. highlight several problems that affected the RCMP's institutional culture during the Cold War. First, the Mounties engaging in counter-intelligence operations were never given a clear directive on how to go about their difficult work, and the lack of policies and procedures in the Security Service provoked anxiety in those required to do it. "Running secret sources and double agents was a very risky business, especially for the sources and agents, but that anxiety could extend to their handlers as well who had to contend with troubling responsibilities, not to speak of moral dilemmas." [85]

A second problem was the culture of the RCMP itself. Giles Brunet, who sold secrets to the Soviets for cash, appears to have gotten away with it for so long in part as the result of his personal connections within the Mounties. Moreover, there was a sense that the honour of the RCMP was a shield from treason: the sense of duty inculcated into Mounties during their training was seen as inoculating them from KGB overtures.[86] Finally, there was a lack of training and a failure to find ways to help Secret Service members transition from police work, with emphasis on immediate results, to the slow and painstaking work of counter-espionage.[87] As such, while the RCMP may have had a strong institutional culture, it does not appear to have been successfully adapted for national security work.

This is why the steps taken in 2016–19 to reform Canada's national security legislation are significant; there are concrete steps towards improvement in all three areas – law, review, and culture – albeit not perfectly. First, there is the creation of a new overarching review architecture with different bodies ensuring that all of Canada's national security activities can be *reviewed* in some way. This includes the National Security and Intelligence Committee of Parliamentarians (NSICOP), Canada's first parliamentary review of national security activities; the National Security and Intelligence Review

Agency (NSIRA) – a body often described as a "super SIRC" that can review all government departments involved in national security; and an intelligence commissioner to review decisions related to cyber-defence and data retention. Second, the new legislation provides legal clarity and sets limits on just how far the government wants national security agencies to go to protect Canada. In particular, CSIS's disruption powers are defined, and the CSE will have its own statute in law that outlines its mandate and responsibilities.

If there is unfinished business here, it is in institutional culture. Importantly, robust accountability and review mechanisms are not a replacement for effective policies, procedures, practices, and good judgment. But who will oversee these "institutional culture" issues is not clear, although NSICOP has started to take promising steps in this direction. While other review entities have a responsibility to check legal compliance, NSICOP has a broader mandate. It can investigate decision-making at a high level to assess the efficacy of national security operations and analysis, as well as its activities. In its 2019 annual report the committee did a study on "diversity and inclusion in the security and intelligence community" – essentially looking at how one element of institutional culture has an important impact on operations. As the report notes, the Canadian national security and intelligence community still struggles to recruit and maintain a diverse workforce: DND and the RCMP have struggled with sexual harassment, violence, and discrimination, and in 2017 CSIS had to settle a lawsuit alleging Islamophobia, racism, and homophobia in a toxic work environment. While all of this has a clear negative impact on operations, the committee also studied the positive relationship between diversity and inclusion with innovative outcomes. It also highlighted what it felt the national security and intelligence community were getting right and made recommendations for improving this element of organizational culture.[88] In this way, although it is new, it seems clear that NSICOP can play a constructive role in promoting a healthy institutional culture within the national security and intelligence community that could be expanded to other areas (such as whistleblowing).

Yet the findings of this chapter suggest that quickly establishing our footing on national security review is key for securing Canada in the twenty-first century. As noted above, espionage threats remain largely the same, but they may be moving into new areas and relying on new tactics. As this is happening, debate about the limits of government and its place in Canadian society is resurfacing. Negotiating this tension and finding a balance is the focus of chapter 4.

4

The Economy and National Security

In the 1990s Nortel was synonymous with Canadian innovation. One of the world's largest telecommunications equipment makers with 93,000 employees, it represented the future of the Canadian economy at the dawn of the internet age. By 2000 the company had $30 billion in sales, a number matched by Apple only in 2007, Google in 2010, and Chinese powerhouse Huawei in 2012.[1]

Today, however, the company represents a cautionary tale. Nortel went fully bankrupt in 2009, was left with billions of dollars in debt, and tens of thousands of employees lost their jobs. A major source of technological innovation became the largest bankruptcy in Canadian history – its assets were sold to pay off creditors in 2013.

For years the story of Nortel's collapse filled Canadian papers. The company was not helped by accruing billions in debt after a buying spree during the "Dot Com Bust" of 2001, and an inability to finance it during the 2008 Credit Crisis.[2] Three Nortel executives would be put on trial for their accounting practices, but were ultimately found not guilty.

But there may be an additional contributing factor: for nearly a decade Nortel had been targeted by hackers "who appeared to be working in China."[3] The perpetrators are alleged to have stolen technical papers, research-and-development reports, business plans, employee emails, and other documents. According to a former Nortel employee who looked into the theft of information, the hackers were able to gain access using stolen passwords from several top Nortel executives, including the chief executive. Nortel, unfortunately, did little to counter the threat other than resetting passwords.[4]

What did the hackers do with this stolen information? Access to intellectual property would certainly help any company looking to compete in the global telecommunications industry. Moreover, having access to its business strategy would ensure that it could beat Nortel's bottom line.

It is likely we will never know the full story behind the alleged Nortel hack, and the connections (if any) to its decline or the extent to which rivals were able to take advantage of stolen information. It is, perhaps, worth noting that as the Department of National Defence moves into the former Nortel Campus as its new headquarters, the media continue to raise concerns about potential bugging of the buildings (senior DND officials maintain that no devices have been found).[5]

So while Nortel might be an important case study for business students, for those interested in national security there may be a different set of lessons to be learned: espionage against Canadian businesses is very much alive and well. Indeed, countries are using the levers of state power to achieve economic ends in new and creative ways that pose a risk to the Canadian economic landscape.

At the same time, the Nortel story is not straightforward; it also raises important questions with no clear answers: Should the Canadian government have intervened in the affairs of a private company? If Nortel took few actions to protect itself after realizing it was coming under attack, did our national security services have an obligation to respond? Should diplomatic officials inform their Chinese counterparts that such interference in a Canadian company will not be tolerated?

These questions are indicative of just some of the challenges Canada faces at the beginning of the twenty-first century on the economy and national security. The risks go beyond the theft of information and economic espionage. Indeed, there are a variety of tools and strategies (legal and illegal) that states are using in an attempt to skew our economic landscape to their benefit. But this means widening our understanding of national security into areas where many think governments should never tread in a free-market society. We are left with two very difficult questions: to what degree is the economy a national security issue, and to what extent should governments attempt to protect it, if at all?

This chapter aims to help readers unpack some of the issues around these questions. First, it will set out the main challenges for Canada in national security and the economy: economic espionage and "geoeconomic" strategies that can affect Canada in less clandestine but more impactful ways. It will then discuss the political and moral challenges of treating the economy as something to be "securitized" by governments. Finally, it will discuss some of the strategies that might be used to mitigate these threats, but ultimately point to the fact that what is really needed is a conversation about what the relationship between the economy and national security should be.

Economic Espionage Threats

Economic espionage is the clandestine or illicit attempt to acquire economic intelligence. This may include trade secrets, intellectual property, financial data, negotiating positions, acquisition plans, or anything that might give a foreign entity an advantage in a matter dealing with markets, industry, or trade.

Although there is much in the news today about economic threats, concerns about this kind of espionage are not new. As discussed in chapter three, during the Cold War there were fears about economic espionage, although these activities were not always described in such terms. In particular, there were fears that the Soviet Union was trying to steal information regarding nuclear secrets, defence technologies, and eventually commercial technology.[6] As the Cold War was coming to an end in the late 1980s and early 1990s, concerns shifted to questions of competitiveness and "industrial espionage" when it was discovered that countries such as France, Germany, China, Britain, Taiwan, South Korea, Brazil, and Japan were likely engaging in such activities against Canadian interests.[7] Canada itself has been accused of engaging in these activities on occasion. Notably, in 2013 it was alleged that the Communications Security

Establishment (CSE) had engaged in similar activities targeting the Brazilian Mines and Energy Ministry, although it was never made clear what, if anything, Canadians were getting out of this activity.[8] Indeed, as the Cold War wound down, the Canadian Security Intelligence Service (CSIS) shifted at least some of its focus to addressing industrial espionage, warning certain Canadian businesses that they were likely to be bugged, have communications intercepted and computers stolen as foreign governments targeted sales strategies, product data, contract bidding, and secret plans.[9]

Interestingly, although CSIS had been relatively open about the fact that China engaged in economic espionage in the 1990s, for most of the post–Cold War period Canadian officials have been reluctant to directly accuse China or other states as engaging in threat-related activities, including economic espionage. Something like a clampdown on publicly naming China seems to have followed the controversy in 2010 first discussed in chapter 3 when CSIS Director Richard Fadden suggested that some municipal officials and Cabinet Ministers from two unnamed provinces were the subject of clandestine foreign influence campaigns.[10] In fact, the first public accusation made against China by the Canadian government did not come until 2014 in the wake of serious cyberattacks against several government departments, discussed further in chapter 5.[11] However, even after this modest step, national security and intelligence officials avoided mentioning China in their public comments. Testifying to the Senate Standing Committee on National Security and Defence in March 2016, CSIS Director Michel Coulombe noted, "A number of foreign states continue to … attempt to gather political, economic, and military information in Canada through clandestine means. Such states will pursue their own national interests through covert means, targeting Canadian businesses, political institutions, and members of the diaspora. And Canada also remains a target for illicit procurement efforts by those pursuing advanced technology including weapons of mass destruction."[12] An Access to Information Request by the Canadian Press reveals that Coulombe's briefing notes state, "Russia and China, in particular, continue to target Canada's classified information and advanced technology, as well as government officials and systems."[13] However, Coulombe did not state these remarks publicly. It was not until December 2018 that Canada made another public cyber-attribution to China, along with its allies in the wake of cyber-intrusions against management service providers. Additionally, it was not until 2019 that China was mentioned as a major source of espionage in a Canadian public document, the National Security and Intelligence Committee of Parliamentarians (NSICOP) first-ever annual report.[14]

Goals of Economic Espionage

Today the goals of economic espionage remain largely the same as concerns raised in the 1990s. Certain states and their corporate partners seek any information that is deemed to provide an advantage in an economic setting. Threat-related activity in this area can be divided into three categories: theft of business strategies, theft of intellectual property (IP), and theft of personal information.

First, there are data that can provide insight into a company's position in negotiations, mergers, acquisitions, and bidding wars. This includes information such as red lines, opening bids, and final offers. When states acquire this knowledge, it allows them to pass along information that gives their national companies the ability to "stack the deck" against Canadian firms in bidding situations or in the global market. If the bottom line of a Canadian firm is already known, it will be easy for the other side to outbid or negotiate around them.

Second, states seek the valuable IP of Canadian firms. Although smaller than the United States, Canada has the second-largest technology corridor in North America between Toronto and Waterloo. Increasingly, Canada is becoming a leader in key areas of innovation such as artificial intelligence and robotics. States seek this knowledge to build or enhance their own native technology companies, without making the costly investment in research and development. In addition, as Canada is home to offices of some of the world's leading technology companies, such as Google and Microsoft, foreign states may seek to target American or global companies through their Canadian offices.

Finally, states seek human resources records on employees or customers that allow them to target specific individuals in order to develop sources. These records provide malicious actors with the knowledge of who has access to what information, allowing them to develop strategies for creating insider threats (discussed below). This and cyber-espionage are two clandestine ways to get information.

Cyber-Espionage

In this book, cyber-enabled threat-related activity is discussed in chapter 5. Still, it is worth briefly noting the extent to which the intelligence and national security agencies of foreign states are using these techniques to benefit companies that are furthering their strategic ends or are in areas the state wishes to protect.

There is not much known about the scale of cyber-espionage against private companies in Canada. Nevertheless, American officials have been very open about the threat and we can draw upon their experience. Since 2013 the U.S. Office of the Director of National Intelligence's "Worldwide Threat Assessment of the U.S. Intelligence Community" has identified cyber-threats as the leading national security threat to the United States, specifically naming China as engaging in large-scale economic espionage. In particular, the assessment noted that such espionage was a significant issue and that their activities continue "despite being publicly identified in detailed private sector reports, public indictments, and US demarches."[15] In 2014 the FBI indicted five Chinese military officers who stole millions of dollars in IP from six American firms in the U.S. nuclear power, metals, and solar products industries. The indictment is clear that the information stolen was provided to the competitors of these American firms, including state-owned enterprises (SOEs).[16]

There is no reason to believe the behaviour of China towards American firms is any different from the way they treat Canadian ones. The allegations made against China in the case of Nortel have already been discussed above, and there is good reason to believe that similar Canadian high-tech firms are the subject of targeted economic cyber-espionage. In January 2011 foreign hackers, believed to be from China, broke into the Department of Finance and Treasury Board's networks as well as law firms to get information that would allow them to influence the sale of Saskatchewan's Potash Corp.[17] A 2013 private sector report on Chinese military hacking identified two Canadian companies (in addition to five more with operations in Canada) as affected by this clandestine activity. The report also noted that three of the servers conducting attacks were based in Canada.[18] Additionally, although it does not name countries specifically, the 2014–16 CSIS public report noted there are continuing attacks in the private sector, especially the "advanced technology sector," research and development, and information "which will give their own companies a competitive edge over Canadian firms."[19]

There is also some evidence that Chinese hackers may use Canada as a base from which to coordinate their activities with national intelligence services. In July 2014 Vancouver resident Su Bin was arrested for helping Chinese military officers hack into the computer networks of U.S. military contractors to steal classified information.[20]

Insider Threats

Matt Bunn and Scott D. Sagan define an *insider* as "a person with authorized access to items that an organization wishes to protect – information, people, and dangerous or valuable materials, facilities, and equipment. Insiders are often employees, but they can also be contractors or certain types of visitors."[21] Importantly, insiders exist at all levels of an organization – from the chief executive officer to the janitor. An insider's status depends more on access to a sensitive facility or information than to rank within a company. Whereas a senior accountant might pass on sensitive financial files, a night guard can facilitate the covert entry of a hostile actor. In having passed on information to the Russian government, Jeffrey Delisle (discussed in chapter 3) was an insider threat.

An insider threat emerges when individuals with this access use it to harm an organization, for whatever reason. They can be self-motivated (betrayal), recruited (bribed), or coerced (blackmailed). Additionally, they may give up information by accident (by leaving sensitive documents or electronic equipment around). Finally, adversarial organizations may seek to infiltrate an organization.[22]

This is where the insights from stolen human resources records (mentioned above) come in handy for states wishing to engage in further economic espionage: it allows them to target individuals who can obtain the information they need. First, it lets them know which employees have access to which sensitive files. Second, they can use personal information to target these individuals. For example, if they are aware of which employees are disgruntled, having financial problems, or in the midst of a divorce, they can use this information to target an individual for blackmail or bribery.

Bunn and Sagan note that insiders can operate in a variety of ways. A *passive* insider threat may simply let an outside organization know about the existence of files, a security vulnerability, or some other weakness but take no part in the plot. An *active* insider takes active part in a plot to steal information or grant outsiders access (such as sending a password or disarming a system), and a *violent* insider is willing to engage in physical harm in order to achieve a particular end.[23]

When it comes to recent, known economic espionage insider threats in Canada, the participants tend to fall in the *active* category. For example, there is evidence China is using insider threats and or theft to steal valuable secrets and intellectual property. During seventeen months between April 2013 and July 2014 there were three reported cases of Canadians and/or Chinese nationals with links to Canada attempting to steal intellectual property or industrial secrets to China. In April 2013 Klaus Nielsen, a former lead researcher with the Canadian Food Inspection Agency and his colleague Wei Ling Yu were charged with trying to smuggle pathogens out of Canada in order to develop and sell testing kits in China against bacteria affecting cows. Nielsen was arrested at the Ottawa airport while Yu is believed to be in China.[24] In December 2013 naval engineer Qing Quentin Huang was charged with trying to pass along classified Canadian shipbuilding techniques to China.[25] Also in December 2013 the FBI indicted Montreal resident Wang Hongwei for trying to steal trade secrets from U.S. seed companies[26] (although in these cases the level of official coordination with Chinese intelligence services, if any, is unknown).

More recently, in July 2019 it was reported that two researchers with ties to China and their Chinese graduate students were escorted out of the National Microbiology Lab (NML) in Winnipeg for what the RCMP called a "policy breach." The NML is a level 4 virology facility, equipped to research serious diseases, and it is one of the very few in North America capable of handling pathogens such as Ebola that require the highest level of containment. At time of publication there were few details known about the allegations against Xiangguo Qiu and her husband Keding Cheng, but the case has the hallmarks of other insider threat cases discussed above. In particular, the seizure and replacement of Qiu's computer by IT specialists and the RCMP referral raise questions about the theft of intellectual property and/or technology at NML.[27]

In summary, as states compete with one another in the global economy, they may turn to clandestine means to achieve their economic goals. Unlike Canada and most free-market economies, adversarial states actively use their intelligence and national security agencies to support their industries. These agencies use their expertise to steal information and then pass it on to domestic companies that may then go on to compete with Western firms without the cost of investing in research and development. This can put Canadian firms at a serious disadvantage.

Yet, while economic espionage may be difficult to detect, it has the strange advantage of being a relatively straightforward national security threat. The theft of information, bribing, and blackmail are all activities that are clearly crimes under domestic law. When a state engages in these activities, we immediately recognize them as national security issues. More difficult to detect are the strategies and policies governments may use to undermine the economic security of another country but, on the surface, appear to be legal. What happens when countries engage in legal activities that allow them to achieve murky agendas? In other words, what happens when states use a series of legal means to achieve more nefarious ends?

Geoeconomics

In calling for widening our understanding of national security, a key argument of this book is that *geoeconomic* strategies represent a major national security challenge. Geoeconomic statecraft is the use of economic instruments to accomplish geopolitical objectives.[28] This is basically the same as what is called "economic statecraft": "the state's intentional manipulation of economic interaction to capitalize on, reinforce or reduce the associated strategic externalities."[29] Rising powers that cannot challenge the United States and its allies in conventional ways are increasingly turning to geoeconomics to achieve state ends. Further, as these rising powers typically have political systems where the state largely has control of production and the use of capital (a situation often described as "state-capitalism"), they can use their considerable financial instruments to carry out geopolitical goals. Given that we live in an era when markets have increasing power over states and the lives of their citizens, the implications of such activities are enormous.[30]

It should come as no surprise that states are utilizing economic leverage to achieve their aims; states have attempted to use economic statecraft for centuries.[31] But the activities being referring to here go beyond what might be described as conventional geoeconomics. Rather, besides conventional foreign and trade policies, states are using a savvy combination of investment and innovation policies that likely amounts to the use of legitimate means to achieve problematic ends. The next section uses China as a case study to explain the challenges of dealing with the rise of new geoconomic strategies and the national security issues that come with them.

President Xi's Vision

At the outset, it is important to recognize that China is not a unitary actor – there are competing interests, factions, and a division between moderates and hyper-nationalists within the Chinese Communist Party (CCP).[32] Nevertheless, CCP leadership is unified around one goal: survival of the party-state. This transcends all things, including the rule of law, and reflects a de facto pact made by the last thirty years of Chinese leadership – increasing prosperity for stability and continued CCP rule. To maintain its end of the bargain, the CCP must deliver and continue to deliver a rising standard of living.[33]

To achieve this goal, the Chinese government has announced several major policies to improve Chinese innovation, facilitate resource extraction, and create more markets for Chinese goods. This includes "One Belt, One Road," which will enhance interconnectivity in Asia and Africa via a network of economic zones, ports, and railways. Further, the "Indigenous Innovation" and "Made in China 2025" strategies are aimed at using the technology of other countries to upgrade and enhance China's manufacturing capabilities, bolster innovation, and establish the dominance of key technological sectors. Indeed, China hopes to reduce foreign technology in the Chinese market to less than 30 per cent by 2025.[34] In the wake of heightened trade tensions with the Trump administration, China has downplayed the Made in China strategy. However, in December 2018 it was reported that China was developing new approaches to promote its own technological dominance.[35]

As such, China has embarked on several geoconomic strategies in traditional foreign and trade, investment and science, and technology policies to enable President Xi Jinping's vision for a rising and dominant China in the twenty-first century in trade and geopolitics.

Foreign and Trade Policy

FOREIGN DIRECT INVESTMENT (FDI) AND LENDING

China has invested abroad in order to feed its growing economy the raw resources it needs to thrive. However, China also uses FDI to persuade other countries to adopt certain policies; within five years of China's first investments in Africa, the number of African states to recognize Taiwan fell from thirteen to four.[36] In addition, China extended billions of dollars in loans to African governments in recent years. One estimate suggests that the Chinese government and its companies and banks loaned over U.S.$94 billion to African governments and SOEs between 2000 and 2015.[37] Further, as an International Monetary Fund report noted, China's share of total external debt in sub-Saharan Africa has risen from less than 2 per cent before 2005 to about 15 per cent in 2012.[38] It is possible that at this rate of growth, Chinese lending to Africa may soon outpace that of the World Bank.[39]

While some suggest that this debt is financing oil and infrastructure and is both welcome and needed by African states, others have argued that this amounts to "debtbook diplomacy," where China has loaned money to countries that have no way of paying them back.[40] This has enabled China to leverage this accumulated debt to achieve its strategic aims. For example, having exerted pressure on Taiwan recognition, there is the possibility that China could use its financial leverage over countries in Asia (Pakistan, Sri Lanka, Cambodia, Laos, and the Philippines) to undermine Western strategic interests, or provide China a proxy-veto in organizations such as the Association of South East Asian Nations (ASEAN).[41] While it may be difficult for China to exert this kind of pressure in Canada, an ability to cultivate diplomatic leverage in parts of the world where Canada has strategic interests is of concern. Policymakers should also consider China's FDI and lending policies as a part of a larger strategy that affects Canada overall.

TARGETED PRODUCT BANS

A frequent way for Beijing to coerce a state is through the use of product bans. This is often carried out through frivolous "public safety" bans that cite far-fetched health concerns over certain goods. Canada has been at the unfortunate end of this trade tactic numerous times. For example, in 2009 and 2016 China slapped a "health and safety ban" on Canadian canola exports. Coincidentally, in both of those years China was dealing with its own bumper crop of canola products.[42] Further, it seems that China has been able to use these bans in their negotiations with Canada – the 2016 ban was put in place in the period leading up to the trade talks between the Canadian and Chinese governments. It is possible China manufactures a crisis in order to extract trade concessions from Canada, while giving up little (if anything) in return.

Following an increase in tension between Canada and China in the aftermath of the arrest of Huawei's chief financial officer, Meng

Wanzhou (discussed below), China began a series of predictable bans on Canadian products, including canola, soybeans, pork, and beef.[43] In some cases the orders have simply stopped, but in others, China said it found "inauthentic" export certificates of Canadian pork shipments which were reportedly found to contain ractopamine – an additive banned in China.[44] While Canadian officials were working to understand how the forged certificates came about at time of writing, using an export ban at a time of tension is consistent with prior Chinese behaviour.

BOYCOTTS

China has also demonstrated that it is willing to use boycotts to achieve strategic ends, especially when nationalist issues are at stake. For example, in 2012 China famously retaliated against economically powerful Japan over its stance on the Senkaku/Diaoyu island group. After days of non-stop anti-Japan coverage in the media, two-thirds of Chinese citizens reportedly agreed to boycott Japanese products voluntarily. Further, it has regularly used rare earth mineral bans against Japan that target its high-tech industries (rare earth elements and metals are essential for making components for mobile phones). Ultimately, these strategies hurt Chinese workers when Japanese foreign investment and goods are suppressed. Yet, the fact that it is willing to take an economic hit underscores the extent to which Beijing is willing to tolerate pain when accepting costs for its geo-economics policies.[45]

Canada has experienced such boycotts by China as well. In 2010 China delisted the University of Calgary as an accredited foreign school after the Dalai Lama spoke on its campus.[46] With an estimated 600 Chinese nationals paying around $36,000 in tuition each, this move was a costly one for the university.[47] It also indicates China's readiness to retaliate against Canada.

Threats to Canadian Individuals

Unfortunately, in December 2018 it became clear that China is willing to engage in another strategy as a retaliatory measure: threats to Canadian persons. That month, Canadian officials arrested Meng

Wanzhou, the chief financial officer for Huawei technologies on a U.S. warrant. The United States alleges that Meng has committed bank fraud, wire fraud, and conspiracies to commit bank and wire fraud as part of a larger effort to circumvent American sanctions on Iran.[48]

Huawei is not a Chinese state-owned enterprise (discussed below), but it can be described as a state-championed enterprise, a private company that maintains close links to the Chinese state and benefits from its active support. President Xi sees Huawei as representing the future of the country. Meng's arrest was therefore met with outrage by China. As noted above, segments of Canadian agriculture were banned. The Chinese ambassador to Canada wrote a hyperbolic editorial in the Hill Times, suggesting Canadians tolerance for the arrest was the result of "white supremacy."[49]

However, the most serious retaliatory actions were the arrest and subsequent charges of two Canadians, Michael Kovrig, a diplomat on leave from Global Affairs Canada working for the non-governmental organization International Crisis Group, and businessman Michael Spavor on charges of breaching China's vague national security laws days after Meng's arrest. Although we do not know much about their conditions, we can expect that they are being held like other detainees – subject to hours of daily interrogation, possibly forced to sit in "tiger chairs" (which amount to stress positions), kept in small cells with twenty-four-hour lighting, denied the ability to speak with their families, and likely threatened with executions.[50] Both men are allowed to meet with consular officials only once per month. And media reports suggest that Chinese officials took away Kovrig's glasses, preventing him from seeing properly, likely to add pressure to "confess" to whatever crime he is accused of.[51]

A few weeks after Kovrig and Spavor were detained, a Canadian convicted on drug charges appealing his sentence suddenly had his trial open to the international press – an event described as rare by China-watchers.[52] Rather than having his sentence reduced, he was handed down the death sentence in an unusually speedy trial, suggesting that the move was political. A few months later in April 2019, a second Canadian was sentenced to death for producing and trafficking methamphetamine.[53]

All of this makes it clear that China is willing to engage in threats to Canadian persons when it is displeased in legal and commercial disputes. Nor was this the first time China has taken such actions. In 2014, following the arrest of a Chinese national, Su Bin, in Canada for extradition to the United States on espionage charges, a Canadian couple, Kevin and Julia Garratt, were suddenly arrested. The couple, who owned a café along the Chinese–North Korean border and engaged in Christian missionary work, found themselves accused of stealing data on military projects with no evidence. Pressured to confess, they were held separately in cells lit twenty-four hours per day, interrogated daily, and also denied full consular services.[54] Julia was not released until February 2015, and Kevin until September 2016 – likely after they were no longer deemed politically useful. Of note, Su Bin was extradited to the United States in February 2016 and pleaded guilty to espionage charges in March of that year.[55] Essentially, China uses strategic arrests in order to circumvent the rule of law.

Investment Strategies

REFUSING RECIPROCITY

While China is eager to invest abroad, it is extremely cautious over allowing foreign companies to invest in China. Indeed, the lack of reciprocity – the fact that Canadian companies do not have full access to the Chinese market in ways that Chinese companies have access to the Canadian one – has been an area of diplomatic contention between the two countries. While most countries have policies on investing in "strategic" areas, China takes a very broad view of what constitutes a strategic sector. This has resulted in a significant trade imbalance between Canada and China (as well as most other Western countries).[56]

JOINT VENTURES

One strategy that Western firms can use in order to get access to the Chinese market is joint ventures – essentially a partnership with a domestic Chinese firm. However, although these partnerships allow for some market access, this policy is often very problematic for Western firms. Since 2016 Beijing has required that these "joint ventures" are majority owned by the Chinese partners. While the requirement is at least 50 per cent, in reality the Chinese share can often reach 70, 80, or 90 per cent.[57] In other words, Western firms lose control over their companies in order to obtain market share: their technology is branded with the Chinese name, manufactured in China, and sold to third countries by the Chinese joint venture.[58] Further, even when a deal is reached to gain access to the Chinese market, companies such as Hewlett-Packard, Cisco, and Microsoft have been forced to sell majority shares in their investments to their Chinese partner, or be forced to leave China entirely.[59] Although it is not manufacturing, American food giant McDonald's now owns only 20 per cent of its business in Mainland China, Hong Kong, and Macao.[60]

FORCED TECHNOLOGY TRANSFERS

One of the most contentious issues between China and the West is the forced transfer of technology from Western firms to Chinese companies as the prices of admission to the Chinese market. For example, as a precondition of staying in business, Bombardier reportedly had to transfer a significant amount of technology on its trains to two Chinese rail companies as well as the designs of its C Series jets to the government's aircraft manufacturing company.[61] The result is the creation of relationships where Chinese manufacturers are simultaneously partners and competitors with Canadian businesses. That competition is occurring not only domestically within China, but internationally.[62] In May 2017 one of Bombardier's strategic partners, CRRC Corporation, beat the company in a bid to make rail cars for the Montreal regional commuter rail service (CRRC Corp, owned by a Chinese SOE, was able to cut its price from $103 million to $69 million).[63]

MERGERS AND ACQUISITIONS

Backed by loans from the state, Chinese firms have engaged in a buying spree of Western firms. While there has been considerable merging of technological firms across the global industry in recent years, this has been mostly to address market weakness and the high cost of research and development. Chinese companies, on the other hand, are making acquisitions in pursuit of government-driven objectives[64] – in particular, the acquisition of Western IP. Consistent with President Xi's innovation policies, the acquisition of IP is a fundamental part of establishing China's technological dominance. Although these companies may be spending hundreds of billions of dollars, as one China analyst observes, "the long-term economic benefit and future scalability of what is being acquired is thought to be a bargain."[65]

Unlike espionage (discussed above) and threats to individuals (which still seem to remain extraordinary), all of these geoeconomic strategies are or use legal tools to accomplish their goals. Yet, when coordinated and used in combination, they have the ability to affect economic relations in such a way as to pose a national security concern to other countries. Here we see the use of legitimate tools to achieve clandestine ends, such as favourably skewing entire industries, if not national economies, to suit China's national interest. Unfortunately, the challenge is that it is very difficult to put a stop to this use of legal tools. Moreover, at a time of global uncertainty, when trade and foreign investment is needed, it is not clear how to proceed. China's SOEs further illustrate this problem for Canada.

State Owned Enterprises: A Case Study in Geoeconomics

Although SOEs are a tool of geoeconomic statecraft, their place in the debate about Canadian national security merits their separate consideration as a case study for this book. Importantly, SOEs indicate the evolving and multifaceted nature of the challenges facing Canada. First, they carry out many of the concerning geoeconomic strategies discussed above for their states. Second, the issues of SOE investment is one where economic and national security interest collide – they cut across many competing areas of government interests, making coordination to deal with this issue, or develop a strategy, challenging.

Defining SOEs is difficult, as they tend to go by many names and have different purposes and status, depending on their country of ownership. SOEs have also been referred to as government corporations, government business enterprises, government-linked companies, parastatals, public enterprises, public sector units or enterprises, etc.[66] The closest thing we have to Canadian SOEs are Crown corporations, but there are important differences from other state-owned corporations. In particular, Canadian Crown corporations were established sporadically and as remedies for market failure.[67] More importantly, they are not instruments of foreign and trade policy.

The nature of SOEs is very diverse and they can be used for any purpose – in China there are SOEs that simply own hotels, manage restaurants, and operate shopping malls.[68] Generally, however, the largest SOEs are in the finance and banking, public utilities (electricity, gas, distribution, transportation, and communication), manufacturing, natural resources (metals and mining), and petroleum.[69] Further complicating definition, however, is the fact that SOEs widely differ in ownership structure, their position in the public administration hierarchy, and whether or not they are listed on a stock exchange.[70] This means that consideration of SOEs, whether for policy or scholarly reasons, is a challenge.

For the purpose of this book, I will utilize the definition used by the OECD and Pricewaterhouse Coopers, where SOEs are defined as "enterprises where the state has significant control through full, majority, or significant minority ownership," including SOEs owned by "the central or federal government, as well as SOEs owed by regional and local governments."[71]

Although free-market liberalism has been the dominant philosophy of international economic affairs since the end of the Cold War, by 2016 the OECD estimated that 22 of the world's 100 largest firms were now effectively under state control – the highest level in decades.[72] A larger survey by Forbes in 2015 found that 326 of the world's largest 2000 companies were SOEs, a third of them located on Mainland China and another 13 in Hong Kong.[73]

A complete history of Chinese SOEs is beyond the scope of this book, but a brief overview is necessary in order to appreciate their implications for national security today. Chinese SOEs had their start in the aftermath of the Communist takeover of China in 1949 as part of a nationalization of private companies and assets. As Duanjie Chen notes, SOEs were "not intended simply to intervene in the market but to replace the market, following the industrialization model of the Soviet Union's centrally controlled economic system."[74] In the 1970s and early 1980s, Chinese leader Deng Xiaoping began to make slow and steady reforms, including to SOEs, many of which were suffering from economic inefficiencies, underinvestment, and long-term decline of productivity.[75] For example, changes were introduced where firms were obliged to produce a certain amount of product to be sold to the Chinese government at a fixed price, but anything produced above this amount could be sold to the domestic market.[76] However, the pace of these reforms was slow, and SOEs were increasingly insolvent, threatening the viability of the quickly growing Chinese economy.[77] As such, further steps were taken to partially liberalize SOEs. By 1994 all SOEs in China were able to keep profits, and through the 1990s steps were taken to commercialize these entities to prepare them for competition on the global market.[78]

Since the reforms of the 1970s and 1980s began, Chinese SOEs have been caught up in a battle between state ideological imperatives and financial viability. There was opposition to the idea of full privatization, particularly on how far and how fast reforms could go. As such, a series of half or partial "privatization" measures took place,[79] which has led to a number of issues with Chinese SOEs, particularly from a Canadian perspective. First, it is not necessarily clear who actually "owns" SOEs. Given the partial privatizations that have taken place, a controlling entity may have the right to "control" a resource or asset, but not necessarily own it.[80]

Second, and relatedly, current arrangements mean that SOEs are often in the hands of Communist Party officials. These officials will often set up their immediate families in SOE businesses to ensure that profits (including bribes or money raised from illicit activities) stay within the family. In this way the officials can remain in their hard-won positions within the Communist Party, but keep the profits from private business.[81]

Third, given this complicated structure, it is not surprising that Chinese SOEs are vulnerable to corruption. Of course, given the number of SOEs and the lack of free press, the full scale of the problem is unknown. However, a survey of reported and prosecuted criminal cases of SOE officials between 2011 and 2014 suggests that most cases involved large sums of money (the average 21 million yuan, approximately $4 million Canadian). This amount is up to five times greater than the average amount that local officials charged with corruption are accused of stealing.[82] Individuals involved in SOEs were typically prosecuted for bribe-taking, embezzlement, and authorized use of public funds, often via financial management, contract bidding, capital raising, and personnel management. Moreover, SOE corruption cases in China involved networks of multiple individuals in large enterprises.[83] One researcher concludes that the potential for corruption is greater in SOEs controlled by the central government, especially when individuals are able to use their political power to work with their family and/or business associates to steal the most valuable assets.[84]

For the purpose of this book, this history is important for two main reasons. First, it suggests that many of the SOEs seeking to invest in Canada are, at best, lacking in transparency and at worst, based on networks of corruption with little to no accountability. Second, the need to maintain control of many, especially the largest and most important, SOEs in China means that they are not regular firms, but seen as instruments of the state with the purpose of furthering geopolitical ends.

China was supposed to liberalize its SOEs after joining the World Trade Organization. However, rather than liberalizing further, recent reforms have seen SOEs merge with one another, concentrating their power in the hands of fewer people in order to avoid competing with one another and "giving them heft to barge into new markets."[85] Indeed, in 2013 President Xi Jinping made it clear that SOEs should continue to play a dominant role in the economy. As the *Economist* notes, "The implication is that [Xi] wants state firms to be better run – hence the emphasis on the market – but only so that they better serve the party by helping it to manage the economy at home and carry China's flag into foreign territory. Mr. Xi has made this point in increasingly strident terms."[86] In other words, China's approach to reforming SOEs has been one of consolidation, attempting to turn them into "gargantuan national champions" that may be opening up to mixed ownership, but remain firmly under state control.[87]

Given the nature of these institutions, it is not surprising that concerns have been raised in Western countries as to whether they should be allowed to invest. This issue has gained prominence since 2008 when Chinese investment in Canada began to jump, from $4.2 billion in 2007 to $12 billion in 2012.[88] However, Canadian governments have struggled to create and/or adapt the right policy tools to address this evolving trend. The result is unpredictability for a market that likes certainty: some bids are approved (such as Nexen) and others are denied (such as the 2018 Chinese SOE bid for Canada's largest construction firm, Aecon) for reasons that are often known only to the government.

The Good, the Bad, and the Economy

Those in favour of SOE investment in Canada have made a number of arguments. For the purpose of this book, it is important to focus on two: that despite their state-owned ties, SOEs are reforming and increasingly behave like normal businesses and that they will be bound by Canadian law.

First, it is argued that Chinese SOEs operate as competitive, domestic firms. It is suggested that Chinese SOEs have learned from their socialist past and should be seen as motivated by profit and commercial in orientation.[89] In other words, we should not worry that SOEs are controlled by the state, because they are increasingly acting in accordance with market forces, not the foreign policy priorities of Beijing. Instead, we should appreciate reforms being made in China that are creating competitive, better-governed, and more efficient SOEs. As such, SOEs should not be treated differently from private firms and that there should be no discrimination of SOEs in the investment review process.[90]

Second, even if SOEs may be the instrument of states, they are bound by Canadian laws. Anti-competitive or predatory behaviour can be addressed by domestic antitrust regulations.[91] Even if SOEs are different from regular firms in that they lack transparency,

Canadian firms will build that risk into the cost of doing business with them.[92] Given our robust institutions, Canada already has enough legislation and policies in place to protect it from China.[93]

It is important to recognize that there is some validity to these two claims. As noted above, not all Chinese SOEs are alike: they vary in stature, purpose, ability, and interests, and this plays a role in their behaviour. Additionally, Beijing is not able to exert the same level of control over all SOEs. In some cases, the centre's control is very direct, while in others the state must work to force an SOE to comply with its geopolitical objectives. For example, if there are a large number of SOEs in a particular industry, it will be hard to assert control over any particular one over the others. Additionally, the Chinese government itself may be divided on a particular goal, making it hard to direct SOEs to one purpose.[94]

It is the contention here that some SOEs raise security issues that may outweigh their benefits, and arguments for treating SOEs as normal firms are flawed. In particular, the idea that Chinese SOEs are and behave like normal firms is easily contradicted by the evidence. It is widely accepted that SOEs are far less efficient than private sector firms. Their profitability continues to fall and the returns are about half of those of their non-state peers.[95] Despite their large presence in China, by 2017 they accounted for less than a fifth of output.[96] While this is a risk for the Chinese economy, there are dangers that these giant SOEs could hurt and distort global markets through their inefficiencies, hurting the potential for growth worldwide as they become the dominant forces in the international economy.[97]

Second, attempts at SOE reform appear to have failed – if anything, SOEs appear to be moving in the opposite direction. The *Economist* observes, "SOEs are getting bigger, not smaller; their management has become more conservative; and their deficiencies are beginning to infect the economy more widely."[98] As discussed above, the trend when reforming SOEs is to make them larger, to remove competition, and to bring them even further in line with Beijing's priorities. This has reached the point where the CCP is now writing itself into the articles of association of Hong Kong's SOEs, just to make it crystal clear who is in charge.[99] While this step essentially formalizes what has been long known, "the changes are the first time the party rather than the government has been named."[100] The promised liberalization of SOEs that their advocates have pointed to are simply not coming.

Third, because of their links to the CCP, SOEs have access to resources that their private sector peers (domestically and internationally) do not. Despite their low productivity, they take about half of all bank loans in China and are responsible for that country's large increase in corporate debt.[101] Moreover, they absorb considerable investment and are able to maintain monopoly or near-monopoly positions in several sectors.[102] They are simply not subject to the same hard budget constraints as private firms.[103] This means Chinese SOEs are not obliged to follow normal business practices and as a result they are unlikely to fail. Backed by the world's largest economy, they can enter into markets, distorting them with large, inefficient corporations that do not have to follow the laws of sound business management. At best, the outcome may be reduced efficiency of the market; at worst, this could lead to the collapse of domestic industries.

Finally, the idea that SOEs are not a threat because they are forced to comply with Canadian business practices and laws is extremely short-sighted. We have already seen that Chinese SOEs are intrinsically linked with the Chinese party-state. As such, any attempt to level the playing field or punish SOEs will likely provoke retaliation in ways that Canadian laws cannot touch. Frivolous "health and safety" claims, discussed above, are frequently used when Beijing is displeased. Repeated bans on canola products, boycotts, threats to more Canadian persons, and perhaps even a cyberattack by Chinese "patriotic hackers" is possible.[104] And clearly, as discussed above, strategic arrests (amounting to a form of kidnapping) is another way China tries to shield its SOEs from the rule of law.

Investment and National Security in Canada

How should Canada deal with geoeconomics strategies? Canada's foreign investment policies originate out of a fear in the early 1970s that foreign (particularly American) firms would eventually buy up and/or effectively trounce Canadian ones. As such, the government of Pierre Trudeau passed the *Foreign Investment Review Act* (FIRA) in 1974. Under the *Act*, all new foreign acquisitions and establishments of business in Canada above a certain size were required to undergo review and approval on whether they were an undefined "significant benefit to Canada."[105] This rather hostile stance towards investment changed under the Conservative government of Brian Mulroney with the *Investment Canada Act* (*ICA*) in 1985. In brief, the new *Act* reflected the government's view that foreign investment was a net positive. Instead of FIRA's "significant benefit test," the *ICA* introduced a "net benefit" test with the criteria that these investments contributed to Canada's global market competitiveness and were compatible with federal and provincial cultural policies.[106] The *ICA* did not distinguish between SOEs and private enterprises until the Ministry of Industry issued a set of "special guidelines" in 2007 that focused on SOE corporate governance and their adherence to Canadian standards and commercial practice.[107]

As unease over Chinese SOE investment grew, the government introduced new national security powers under the *ICA* in 2009. These new measures stipulated that if the Minister of Industry (now the Minister of Innovation, Science and Economic Development [ISED]) "has reasonable grounds to believe that an investment by a non-Canadian could be injurious to national security," the government may review any investment in a Canadian business by a non-Canadian.[108]

A catalyst for debate and consternation, however, was the announcement that the Chinese National Overseas Oil Corporation (CNOOC), a Chinese SOE, was going to purchase Nexen, offering a very large sum – 61 per cent over the share price – to investors. This was not the first Chinese foray into Canadian national resources – the Chinese National Petroleum Corporation (CNPC), on its own initiative, signed an agreement to cooperate with Alberta on exploring the oil sands as far back as 1991. And in June 1993 CNPC acquired 15.9 per cent of an Alberta gas processing plant, marking CNPC's first equity stake and reportedly China's first overseas oil production.[109]

The scale of the proposed CNOOC-Nexen takeover bid immediately stood out; the $15.1 billion deal was the single largest foreign takeover by a Chinese company at the time.[110] After subjecting the takeover to a national security review, the deal was approved by the Conservative government in December 2012. Indicating the unease with which the decision was made, however, it came with an announcement of future restrictions on investments in Canada by SOEs, clarifying the government's new priorities and the challenges it faces when dealing with SOEs in the Canadian context: "First, foreign SOEs are, although to varying degrees, inherently susceptible to foreign government influence that may be inconsistent with Canadian national industrial and economic objectives. Second, SOE acquisitions of Canadian businesses may also have adverse effects on the efficiency, productivity and competitiveness of those companies, which may have negative effects on the Canadian economy in the longer term. The continued growth of foreign SOE transactions, with a particular increase in acquisitions of control of Canadian businesses, suggests that further clarification would be useful for the marketplace." The government also noted, "While the vast majority of global energy deposits are state-controlled, Canada's oil sands are primarily owned by innovative private sector businesses. If the oil sands are to continue to develop to the benefit of all Canadians, the role of private sector companies must be reinforced." Or, as Prime Minister Harper argued, "To be blunt, Canadians have not spent years reducing the ownership of sectors of the economy by our own governments, only to see them bought and controlled by foreign governments instead."[111]

The new policy amounted to adding extra burdens to SOEs, including satisfying the Minister of Industry (now ISED) that the investment is based on a commercial orientation and free from political influence, adheres to Canadian laws, and makes positive contributions to the efficiency of the Canadian business. The Minister will also examine the degree of control or influence an SOE would likely exert on a Canadian business and how the industry in which the Canadian business operates would be effective and whether or not the private sector orientation of an industry could be put at risk. Essentially, the statement seemed to make it clear that future SOE investment in the oil sands would be an exception, not the norm: "Each case will be examined on its own merits; however, given the inherent risks posed by foreign SOE acquisitions in the Canadian oil sands the Minister of Industry will find the acquisition of control of a Canadian oil sands business by a foreign SOE to be net benefit to Canada on an exceptional basis only."[112] These new restrictions/policy clarifications were met with resentment, not least from those with shares in the oil sands (and their law firms).

A second approach taken by the government to mitigate some of the negative externalities of doing business with China was through the Canada-China Foreign Investment Protection Agreement. In theory, this agreement (which came into effect in 2014) protects investors by creating a mechanism for investor disputes in each country for thirty-one years. Yet the agreement keeps existing investment restrictions in place and specifies that arbitration will be overseen by a panel that may keep the process secret to the parties being sued. In this sense, it does not address concerns over existing unfair practices and transparency in a system that does not respect the rule of law.[113] In this sense, it is far from certain that Canadian investors will truly benefit from this agreement.

Huawei or the Highway?

Since the CNOOC-Nexen takeover the situation has become more, not less, complicated. As noted above, Canada is dealing not only with Chinese-SOEs but also with Chinese state-championed companies. China has exerted increasing control over its private sector under President Xi, and it effectively champions certain enterprises as flag-waving winners and hallmarks of a future where that country is able to dominate global manufacturing as well as research and innovation in high-technology. These companies have access to many of the same resources as SOEs but are also expected to serve Chinese ends where necessary. Nevertheless, their status as "free" enterprises often means that they can claim that they operate independently from the Chinese state, complicating enforcement rules in Western as well as other states.

The most prominent example of this challenge for Canada is the complex matter of Huawei technologies. Although a decision about the future of the company's presence in Canada may be made by time of publication, Huawei represents a cautionary tale in how it combines concerns over how Chinese companies with close ties to the state operate in Canada, their access and/or control over Canadian critical infrastructure, the risk of retaliation by China for taking actions against it, and the need for foreign investment for research and development.

Even before Meng's arrest, Huawei has been a major challenge for Canadian politicians and policymakers. In particular, there is the question of whether the company should be allowed to participate in Canada's 5G network – the technology that will likely power the next industrial revolution. There are two immediate national security issues that arise. First, all Chinese companies are subject to the national security laws, which compel them to assist the Chinese state in conducting their activities. While Huawei and the Chinese government have argued that the company is not obliged to act against its legitimate business interests, the law is, at best, ambiguous and there are few publicly known examples of companies standing up to the Chinese government requests for information.[114] Will giving Huawei access to Canada's telecommunications infrastructure threaten our cybersecurity and facilitate espionage? Second, should there be hostilities or even simply further antagonistic relations between Canada and China, would the latter require Huawei to shut down its equipment? Or hand over control to the Chinese state?

On the other hand, few companies can provide the equipment that is needed to develop 5G networks, except for two or three other European/Asian firms. Huawei offers a cheap option for Canadian telecommunications companies seeking to bring 5G to Canada. Indeed, from a vulnerabilities perspective it makes sense to have many companies operating within a larger network, because cutting down on the number of suppliers can have real risks. Less competition means there is a reduced incentive for remaining companies to improve cybersecurity in their products. Further, if telecommunications networks are built in a way where the compromise of one supplier could result in 30–50 per cent of the market being affected, it could cause catastrophic national harm.[115] There are real incentives for governments to have many, not fewer companies building communications infrastructure. In this sense, Huawei may represent a threat, but one that might best be managed through a "defence in depth" approach to Canada's telecommunications infrastructure. This a method of cybersecurity that uses layers of detection and protective measures "designed to impede the progress of a cyber intruder while enabling an organization to detect and respond to the intrusion with the goal of reducing and mitigating the consequences of a breach."[116]

There is also the question of Huawei's role in Canada's research and development community, especially at Canadian post-secondary institutions. The company provides millions of dollars in funding to Canadian universities, often paired with government grants to develop technological breakthroughs and intellectual property.[117] However, despite the advances taking place on Canadian soil and with taxpayer support, the intellectual property belongs to Huawei and is shipped back to China for development into products. While Canadian professors, researchers, and their students benefit from funds, Canada is not necessarily benefiting from their work.

In this sense, Huawei represents a complex dilemma that goes to the heart of the troubles at the Sino-Canadian relationship: what should the Canadian government do when Chinese companies engage in legitimate transactions that may cumulatively create a negative impact on certain sectors of the Canadian economy?

In dealing with the narrow technical threat, the answer comes down to a choice between risk mitigation and ban. At present, the security for Huawei equipment is tested in a "white lab" under the Security Review Program overseen by the CSE. In these labs, funded by Huawei itself, cybersecurity specialists test the company's equipment for vulnerabilities that would give the Chinese state deliberate or accidental access to Canadian systems. The effectiveness of such systems, however, remains up for debate.[118] Trying to mitigate the risk is complicated and requires constant testing and updating. Countries can never be entirely sure their infrastructure and information are not at risk. Such an approach always leaves open the possibility of failure – and once Huawei technologies are in Canadian networks, it will be very difficult to remove them if a threat should suddenly arise. But there are problems with a ban as well. It will make telecommunications more expensive, result in the elimination of millions of dollars of funding to universities, and, as discussed above, potentially leave our 5G networks vulnerable through relying on only one or two suppliers.

However, as this chapter makes clear, the issue goes beyond just technical questions – it is fundamentally geoeconomic. Is it a national security concern if state-championed enterprises with vast state backing and support can enter into our economy with market-distorting effects? Normal companies are subject to the consequences of their decisions and poor management practices. On the other hand, SOEs and state-championed enterprises simply cannot fail. This enables them to take risks and/or engage in behaviour that undermines their competition by out-bidding others, offering cut-rate prices at a loss, etc. Ultimately, such behaviour skews the economic landscape in such a way that enables these entities to dominate the market, achieving the political ends of their sponsoring state. Moreover, for Canadian companies, it can undermine their research and development, and result in the loss of IP and jobs and even their collapse.

Additionally, it is not even clear that SOEs or state-championed companies can truly be held accountable for their actions. Spokespersons for Huawei Canada have frequently stated the company will abide by Canadian law.[119] However, as the Meng case has demonstrated, China is able to use its size and geoeconomic tools to circumvent attempts to apply Canadian laws and regulations if it chooses. Should Canada try to investigate a company like Huawei (or others like it) in the future, China may very well try to retaliate economically (targeting Canadian agricultural products) or by arresting more Canadians on trumped-up espionage charges. In this way, the cost of pursuing justice and the rule of law are blows to vulnerable segments of our economy or even the lives of Canadians. While Canada may be able to mitigate technical threats, it is not yet clear that we have a strategy to manage geoeconomic ones.

Conclusion

The above sections have described the clandestine and legitimate means that China is using in order to achieve its geoeconomic goals. It has also shown that China is more than willing to use a series of strategies to obtain what it wants from the Canadian economy. Still, we are left with the question of whether this is a national security problem.

This is one of the most serious policy challenges Canada faces in the twenty-first century, and there is no clear answer on how we address it. It can be argued that the issues raised in this chapter are simply the price of doing business in our era, that the need for investment and growth outweighs any security risks that may accompany SOEs, state-championed companies, and/or foreign direct investment. Others point to the fact that it is simply not a national security problem if businesses make bad decisions. It stands to reason that the government of Canada did not spend so much effort de-nationalizing Canadian firms in the 1980s simply to have it come back and make decisions for businesses all over again. There are clearly serious risks to the health of our economy if we choose to securitize too many elements of it.

So, what are the security concerns that can be raised? A narrow approach to national security would highlight the use of clandestine means by states to damage our economy: cyber-espionage and insider threats to steal IP and to affect the outcome of negotiations. These are clearly illegal actions where there is likely universal support for action by the government to prevent such activity, whether through diplomacy or technical means. But essentially this is where the concern ends.

On the other hand, a wider approach to national security highlights how a combination of seemingly legitimate tools can be applied for covert ends that are not necessarily in Canadian interests. As CSIS delicately discussed the issue nearly a decade ago in its 2010–11 public report, "While the vast majority of foreign investment in Canada is carried out in an open and transparent manner, certain state-owned enterprises (SOEs) and private firms with close ties to their home governments have pursued opaque agendas or received clandestine intelligence support for their pursuits here."[120]

Free market/capitalist systems require a level playing field and the rule of law in order to operate efficiently. However, China's strategies and tactics combined are aimed at skewing the Canadian economic landscape in ways that favour it and disadvantage Canada. As this chapter illustrates, China seeks to introduce into our economy uncompetitive, inefficient enterprises that cannot fail because they are backed by unlimited loans and the interests of the Chinese state. These entities can outbid and undercut because they are often responsible to state interests and not shareholders. This undermines competition in the Canadian market place, hurting domestic businesses.

Additionally, China continues to discriminate against Western businesses through its joint venture and technology transfer policies as well as its lack of reciprocity. Again, some companies may believe this is a fair deal to gain access to one-sixth of the world's population in a growing economy. For others, however, these practices amount to an attack on World Trade Organization rules, the foundation of our modern trading system. As one commentator notes, this Chinese practice means giving Western firms "an offer that Don Corleone would have recognized."[121]

Finally, there is the risk of retaliation. China is not afraid to use its economic and political might to send strong signals to states. Norway suffered China's wrath when it awarded the Nobel Peace Prize to dissident Liu Xiaobo, sparking a sharp fall in Norwegian imports such as salmon.[122] Any attempt by Canada to respond or retaliate against a Chinese company in a core-interest area could very well result in a harsh economic punishment from China. As Canada's former ambassador to China, David Mulroney notes, "China seems to be the only country in the world that can have its feelings hurt.... Senior Chinese officials claim to be wounded, deeply and personally, by criticism from the media, local communities or NGO groups.... Some SOE managers appear to confuse the SOE and its interests with China itself, allowing any bump in the road of negotiation to be transformed into an insult to the nation."[123]

Essentially when China (or its SOEs or state-championed companies) is hurt, it lashes out, using whatever instruments it has at its disposal, including the SOEs themselves. All of this paints a troubling picture from a widened national security perspective: if Canadian firms are undermined, there will be job losses; if inefficient SOEs dominate certain areas of the market, our economic growth may be hurt; if another country controls our strategic resources, we may lose part of our sovereignty; and if China gains access to sensitive or military IP through mergers and acquisitions, our future security could be at risk.

The question for Canada is what to do about this. For some, the idea of securitizing our markets is a cure worse than the disease. For others, protecting our economy is an essential part of protecting our way of life – a country cannot be secure if its jobs are threatened and its economy is being undermined. But realistically, in an era when traditional trade alliances are under pressure from protectionism, Canada will need to expand its circle of trading partners to countries who have different ideas about the rule of law and the proper role of the state in the economy.

The reason the questions raised in this chapter are so hard to answer is that the nature of our country makes it difficult. While Canada benefits from being a free market and trading nation, one drawback is that we have not had to confront the relationship between the economy and national security for some time. The idea that the government should be minimally invasive has been largely adopted by all political parties (albeit to different degrees). Moreover, as a large country with a relatively small population, Canada needs to be open to investment from abroad.

Therefore, a very basic starting point is to simply ask ourselves, What should the role of national security agencies be in protecting our economy? And how can we develop policies that meet the challenges discussed in this chapter without burdening our economy with surveillance and monitoring that could do more damage in the long run?

This chapter has focused on China, but the lessons of its SOEs (and state-championed enterprises) could easily apply to Russia (when it is not under heavy financial sanctions) or to other countries. At the same time, China is not Denmark. It is an autocratic party-state with one-sixth of the world's population. It cannot simply be ignored. Canada will have to figure out a way to live and trade with a rising and aggressive China, but must do so carefully and with its eyes open.

But more importantly, this chapter echoes the core theme of this book: that Canadians must widen their understanding of national security threats. The idea that espionage is only the threat of spies playing a game of "cat and mouse" around the streets of downtown Ottawa is no longer sufficient. The information that states now seek is often corporate records and IP. States may still be interested in our ships, but they are more interested in selling us cheaper phones made from our own technology.

5

Cybersecurity

Spies do not like the spotlight. They prefer their world to be closed from public view, answering the occasional media request with a typically bland statement while focusing on the mission at hand.

This makes it extraordinary that on 4 December 2018, CSIS Director David Vigneault showed up in the heart of Canada's financial capital, Bay Street in Toronto, to give a speech. Even more unusual for a civil servant, Vigneault was prepared to say something interesting: for the first time since 9/11, CSIS declared that "the greatest threat to our prosperity and national interest" is foreign influence and espionage. While terrorism remained the number one threat to public safety, "other national security threats – such as foreign interference, cyber threats, and espionage – pose greater strategic challenges."[1] As such, he urged the corporate executives in his presence to review their cybersecurity, think hard about who their business partners abroad were, and, importantly, think of themselves as partners in keeping Canada safe.

Vigneault's remarks followed a year of change in how Canada was responding to cyber threats. In the previous twelve months, Canada (along with its allies) very publicly attributed three serious cyber-incidents to the states that sponsored them, North Korea and Russia. (Although not a formal attribution statement, the Communications Security Establishment or CSE also acknowledged a fourth incident by Iran to Vice Media.[2]) Shortly after Vigneault's speech, Canada (along with several other allies) attributed yet another serious cyber-intrusion to China's Ministry of State Security. Significantly, this move followed the detention of Huawei's chief financial officer, Meng Wanzhou, by Canada on a U.S. warrant for her arrest for violating Iranian sanctions – a move that had garnered international headlines and stoked Chinese outrage (as discussed in chapter 4).

All of this suggests that 2018 marks a turning point for Canada's national security policies in relation to cyber-threats. But why? What brought about this sudden change when so much of the Canadian public's attention was still attuned to media stories about foreign fighters returning to Canada and the ongoing threat of the Islamic State? This chapter seeks to answer that question by providing a survey of cyber-threat-related activity that affects Canada daily. It looks at trends in how this activity has changed since 2000 and how Canada has tried to keep pace with the evolving nature of threats in this space.

What Do We Mean by "Cyber"?

In contrast to other topics discussed throughout this book, cyber is best understood as a threat-vector (basically, a method) rather than a threat in and of itself. The concern from a national security perspective is that while we benefit immeasurably from cyber-technology in our daily lives, it is also the source of insecurity as violent extremists, foreign actors, and criminals find ways to use this tool to further their own ends.

Like violent extremism and espionage, cyber is a contested concept with no set definition. The term originated from "cybernetics," the science of electronic communications and control established by Norbert Wiener in the late 1940s. "Cyberspace" was popularized in the fiction of William Gibson to describe the virtual reality "space" between computer networks. By the 1990s, the term "cyberspace" had become synonymous with the internet itself. Today, "cyber" typically refers to more than just this virtual space, encompassing the physical computers and networks, as well as the individuals using them.[3]

Therefore, for the purpose of this book, the "cyber realm" that national security agencies aim to protect against threat-related activity will be considered to have three components: the virtual informational environment, the physical networks and computers that form the worldwide "web," and the humans who use both. All of these components are essential to the operation of the network, and each present its own risks and vulnerabilities within this system.

Strategists have long argued that control over information is fundamental to military victory and a secure state. However, the proliferation of cyber-technologies has redefined the ways information can be used to help and harm our societies. Information in cyberspace is increasingly a tool of statecraft as well as a target. The U.S. government suggested that by the end of 2016 there were more than thirty countries developing offensive cyberattack capabilities.[4] But the threat goes beyond that posed by states: proxies and even lone actors are increasingly able to cause disruption and destruction on a growing scale.[5]

Yet, understanding how these actors pose a growing threat and who these actors are is confusing. As such, for the purpose of this chapter, they will be broken down into four categories: attacks, espionage, crime, and clandestine foreign influence. It is important at the outset to recognize that these activities do not operate in isolation from one another – state actors may use a combination of these threats to achieve a specific aim. (Foreign influence using cyber will be discussed in the following two chapters.)

Cyberattacks

A cyberattack is simply an attack by one computer system against another in order to cause disruption or damage. While it is not unusual to hear concerns about "cyber-9/11" in the media, there is a tremendous range in the power of such attacks and the kinds of actors who engage in them.[6] In this sense, it is useful to think of these events along a spectrum in their severity, from annoying inconveniences caused by politically motivated activists (defacing a website, for example) to attacks that may destroy data completely or cause physical damage by targeting industrial control systems. Below is a discussion of the tools that can be used along this spectrum with various levels of sophistication, depending on the resources and capability of the attacker(s). Attacks typically occur through one of two ways – through installing malware on a target's computer or through denying access.

Malware

Malevolent software or "malware" refers to computer programs designed to attack, disrupt, or compromise data and computer networks. Such programs often (but do not necessarily) contain a "payload" or instructions for what it should do after it is able to access a system, which may include everything from replicating itself to finding and destroying data.[7] There is malware that compromises systems but does not necessarily hurt them. Adware, for example, generates revenue for its developer by showing ads on digital devices. Adware can also use spyware that tracks and gathers user and device information, including location data.[8] Malicious crypto-miners use system resources (including electricity) of compromised machines to "mine" crypto-currency (such as Bitcoin), which requires massive levels of processing power to function on a large scale. Compared to other types of cyber threats, these programs are more of a nuisance than harmful.

Early forms of harmful malware include *viruses, worms,* and *trojans*. Viruses spread by attaching themselves to other programs and alter the way a computer or system operates. They spread using host files, leaving infections behind that may delete or damage files. One of the most famous attacks occurred in 2001 when the Anna Kournikova Virus spread across computers around the world, tricking email users into opening a file that was said to contain a picture of the tennis star. Instead, the file accessed the user's email account and sent copies of itself to all of their contacts.[9] Worms are similar to viruses in that they can replicate themselves and cause damage, but they do not need to attach themselves to a file in order to spread. Instead, they are standalone programs that are able to travel through networks or trick users into downloading them. The 1988

Morris Worm was unleashed when a graduate student named William Morris created a program to map the size of the internet. His "worm," however, quickly replicated throughout the early internet, clogging it, rendering it inaccessible for many users. (Ironically, Morris, who meant no harm, was the son of the chief scientist of the NSA's Computer Security Center.) [10] Trojans, (named after the famous Trojan Horse) are malware programs that are disguised as something benign. They are similar to viruses and worms in that they cause damage, or allow access to a user's system, but they cannot self-replicate and must somehow trick a user into executing them in order to work. The ZeuS/Zbot Trojan uses keystroke logging (using software or a device to record the keystrokes on a computer's keyboard, also known as "keylogging") to steal account passwords and other sensitive information, such as bank account numbers.[11]

Today, one key concern for cybersecurity experts is "zero day" vulnerabilities and exploits. In these cases, malware targets a *vulnerability* (often called a "bug") in software that weakens its performance and/or operation. While software developers aim to avoid having such vulnerabilities in their code and work to prevent them through testing prior to use, it is extremely difficult, if not impossible, to create flawless software. These vulnerabilities, which exist but are unknown to designers, system administrators, and users, get their name from the number of days that the flaw is known to the software vendor – "zero days." At this point no "patch" is available to fix the vulnerability.[12] Malware programs that target vulnerabilities are typically called *exploits*. These take advantage of the vulnerability, allowing malicious actors to install the payload, which can be used to take control of a machine or cause damage to it. Unfortunately, given that individuals and system administrators may not immediately download software updates made available by vendors, zero-day exploits may continue to affect computers long after they are discovered. According to one survey of known zero-day exploits and underlying vulnerabilities, their lifespan can be as long as 6.9 years.[13]

Nevertheless, in order to carry out an attack, malware needs to reach and be installed on a target computer or system. In order to do this, an attacker has a number of options to pursue.

INSIDERS

Insider threats were discussed in chapter 4. For the purpose of this discussion, there are a number of ways witting and unwitting insiders can be used to install malware on a device. The first is simply gaining physical access. This is important for when target systems are "air gapped," or not connected to the internet and separated from other co-located computer networks. For example, they can find an insider to deliberately install the malware by sneaking it into a facility or allowing someone into the facility to do it.

SOCIAL ENGINEERING

Frequently attackers seek to create unwitting "insiders" by tricking otherwise well-intentioned individuals into putting malware on their systems. In the first instance, this is done by social engineering – gaining individuals' trust in order to convince them to perform an act that will assist a malicious actor in carrying out an attack. Essentially, social engineering takes advantage of the natural, human tendency to trust individuals, especially if they pose as something already familiar to us. In the case of cyberattacks, by far the most popular way of doing this is "phishing" – convincing someone to download a legitimate-looking file that contains malware. This can be done by using an attachment (such as a document) or inviting someone to click on a link to a website where the file will be downloaded. Spear-phishing refers to emails that specifically target a recipient or group of recipients. "Whaling" is spear-phishing that targets senior executives or other high-profile recipients with privileged access to sensitive information.[14] Malicious actors have also been known to convince individuals to give up passwords through impersonating IT or security departments or simply asking for them in person or over the phone.[15]

INFECTED HARDWARE

Another way unwitting insiders assist in attacks is through using infected hardware that is then installed on targeted systems. In 2008 it was discovered that U.S. classified systems in Afghanistan had been compromised by what was likely an infected USB flash drive bought in Kabul, stuffed into a briefcase, or dropped in a parking lot. It was later established that many of the thumb drives sold in Kabul had been supplied by the Russian government, likely in the hope that one day an individual would use it on a secured system.[16]

DRIVE-BY DOWNLOADS

Malware can be installed by unwitting individuals on their devices by simply visiting websites with malware that takes advantage of security gaps in web browsers or device security. Such methods take advantage of vulnerabilities in software, as discussed above.

UNAUTHORIZED ACCESS

While all malware attacks require some kind of unauthorized access, attackers may try more direct ways to obtain it. Attackers may seek to take advantage of lax physical security in order to gain access to systems to either install or download software onto a computer themselves. In such a case an individual could install a hardware keylogger device in order to steal information such as passwords that can be used to further compromise a system. Some attackers simply attempt to guess passwords. This is possible, as many devices come with pre-set passwords that some users do not bother to change. Other users may have easy to guess or "weak" passwords such as "123456" or "password." A more sophisticated method is to use "brute force" – automated scripts that can run through thousands (if not millions) of possibilities to guess a password in a relatively short period of time. (Such programs can usually be defeated by limiting the number of failed login attempts allowed on a given account.)[17]

Threats to Critical Infrastructure

A noted above, a wide range of attacks result from malware that vary in degree and sophistication. Some may simply seek to cause a nuisance – closing windows or making it harder for computers to operate. Others such as the Morris Worm and Anna Kournikova virus clogged servers, making them inaccessible to their users for hours or even days. However, other kinds of attacks have far more devastating consequences, wiping out thousands of computers and networks. Such attacks target the systems that control industrial machinery and critical infrastructure known as supervisory control and data acquisition (SCADA) systems. The potential for harm to critical infrastructure such as electrical grids, dams, pipelines, and traffic controls is considerable. It is important to note, though, that in December 2018 the Canadian Cyber Security Centre assessed that "it is very unlikely that, absent international hostilities, state-sponsored cyber threat actors would intentionally disrupt Canadian critical infrastructure." Nevertheless, the proliferation of malware is enabling less-sophisticated actors to have some success in disrupting critical infrastructure in less severe attacks.[18] Disruptive "attacks" on critical infrastructure are far more likely to be the inadvertent result of malware or ransomware attacks (discussed below) making their way online and through networks.

So is there a reason to be concerned? Unfortunately, the world has seen a rising number of these serious attacks in recent years. Most famous is the Stuxnet virus, discovered in 2010, which targeted the Iranian nuclear program. The attack, believed to be carried out by American and Israeli security agencies, was extremely sophisticated, allegedly taking eight months for planners to design and build a worm to carry it out. The attack used many of the methods discussed above: an infected piece of hardware to install the malware and a worm that spread in order to destroy centrifuges necessary to create weapons-grade uranium, utilizing five zero-day exploits to do so. While the program caused the centrifuges to spin at varying rates, often out of control, the compromised computers reported back to the Iranian scientists that everything was fine. The result was that Stuxnet destroyed thousands of centrifuges and set back the Iranian nuclear program, at least temporarily.[19] In the spring of 2012, the Flame (aka Wiper) virus – malware related to Stuxnet– wiped out nearly every hard drive at the Iranian National Oil Company.[20]

While some may agree with the purpose and target of the Stuxnet attack, it does highlight at least three future challenges in cyber-threats. First, *there is a growing risk of real-world effects*: Stuxnet was the first prominent case of a cyber weapon designed not just to steal, delete, or compromise information, but to cause physical damage using cyber means. As P.W. Singer and Allan Friedman note, "Its makers wanted it to break things in the real world, but through action only on digital networks."[21] While the Stuxnet attack's sophisticated nature required considerable resources and development, future actors will likely learn from it, incorporating such methods into their own attacks. This increases the risk to critical infrastructure globally.

Second, the discovery of Stuxnet demonstrated *the power and unpredictability of cyber weapons*. Despite being designed to attack Iranian systems only, the Stuxnet worm was able to jump back across the Iranian nuclear facility's "airgap" and infect computers worldwide. Cybersecurity specialists were able to find and identify a bizarre piece of code that constituted the malware and presented it to the world without knowing what it was for.[22] The fact that the code was able to travel well beyond what its creators had intended shows that the impact of cyberattacks is hard to predict and may create future problems. If states cannot predict the outcome of their most sophisticated cyberattacks, are such tools/weapons making our societies more or less safe?

Third, *states can develop a considerable cyber capacity quickly*. After Stuxnet was discovered, it was not long before Iran hit back with cyber weapons of its own. The cyberattack spurred the Iranians to create their own cyberwar unit through the Basij, a volunteer military group organized within the Iranian Revolutionary Guards. The group was said to be operational as of March 2011 and allegedly launched a series of attacks against Google, Microsoft, Yahoo, Mozilla, and Skype eleven days later.[23] This means that Iran was able to go from having a very minimal capability to being able to launch relatively sophisticated cyberattacks by 2011 – a significant, if scary, achievement.[24] More frightening, in 2012 the Iranians unleashed what appears to be a "copycat" malware called Shamoon, using some of the elements of other Western cyber-weapons. The virus targeted the U.S.-American Saudi Aramco oil company, wiping out 30,000 hard drives and planting on every one of its computer monitors the image of a burning American flag. In addition, Iran has mobilized "patriotic" hackers as proxies, launching attacks against American banks, and remote access to a dam in New York State in the late summer of 2013.[25]

We are already seeing these three trends in other malware attacks around the world. On 24 November 2014 hackers calling themselves the "Guardians of Peace" hacked into Sony Pictures Entertainment, stole information, uploaded unreleased films to file-sharing sites, and damaged two-thirds of the company's servers and computers. Sony employees were forced to communicate using personal Gmail accounts and old mobile phones. Others worked on legal pads of paper, as their computers were no longer functional. The "Guardians" were revealed to be North Koreans, probably working from Thailand, in revenge for the mildly funny comedy *The Interview*, which poked fun at "Dear Leader" Kim Jong Un.[26] Additionally, in 2015 a major cyberattack attributed to Russia gained unauthorized access to France's TV5 computer network and, under the guise of an ISIS-directed "cyber caliphate," launched a cyberattack that sought to destroy the computers it infected. The television network spent millions of dollars trying to repair the damage, disrupted broadcasting for days, and kept much of its staff offline for weeks.[27]

Importantly, while these later attacks did not cause the physical damage that Stuxnet did with the Iranian centrifuges, they still had important real-world effects. In the first instance, both attacks destroyed computers, causing millions of dollars in damage. They also attacked entertainment companies, events that were seen by leaders in France and the United States as attempting to shut down free speech.[28] Further, unlike more general malware, which seeks random targets as they propagate themselves through networks, in all of these cases the targeting was very specific.

DDoS Attacks

A second kind of cyberattack is referred to as *distributed denial of service* (DDoS). Essentially, a DDoS attack bombards certain websites and servers with traffic in order to deny access to others. In these cases, a flood of traffic temporarily disables a website or server by bombarding it with such high levels of internet traffic that it is unable to respond to normal requests. The situation is not unlike the impact of crowds at a Black Friday or Boxing Day sale. On other days the doors to a store work fine and customers can enter and exit the store without hassle. On these sale days, however, an increase in demand brings a flood of people to the store at the same time. Similarly, DDoS attacks create an artificial surge of traffic to jam access to websites.

DDoS attacks can be carried out by groups of individuals working together – say, a network of hackers all trying to download from the same site, creating a surge of demand. Frequently attackers create a robotic network or "botnets," a network of computers to drive traffic towards a particular target. The botnet is typically created through malware that is able to take command of the processing power and/or resources of a digital device or computer (unbeknownst to the owner or user) and direct it towards a certain use or target.

The vast majority of DDoS attacks are more properly categorized as a nuisance rather than a true national security threat. Unlike the cyberattacks described above, they do not steal or destroy information, nor do they destroy computers or seek to damage infrastructure. Instead, they serve as a way to make a statement – whether for political reasons or because it amuses someone or some group. Activists (sometimes called "hacktivists") may use DDoS attacks to protest or draw attention to a certain cause. For example, in June 2015 a hacker attacked three government websites, including that of CSIS, in order to draw attention to the Conservative government's Bill C-51's changes to national security law in Canada.[29]

In recent years, though, these techniques have become more sophisticated and may be used to create a more advanced form of threat. In particular, large-scale DDoS attacks applied against key components of the internet, such as domain name registry services and internet service providers (ISPs) have had a far more dramatic impact. Some have come from state-actors. In what is often described as the first incident of "cyberwar," Russia used a sophisticated DDoS campaign to attack Estonia in 2007 and Georgia in 2008. Through a massive bombardment of information, the attacks effectively took both governments offline. In the first instance, it sent a strong political message to Estonia about the treatment of ethnic Russians in that country.[30] In the second case, the DDoS attacks were part of a larger military operation that sought to degrade the Georgian communications systems. This gave the Russians information dominance in theatre, preventing Georgians from communicating with one another, allowing Russians to establish the first and dominant narrative, and to generate a sense of helplessness.[31] DDoS attacks have also been a prominent feature of Russia's information and hybrid warfare against Ukraine since 2014.[32] (Ukraine, however, has cyber-hackers who have been able to fight back to a limited but not insignificant effect.[33])

In October 2016 attackers were able to send so much traffic to Dyn, a domain name registry service, that it took most of the U.S. Eastern Seaboard offline for a day. The domain name registry service essentially serves as a directory for the internet, helping to direct computers to traffic. Once it was clogged, users were unable to access the websites they were looking for. This attack was accomplished through the use of malware called "Mirai" that was able to find and take control of networked devices, turning them into "bots" as part of a larger network (or botnet) and redirecting their traffic towards a target.

But there is a further twist to this story. Strangely, the creators of Mirai appear to have been far more interested in profitable hijinks than creating a major weapon to be used against infrastructure via the internet. Indeed, the malware seems to have been designed to help players cheat at the popular game *Minecraft*: individuals could pay DDoS services to attack servers to effectively boot opponents off the internet, rendering them incapable of defending themselves in a head-to-head fight.[34] The desire to win online appears to be creating a digital arms race of botnets and DDoS tools to provide a competitive (if cheating) edge. Even government prosecutors do not believe that the three university students charged in the creation of the software meant to cause such harm. (In fact, their sentencing appears to have been to work with the U.S. government on cybersecurity rather than serve jail time.[35]) This episode shows that malware creators may not understand the power of the tools they are creating, or appreciate how others may use their de facto weapons, adapt and use them for more nefarious ends. In this case, the attack on Dyn, which used millions of hijacked digital devices by an unknown person or entity, may have been an attempt to punish – if not silence – Brian Krebs, a journalist with an important blog on cybersecurity, possibly in retaliation for his investigative reporting.[36]

Mirai is almost certainly a harbinger of problems to come in a world of connected devices that are designed for ease of use and convenience rather than security. Further, developments in DDoS attacks mirror some of the worrying trends with malware attacks: ability to cause real-world effects (mass disruption, if not damage), unpredictability, and the fact that actors can learn to develop and use such tools relatively quickly. For example, in April 2020 reports emerged about a new advanced, robust botnet called dark_nexus, likely to be used in DDoS attacks, but with the ability to disguise malicious traffic as benign. Researchers were able to link dark_nexus to a Youtube account selling malware services, suggesting the motivation behind the botnet.[37]

It bears repeating that while there may not be any harm done to computer systems during DDoS attacks, great harm can occur during such attacks in the real world. DDoS attacks can financially hurt companies by taking them offline, making it impossible for them or their customers to conduct business. The Russian DDoS attacks against Georgia in 2008 show how a well-timed, large-scale DDoS attack can create further panic and confusion during a crisis. Russia was not only able to prevent the Georgian government from communicating with its citizens, it was able to ensure only its messaging and narratives reached the airwaves. In Canada a malevolent actor could take advantage of a natural disaster, serious accident, or terrorist attack in order to spread further panic and/or to discredit the government. Finally, an adversary might use a massive DDoS attack against key domain name servers (like the October 2016 attack described above) during an election to prevent voters from finding information about their polling station, and/or to generate a sense of panic that could be used to delegitimize the results.

Cyber-Terrorism

In the post-9/11 era, much has been made of the potential for serious or even deadly cyberattacks from terrorists. Such an idea conjures up the image of a violent extremist finding ways to attack critical infrastructure from behind a computer screen in a far-off country.

Thus far, the reality is far more benign: for all of the concern, no one has ever been killed or harmed in a "cyber terrorist" attack.[38]

This does not mean groups like the Islamic State are uninterested in cyberattacks. In 2015 the U.S. government acknowledged that the group was attempting to hack into the U.S. electrical grid, although it was failing. (An official with the FBI described the group as having "strong intent. Thankfully, low capability."[39]) Also in 2015, the U.S. Department of Justice charged a terrorism suspect with hacking for the first time: Kosovo citizen Ardit Ferizi was arrested in Malaysia and extradited to the United States for having provided material support to the Islamic State. Ferizi, who may have been recruited online, hacked into a private company and passed on 1,300 names and personal details of U.S. government and military personnel to the Islamic State. The terrorist group then published the names with a threat to attack. For these actions, Ferizi was sentenced to twenty years in prison.[40]

Nevertheless, "cyber-terrorism" remains rare, as these groups simply do not yet have the technical sophistication to conduct serious attacks. As the Co-Director of the Cyber Policy Initiative of the Carnegie Endowment for International Peace, Tim Maurer, notes, technical sophistication matters for three reasons. First, it gives actors the ability to effectively stick around within a computer system and discover how it works in order to do damage. (This is often called "persistence" or the ability of the actor to maintain access to an infiltrated system.) Second, technical sophistication allows an actor to have stealth – or remain undetected and hide the malicious activity. Finally, technical sophistication allows for a degree of precision, ensuring that the malware successfully attacks the target it is aiming for and possibly limiting the effect to that specific system. In other words, while it might be easy to access a system remotely, doing long-lasting, targeted damage remains very hard and often takes the resources of states.[41]

Instead, violent extremist groups tend to engage in relatively unsophisticated activity that may still have an impact and get them attention. Notoriously, in April 2013 the Syrian Electronic Army (SEA), a pro-Assad group, was able to hack the Associated Press Twitter account. It sent out a tweet indicating that there had been an explosion at the White House and President Barack Obama had been hurt – a message that sent the stock market into a dive until the hoax was dispelled.[42] Besides the Ferizi case, individuals either identifying or affiliated with the Islamic State have likely used "web crawlers" to scan the internet for references to the names of random individuals to put them on a "kill list." (This is different from the Ferizi case in that there was likely no hacking involved.) In 2016 the "United Cyber Caliphate" (a pro-Islamic State hacker group) released several "kill lists," including one with at least 150 Canadian "targets."[43] Violent extremist groups have also tried to "hijack" popular hashtags in order to draw attention to their cause by bombarding them with messages. In November 2014 Islamic State supporters used the hashtag of the Halifax Security Forum to circulate a propaganda video featuring a British hostage.[44]

Online access remains crucial for violent extremist activity. As discussed in chapter 2, violent extremist groups engage in five activities: attack planning, facilitation, financing, travel, and attack planning. Cyber is an important, if not critical, component of each of these activities. Social media has been the oxygen of extremist movements, allowing groups to spread their propaganda and bringing together like-minded individuals. Likewise, digital devices are key for the facilitation of violent extremist activities, such as ordering goods, coordinating logistics, operational communication, etc. One study found that violent extremist jihadist groups use secure browsers (like Tor), virtual private networks (VPNs), and proxy servers to secure their online activities, protected email services (like Hush-mail, Protonmail), mobile security applications that disguise physical location, secure phones (with features such as disabled cameras and microphones, that destroy data after several failed log-in attempts, etc.) and (as discussed in chapter 2) encrypted messengers like Telegram and WhatsApp.[45]

In terms of financing, groups from ISIS through to white nationalists have been experimenting with cryptocurrency in order to raise funds and make payments. Much of the evidence of this, however, is fragmented and anecdotal, with only a few examples to draw from at the time of writing.[46] For example, in December 2017 the U.S. Department of Justice charged Zoobia Shahnaz with sending U.S.$85,000 worth of Bitcoin and other cryptocurrencies to support the Islamic State.[47] Additionally, after being shut out of mainstream financial institutions, and drawn to its promised anonymity, it seems that white supremacist groups turned to cryptocurrencies as a source of investment and fundraising.[48] Cyberspace is used to help coordinate travel to conflict zones and is a way for violent extremist groups to research and even do reconnaissance on potential terror attacks.[49] In Syria, the Islamic State has been known to use remotely guided aerial vehicles to carry out such missions.[50]

In this way, cyber – digital devices, networks, social media, etc. – has become essential for modern violent extremist groups. Some analysts have suggested that as the Islamic State loses territory in the real world, it could transition to a "virtual caliphate," transforming into an online base from which to continue its efforts.[51] Whether or not the loss of physical territory will affect the quality of output and messaging by the Islamic State remains to be seen. While acknowledging the continued importance of a "virtual caliphate," Charlie Winter, an analyst of the group's propaganda since 2014, notes that there has been a decline in the quality and quantity of the propaganda as the group has lost territory. Instead, there has been a shift from mass propaganda to survival, "prioritising operational education over recruitment propaganda."[52] In this way, we should expect greater emphasis on the recruitment of lone actors using digital tools.

In summary, while violent extremist groups have shown interest in developing cyber-terrorism capabilities, the ability to conduct a devastating attack is beyond their capabilities *for now*. While they could spend the thousands of dollars and invest the effort needed to develop cyber-capabilities that *could* pay off in the future, it is far easier to put these resources towards low-cost, smaller, but still deadly terrorist plots in the real world. It seems likely, though, that Western intelligence agencies will continue to monitor violent extremist groups for signs that they are moving in this direction.

Proxies

If there is a threat from violent extremist groups, it is that they may partner with a state actor prepared to support them. Tim Maurer defines "cyber proxies" as "intermediaries that conduct or directly contribute to an offensive cyber action that is enabled knowingly, whether actively or passively, by a beneficiary."[53] He delineates three ideal-types of proxy relationships: *delegation*, where the beneficiary has significant or overall effective control over the proxy (such as the use of private contractors by the U.S. military); *orchestration*, where proxies are "on a looser leash, where the state supports the proxy without necessarily providing specific instructions" (such as Iran's use of networks of hackers who perform work on behalf of the Islamic Revolutionary Guard Corps);[54] and *sanctioning* or passive support, where a state provides an enabling environment by non-state actors for malicious activity by turning a blind eye to their activities.[55] (For example, the Russian government has clearly sanctioned the actions of "patriotic hackers" who have taken part in cyberattacks against Estonia in 2007 and Ukraine since 2014.[56])

So far there are no known examples of a state supporting a terrorist group like Al Qaida or the Islamic State to develop cyber-capabilities. As discussed above, it may simply be easier to provide money and arms for a more immediate effect rather than cyber-capabilities. Further, given the money, resources, and time that goes into developing cyber-weapons – and the risks that they pose – it may not make sense for states to do so.

Instead, as Maurer notes above, it is more likely that states will use hackers with whom they can pressure or develop links to help develop or enhance capabilities they do not have, or to create plausible deniability. One of the more famous recent examples of this the SEA (mentioned above). By its own description, the SEA began as a group of pro-Assad youth who sought to counter what they saw as disinformation about the conflict in their country. It launched DDoS attacks against media outlets and targeted regime opponents with spyware. However, information leaked by the hacker group Anonymous revealed that, between 2011 and 2013, the SEA was likely a hierarchically organized group that disappeared in 2013. After this period, the "SEA" appears to have been replaced by a group of hackers who function as a "loose hacking collective" rather than a state-sponsored brigade. In this way, Maurer assesses that the SEA appears to be *orchestrated* with the Syrian government rather than coordinated by it.[57]

The Syrian government is not alone in its use of proxies. Russia and China have used arm's-length "patriotic" hackers to achieve state ends – often engaging in DDoS operations and website defacements in response to a national outrage. China has exerted increasing control over its non-state hacking group (likely fearing that such activities might one day be used against its own government), directing activities from such attacks to data theft against rival states and companies using state-controlled hacking militias.[58]

An important aspect of proxies that Maurer notes is how transnational they can be. Significantly, Canadians have been caught in several proxy groups who benefit adversarial countries. Members of an Iranian hacking group "Cutting Kitten" are assessed to be located in Canada by at least one cybersecurity firm.[59] Similarly, Karim Baratov, a young Canadian, was arrested in March 2017 as part of an investigation into Russian cyber-criminals working on behalf of Russian intelligence to hack Yahoo email accounts. Here we see that Canada can be home to hackers working as proxies for countries that may pose a national security threat beyond our borders.

Cyber-Espionage

Chapter 3 defined espionage as "activities with the purpose of acquiring information through clandestine means and proscribed by the laws of the country in which it is committed." In this sense, "cyber-espionage" can be understood as the act of espionage carried out through cyber means – essentially gaining unauthorized access to information and exfiltrating it through online networks.

Recall that in chapters 3 and 4 we looked at the reasons states engage in espionage: they seek information to inform their own decision-making, gain an advantage in negotiations, discover (and counter) military plans. Economically, they are searching for information that may help their own domestic industries or companies, including bottom lines, intentions, and intellectual property. Intelligence services have also used cyber-espionage to infiltrate newspapers and media organizations to obtain intelligence on sources for stories that are perceived as embarrassing. In 2013 the *New York Times* went public with a story on how it had been hacked, likely by the Chinese government, in response to stories about corruption linked to the relatives of the Chinese Prime Minister.[60] States are also known to look for information that can be used for blackmail (such as evidence of wrongdoing, marital affairs, and financial difficulties) to create insider threats they can use to their advantage. Recently, state and non-state actors have sought information that is or can be made to seem embarrassing for the purpose of making it public to disrupt political processes, including elections.

The most prominent cases of cyber-espionage have been undertaken by "advanced, persistent threats" or APTs, normally by state actors or well-orchestrated proxies. As the name suggests, APTs are "advanced" in their sophistication and "persistent" in their ability to remain undetected within systems for long periods of time. This means that once cyber-spies have access to a system, they are typically able to remain inside it, taking time and care to search for and select information and then exfiltrate it without the target's knowledge. These are not "smash and grab" operations but methodologically plotted missions to get certain desired information. Cybersecurity firm Symantec describes the features of an APT as customized to a specific target, stealthy ("low and slow"), tailored to long-term strategic objectives rather than an immediate need, and specifically aimed at certain targets rather than a broad range of actors.[61] These features make such attacks different from other cyber-threat-related activities discussed thus far.

Importantly, while APTs are most famous for engaging in espionage and the theft of information over long periods of time, they may also engage in serious cyberattacks. As these activities are normally discovered when the attack occurs, the stealth element involved in cyber-espionage is typically less important. For example, it is believed that the attack on TV5 discussed above was carried out by APT 28, attributed to Russian military intelligence.

The "life cycle" of an APT is typically broken down into several phases.[62] First, adversaries will engage in reconnaissance in order to learn about their target, to create convincing social engineering tools to trick individuals into downloading tailored malware onto their systems. This phase can be resource-intensive; attackers will spend considerable time investigating and developing their plan before putting it in motion, particularly if they are engaging in spear-phishing or whaling (as discussed above). Next, once the malware has been downloaded, attackers will use it to gain access to the system and research its structure and discover where sensitive files may be. Further, the attackers may create additional points of compromise in case the original source is blocked, effectively reinforcing their operations. Once an understanding of the network/system is achieved, attackers will then gather the information they want and exfiltrate it out of the system while attempting to cover their steps. Unfortunately for the victims of such attacks, they are usually sophisticated enough that even when they are discovered the cyber-spies are able to maintain some form of access for a considerable period afterwards.[63]

While APTs refer to the methodological approach described above, it is common for major cybersecurity firms and governments to describe cyber-spies of rival countries as APTs. Of those publicly identified actors, China is assessed as being responsible for most, with at least twenty attributed to that country by some cybersecurity firms by 2013.[64] This includes APT1, also known as Unit 61398 of the Chinese People's Liberation Army, and "Comment Crew" – famous for "systematically" stealing "hundreds of terabytes of data from at least 141 organizations" since 2004.[65] However, APT3, APT10, APT12, APT16, APT17, APT18, and APT30 are also suspected of being linked to the Chinese government, and APT19 is suspected of being a proxy or freelancer.[66]

Of course China is not alone in using APTs. Several have been associated with countries that have been known to engage in threat-related activities against the West, including Iran (APT33 and APT34), and North Korea (APT37). Two notorious APTs, APT28 and APT29, are believed to be directly connected to and orchestrated by Russian intelligence. APT28 (also known as "Fancy Bear") is associated with the GRU, and APT29 (also known as "Cozy Bear") is associated with the SVR.

Cyber-Espionage and Canada

It is difficult to understand the scale of the problem of cyber-espionage cases in Canada, as victims do not necessarily come forward, and the government may not wish to reveal what they know about hostile foreign activity. In 2018 it was reported that between July 2016 and July 2017 federal cyber-defences blocked an average of 474 million "malicious cyber activities" per day. These activities reportedly cover everything from sophisticated state-sponsored attempts to gain access, through to automated and continuous probing of systems to look for vulnerabilities that can be exploited using more sophisticated means.[67]

Some basic indicators of cyber-espionage-related activity are available: data from CSE suggests that between 2013 and 2015 the Government of Canada detected on average more than 2,500 state-sponsored cyber activities against its networks per year. Of these attempts, approximately 6 per cent were successful in 2013, but only 2 per cent in 2015.[68] Of these cases, the two most prominent are the 2011 and 2014 attacks that have been attributed to China. In 2011 it was publicly revealed that the Department of Finance, Treasury Board and Defence Research and Development Canada (DRDC) had been compromised dating at least back at least as far as 2010, allegedly from servers in China. Media reports indicate that the hackers used social engineering to obtain access: they sent emails posing as federal executives to technical staff to obtain access to key passwords that unlocked access to government networks. Other staff were reportedly sent emails with viruses disguised as attachments that also provided the hackers with the opportunity to seize information and exfiltrate it to China.[69] In 2014 the National Research Council was compromised, although the government has never been clear about what information or intellectual property was stolen, if any. Official documents suggest the federal government believes the ultimate cost of the 2014 hack was in the hundreds of millions of dollars, with the first year of fixes to the NRC's network alone pegged at $30 million.[70] Like normal spying, we can expect cyber-espionage to continue for the foreseeable future simply because it is effective.

Cybercrime

For the most part, cybercrime is not *usually* considered to be a national security threat and therefore not a central focus of this book. Nevertheless, the Canadian Centre for Cyber Security notes, "Cybercrime is the cyber threat most likely to affect Canadians and Canadian businesses."[71]

The Canadian government takes a very broad view of the term, describing "cybercrime" as "a crime committed with the aid of, or directly involving, a data processing system or computer network. The computer or its data may be the target of the crime or the computer may be the tool with which the crime is committed."[72] Therefore, this definition includes a wide range of activity – essentially any crime that involves a computer in some way.

For the purpose of this book, we can unpack this term in two ways. First, in the same manner that violent extremists mostly use the internet to facilitate attacks in the real world, there are criminals who use the internet to facilitate their activities. This might be researching a company, facility, or person before robbing them, procuring necessary tools to commit a crime, recruiting others, etc. Some criminals use the internet to reach a specific audience. For example, some use the "dark web" to sell drugs and other illegal goods.[73] Second are novel forms of crime that have been enabled by cyberspace. Ransomware – a form of malicious software that prevents or restricts usage of digital devices or applications, or access to certain data until a ransom (usually a form of money) is paid – is one example.[74]

There are several ways in which cybercrime intersects with national security concerns. At a basic level, all of the online threat activity discussed so far in this chapter is illegal and therefore criminal. Just as they can in the "real" world, individuals can be prosecuted and punished for attacks or espionage, even if they occur on digital devices. As such, some cyber-criminals take advantage of locations where there is lax enforcement of the rules or difficulties obtaining extraditions due to a lack of will, capacity, or both.[75]

Cybercrime can also be used to fund other malicious activities. The United States (supported by the other Five Eyes countries – Australia, New Zealand, the United Kingdom, and Canada – and

Japan) has attributed the WannaCry ransomware to North Korea.[76] The malware was created by repurposing an NSA tool that had been leaked on the internet and was released in May 2017. Over several days, WannaCry was able to infect more than 200,000 computers worldwide, including hospitals, manufacturing plants, and telecommunications companies. (Although the ransomware demanded a $300 ransom in bitcoin, only $50,000 appears to have been collected.[77]) It is not clear that North Korea used these funds towards any illegal purpose, but the country has often supported itself by engaging in a range of illegal activities. The ransomware may have been a test of capabilities.

Even though cybercrime may be driven by profit, it can target critical infrastructure and even national security institutions, affecting their operations. As discussed above, WannaCry was able to target several areas of critical infrastructure, including the mobile operations of two large companies. In the case of the UK hospitals affected, the attack closed emergency rooms and cancelled operations.[78] In the spring of 2018, the City Hall of Wasaga Beach, Ontario, found its computers and back-up systems encrypted and over a period of weeks had to negotiate a ransom settlement with the criminals for $35,000 – after paying $50,000 to cybersecurity consultants.[79] Should cyber-criminals attack during a natural disaster or find ways of encrypting critical infrastructure responsible for delivering heat and electricity in the winter, lives could be at risk.

An additional concern is that cybercrime diverts resources away from national security institutions. While trying to deal with the other issues discussed so far in this book (violent extremism and espionage), more resources are required to set up specialized units and agencies to counter this specialized area of criminal activity. At a time when the RCMP is already stretched in capabilities to deal with national security problems such as foreign fighters, it is also expected to deal with cybercrime. In recent years governments have found themselves having to invest millions (if not billions) in cybersecurity. In 2018 the Trudeau government established a National Cybercrime Coordination Unit "to expand the RCMP's capacity to investigate cybercrime, establishing a coordination hub for both domestic and international partners." The new centre is being given a budget of $116.0 million over five years, and $23.2 million per year afterwards.[80] Unfortunately, the unit is not scheduled to be fully operational until 2023.[81]

Finally, and perhaps most importantly, although this chapter has tried to unpack and discuss cyber-threats separately, adversaries often combine attacks, espionage, and crime to achieve their objectives. In this sense, cybercrime is often used as a part of campaigns by state and non-state actors against a target.

A good example of this phenomenon is the NotPetya ransomware that affected computers around the world in June 2017. The malware, publicly attributed to Russia by Canada along with Australia, Denmark, Estonia, Lithuania, New Zealand, the United Kingdom, and the United States in February 2018, was designed to disrupt financial software used in key Ukrainian institutions. (Its name comes from its similarity to ransomware known as Petya.) Hackers used two powerful exploits: EternalBlue, a U.S. National Security penetration tool leaked in 2017, as well as Mimikatz, which allowed hackers to discover leftover passwords in a computer's memory. Used in tandem, the ransomware would attack unpatched computers and then grab network passwords to attack computers that were patched.[82] Moreover, the ransomware was designed to spread automatically across many computers as quickly as possible. The result was a devastating code that was indiscriminate in its attacks across the world. A network of a large Ukrainian Bank was brought down within forty-five seconds. It also dramatically affected pharmaceutical company Merck, Danish shipping company Maersk, and parts of FedEx for weeks, if not months. The White House estimates the cost of the attack at approximately U.S.$10 billion.[83]

NotPetya is an example of how a state can combine crime and attacks to engage in clandestine foreign influence. The attacks were not only financially devastating, they furthered the broader and ongoing campaign against Ukraine. It is a good indicator of what future attacks in this space will look like.

Closer to home, in March 2017 Karim Baratov, a Canadian who had immigrated from Kazakhstan with his family, was arrested and charged with hacking into thousands of email accounts. Baratov, who had a penchant for fast cars and owned a $650,000 house, was different from other cyber-criminals – in this case, the FBI and RCMP claimed that he had been actively assisting the Russian FSB (the successor to the Soviet-era KGB) in their efforts to spy on U.S. and Russian journalists and political figures.[84] In late 2014 Russian hackers associated with the FSB's Centre for Information Security were able to compromise Yahoo Mail servers and obtain access to approximately thirty-two million in-boxes. Not only were they able to spy on dissidents, they stole money and gift cards from average people who had no idea where the money went.[85]

Baratov came into this arrangement when the Russian hackers realized that they had discovered the other email accounts of their targets through the Yahoo hack. Having developed a reputation for breaking into Gmail accounts, Baratov was hired to target certain accounts of interest to the Russian spies. It is not clear if Baratov realized the full extent to which he was a part of a large-scale FSB operation. Nevertheless, the FBI indictment against him indicates that he breached the email accounts of several Russian officials, including the deputy chairman of the Russian Federation, officials with a Russian cybersecurity firm, an expert working with the Russian Ministry of Sports of a Russian republic, officials within banks and financial firms, private companies, an International Monetary Fund official, and government advisors from other countries.[86]

Canadian Trends

Canada and Canadian citizens are affected by all of the incidents discussed above. A report by the Standing Senate Committee on Banking, Trade and Commerce found that at least ten million Canadians had their data compromised in 2017 alone.[87] Despite these numbers, most malicious cyber activity in Canada goes unreported. Neither the private sector nor the government knows the full scale of the problem, which makes it challenging to state anything definitive about cyber trends.

While quantitative data about malicious cyber activity may be hard to come by, it is possible to identify trends in how these issues have been covered in the media. In an attempt to get a better understanding of how malicious cyber activity has been affecting Canada, a survey of media reports about such incidents between 2000 and 2018 was compiled for this book. It includes global attacks that affected Canada, as well as attacks that only targeted Canadians.[88] Importantly, such an approach does not provide an accurate scope or scale of the problem, but it does offer some useful context and description as to how cyberattacks have changed between 2000 and 2018.

The survey found reporting on ninety-five incidents that affected Canada during this period, forty-three global attacks and fifty-two Canadian-specific attacks. The survey revealed that reporting on cyber-incidents greatly increased after 2011. Between 2000 and 2010, one to four incidents were reported per year, while six to twelve incidents were reported annually between 2011 and 2018. Whether this is due to a growing number of attacks, an increase in severity in cyber-incidents, a growing interest in cyber-related issues, or more dedicated journalism to cyber issues is unclear. Of these incidents, only 40 per cent were attributed to a specific actor.

Although the dataset is limited, it is possible to identify three emerging trends in reporting on cyber issues. First, after 2011, the coverage was increasingly focused on incidents that affected Canadian rather than global targets. Between 2011 and 2018, over half of reported incidents affected a Canadian target (with the exception of 2013). This may be due to a lack of data prior to 2011, a trend towards more localized attacks, and/or an increase in ransomware attacks.

Second, of the attributed attacks, there appears to be movement away from individual perpetrators to groups. Between 2000 and 2009, reported and attributed cyber-incidents appear to be conducted by individuals such as those carried out by Michael Calce, a Canadian teen who went by the handle "Mafia Boy." Calce used DDoS attacks to flood major websites with fake messages, causing the sites to shut down, including Yahoo!, eBay, Amazon.com, CNN, ZDNet, Buy.com, Etrade and Excite, and HMV Canada.[89] After 2010, state actors are increasingly reported as responsible for attacks. Additionally, by 2011, hacker collectives (such as those acting on behalf of "Anonymous") begin to appear.

Third, the first report of a financially motivated attack affecting Canada appeared in 2016, although ransomware had been around for a considerably longer period than this. Whether the lack of reporting is due to few attacks affecting Canada prior to 2016, or that many attacks were dealt with privately, is not clear. Nevertheless, since 2016, there has been a significant increase in reported ransomware attacks affecting Canada. When combined with reported cyber-incidents aimed at theft (such as bank and credit card fraud), there appears to be a movement towards financial gain as a motivation for malicious cyber activity.

Canada's Evolving Cyber Policy

As cyber has become an increasingly prominent national security and economic issue, the Canadian government has enacted policies to respond. The period between 2016 and 2018 saw major initiatives to combat some of the threats identified in this chapter, including legislating new powers for national security agencies, the creation of government cyber-centres, a new national cyber strategy, and coordinated diplomatic responses to major cyber incidents.

New Legislative Powers

The first step the government took in this direction was its massive overhaul of the architecture of Canada's national security services in Bill C-59. Three major changes are pertinent here. First, the bill outlined a legal strategy for CSIS to collect, store, and search "datasets," which, in an era of digital media, is necessary to ensure that all intelligence operations have a sure legal footing. (The ability of CSIS to hold onto and use such bulk data had been put in jeopardy by the Federal Court decision Re X 2016, which described previous practices as unlawful.[90]) Second, C-59 gave the CSE its own statutory footing by creating the *Communications Security Establishment Act*. The *Act* is the first to provide a more transparent description of the powers and duties of the CSE to the Canadian public.[91]

Third, C-59 created new powers for the CSE, specifically "active" (offensive) and "defensive" cyber operations. The first is the more controversial of the two, as it will allow the CSE to conduct offensive cyber operations for the first time. Section 19 of the *Act* defines these as "activities on or through the global information infrastructure to degrade, disrupt, influence, respond to or interfere with the capabilities, intentions or activities of a foreign individual, state, organization or terrorist group as they relate to international affairs, defence or security." This will put the CSE on more equal footing with most of its Five Eyes partners, especially the American National Security Agency (NSA) and the British Government Communications Headquarters (GCHQ). Practically, it will allow the CSE to disrupt malicious cyber activities (such as a foreign influence campaign) aimed at Canada before they begin.

While CSE already had the mandate to protect government communication systems, defensive cyber allows the CSE to defend Canadian critical infrastructure designated by the Minister of National Defence "as being of importance to the Government of Canada."[92] This includes any "electronic information, any information infrastructures or any class of electronic information or information infrastructures as electronic information or information infrastructures." How these infrastructures are chosen is not yet clear at time of writing.

Although Bill C-59 was received with less criticism and controversy than Bill C-51, these three policies have been the focus of much of the commentary on the bill. Supporters generally argue that C-59 balances these new powers with increasing levels of review and oversight.[93] Detractors highlight concerns over whether or not there is appropriate oversight of active and defensive Cyber provisions and worry about the lack of a definition for "dataset."[94] The main takeaway, however, is that Canada is substantially enhancing the powers of its national security agencies in the cyber realm, with the concomitant expectations they will be able to protect Canadians from malicious activity online.

New Cybersecurity Institutions

The March 2018 budget announced the creation of new government cyber-centres: as noted above, the National Cybercrime Coordination Unit within the RCMP, and a new public-facing Canadian

Centre for Cyber Security run by the CSE. The latter organization "is designed to be a single unified source of expert advice, guidance, services and support on cybersecurity for government, critical infrastructure owners and operations, the private sector and the Canadian public."[95] In this way, the new public-facing centre is meant to address a key problem that has plagued governments for years – how to translate knowledge of cyber threats from intelligence services to the private sector and public at large. It will also serve as a key point of contact to "enable faster, better-coordinated, and more focused Government responses to cyber threats."[96] When fully operational it will provide security advice and assistance as well as regular threat assessments. The centre opened in the fall of 2018 and it is envisioned that it will be fully operational by 2020, although this has been delayed by the COVID-19 pandemic.

New Strategies/Policy

In 2016 the Trudeau government began consultations with the Canadian public to develop new strategies in areas that affect cyber. A major consultation on a new defence strategy as well as deliberations on cybersecurity with business and researchers sought input on the direction the government should take.[97] The result was two new strategies that have major implications for the government's approach to cyber.

2017 DEFENCE STRATEGY

In mid-2017 the Trudeau government released a new defence strategy outlining the Department of National Defence's (DND) understanding of new and emerging threats, gaps, capabilities, and procurement plans for the next twenty years.[98] Cyber-related issues feature prominently throughout the document, including emerging challenges (hybrid warfare and a changing cyber environment), implications for human resources (new part-time cyber-operators), as well as research and development. The defence strategy, named "Strong, Secure, Engaged," notes that the threat from the foreign intelligence and military services of foreign adversaries is likely to grow. As such, "a purely defensive cyber posture is no longer sufficient. Accordingly, we will develop the capability to conduct active cyber operations focused on external threats to Canada in the context of government-authorized military missions."[99] This is a clear indication from the Trudeau government that Canada will be playing a more active role in cyber operations. In addition, cyber (along with space and remotely piloted systems) are identified as one of three areas of technology that will not only have an impact on military operations, but also where Canada is well placed to further develop its capabilities.[100]

2018 CYBER (SECURITY) STRATEGY

June 2018 saw the launch of a new National Cyber Security Strategy, the first such policy document since 2010.[101] While the strategy outlines the threat environment, it spends considerable time discussing the need for innovation and international leadership in cyber, developing skills, and stressing the benefits of digital technology. In this sense, it was more of a statement of principles that underpin the Trudeau government's approach to cyber generally, than a robust cybersecurity policy. Indeed, there are few steps, if any, outlined on how the government plans to implement its strategies. Although a number of legislative and institutional steps have been taken, it remains difficult for observers to say what, exactly, Canada's cybersecurity policy is and how it is being implemented. We do know, however, the National Cyber Security Strategy has an international component with plans to increase diplomatic engagement with the United States, and regional organizations that are working on cyber issues. There is also the creation of a Cyber Engagement Working Group within GAC to coordinate the activities of different government organizations with a mandate in this space.[102]

Diplomacy: Agreements, Naming and Shaming

One method Western countries have experimented with to mitigate the problem of corporate espionage is signing agreements that seek to ban such activities. These agreements seek to address the uncompetitive advantage Chinese firms have when they receive intellectual property from Western countries that has been stolen by Chinese government agencies. Given that the intelligence services of Western countries do not steal IP to provide to their corporate entities, such agreements do not require them to give up much in exchange.

The first country to sign an agreement with China was the United States in 2015, following a series of high-profile attacks. Although some question whether an agreement is robust enough to put a stop to such malicious activities, some cybersecurity firms believe that the treaty signed between the United States and China resulted in a notable drop in the amount of cyber-espionage in the United States. Cybersecurity firm FireEye observed that within a year of the agreement being signed there was a "notable decline in China-based groups' overall intrusion activity against entities in the U.S. and 25 other countries."[103] Even in late 2018, with tensions rising between China and the United States, FireEye was still describing the treaty as "successful" – although the firm predicted a rise in espionage generally as great power competition intensifies in Asia.[104] With such a finding, there is incentive for other countries to follow suit and the Trudeau government signed a similar agreement with China that would ban cyber-espionage against private companies in June 2017. (At time of publication it is unknown how successful this agreement has been.)

Nevertheless, these agreements are not panaceas and there may be limits on how far they can go to solving the problems of cyber-threats. Although there may have been a decrease in cyber-espionage, it has certainly not disappeared since 2015. Indeed, amid rising trade tensions between China and the Trump administration, the National Security Agency accused China of violating the terms of the agreement in November 2018 and indicated they had detected a resurgence of this activity since 2017.[105] Additionally, even when these treaties work, it may only be with a limited range of actors and activity. In particular, it is not clear that such treaties would work for cyber-threat-related activity outside of corporate espionage. Given their success in influence operations and other malicious cyber-threat-related activity, it seems unlikely that Russia would sign such an agreement. Nor is it clear that online threat-related-activity by Iran or North Korea could be curtailed in this way. The incentive for China to cooperate is its integration into Western economies and a desire for its technologies to be regarded as safe and secure. Russia,

Iran, and North Korea do not have this incentive. And while they may have demonstrated some willingness to negotiate sanctions, it is not clear that there is a political will to strike such agreements limiting malicious cyber activity.

Given the limitations of these treaties, Canada has increasingly engaged in coordinated diplomacy with its allies to call out malicious cyber activity by states, specifically Russia and China. This differs from the approach to attribution taken by the Harper government, which either confirmed attributions made by the media or saw lower-level officials make statements. For example, in 2014 the government attributed the NRC hack to "a highly sophisticated Chinese state-sponsored actor" in a statement made by the chief information officer for the Government of Canada at the Treasury Board.[106] In 2015 the Harper government confirmed that Iran had successfully hacked into a government agency as part of a broader cyber-espionage campaign.[107]

As noted at the beginning of this chapter, there were four official attributions made by Canada between December 2017 and December 2018, all of them repeating or reinforcing similar statements made by allied countries. These include accusations made against WannaCry (North Korea) and NotPetya (Russia).[108] In October 2018, Canada – along with the United States, the United Kingdom, and the Netherlands once again called out Russia as the site of a global hacking campaign targeting anti-doping agencies and the Organisation for the Prohibition of Chemical Weapons (OPCW), of which Canada is a member.[109] In December 2018 Canada joined its Five Eyes partners, in addition to Finland, Sweden, the Netherlands, and Japan, in attributing a global hacking campaign against managed service providers (MSPs) to China.[110] While no formal statement has been issued, officials have confirmed an Iranian-sponsored cyber intrusion into Canadian universities in March 2018.[111]

No single factor is driving this particular evolution in Canada's (unofficial) cyber foreign policy. One is an agreement among likeminded countries to begin to take a more vocal stance against states that engage in malicious cyber activity. During the 2018 G7 summit, participating countries agreed that they would "strengthen G7 cooperation to prevent, thwart and respond to malign interference by foreign actors aimed at undermining the democratic processes and the national interests of a G7 state."[112]

These diplomatic moves are significant. While the coordinated, multilateral approach Canada is taking in "naming and shaming" diplomacy may take time and require diplomatic resources, there are several advantages to working with like-minded countries in this way. In particular, it amplifies Canada's voice, making it harder for countries like China and Russia to ignore. Moreover, a coordinated approach helps to establish and reaffirm international norms against such activities, even if they continue to happen. As a country that supports the rule of law, speaking up against corporate espionage and malicious attacks is important for Canada's role in the world.

Conclusion

The underlying argument of this book is that Canadians need to responsibly widen their understanding of national security in order to grapple with twenty-first-century threats. In the case of cyber, responsibly widening implies a need to not only understand the range of interests that are affected by malicious cyber activities, but to understand the need to establish and build trust between the public and private sectors as well as the general public. Although the government has made progress in enhancing Canadian cybersecurity in recent years, a number of challenges remain. In particular, there are trends and challenges that all Western governments will have to address as they seek to promote innovation while deterring threats in the cyber realm.

The first challenge relates to the "internet of things" and the extent to which Canadians are increasingly living their lives online. Constantly connected, Canadians are vulnerable to hacking, and the risk of personal privacy being compromised is greater than ever before. Relatedly, individuals and companies are increasingly putting their information in the "cloud." Rather than maintaining their own expensive IT and servers, it is now possible to hire companies to manage and store information and provide the software platforms to access it – all offsite. This not only saves companies money but provides the infrastructure to allow employees to access the data they need no matter where they are in the world. Unfortunately, this is also true for hackers. While firms such as Google, Amazon Web Services, and Microsoft typically have excellent security, online information remains a target-rich environment for those engaged in corporate espionage.

Individuals and groups commissioned by countries to quickly and cheaply achieve a political end may be the ones doing the hacking. As noted above, Iran was able to rapidly gain a cyber capability, in part by leveraging a network of hackers throughout the world. And private cybersecurity firms have identified freelancers working on behalf of the Chinese government.[113] It is not clear if governments in the future will prefer to have full control over their hackers or if they will be willing (and able) to hire cyber-proxies. As the trend towards blended battlespaces (so-called hybrid warfare) continues, it is likely that states will find an incentive to use actors with whom there is some degree of plausible deniability.

Another reason states may use proxies in the cyber realm is that many countries are experiencing a skills gap. Already national security services in Western countries are struggling to recruit individuals with strong IT and information security skills. Opportunities to earn a large salary and work for a dynamic company like Google or a new start-up make it increasingly difficult for intelligence and security agencies to recruit from a limited talent pool. (And that is before the often lengthy security screening process.) Chronic human resources problems could have a serious impact on Canada's ability to protect itself from malicious cyber activity in the future.

If the internet of things, cloud computing, proxies, and human resources issues are already creating serious problems, what are the implications of future technologies such as quantum computing and artificial intelligence? AI is already being used in cyber defence (combatting the 600 million cyberattacks made against the Canadian government daily), but rapidly changing technology leads to more sophisticated malware that can adapt to and counter security measures. Quantum computing, which will enhance computational speed and power by an order of magnitude, has not yet matured at time of writing, but countries are in a race to develop the technology, which has serious implications for national security. At present, public encryption is based on very hard math problems that are difficult for computers to solve and therefore hack into. Quantum computers, however, will be able to solve these math problems quickly, potentially within a matter of seconds. As the CSE notes, this means that if an adversary is able to steal encrypted information, it might be able to decrypt it within ten to twenty years. If that information is still sensitive or classified, this poses a serious national security problem.[114] As such, while working on developing quantum computing, governments around the world are also working on developing quantum resistance cryptography (QRC).[115]

Finally, moral and ethical questions are raised that governments need to answer at the same time as they are trying to ensure national security. Perhaps the most pressing of these is how they should balance privacy rights against a need to counter violent extremists using encrypted apps, discovering spies online, and protecting designated critical infrastructure. In the United States, there have been calls for companies to create a "backdoor" to encrypted social media apps that would allow them to follow the conversations of suspected violent extremists. Australia has gone so far as to introduce legislation requiring it.[116] Privacy consumers argue that keeping apps secure is hard enough – introducing a deliberate weakness makes this job harder. Worse, weakening encryption could be taken advantage of by adversarial states for espionage or by repressive regimes to crack down on dissent.

Additionally, we do not know how the increasing use of offensive cyber capabilities by states will affect norms in cyberspace. Canada has always been a country that benefits from the international rule of law. Is getting into "active cyber" contributing to the creation of legal norms that are antithetical to the values Canada traditionally ascribes to? What might be the broader implications for Canadian national security and international relations? And what will happen to Canadian companies or citizens if an adversarial state is able to strike back?

It is unlikely that any of these issues will be definitively answered. As technology changes, so does our understanding of what constitutes privacy, even as we are willing to make more information about ourselves public. But it is understandable that the information we want to share with our friends is not the same information we are comfortable handing over to CSIS. Governments need robust powers to limit the harm malicious actors can cause in cyber space, but they also need clear guidance on how far they can go when investigating national security threats, and review to ensure that they are staying within those limits. After all, innovation requires not just a secure internet, but an open one where individuals feel they can be confident doing business.

Nevertheless, the nature of cyber – the ability to hide one's identity, to use stealth, to gather wide swaths of data and process it with algorithms – means that cyber is one of the hardest areas in which to generate trust. And, as noted above, just when Western states think they have figured it out, technology evolves, raising new concerns and challenges.

The Canadian government has taken an approach to these problems that seeks to grant national security agencies social licence by matching enhanced cyber powers with more oversight and review. It remains to be seen if they have struck the right balance. Nevertheless, for other states, this technological turmoil is less a challenge than an opportunity. While increasingly using surveillance and repressive techniques to clamp down on internet freedoms at home, adversarial states are using the openness of the internet in Western countries to achieve political ends, including undermining trust between governments and their citizens. Why this is such a pressing national security problem is the focus of the next two chapters.

6

Clandestine Foreign Influence

> I am really worrying about my son's safety....
> I don't know what they are planning, it's quite disturbing.

Rukiye Turdush, a Uighur activist and human rights campaigner explained to the reporter that she was afraid not only for her own life, but that of her son, a student at McMaster University in Hamilton, Ontario.[1] A few days earlier, Turdush had given a talk on the scale of the repression of Uighurs in China. Word of the talk spread quickly among Chinese students on campus through WeChat, the popular Chinese-language messaging app – sparking instant outrage.

Uighur human rights advocates are seen as violent separatists in the eyes of Beijing. In fact, "East Turkmenistan" independence movements were listed as a serious threat in the 2019 Chinese Defence White Paper.[2] China has spent billions of dollars in trying to supress Uighur culture and religion, torturing and detaining millions of people. It arguably has made the population of Xinjiang the most surveilled in the world, with the use of internet monitoring, facial recognition, and heavy police monitoring to stamp out any sense of independence.[3]

Reports of what happened next indicate the lengths to which some Chinese students at McMaster were willing to go to disrupt the talk. Some engaged in what can be seen as typical campus political behaviour: Chinese student groups at McMaster published a "bulletin report" about the talk. Others went to the talk to protest the event and to shout at Turdush before marching out. So far all of this could be categorized as disruptive but normal student behaviour.

But many of the other student actions went far beyond the mere expression of dissent. On WeChat, some students indicated that they had been in contact with Chinese diplomatic officials about Turdush's talk. These students reportedly said they were told to watch and report on any university officials who were present. Some students videotaped and took photographs of the event, sending them on to the Chinese consulate in Toronto. After noting the Chinese consulate was aware of the event, one student on WeChat suggested that the group "find out about [her] son."

University campuses should be the location of robust and informed debate and discussion. But the indications that some of this activity was done in conjunction with Chinese diplomatic officials is disturbing. Both the students and Chinese diplomatic officials deny any coordination, but it is clear that at the very least the activities of the former are approved and encouraged by the latter. Asked to comment about the incident, the Chinese embassy said, "We strongly support the just and patriotic actions of Chinese students."[4]

This was not the only incident of Chinese meddling on Canadian campuses in 2019. In February Chemi Lhamo, a Tibetan-Canadian student, was subjected to thousands of hateful messages and threats after she was elected Student President of the University of Toronto's Scarborough campus. A petition with ten thousand signatures was circulated among Chinese students to demand her resignation. Shortly thereafter, Lhamo was forced to close her office in response to security concerns.[5] In March, the Chinese consulate in Montreal pressured city officials to cancel an event featuring a Uighur-rights activist at Concordia University.[6]

These actions are similar to what has occurred elsewhere in the world: having clamped down on dissent within its own borders, China is increasingly working to suppress views that contradict Beijing's political lines beyond its borders. This includes on university campuses, in the media, and at public events. To do so, it uses a range of tools, including civil society organizations with links to the Chinese Communist parties, threats against the livelihoods and lives of individuals and family members in mainland China, and seeking to control Chinese-language publications and social media.

Is this a national security threat? Threats of violence and intimidation are clearly illegal, but what about attempts to control the conversation on campus or in the media? After all, governments, businesses, and non-governmental agencies around the world hire public relations firms to improve the way they are seen domestically and internationally all the time. Trying to spin a positive image to drown out negative messages is hardly unique to China.

The answer to this question is yes. Attempts to influence populations in a clandestine manner that is detrimental to Canadian interests or involve threats to persons are understood as "clandestine foreign influence" operations. If Chinese diplomatic officials are trying to control the narrative through clandestinely organized activities, or threatening individuals, it is detrimental to the rights and freedoms that Canadians enjoy: freedom of speech, assembly, and belief. It harms our society when persons in Canada cannot be free to live their lives or advocate for their views.

Yet this is far from the first case of clandestine foreign influence in Canada. For decades, states and non-state actors have sought to influence individuals residing in Canada for their own ends. Over time this has included the Soviet Union (later Russia), India, the Tamil Tigers, the Islamic State, and China. Taken as a whole, clandestine foreign influence activities have involved all of the other threats discussed in this book: violent extremist groups, espionage, and, increasingly, cyber means.

Nevertheless, until recently, clandestine foreign influence was not well understood among the Canadian public. This has changed in the aftermath of the 2016 U.S. election, with allegations of electoral interference by Russia. Now the general public is aware that these operations exist, but the understanding of the threat is framed largely in those terms: online operations with thousands of "Russian bots" bombarding individuals with scary messages. This is misleading: as noted, there are a range of actions states and non-state actors can engage in to attempt to control the information sphere.

As such, the next two chapters seek to unpack what "clandestine foreign influence" national security threats are and how they have manifested in Canada since the end of the Second World War. While the next chapter will explain how such threats have evolved online in recent years, this chapter will focus on case studies that examine "traditional" clandestine foreign influence activities that continue to exist.

What Is (Clandestine) Foreign Influence?

Before diving deep into the concept of clandestine foreign influence and how it is defined in Canada, a contextual discussion is important. First, in case it needed to be said, foreign interactions and exchanges are good things for a country. It is beneficial for Canada to learn from other nations and for our country to share our experiences and values in return. In this way, it is fundamental from the outset to note that foreign influence is not in and of itself a bad thing. Indeed, countries, including Canada, set up embassies, high commissions, and consulates abroad for the express purpose of trying to influence others to take a more favourable view of their interests. This may include the promotion of trade, culture, tourism, or joint cooperation on certain initiatives, such as environmental programs or international agreements.

Second, the discussion of beliefs and opinions in relation to threat-related activity is very difficult. As noted in the previous discussions of violent extremism and espionage, Canadians have the right to hold views that are not seen as mainstream. And, as seen in chapter 3, Canada has had a history of harassing individuals because they were gay or monitoring them because they were seen as subversives for their political beliefs alone. Therefore, in discussing beliefs, opinions, and foreign influence, it is crucial to frame the discussion around the fact that part of being Canadian is having the right of free speech and the freedom of belief. Citizens and residents can support the rights of other countries and even take their side in a dispute. The fact that people believe that sanctions on Russia cause more harm than good does not make them agents of the FSB.

So what is the problem if states try to influence one another, and their citizens, all the time? Simply put, it is when these influences take place in a clandestine matter in a way that creates a harm that a national security concern arises. The clandestine element suggests not only secrecy about an influence campaign, but an effort to hide who is behind it. Bot campaigns often use accounts set up to look like citizens of a target country. Alternatively, states may set up and clandestinely support (often financially) organizations that will claim to be independent, but are championing a predetermined line. Such efforts raise questions about the purpose of setting up these operations, what the ultimate goals of the sponsoring state or organization are, and whether or not our democratic institutions are being threatened. However, the clandestine nature of these operations also makes them the most difficult to detect and prevent out of all of the national security threats presented in this book, especially given the challenge of establishing proof, and a lack of laws and tools to stop them from happening in the first place.

Foreign Influence in Canadian Policy and Law

While foreign influence is acknowledged to be a national security threat, there is no set definition in Canadian law, nor any law explicitly banning states and other entities from engaging in such activities. The closest thing to a definition comes in section 2(b) of the *CSIS Act*, which allows the Service to investigate "foreign influenced activities within or relating to Canada that are detrimental to the interests of Canada and are clandestine or deceptive or involve a threat to any person." In a 2005 document CSIS further explained its understanding of foreign influence as "activities detrimental to the interests of Canada, and which are directed, controlled, financed or otherwise significantly affected by a foreign state or organization, their agents or others working on their behalf."[7] In its 2019 annual report, the National Security and Intelligence Committee of Parliamentarians (NSICOP) uses "foreign interference" when discussing activities that would be considered "foreign influence" under the *CSIS Act* as, in their view, the term "has become common in Canada and among its allies to better distinguish between acceptable diplomatic practices and hostile or illegal practices." However, the report emphasizes that its definition of "interference" is identical to that of "foreign influence" in the *CSIS Act*.[8]

Beyond this, there is little in the law to work with on a domestic legal basis. Craig Forcese and Leah West note the concept is an "emerging legal preoccupation" and that applicable law is mostly international; certain foreign influence activities can be considered a violation of state sovereignty or territorial integrity, and "therefore, an intentionally-wrongful act."[9] Unfortunately, like many international legal principles, enforcement is challenging. Diplomats believed to be engaging in clandestine foreign influence activities may be declared persona non grata (PNG), effectively stripping them of their diplomatic status and immunities, and requiring them to leave the country.[10] As will be discussed in the next chapter, Canada expelled four Russian "diplomats" believed to be engaging in intelligence operations and threat-related activity against Canada in March 2018.

In addition, individuals may break Canadian laws while engaging in clandestine foreign influence activities. For example, Russian efforts to meddle in the 2016 U.S. election involved hacking into the computers of the Democratic National Committee. Such hacking operations are illegal in most countries and could serve as the basis for prosecution. Similarly, efforts to force individuals to hand over money to a particular cause (discussed further below) would be a form of extortion and uttering threats. Unfortunately, if these activities occur overseas, prosecution in a Canadian court is unlikely, given that these individuals are unlikely to travel to Canada – or places where extradition is possible.

Nevertheless, based on the *CSIS Act*, there are four components to clandestine foreign influence that can be unpacked: the influence must be *foreign directed*. In other words, Canadians attempting to influence other Canadians may still be harmful (such as the case of radicalization) but it is obviously not foreign influence. Second, the activity must take place *within or relating to Canada* – keeping with CSIS's domestic mandate.[11] Third, the activity must be *detrimental to the interests of Canada*. In other words, if the activity does not harm Canadians or Canadian interests, it cannot be seen as a national security threat. For example, efforts of a company, backed by a state-funded organization, to promote a foreign film in Canada would not likely meet this threshold. However, interests may be interpreted broadly and could include protection of Canadian assets (public or private) domestically or abroad, the protection of Canadian citizens or even values.

Finally, the activity must fall into one of two categories: it must be clandestine or deceptive (as discussed above) or it must involve a threat to any person. The former category has already been briefly discussed and will be elaborated on below. Suffice to say, it covers propaganda-style activities where the foreign originator is hidden. The latter category refers to threats against citizens, residents, or anyone residing in Canada by a foreign state or entity to either do or refrain from carrying out an action. In most cases, this involves some form of monitoring of a diaspora group on Canadian territory.

Importantly, not all "clandestine" operations are hidden from view. In chapter 4 we saw how states use a range of seemingly legitimate tools to pursue opaque economic agendas. The same is true with clandestine foreign influence. For example, it is not unusual for a Beijing-friendly organization to purchase a newspaper to share pro-China information – sharing views is a part of participating in a democracy. However, a campaign to quietly purchase all Chinese-language newspapers in a particular area or country so that no other views can be heard is problematic from a clandestine foreign influence perspective. Similarly, taking government officials on an all-expenses paid trip is not in and of itself "hidden influence," but when travel perks create the expectation of having favours repaid or obligations fulfilled among a group of politicians, a clandestine foreign influence risk arises.

Clandestine Foreign Influence Activities in Canada: A Brief History

The nature of clandestine foreign influence in Canada makes it difficult to know the extent of the problem. We do know that sources of concern have evolved over the years, with many preoccupied with American influences in Canada as a possible threat – not to national security, but to the health of Canadian society. We have already seen in chapter 4 that the first modern efforts to control foreign direct investment in Canada were aimed at the United States. But there has also been long-standing concern that American media would dominate Canadian airwaves. This led to the creation of the Royal Commission on National Development in the Arts, Letters and Sciences (otherwise known as the Massey Commission) in 1949, which issued a report in June 1951. The commission's findings led to the government supporting Canadian cultural and educational institutions in order to promote a distinct culture and identity. While it cannot be removed from its Cold War context (the report argues that there is a link between the democratic health of a country and its culture), this is seen mostly in societal rather than national security terms.

Soviet Foreign Influence Efforts in Canada

While the Americans may have been seen as a problem at one point, the Soviets were clearly another. Following the Gouzenko Affair (discussed in chapter 3), it became clear that the Soviet Union was not only making efforts to spy in Canada, but was engaging in an influence and subversion campaign as well. By the 1950s it was well appreciated that Communists had effectively propagandized the masses in their own states, as well as increasingly in developing countries. Concern was raised that this could then be used to mount subversion campaigns aimed to foster more Soviet-friendly or even Communist governments around the world.[12] Unfortunately, as we also saw in chapter 3, over-reaction to this fear led to a Red Scare, which saw thousands fall under suspicion and onto RCMP monitoring lists. At the same time, the Soviet Union was involved in directing or leading a clandestine foreign influence campaign in the West, including Canada, to achieve its goals.

Although policy and responsibility for influence operations changed over time, Soviet actions in this space are often referred to as "active measures" – a rough translation for *aktivnyye meropriatia*, or the name of Soviet KGB unit in charge of implementing these activities by the 1960s (the Active Measures Department – or Department A for short).[13] During the Cold War, Richard H. Shultz and Roy Godson described "active measures" as "certain overt and covert techniques for foreign influencing events and behavior in, and the actions of, foreign countries.... Active measures may entail influencing the policies of another government, undermining confidence in its leaders and institutions, disrupting relations between other nations, and discrediting and weakening governmental and non-governmental opponents. This frequently involves attempts to deceive the target (foreign governmental and non-governmental elites or mass audiences) and to distort the target's perception of reality."[14]

Active measures covered a wide variety of activities, including disinformation efforts (*dezinformatsia*), political influence operations, as well as coordinating the activities of Soviet front groups and foreign Communist parties.[15] Although the two are not mutually exclusive, Soviet active measures should be distinguished from intelligence collection. While the latter aimed to obtain information, the former sought to wield it as a strategic tool to alter opinions and sow discord and mistrust of the West. Shultz and Godson identify six main themes of Soviet efforts during the Cold War: (1) to persuade Western opinion that the United States was the major cause of international conflict and crisis; (2) to demonstrate that the United States is aggressive, militaristic, and imperialistic; (3) to isolate the United States from its friends and allies, especially in NATO, and to discredit any state that cooperates with the United States; (4) to discredit Western military and intelligence establishments, especially NATO; (5) to discredit U.S. policy vis-à-vis the developing world; and (6) to confuse public opinion concerning Soviet global ambitions, creating a favourable environment for Soviet foreign policy.[16]

These activities date back as far as the Soviet Union itself: following its 1918 Revolution, Russia was diplomatically isolated and weak. As such, it depended on its new intelligence services to spread disinformation about the strength of its military capabilities.[17] During this early period, the Soviet Union established Communist International (Comintern) to spread the Bolshevik revolution around the world, and various (often competing) intelligence services also ran covert terrorist and sabotage operations against hostile states.[18] In addition, disinformation efforts were used in the 1920s in Europe, often to lure émigré activists back to Russia using subterfuge, and to sow dissent among émigré groups.[19] By the 1930s disinformation efforts shifted to trying to convince the West that industrialization had been a success and that the Soviet Union was a rising industrial power.[20]

Although the Soviet Union found itself in a different security situation after the end of the Second World War, globally the threat-related activities it engaged in were similar to its pre-war approach. Within Canada they broadly fall into three main categories: propaganda, front groups, and links to political parties. Although the success of these operations is not obvious – insofar as they did not lead to major policy changes or shifts in the attitude of the Canadian public, it is clear that the Soviet Union provided significant resources to these efforts.

FRONT GROUPS

As noted above, among some of the first steps the Soviet Union took in order to promote its interests (if not export its revolution abroad) was the creation of international movements. Following the Second World War, the Communist Information Bureau (Cominform) was responsible for coordinating these organizations. The World Peace Council, an organization created out of several Communist-organized international peace summits in the late 1940s, is often pointed to as an example of a front group that existed largely to serve Soviet ends.[21]

Within Canada the Canadian Peace Congress was affiliated with the WPC. Founded in 1949, the Congress campaigned for nuclear disarmament and drew crowds across the nation. As in other Western countries, Communist Party members rushed to join or work with the organization.[22] While there is no indication that the leader of the Congress, Reverend James Endicott, was a member of any Communist party, he did echo Soviet speaking lines about foreign affairs, including the lie that the United States was engaging in "germ warfare" in North Korea. He also received the Stalin Peace Prize in an act that outraged many Canadians, just as the group began to fall into decline in the 1950s.[23]

Soviet active measures also included efforts to control and promote "friendship" societies. Within their host countries, these societies served a number of purposes. One of the most important was laundering the Soviet strategic narratives discussed above through organizations that attempted to present themselves as more neutral, academic, or even intellectual. Second, these groups served as a way to disseminate propaganda, such as books or films to audiences in the West, promising them the "real story" that conventional news sources were allegedly not showing them. Third, friendship societies would arrange for cultural exchanges. This might include bringing Soviet artists to the West, or bringing interested individuals to the Soviet Union itself – although they were almost certainly shown a sanitized facade of a village.

Within Canada, the most prominent of these groups was the Canadian-Soviet Friendship Society (CSFS), which aimed to convince progressive-leftists in North America that the Soviet Union was an enlightened and egalitarian state.[24] In the 1950s the RCMP assessed the CSFS as a communist-front organization largely under the control of the Communist Party of Canada (the Labour Progressive Party) that served as a "clearing house" for invitations to the USSR and the promotion of Soviet propaganda as well as to persuade Canadians to view Soviet-style communism favourably.[25] In her history of the CSFS, Jennifer Anderson argues that the organization's main legacy was its consistent attempts to soften Canadian antipathies toward the USSR.[26]

PROPAGANDA/DISINFORMATION

As noted above, a key strategic goal of the Soviet Union was to discredit the United States and NATO to other Western countries, including Canada. These efforts can be divided into two categories – straightforward endeavours to propagate the Soviet perspective and more clandestine or covert attempts to plant stories in the West to insert a strategic narrative using disinformation. These latter campaigns attempted to plant bogus stories in (typically) left-leaning papers in the hope that other outlets would pick up the story or that it would gain traction through repetition. For example, the Soviets put considerable effort into linking the CIA to the assassination of President John F. Kennedy and Martin Luther King. More infamously, the Soviet Union created a rumour that the United States had created HIV/AIDS as part of a biological weapons laboratory, using an "anonymous" letter to a left-leaning Indian newspaper as well as the suspect report of a retired East German biophysicist (who was reported as being French). This campaign, called Operation Infektion, reportedly persuaded newspapers in up to thirty countries to print the story.[27] In Canada the *Montreal Gazette* reprinted a *Baltimore Sun* story that repeated the Soviet allegation, but noted it was an East German talking point with little support in the AIDS research community. Nevertheless, the story carried an allegation that there was a conspiracy to silence the story without clearly stating that the AIDS-conspiracy theory was false.[28]

While the AIDS story used questionable experts and anonymous letters, the Soviets also used forgeries in the 1980s as "evidence" to support fake stories they were trying to plant. This included several fake plots that the United States was planning to overthrow governments or assassinate individuals, including the pope. Forgeries included fake diplomatic telegrams, military field manuals, pamphlets, and official plans.[29]

Sometimes the efforts were more direct: in the 1940s some Canadians began to receive letters, usually from Russia or the Soviet Bloc, from individuals who said they were interested in learning more about Canada and establishing a pen-pal relationship. Many of these letters requested sensitive materials, including maps, pictures of military bases, and other information about the armed forces and phone directories. While this campaign appears to have been part of an effort to obtain strategic information, it also seems to have been a genuine attempt to engage in foreign influence. After a Montreal automobile club responded to a letter it received from Czechoslovakia, they received 100 anti-nuclear pamphlets that encouraged people to stand up against the U.S. nuclear program.[30]

Although these campaigns may have caught some followers in Canada on the fringe-left, Soviet propaganda arguably succeeded more in the efforts of front groups to bring propaganda to Canadians and into the mainstream media. The CSFS printed thousands of documents for its members as well as interested outlets. This included

"Photo-Facts" – idealized pictures of life in the Soviet Union with factoids on the other side that CSFS members were requested to purchase for friends or to leave in public locations. Some of the "Photo-Facts" showed the various "freedoms" citizens supposedly enjoyed, such as the "freedom of race and religion," "freedom for women," and "freedom from slave labor."[31] In addition, the CSFS published books about their visits to the Soviet Union as well as a monthly publication, *Northern Neighbours*, which presented a heavily sanitized look at life in the USSR that parroted approved Soviet lines.[32]

LINKS TO POLITICAL PARTIES

Significant Soviet effort was spent on controlling and clandestinely supporting foreign Communist or far-left leaning parties, although this was done with different degrees of success globally.[33] Within Canada, the Communist Party of Canada (CPC) was founded in 1921 in Guelph, Ontario. In its first two decades the CPC had a precarious existence, and many of its leaders had to go into hiding during the first years of the Second World War to avoid internment.[34] However, the CPC rebranded itself as the Labour Progressive Party in 1941 when the Soviet Union joined the Allies. Hopes for post-war influence faded with the Gouzenko spy scandal, which saw several Canadian Communists, including the only Communist MP ever elected, implicated in espionage.[35]

Clearly, not every communist was a spy or agent of foreign influence, but many of the spies and agents of foreign influence in Canada were members of the CPC. Other members of the CPC served as talent spotters for the KGB, or assisted in operations in any way they could.[36] In addition, others would join the Canadian Peace Congress and Canadian-Soviet Friendship Society, where they could advocate for more friendly policies towards the Soviet Union.[37]

Tamil Tigers and Threats to Persons as Clandestine Foreign Influence

Of course the Soviet active measures are not the only case of foreign influence activities in Canadian history. As a nation with a large immigrant population, Canada has several large and small diaspora groups that have been the objects of clandestine foreign influence campaigns by extremist groups and states. In these cases the foreign influence campaign is less to shift a narrative or change popular opinion and is directed towards threatening individuals into compliance with the aims and objectives of a foreign entity. This may include trying to silence critics through threats of violence to individuals in Canada or family members overseas, coercing individuals into public displays of support, attempts to infiltrate other organizations to support extremist ones, and forced remittances.

A number of groups have engaged in such activities, but one of the most prominent in the recent past has been that of the Liberation Tigers of Tamil Eelam (LTTE or Tamil Tigers). The overarching goal of the LTTE in Canada was to create support for a separate Tamil state as well as the infrastructure (clandestine and open) to finance political and military efforts to achieve these ends. However, in order to accomplish this goal, the LTTE needed to ensure that they spoke for the Tamil community, that they controlled any potential rival who could put out an alternative message, that they were able to effectively silence dissent, and they needed to convince Canadian politicians that they were a group of noble freedom fighters looking to create a state free from oppression.

FRONT GROUPS
Both chapters 1 and 2 have already highlighted some of the activities of the LTTE in Canada. In chapter 1 it was observed that the World Tamil Movement (WTM) was set up as a front organization in Canada, although its support for the LTTE was no secret – it publicly fundraised for the terrorist group.[38] Nevertheless, the WTM successfully presented as a normal political movement, with its own addresses and institutions in several cities that anyone could access or go to. As discussed below, it wasn't until the group was listed as a terrorist entity that the group was forced to close down publicly.

CONTROL OR SUBVERSION OF COMMUNITIES AND INSTITUTIONS
The LTTE actively worked to infiltrate other Tamil organizations and subsume them under their control. In the early 1990s an attempt was made to create an umbrella organization for the different Tamil move-

ments in Canada called the Federation of Associations of Canadian Tamils (FACT). While outwardly the motivation behind FACT was said to be unifying voices within the movement and working toward common goals, by the late 1990s it was seen by officials in the U.S. and Canada as a front organization for the LTTE. The leadership of the constituent organizations that belonged to FACT were increasingly hardliners who outright supported the LTTE or believed they were the Tamils' only hope.[39] The LTTE also sought to control Hindu temples in Canada, as they "provide both ready access to the Tamil community and to a potential source of funds, the LTTE has sought control over temple events, management, and revenue." With the "capture" of these temples, extremists and Tiger sympathizers could use them to display propaganda, quell dissent, and direct funds to militants.[40]

THREATS OF VIOLENCE

One way the LTTE and its supporters were able to assert their authority was to threaten violence to those who resisted its demands. In chapters 1 and 2 it was noted that the Tigers used a variety of criminal means to obtain money. When individuals refused to donate, they turned to aggressive measures to extort funds. For example, in interviews with Human Rights Watch in the mid-2000s, it was reported that Tamils in the West were told they would not be able to visit Sri Lanka to see their friends and families or that they or their families would encounter "trouble" if they did not contribute.[41] There are allegations that much of the threat of violence came from criminal gangs who engaged in arson and extortion, and served as an enforcement arm of the LTTE's political representatives in Canada.[42]

SILENCING DISSENT

Threats of violence were also used to harass critics. In a report on LTTE harassment and foreign influence, Human Rights Watch reported that such threats have "created a climate of fear for many within the Tamil diaspora, discouraging statements, activities, or even social interactions that may be perceived as critical of the LTTE."[43] Journalists in Canada covering events in Sri Lanka that were critical of the LTTE or reported their military defeats received threats and harassing calls. Stores carrying newspapers with news of LTTE's military defeats were targeted, and harassment campaigns resulted in the shuttering of at least one publication in Toronto.[44] And as Human Rights Watch notes, the harassment went beyond journalists: "Tamils in the West have been subject to death threats, beatings, property damage, smear campaigns, fabricated criminal charges, and even murder as a consequence of dissent. Although incidents of actual violence have been relatively rare, they reverberate strongly within the community and effectively discourage others from expressing views that counter the LTTE."[45] When a Tamil organization in Toronto publicly mourned the death of a journalist killed by the LTTE in Paris after he had been critical of their leadership, the library of the organization, containing 2,000 rare manuscripts, was burned to the ground.[46]

DIASPORA MONITORING AND SURVEILLANCE

To support its activities, the LTTE and its supporters engaged in the monitoring and surveillance of Tamils in Canada. The LTTE is reported to have kept records of where Tamils in Canada were located in order to keep track of them.[47] In this way the Tigers could continue to monitor and follow up with recent immigrants to whom they could continue to turn for support and donations, even if this attention was unwelcome.

One way the Tamils were able to accomplish this was by controlling the system of migration to the West, including Canada. Tamils wishing to emigrate were forced to move through channels and processes carefully managed by the LTTE. Simply leaving Tamil-controlled territory during the conflict is said to have required permission from the Tigers and may have required selected individuals to provide some sort of leverage in order to do so, such as ensuring relatives remained in the country or assets in Sri Lanka were turned over to the LTTE. According to one analyst, this gave the LTTE a "stranglehold" over refugees after they left the country.[48]

POLITICAL INFLUENCE

Understanding that the support of mainstream politicians would aid their cause, the LTTE sought to extend their reach beyond the diaspora. As such, they ran a propaganda campaign with three key messages aimed at the West and Western politicians that (1) Tamils are the innocent victims of a government dominated by Sinhalese; (2) Tamils in Sri Lanka are subject to constant discrimination and military oppression; (3) peaceful co-existence between the Tamils and Sinhalese in a single state is not possible.[49] To do this, the LTTE campaigned under a "peace card" in order to garner the support of politicians and NGOs, which in turn could be used to garner further political support.[50]

The LTTE's influence campaign was broadly successful. Despite their links to violent extremists, LTTE supporters, including the World Tamil Movement, lobbied municipal, provincial, and federal politicians to support their cause. As one analyst wrote in 2000, "By permitting the LTTE to open offices and establish representation, Western countries have unwittingly blessed the group's political and military agenda."[51] In Canada, LTTE sympathizers held political rallies at the Ontario legislature, and politicians appeared in WTM publications, such as business directories.[52] In May 2000 two federal Cabinet Ministers, including future Prime Minister Paul Martin, attended a dinner sponsored by FACT, despite being reportedly warned by national security agencies to not attend the dinner.[53] Public outrage over this incident contributed to the growing awareness of Tamil activities in Canada, which led to WTM's listing as a terrorist entity in 2006.[54]

As the LTTE and WTM lost credibility in Canada and the LTTE was militarily defeated in 2009, Tamil extremism became a lesser national security priority. While there is still a strong sense of Tamil nationalism in Canada and in Tamil diaspora around the world, research on the attitudes of Tamil youth by Amar Amarasingam reveals that most have taken a different path away from violence to achieve their goals.[55]

This case study is important because it indicates the kinds of activities that state and non-state entities have and engage in. This includes groups such as the Mojahedin-e Khalq (People's Mujahedeen of Iran, or MEK), a former leftist terrorist group that is now often described as an Islamist-Marxist-feminist cult centred upon its leaders, the Rajavi family.[56] Having participated in the 1979 Iranian Revolution that overthrew the shah, the MEK was seen as a threat to the new Islamic Republic and it took on the sponsorship of Saddam Hussein. During the 1970s the MEK actively targeted the West, but soon after the Revolution, once ousted by the Supreme Leader, re-directed their efforts inside Iran, killing over seventy officials, including the President and Prime Minister in August 1981, according to the U.S. State Department. The group also fought against their home country in the Iran-Iraq War.[57]

We briefly encountered the MEK in chapter 2 as a formerly listed terrorist entity that Canadians joined as foreign fighters up to the mid-2000s.[58] Notoriously, it orchestrated attacks against Iranian embassies in the West in 1992, including Ottawa. In addition, the organization has engaged in its own clandestine foreign influence operations. They include using Canada to raise funds to support its violent overseas tactics[59] and a political campaign to establish legitimacy among Canadian MPs who, despite warnings from CSIS, see the organization as a viable alternative to the Iranian government.[60] There have also been multiple allegations that the group continues to terrorize its members, potentially detaining them overseas and mistreating members with dissenting opinions or who tried to leave.[61]

Another example of state-led clandestine foreign influence involves India and actions allegedly carried out against the Sikh diaspora in Canada. This should not be a surprise: India has very capable intelligence services and sees Canada as a national security threat, providing safe harbour to individuals it views as Sikh separatists. For decades India has expressed concern about supporters of violent Sikh movements abroad who have financed, facilitated, or supported attacks against it from Canadian territory.[62] To mitigate this threat, India frequently raises its concern with the Canadian government.[63] However, seemingly untrusting of Canadian authorities to take the threat seriously, the Indian government also engages in clandestine actions, including the active monitoring of the Sikh diaspora and political influence, in order to achieve its ends.

India has monitored Sikhs in Canada since at least the 1980s, especially in the aftermath of the Air India bombing.[64] During this time it was reported that these activities by India were carried through its consulates in Canada and indirectly through infiltration into the Sikh community in Canada. The range of reported clandestine foreign influence operations runs from recruiting and directing sources to report on the activities of the community, and disinformation operations, to influence operations that seek to discredit the Sikh movement in Canada.[65] Decades later, the Indian press continues to run stories that are critical of the Canadian government and highlight perceived threats within the Sikh community in Canada. These stories are sometimes picked up the Canadian media and have tended to resurface during official meetings between the two countries.[66]

India's continued recourse to clandestine foreign influence has been confirmed in recent media and government reports, including an NSICOP report into national security questions surrounding Prime Minister Justin Trudeau's controversial trip to India in 2018. During the visit, an individual convicted of attempted murder was invited by Member of Parliament Randeep Singh Sarai to attend a reception for the Prime Minister. While most sections on clandestine foreign influence were heavily redacted, the report's recommendation that "members of the House of Commons and the Senate should be briefed upon being sworn-in and regularly thereafter on the risks of foreign interference and extremism in Canada" suggest that at least some of the activities alleged since the 1980s are real and ongoing.[67] Additionally, in July 2019 a Canadian Press news story revealed that Deputy Ministers were warned about China and India trying to use their respective ethnic communities in Canada to advance their own agendas.[68]

None of this should detract from the real threat of individuals based in Canada who wish to carry out attacks against India. In 2018, in two official documents, the government noted an increase in the number of "extremists who support violent means to establish an independent state within India."[69] However, there is clearly a difference of opinion between Canada and India over what constitutes a threat. In Canada, the Charter of Rights and Freedoms protects most actions that promote the peaceful advocacy of views, including those of separatist movements. Put plainly, it is not against Canadian law to argue that Sikhs should have their own country. Where these activities cross a line is when these views intersect with the threat-related activities described in chapter 2: radicalization, facilitation, financing, travel, and planning attacks. India clearly believes the threshold for extremist activity should be lower than what exists in Canada, and it seems likely that the government will continue to engage in these activities so long as they perceive a threat to their safety and sovereignty.

Traditional Clandestine Foreign Influence Operations in Canada Today

The previous discussion sets the stage for an overview of what traditional clandestine foreign influence looks like in Canada today. While there continue to be a variety of state and non-state actors operating in this space, the major threat of in-person campaigns is perceived to come from China. China has already been extensively discussed in this book relative to its economic and cyber-espionage activities in Canada. A third set of threat-related activities is its foreign influence campaign used to create pathways for Chinese foreign investment, promote acceptance of a rising China's place in the world, quell dissent abroad, and monitor the Chinese diaspora.

It should be acknowledged at the outset that while this section discusses the actions of the Chinese state, it really refers to the actions of the Chinese Communist Party (CCP). In chapter 4 it was noted that while the CCP is not a unitary actor – it has internal divisions and competition – it is united around a single goal, the survival of the party-state. In this sense, while this chapter will speak about "China," it is really referring to the actions of CCP officials in support of its goals.

Within the CCP, there is no single entity responsible for clandestine foreign influence. Although the "United Front Work Department" (UFW, discussed below) has received considerable media attention in recent years, there are a variety of actors known to engage in this space. These include the Foreign Affairs Commission, the External Propaganda Leading Group/State Council Information Office, the CCP Propaganda Department, and the CCP International Liaison

Department of the People's Liberation Army General Political Department. In March 2018 the Overseas Chinese Affairs Office of the State Council, which reportedly worked to influence recent Chinese immigrants to the West, was merged with the UFW.[70] Together, these groups are responsible for the formulation and implementation of influence policies, both public and clandestine.[71] The Ministry of Foreign Affairs is also important in that it is responsible for China's embassies, where bureaucrats from the above-mentioned organizations are stationed abroad.[72]

A specialized body of the CCP, the UFW, is tasked with building support for the CCP and its policies abroad. The UFW was formed at the behest of the Soviet Union in the pre-Chinese revolutionary period to co-opt control of Chinese political movements and strengthen the CCP against the nationalists. Later Mao used the UFW to consolidate power as well as educate and train the socialist successors of the Chinese revolutionaries as well as control religious movements inside China.[73] In addition, along with the International Liaison Department, the UFW supported and nurtured revolutionary and nationalist movements abroad, as well as pro-China organizations during the Cold War.[74] Following the collapse of communism in other countries around the world, and the widely publicized government crackdown against protestors in Tiananmen Square, the UFW became seen as an important tool to influence ethnic populations abroad as a way to restore and promote China's position in the world. This included strategies to discourage support for Chinese dissidents abroad as well as the Falun Gong (a Chinese new religious movement seen as a threat by the PRC), discredit China's democratic model, stir patriotism among the diaspora, and generate support for China's economic goals.[75]

Within the increasing body of writings on the UFW, there is some dispute about the range of its activities, particularly those directed against the ethnic-Chinese diaspora.[76] There seems to be a consensus, though, that UFW activities have increased and expanded under Chinese President Xi, who, in a 2014 speech, described the work of the Front as "magic weapons."[77] In this sense, the UFW should be seen as a major but not exclusive player in Chinese efforts to target the Chinese diaspora, as well as in attempts to positively influence views of China more generally.

While it is not possible to discuss the full range of Chinese foreign influence activities in Canada, much of these efforts can be categorized along the following lines.

Front Groups

A number of Chinese associations in Canada are believed to be under the control of the UFW or other Chinese government agencies. This includes myriad "friendship societies" and organizations that typically champion Beijing's talking points. For example, the Chinese Association for International Friendly Contact is widely understood to be a front for the International Liaison Department.[78] In other cases, organizations that claim to be representing the ethnic diaspora in Canada are often controlled by the Chinese government. The Tibet Association of Canada, for one, has been accused of being a front group. Unlike other Tibetan groups in Canada who generally advocate for the freedom of Tibet from Chinese rule, the association accepts and promotes Beijing's lines on Tibetan independence and advocates for its policies there.[79]

There have also been accusations that Chinese Students and Scholars Associations (CSSAs) serve as front groups for the CCP. While the CSSA help Chinese students adjust to life in the West (among other useful social services), there have been accusations that these groups receive guidance from the CCP through embassies and consulates, and engage in work that is consistent with UFW goals.[80] As discussed above, in February 2019 there were two incidents where Chinese students coordinated protests to advance Chinese-state interests on university campuses. Both of these activities serve Beijing's goals and appear to have been coordinated with the Toronto Chinese consulate (although this was officially denied), and in the case of McMaster, in part coordinated by the CSSA.[81]

Control or Subversion of Communities and Institutions

Where Beijing has not been able to establish front groups, it has worked to monitor, if not establish effective control over different Chinese organizations based in the West, including Canada.[82] There are hundreds of such organizations in Canada, including community associations, business societies, educational and cultural institutes, and athletic associations. Importantly, China does not direct or control these organizations. They have, however, been known to coordinate their activities to advance the priorities of Beijing. In the wake of the 2019 protests in Hong Kong, advertisements ran in two large Canadian Chinese-language newspapers criticizing foreign intervention in Chinese affairs. This action was coordinated by the Chinese Benevolent Association of Vancouver, an umbrella group of more than 100 business and cultural associations whose names also appear on the advertisement.[83] While there is no evidence that this action was ordered by Chinese consulate or CCP officials, some argue it is indicates the kinds of campaigns CCP and UFW groups regularly engage in.[84]

Controlling the Media/Message

As noted above, since the fallout of the 1989 Tiananmen Square crackdown, a key priority for China has been defending the CCP and its policies, promoting favourable coverage, and stamping out criticism. Chinese authorities appear to be doing this in two ways: by distributing propaganda through its own media channels and attempting to control the narrative in Chinese-language media in the West, including Canada.

There are several official Chinese institutions and media outlets through which Beijing's views are distributed. In 1991 China established the State Council Information Office and, shortly thereafter, an English-language news channel, China Central Television (CCTV), later renamed CCTV International and eventually China Global Television Network (CGTN). In addition, China Radio International (CRI) and Xinhua News Service expanded their global presence, beginning in the 2000s, with the latter now having approximately

200 bureaus around the world.[85] In 2015 a Reuter's investigation found that thirty-three radio stations in fourteen countries had concealed the fact that their majority shareholder was CRI.[86] In 2018, CGTN, CRI, and China National Radio were consolidated under one management structure called "Voice of China." This allows the separate news brands to exist but brings them all under the control of the CCP's Publicity Department, an agency in charge of propaganda and media censorship.[87]

In 1997 the *People's Daily*, an official publication of the CCP, began hosting a website, which has expanded to publishing in at least twelve languages over the past three decades, and recently created mobile phone apps in Chinese and English. China has also established newspapers or English-language editions in Western countries, such as the *China Press* and *China Daily* – the latter directly distributing content as advertising supplements in major newspapers such as the *Wall Street Journal* and the *Washington Post*.[88] Importantly, while these media outlets are promoting Beijing's world view, they are typically doing so openly and within Canadian laws (although there have been allegations that China has used its media outlets as cover for espionage, causing the government to strictly control who may come to Canada for reporting purposes[89]).

More worrying from a national security perspective is the allegation that China has been working to assert control over non-official Chinese-language media outlets in the West. In particular, there is concern that Beijing has been able to control the coverage of China in Chinese-language media in Canada. This has been done through acquiring ownership of publications by CCP-friendly organizations, financial pressure, or even threats and intimidation. A 2016 report by the *New York Times* noted that of the thirty free Chinese-language newspapers in Ontario, very few published any content that would be viewed negatively by the Chinese state.[90] Even major Chinese-language media outlets have been affected. Several once independent media outlets with distribution in Canada increasingly have come under the control of Beijing, including *Sing Tao*, *World Journal*, and *Ming Pao* over several decades.[91]

When Chinese-language sources are not under direct or indirect control, there are other ways China can "harmonize" the material from media outlets with that of official state sources. With a competitive market, news outlets fear a boycott by pro-Beijing businesses and organizations, as well as a loss of distribution deals with Chinese state media publications.[92] It has been reported that Chinese diplomatic staff have called Chinese-language outlets in Toronto, asking them not to accept advertisements from the Falun Gong or delete content they view as countering Beijing's official lines or portraying China in a negative light.[93] In addition, journalists viewed as critical of China have frequently been harassed. Some believe they have been fired from their jobs for being critical of China. Worse, some claim to have faced threats to their and their family's safety, sometimes from Chinese state security officials.[94] In this way, China has been able to increasingly dominate traditional Chinese-language news outlets in Canada, ensuring that the diaspora population, particularly newcomers to Canada, continue to receive the CCP's preferred version of human events.

Finally, China has used its economic might to intimidate foreign companies into adopting its world views. In May 2018 clothing company Gap Inc. was forced to apologize when a shirt displaying a map of China did not include Taiwan and what China calls "southern Tibet" (a swath of disputed territory with India) on it. In a statement to the CCP's *Global Times* newspaper, Gap Inc. stated, "As a responsible company, Gap Inc. strictly follows Chinese laws and rules," and the apology was quickly tweeted, in English, by the media outlet.[95] In that same month, China's Civil Aviation Administration demanded that thirty-six foreign airlines list Taiwan as a part of China in their ticket-booking processes as well as in the maps they use. Air Canada, one of these airlines targeted by China, complied with the demand.[96] As we can see, it is not just Chinese-language companies that bow to CCP orders; global companies must as well.

Silencing of Dissent

In order to enhance its image abroad, China cracks down on dissent within its borders and increasingly seeks to do so overseas. As such, it engages in a variety of activities to silence critics in Western countries, particularly advocates of independence for Tibet, Xinjang, and

Taiwan, advocates for democratic reform, and the Falun Gong.[97] As noted above, journalists from Chinese-language media outlets who report on these issues but stray from the Beijing line are subject to harassment. But the activists for these causes are often subject to worse: surveillance, and threats to themselves and their families abroad. A confidential assessment of these activities by Amnesty International and the Canadian Coalition on Human Rights in China for Global Affairs Canada found that while it may be difficult to directly attribute this harassment to Chinese authorities, "credible reports of an organized and sustained pattern of harassment and intimidation are consistent with allegations that they are part of a coordinated Chinese government-sponsored campaign to target certain groups and individuals outside of China opposed to Chinese government policies."[98]

These harassment campaigns take on a variety of forms. Targeted individuals have reported being digitally harassed, sometimes in the form of emails with attachments containing malware. It is believed that the purpose of the malware is to conduct surveillance on activists, particularly the Canada Tibet Committee.[99] In other cases, the harassment takes place on social media, with the Tibetan student elected President, mentioned above, receiving hundreds of pro-China messages on her social media account as well as others that were more directly threatening.[100] There are also reports of defamatory websites and fake social media accounts being created to target Falun Gong activists[101] and pro-democracy advocates.[102]

Offline, activists report having received a series of phone calls that include recorded hateful messages and even death threats.[103] There have also been reports of in-person harassment, particularly at demonstrations protesting Chinese policies. This includes photographing and surveilling protestors, and attempting to block or hide protest banners through coordinated counter-protests that interfere with the right to freedom of speech and assembly.[104]

Dissidents in Canada have had their families targeted by the Chinese state. Uighurs in Canada frequently report having had at least one family member in one of the many large Chinese detention centres in Xinjiang. These individuals fear that their families are effectively being used as hostages to prevent them from engaging in any form of activism or protest against Chinese policies abroad.[105] They are also concerned that they will be subjected to re-education camps in Xinjang should they return home, especially if they engage in democratic activities abroad. Simply living overseas seems to be reason enough for an individual's family members to be detained.[106]

Finally, it should be noted that China has also targeted Canadian academic institutions that offer a platform to critics or an alternative view to the official CCP line. As noted in chapter 4, after a visit by the Dalai Lama to the University of Calgary in 2013, China suddenly no longer recognized its degrees. Given that Canadian universities make considerable money from Chinese students, this was a serious economic blow and it took nearly a year for the decision to be reversed. As former ambassador to China, David Mulroney, observes, "This was a skirmish in a larger, global campaign to intimidate governments and universities and thereby diminish the international space available to the Dalai Lama."[107] He adds that Chinese authorities know they can "trade access" to China for academics through their visa process. Scholars seen as too critical or too outspoken risk being barred from visiting, which can hurt their careers and research. In this way, they are able to extend Beijing's authority beyond China's borders.[108] Indeed, as seen in the next section, China applies considerable effort to monitoring the messages given and received on campus, especially to Chinese students.

Diaspora Monitoring

While the overseas Chinese security apparatus and UFW dedicates much of its efforts towards dissidents, they are also concerned with monitoring average citizens who happen to be in the West, particularly at universities. Universities have played a key role in establishing and developing relations between China and the West, but in recent years Beijing has enacted policies, with moderate success, to ensure that Chinese and Western students are predominantly exposed to CCP-approved information. Sometimes their strategies are very direct; above it was noted that there is reason to believe Chinese consulates were involved in harassment of Tibetan and Uighur students. In at least one other instance, an institute at Concordia

University and the City of Montreal received emails from China's Montreal consulate demanding that a Uighur speaker not appear at an event.[109]

There are other strategies used to monitor students and ensure that pro-Beijing lines are dominant on campuses in the West. The CSSA has already been discussed in its relation to allegations that it coordinates influence operations with Chinese embassies and consulates, but there are allegations it plays a role in supervising Chinese students as well.[110] Between 2015 and 2018, Human Rights Watch interviewed over 100 academics and scholars in Australia, Canada, France, the United Kingdom, and the United States on their experiences of being monitored by the Chinese state. In multiple cases the families of students were threatened on the basis of the views expressed by their relatives in Western classrooms. Others remained silent out of fear that their remarks would be reported to Chinese authorities.[111]

One of the most prominent ways China seeks to influence campuses is through Confucius Institutes. These are nominally sponsored by the Chinese Ministry of Education but are effectively directed by the CCP through the CCP Propaganda Department, linked to the UFW.[112] On the surface, Confucius Institutes are centres that teach the Chinese language, culture, and history at the primary, secondary, and tertiary level around the world, including Canada.[113] Teachers, students, and school board members are often taken on government-approved trips to China, some of which are fully paid for.[114] While it is common for countries such as France, Germany, and the United Kingdom to establish and sponsor language and cultural institutions in other countries as a part of "soft power" initiatives, Confucius Institutes are known to play a more clandestine role. Agreements between Confucius Institutes and host universities in the West forbid these universities from contravening Chinese law.[115] This would presumably include laws about assisting Chinese security agencies. Confucius Institutes use only approved CCP materials that promote their world view and talking points. There are concerns that the institutes govern which topics may and may not be addressed in classrooms, including Tibet, Taiwan, and Xinjiang.[116]

Alarm has also been expressed about the opaque nature of the agreements between host educational institutions and Hanban/Confucius Institute Headquarters (a public institution affiliated with the PRC Ministry of Education), leading to criticisms about a lack of transparency from critics concerned about academic freedom at Confucius Institutes.[117] This issue was raised in 2011 when an employee of a Confucius Institute at McMaster University complained to the Human Rights Tribunal of Ontario that her employment contract forced her to hide her adherence to Falun Gong teachings.[118] By late 2013 the Canadian Association of University Teachers (CAUT) passed a resolution calling on any academic institution playing host to Confucius Institutes to sever ties with them unless they became more transparent and followed the norms of academic freedom in the West. In 2014 the American Association of University Professors voiced similar concerns.[119] Although several higher education institutions in Canada continue their relationship with Confucius Institutes, several others have now severed their relationship, including McMaster and Sherbrooke Universities, often citing concerns about academic freedom and other practices.[120] In addition, the Toronto District School Board cancelled its plans to establish a Confucius Institute, and New Brunswick announced plans to terminate its contract with the Confucius Institute programs in early 2019.[121]

Political Influence

As noted in the beginning of this chapter, state representatives and diplomats often meet with politicians, community leaders, and other individuals seen as influential to advocate their interests and increase their nation's soft power. These activities are normal and legal. However, there are concerns that China has engaged in political influence that crosses a threshold into more clandestine activity. The challenge for national security agencies is knowing when this happens. Moreover, even if it can be determined that a state has engaged in political interference, it is not always possible to assess whether or not it has been effective – just that an attempt has taken place. There is little national security services can do other than advise governments that these activities are going on.

Indeed, the issue of Chinese clandestine political interference has been very difficult to address in Canada – many are rightfully concerned about seeming to scapegoat the Chinese community, especially given Canada's history of racist and discriminatory policies against Chinese immigration that continued well into the twentieth century. Striking the right balance between expressing concern about political interference and seeming to incriminate an entire community is difficult. It is clear, though, that the CCP is trying to influence Canadians – although it is difficult to measure how effective these activities are.

An example of the challenge to explain clandestine foreign influence to the Canadian public occurred in 2010, when former CSIS Director Richard Fadden was widely condemned for stating that Canadian politicians were being influenced by Chinese agents (discussed in chapter 3). This seemed shocking at the time but is now largely accepted to be true. At the time, however, Fadden was roundly condemned. He was forced to testify in an unclassified parliamentary hearing where he could not divulge the information he had and was admonished in a report by members of Parliament that called on him to resign. Nearly a decade later, in 2019, an NSICOP report acknowledged that he was correct.[122]

What exactly did Fadden say that caused such outrage? In a speech at the Royal Canadian Military Institute in Toronto, Fadden noted that the Service believed "there are several municipal politicians in British Columbia and in at least two provinces there are ministers of the Crown who we think are under at least the general influence of a foreign government." He went further in a TV interview shortly thereafter, noting that the agents of influence were Chinese and that "they haven't really hidden their association, but what surprised us is that it's been so extensive over the years and we're now seeing, in a couple of cases, indications that they are in fact shifting their public policies as a reflection of that involvement with that particular country."[123]

Although it may have been shocking then, there can be little doubt today that China seeks to engage in political interference in Canada. In 2017, the *Financial Times* published a report on a UFW training manual that touted successes in the 2006 Toronto City Council elections, with ten of forty-four candidates elected. The manual continues, "We should aim to work with those individuals and groups that are at a relatively high level, operate within the mainstream of society and have prospects for advancement."[124] Although there is not much evidence to say whether the UFW was ever successful in its targeting, the findings from the manual reveal that political influence operations in Western countries target not just federal, but provincial and local politicians, aiming to groom them to be receptive to China's world view and to assist in achieving CCP objectives.[125] Indeed, sub-national authorities often have jurisdiction over issues that are important to China, such as education (approving Confucius Institutes as part of the educational curriculum) or natural resources (energy and mining operations.)

There are a number of ways that China may be engaging in these activities. One is to offer lavish free trips and gifts to a wide range of authorities across Canada. Former diplomats and national security officials have indicated that such trips may pose a risk to political leaders, as China likely views these individuals as being potentially manipulated by benefits such as travel and business opportunities to support the interests of China in Canada.[126] Most public knowledge about such travel is at the federal level, given requirements to disclose and report. In January 2018 it was revealed that between 2007 and 2017 China was the third-most-visited destination by Canadian MPs (with Taiwan – actively seeking to influence Canada away from China – and Israel as the top two). As noted above, however, China also reaches out to local school board officials through its Confucius Institutes and other programs.[127] This illustrates the fact that China is not aiming its influence solely at the top political levels in Canada: it targets local politicians and seeks to build relations in communities as well.

A second issue that has raised concern in Canada is political donations. It was reported in 2016 that wealthy Chinese business leaders with close connections to the CCP were making political donations in Canada. For example, during $1,500 per ticket fundraisers for the Liberal Party of Canada, Canadian-Chinese business people brought along contacts from China, including representatives of Chinese SOEs with alleged links to the CCP.[128] Again, it is not clear what – if anything – came out of these donations or political contacts. The situation in Canada does, however, mirror developments in other countries, albeit to a lesser extent. In Australia, CCP-linked funding of politicians and political parties has become a major political scandal[129] (although it should be noted that until 2018 Australia had comparatively weaker political donation laws than other Western countries[130]).

A third method may be through attempts to mobilize ethnic-block voting. In this case politicians or candidates are believed to be mobilizing community organizations or using Chinese-language social media to encourage Chinese-Canadians to vote for certain candidates.[131] Deputy Ministers were warned by national security analysts in March 2018 that China and India were attempting to "directly and indirectly work to influence diaspora communities across the country.... [T]he lines between legitimate advocacy and lobbying and pressures imposed to advance the economic and political interests of foreign actors are becoming increasingly blurred."[132]

Of course political parties trying to mobilize ethnic blocks is nothing new in Canada – and political nomination fights can be notoriously murky. It is, however, a problem if these individuals either running or supporting candidates have undisclosed ties to the Chinese state or the CCP. In 2017 David Mulroney stated that China was known to mobilize Chinese students and would attempt to tap into the Chinese diaspora in Canada to achieve its interests, which include electing politicians seen as pro-Beijing.[133] In October 2018 the RCMP announced they were investigating allegations that the Canada-Wenzhou Friendship Society used the Chinese social media platform WeChat to offer voters twenty dollars as a transportation subsidy if they voted for certain candidates of Chinese descent in Vancouver, Burnaby, and Richmond, British Columbia. Subsequent police and media investigations turned up few individuals claiming to be victimized, or clear evidence of meddling on a mass scale. Nor was there any evidence that the head of Canada-Wenzhou Friendship Society had any leadership roles in any group with ties to the Chinese government. However, the group met with the Overseas Chinese Affairs Committee under its former leader.[134]

In the end, what makes assessing the effectiveness of Chinese foreign influence so difficult is that it is often hard to know where threats end and begin – on an individual basis certain activities may seem innocuous, but put together, the cumulative impact and ultimate ends are unknown. This national security concern was already raised in chapter 4 – the takeover by an SOE here and there, and a few joint ventures between Chinese and Canadian companies may not seem significant, but in the long run they may add up to something more problematic. The same is true for clandestine foreign influence: a few MPs are given free visits, students use textbooks approved by the CCP, and airlines are forced to un-recognize Taiwan on the maps they use. Can all of this be said to amount to a campaign to soften Canada to China's larger foreign policy goals? And if so, what can we do about it?

Conclusion

For years, Canadians have turned a blind eye to clandestine foreign influence aimed at new Canadians or diaspora groups. We have not had much interest in foreign disputes with origins thousands of miles away, even some elements may be being carried out on our shores. We have been content for such matters to be played out in the restaurants, communities, religious institutions, and halls of those affected while most Canadians focus on the domestic political issues of the day.

At the same time, it is difficult to know when such operations are being conducted on our shores. In the first instance, there is seldom, if ever, a consensus on anything within a diaspora community: like other groups, there may be heated debate and discussion over national and international events. There is no single Chinese-Canadian or Indian-Canadian view – and as such it is challenging to know when a national security issue may arise. As noted above, advertisements in Chinese newspapers in Vancouver supporting Beijing during the 2019 Hong Kong protests have the hallmarks of the kinds of operations run by state-linked individuals or groups, but there is little hard evidence to state this with full certainty. On the one hand it mirrors the kind of threat-related activities that have come before, while on the other it is likely there is genuine division within the Chinese-Canadian community over how this issue is being handled, and different groups may have simply come together to act.

More disturbingly, individuals may be too frightened to come forward with their concerns – fearing for their position in the community or their livelihoods. In worst case scenarios, they worry that coming forward will threaten their lives or the lives of their families still living overseas. By preventing individuals from speaking up, states and non-state actors are able to keep their activities out of the view of most Canadians.

There is no one-size-fits-all solution to the threat of clandestine foreign influence – it depends on who is engaging in the activities, the nature of the threat, and how it affects national security. Nevertheless, there are a number of steps Canada should be taking to support victims of harassment campaigns or that target Canadian institutions.

First, government and national security officials should disaggregate clandestine foreign influence operations into those intended to persuade and those that involve genuine threats to life and livelihood. One great challenge of countering clandestine foreign influence is the fact that states can take advantage of Canada's laws protecting freedom of speech, belief, and right to protest. In these cases, it may be more difficult to stop the activities from taking place. Nevertheless, Canada should consider being more active in declaring embassy or consulate staff persona non grata when they are known to be engaging or encouraging these threat-related activities, particularly when they involve threats of violence or harm.

Second, Canada should be more proactive in supporting victims of clandestine foreign influence. An obvious way to do this is to take a more active stance on human rights, especially in populations facing repression at home. As with other international issues, Canada's voice will be amplified if it works with its allies in calling out repression. In July 2019 the UN ambassadors of twenty-two states (including Canada) came together to condemn China's treatment of its Uighur minority.[135] More of these kinds of actions should be encouraged.

Within Canada, the government should create spaces for victims to come forward without threat of criminal charge or threat to their immigration status. These could be set up at or near community institutions, schools, and universities.

Perhaps the most pressing case here is that of the Uighurs in Canada who face tremendous discrimination at home and, as this chapter has made clear, attacks through CCP-linked officials and entities. The international community has not done enough to speak up against the extreme brutality and repression that Uighurs face in China. Moreover, Canadian officials and politicians should do more to defend their rights in Canada when they are attacked.

Third, Canada should be extremely careful when outsourcing its education to state-linked institutions. While there is likely little to fear from France's Alliance Française or Germany's Goethe Institut, the Confucius Institute goes well beyond a normal educational centre with its requirements to follow Chinese law and potential threats to academic freedom. The federal government should encourage the provinces to fund independent language and area studies programs – ones that allow students to come to their own conclusions after being presented with evidence and knowledge in an environment where they are free to ask questions.

Fourth, the NSCIOP's 2019 study of the government's response to clandestine foreign influence argues there needs to be a more coordinated, comprehensive, and permanent approach to foreign influence in Canada. The committee notes there are several working groups that involve different departments and agencies trying to counter this threat. Unfortunately, the participants tend to have different understandings and perspectives of what influence activities are and how they affect Canada. NSICOP also notes that government reaction to foreign influence has traditionally been reactionary and "piecemeal, responding to specific instances of foreign interference but leaving unaddressed the many other areas where Canadian institutions and fundamental rights and freedoms continue to be undermined by hostile states."[136] In this sense, the committee made recommendations to create a more permanent approach.[137] This includes the development of "practical, whole-of-government, operational and policy mechanisms" to enable a more comprehensive approach nationally. In addition, they suggest the creation of regular mechanisms to work with sub-national units, providing security clearances if necessary in order to better share information about foreign influence activities. As an example of such mechanisms, NSCIOP suggested that it would appropriate for Canada to examine appointing a "National Counter Foreign Interference Coordinator" position such as the one that Australia created in 2018 who is able to lead in whole-of-government initiatives.[138]

In the conclusion to chapter 4 it was noted that the PRC represents a serious dilemma for Canada – with a population of over a billion there is no realistic option to cut ourselves off from China in a meaningful way. Nor is it clear that there would be any real benefit in doing so. Although this conclusion has called for a tougher approach to clandestine foreign influence activities, Canada is faced with many of the same problems in handling China's threats to economic national security: balancing the need to stop such operations while maintaining freedoms (such as freedom of speech and freedom of assembly); and the threat of retaliation against Canadian interests. As the University of Calgary discovered, challenging China may cause it to remove some (or all) Canadian universities and colleges from the list of officially recognized international degree-granting institutions. This would be a serious blow to our higher education system, which increasingly relies on fees from foreign students. Challenging clandestine foreign influence is risky business.

Yet, while this challenge is considerable, we have strengths we can utilize. We can better deploy our democratic culture to support the idea of human rights at home and abroad. We can choose to better coordinate with ourselves and our allies and speak up about the conditions that drive clandestine foreign influence operations. We can demand more transparency and accountability from our political parties and candidates at all levels of government in their fundraising activities. And we can fund and promote our own foreign language, culture, and area studies programs in high schools and at higher education institutions. None of this will eliminate clandestine foreign influence, but it will go some way to partially mitigating the threat.

Like all threats described in this book, however, clandestine foreign influence activities are constantly evolving. We have already seen how China is willing and able to use Chinese-language social media apps to engage in influence operations. But these activities are directed largely to the Chinese-Canadian diaspora who remain the primary audience for Beijing's messaging. Since 2016 it has become clear that other states are willing to go well beyond their own nationals and target the general population of a country. In this sense, the internet is being used not only to attack people, but the very institutions that make our democracy work. How states, specifically Russia, engage in sophisticated disinformation operations, and how this has created new threats to Canada's national security, will be the focus of chapter 7.

7

Disinformation and Threats to Democratic Institutions

> The new joke in town is that Russia leaked the disastrous DNC e-mails, which should never have been written (stupid), because Putin likes me.[1]

Presidential candidate Donald Trump may not have known at the time, but the premise of his tweet was not a joke. We now know that as early as 2015, Russia had decided to interfere in U.S. politics and by July 2016 was directing its efforts to convincing the American electorate to elect Trump as President of the United States. Western countries were still dealing with the shock "Leave" victory in the Brexit referendum earlier that year when Trump managed to defeat Democratic candidate Hillary Clinton, defying the expectations of the majority of commentators. Indeed, at the time, Trump's election seemed to be the culmination of a rising far-right/populist wave that admired his economic populism and his appeals to anti-immigrant sentiments.

Perhaps nothing has brought the national security threat of "clandestine foreign influence" into the mainstream more than the subsequent investigation into Russian efforts to influence the 2016 U.S. election. Governments and security services had spent most of the previous four years focused on problems related to the Islamic State, foreign fighters, and cyber-espionage. Information technology was supposed to be disrupting autocratic power, not enhancing it: Twitter and Facebook should be challenging Putin, not shaking the basis of democratic institutions in the West. Now it was being turned against them.

Chapter 6 detailed the extent to which states engage in in-person clandestine foreign influence operations. Today, several states, particularly Russia, have adopted online tools to enhance their clandestine foreign influence operations. In the 1980s it may have taken years for a Soviet spy to circulate a conspiracy theory, using obscure left-leaning newspapers during the war. Now, notions of impending civil war and economic calamity in the West can be circulating in hours.

This chapter will examine the threat of online clandestine foreign influence by examining the methods used by Russia to interfere in the politics of the United States and other Western countries as well. It is a bit different from other chapters in this book, which have often started with a historical overview of the problem in the Canadian experience. However, in this case such an approach does not make much sense: online clandestine foreign influence activities are less than a decade old and have only really begun to manifest in a directly harmful way since around 2014. In this sense, the nature of the threat and how it has developed over the last decade will be emphasized below. This includes the salience of hybrid warfare, a proliferation of like-minded online communities receptive to information that confirms their beliefs on social media, and the opportunity to practise these new techniques on an unsuspecting American public in the lead up to the 2016 election. The chapter then looks at how this has manifested in Canada in recent years as well as steps the government is taking to counter the threat. It concludes by looking at how this threat is likely to evolve.

Bot or Not? A Preliminary Note of Caution

As details about the Russian clandestine foreign influence operation targeting the United States have become public, much has been made of the social media element – especially the idea that there are powerful Russian "bots" capable of targeting and changing the minds of millions. In this sense, what we know of Russia's efforts has been surrounded by a narrative about social media, algorithms, and technology interacting with propaganda as having hacked minds and attacked our democracy.[2]

Several scholars have pushed back against this narrative. Researchers at Harvard point to the fact that the American "right-wing media ecosystem," which they argue operates differently from other mainstream sources of information, had a greater impact in 2016 than either Russian disinformation efforts or far-right conspiracy theorists. In this sense bots act as "background noise, and do not change the structure of the conversation."[3] Alexander Lanoszka argues that despite the concerns over disinformation, there is no evidence that it changes behaviour at a strategic level (a state's alignment or armament decisions), or that it changes the pre-existing ideological commitments of a population.[4]

While this chapter presents the role of social media as very important to Moscow's disinformation operations since 2014, I agree that it is important to avoid technological-determinist explanations for what took place. There were almost certainly a range of factors that contributed to Brexit, the success of far-right parties across Europe, and the election of Trump. Human agency is important and cannot be ignored: whole personalities are not changed by a few advertisements on Facebook or a series of tweets spreading misinformation about Hillary Clinton's health. It is hard to hack a human brain.

Nevertheless, from a national security perspective, such arguments miss the key point of why states are concerned: it is not that clandestine influence operations are successful, but that these efforts exist at all. Indeed, it would be inappropriate (at best!) for national security and intelligence agencies to assess how and why voters chose one political candidate over another in their own country. But once an attempt to engage in clandestine foreign influence operations is discovered, it is the job of a state's security services to get to the bottom of it and (potentially) stop it from occurring in the first place. No matter the impact of Russia's efforts to meddle in the democracies of the West, it is worth understanding how such operations work and trying to disrupt them.

Here an analogy may be made with terrorism: if a security service discovers a bomb plot, it will likely do something about it, even if the wannabe violent extremists are not exactly competent. From a national security perspective, it is problematic that they are involved in this activity at all – and there is always the risk they could get lucky. Similarly, states will want to monitor and counter most clandestine foreign influence campaigns, regardless of their effectiveness; the attempt is a threat and the malicious actors could have an effect.

Clandestine Foreign Influence in the Digital Age

For decades states have recognized the transformational power of the internet. Since the creation of ARPANET (named for the U.S. Advanced Research Projects Agency that developed it) in southern California in the 1960s, the ability to link computers and store and share information was seen as revolutionary and likely to transform most aspects of society – although no one was quite sure how.[5] Would the internet be a lawless, anarchical space, free from government power, or an enabler of a surveillance society where authorities could seize control and track their citizens even more effectively?

So far the material in this book suggests the answer to this question is not yet clear – the internet has provided violent extremist entities with platforms upon which to spread their propaganda and recruit members, but it has also enabled states such as China to directly monitor its population, inside and outside its borders. It also creates new challenges that democratic states must grapple with – such as ethically managing large amounts of available data on its citizens. At the beginning of the 2020s, the West is in the throes of intense debates over privacy and security while, concomitantly, authoritarian states are engaged in a game of cat and mouse played between the establishment and online activists.

At the very least, it can be said that the internet has required states to adjust almost every aspect of the way they do business. Taylor Owen notes that while digital technologies do not mean the end of the state, their powers are now in question. "The state is losing its status as the pre-eminent mechanism for collective action. Where it used to be that the state had a virtual monopoly on the ability to shape the behaviour of a large number of people, this is no longer the case. Enabled by digital technology, disruptive innovators are now able to influence the behaviour of large numbers of people without many of the social constraints that have developed around state action."[6]

There is much to be said for this argument, but developments since 2015 (when Owen's book was published) mean it requires qualification. States have reacted differently to the disruptive power of digital technologies – and some have had a lot more success in countering them than they had ever been anticipated. It was once thought impossible to control the internet – that the amount of technology and labour required would make such a goal unachievable. President Bill Clinton famously stated in 2000 that trying to censor the digital world was like "trying to nail Jell-O to a wall." And yet, some states have done just that – China has championed "internet sovereignty," effectively an unprecedented censorship and surveillance project that has made divergence from the party-state line in the digital realm extremely difficult, not to mention very risky for those who dare try. Chinese authorities were able to accomplish the seemingly impossible through what has come to be known as the "Great Firewall of China," which effectively keeps foreign content out. It pressed major internet companies like Google to follow a strict set of censorship guidelines, forcing the company to mostly (but not entirely) abandon its business in that country.[7]

Moreover, as a country without significant privacy rights or protections, China requires all internet service providers and mobile companies to hand over information at the government's request. It also requires users to register social media accounts with their real names and phone numbers, creating a drop in anonymous posting. Those accused of spreading "online rumours" are arrested and publicly prosecuted for their transgressions.[8] In 2018 China passed a sweeping cybersecurity law that centralizes all internet policy within the Cyberspace Administration of China (CAC). This has been followed by near-daily directives that dictate what individuals can and cannot do online and worked to eliminate virtual private networks

(VPNs) that could potentially hide a user's identity and location.[9] There are also concerns that private "social credit" systems are being used to control and monitor Chinese citizens.[10]

Russia shares similar authoritarian goals for cyberspace, albeit not to the same extent as China. There is credible opposition to Putin in Russia, but it is often met with a determined effort to suppress it.[11] Russian law requires that ISPs have monitoring devices (known as SORM boxes, a Russian acronym for "operative search measures") that monitor phone calls, emails, internet usage, video chats, text messages, and social networks.[12] This gives security services the ability to heavily monitor their population or use collected information as blackmail or in disinformation operations to discredit opponents and ideas. Similar to China, Russia has put pressure on foreign social media companies, such as Google and Twitter, as well as Russian-owned ones, VKontakte and the search engine Yandex.[13] In July 2017 Russia took steps to restrict VPNs and banned the social network platform Telegram, as it refused to make encrypted data accessible to the FSB.[14]

In both Russia and China, efforts to control the online space have mirrored those to control television, radio, and other forms of traditional media.[15] Given the lofty talk of free-flowing information and challenges to authority, it should come as no surprise that authoritarian countries try to limit the impact of the technologies they have been warned about. What is surprising, however, is the success they have had in doing so. Certainly these are not perfect systems of control, and protestors find ways to get around heavily monitored systems. One need think only of the open-source investigators who discovered Russian soldiers posting pictures from Crimea, despite state insistence that there were no troops in the region.[16] Or the efforts of journalists at the investigative reporting site Bell¿ngcat who used open-source information to track down the names, positions, and even the passports of Russian intelligence officers linked to the 2018 chemical attack on UK residents in Salisbury.[17] Nevertheless, there has been an obvious negative impact on freedom of speech and expression in these countries. Indeed, far from challenging the state, the internet has enabled the surveillance and control of citizens in many parts of the world. If disruptive technologies have forced states to choose between seeking absolute control and accepting greater uncertainty,[18] authoritarian states are choosing the former – and it seems to be working.

So how is this relevant to a book on Canadian national security threats? Two main issues should concern Western states, including Canada. First, Russia and China are not only working to control the internet in their own countries, they are exporting the software and techniques they have learned to other aspiring authoritarian states who also seek "internet sovereignty." This, according to a 2018 report by Freedom House, includes supplying telecommunication hardware, advanced facial-recognition technology, and data-recognition tools to a variety of governments, many of which have poor human rights records.[19] Countries that have purchased this equipment include Azerbaijan, Ecuador, Kazakhstan, Kyrgyzstan, Malaysia, Pakistan, Rwanda, Uzbekistan, Venezuela, and Zimbabwe.[20] This goes against Canada's interest in ensuring a free and fair internet and the protection of human rights worldwide.

Moreover, there are concerns that the systems being sold may be accessible to the intelligence systems of the countries that built them, especially China.[21] In addition, Ukraine and former Soviet states are believed to use Russian-designed systems to maintain control over digital technologies.[22] In this way, far from just a business opportunity, selling this technology to countries throughout the world helps to strengthen the arguments of Russia and China for vast internet censorship and authoritarian repression.

A second reason that this is important is that both China and Russia have learned how to manage, if not control, the information space, by experimenting on their own countries. Increasingly, they are adopting these tactics and using them beyond their borders. In chapter 6, China's willingness to use Chinese-language social media to target people outside its borders was reviewed. And as discussed above, Russia has used its control over the physical infrastructure of the internet to control the way its citizens are able to access and engage online. Interference in the U.S. election of 2016 represents evidence that there has been a significant evolution in how clandestine foreign operations are conducted. Here it is not simply diaspora populations that are targeted. Through cyberattacks and clandestine efforts, Russia sought to undermine the integrity of democratic institutions and processes more broadly.

Online Clandestine Foreign Influence: How Did We Get Here?

Several books and studies have examined the history of how disinformation has come to dominate contemporary Western politics.[23] Rather than repeat this history, I will focus on three important trends that contributed to the rise of the current national security threat of disinformation in Canada: the salience of the hybrid warfare concept, the formation of like-minded communities via social media, and the early successes of state and non-state actors in exploiting these two trends.

Hybrid Warfare

Since 2014 it has been common to use the concept of hybrid warfare to describe a sequence of overt, clandestine, and covert measures taken by states and non-state actors across domains to achieve their political ends. Not that the concept is universally accepted: there is a divide among those who study the concept about whether it is something new,[24] something old,[25] something conceptually incoherent,[26] or a distraction.[27] If there is anything those writing about hybrid war agree upon it is that there is no standard definition, and that the term can be applied to a range of conflicts, actors, and tactics.[28]

Nevertheless, the concept has become useful for describing the way that Western countries have perceived and responded to threats and challenges that do not easily meet conventional definitions. Frank Hoffman, a retired lieutenant colonel and fellow at National Defense University in Washington, DC, is perhaps the greatest champion of the concept in the West. Hoffman describes hybrid wars as incorporating "a range of different modes of warfare including conventional capabilities, irregular tactics and formations, terrorist acts including indiscriminate violence and coercion and criminal disorder."[29] Other definitions take a similar view, typically highlighting the blending of different forms of warfare and destabilization. Guillaume Lasconjarias and Jeffrey A. Larsen at the NATO Defense College in Rome describe hybrid warfare as "the true combination and blending of various means of conflict, both regular and unconventional, dominating the physical and psychological battlefield with information and media control, using every possible means to reduce one's exposure."[30] Robert Wilkie suggests, "It is conflict in which states or nonstate actors exploit all modes of war simultaneously by using advanced conventional weapons, irregular tactics, terrorism, and disruptive technologies or criminality to destabilize an existing order."[31] Writing from a Canadian perspective, researchers at Defence Research and Development Canada (DRDC), Neil Chuka and Jean François Born take a (deliberately) broad view of the concept suggesting it is "a conflict in which at least one belligerent employs organized military, paramilitary, and non-state (irregular) forces simultaneously, coordinating multiple forms of warfare as one means in a more-or-less comprehensive strategy meant to achieve a political end."[32]

While there is variation, ideas of what constitutes "hybrid warfare" tend to converge on the following four points:

1. the blending of different (or all) forms of warfare: the lines between regular and irregular forces are blurring and bending into new modes of conflict, increasing the lethality and agility of hybrid forces;
2. the blending of battlespace: hybrid forces are seen as not just present on the battlefield, but in the virtual realm, using cyberspace, targeting social and traditional media, as well as financial institutions and critical infrastructure;
3. the rejection of the traditional distinction between the military, criminals, and civilians: the nature of hybrid tactics requires viewing civilians as targets, exploiting criminals and criminal networks and utilizing special operations forces, guerrillas, and/or irregular troops (clandestinely supported by conventional forces) who hide within the other two; and

4. the rejection of the traditional limits on warfare: given all of the above, hybrid actors neither respect nor follow the law of armed conflict. There is little to no differentiation between soldiers and civilians in physical and virtual targeting. Indeed, many efforts are aimed at civilian populations.

Although aimed at militaries, there is a clear overlap with the themes of this book: the blending of battlespaces, rejection of distinctions and limits, and targeting of civilians (particularly through information operations) means there is a clear national security nexus to hybrid war. In this sense, the response to hybrid warfare does not rest solely with the military. It necessitates a range of government tools to counter these efforts.

NON-STATE ACTORS AS HYBRID WARRIORS

Although hybrid warfare is typically associated with Russia's efforts in Ukraine and in its attempts to meddle in Western democracies today, the first uses of the term were applied to non-state actors, especially Hizballah's tactics in the 2006 Lebanon War.[33] During the fight, Hizballah drew the militarily superior Israel Defense Forces into a ground campaign where they struggled to deal with the militia. The group was able to do so by fusing militia units, specially trained fighters, and anti-tank guided missile units, the use of information warfare, signals intelligence, operational and tactical rockets, and armed UAVs. Of this campaign, Hoffman notes, "Hezbollah's leaders describe their force as a cross between an army and a guerrilla force, and believe they have developed a new model."[34]

The success of the Islamic State in Iraq and Syria has also been characterized as an example of hybrid warfare.[35] Declaring itself independent from Al Qaida in 2014, the group quickly demonstrated that it could combine traditional military tactics, insurgency, and information warfare to achieve its aims, albeit temporarily. With plausible claims of having up to 100,000 fighters, the group utilized combat capabilities, as well as considerable intelligence and reconnaissance skills based on sophisticated networks of informants and supporters.[36] As such, it was able to overwhelm Iraqi forces in the north of that country and take advantage of the Syrian civil war to establish a territory that at one point was as large as Britain.

Moreover, to support its efforts, the group demonstrated tremendous aptitude and proficiency in wielding social media to spread its propaganda in ways that had not been seen before from a nonstate actor. By one account, the Islamic State had almost fifty different media hubs, targeting different regions and audiences that were pushed out by thousands of social media accounts.[37] As social media companies began to crack down on the Islamic State's online presence, the group turned to widely available encrypted messaging platforms like Telegram to spread its message. While success on the battlefield helped its reputation among aspiring-jihadi audiences, the Islamic State was well aware that its propaganda operations were central to its operations.

In April 2016 the group circulated a document on its encrypted social media channels called "Media Operative, You Are a Mujahid, Too," updating its guidance on how individuals around the world could support the Islamic State's operations. According to terrorism researcher Charlie Winter, the document served two ends: it reassured individuals involved in propaganda, rather than direct fighting, that they were full participants, and it re-engaged a virtual caliphate in the struggle. This was helped by the fact that ISIS did not differentiate between "official" and "unofficial" efforts.[38] Moreover, the document makes clear that the Islamic State's approach to media was well planned and strategic. It called for a three-pronged strategy, using a combination of positive messages, "counterspeech" operations that targeted the media of "the enemy," and a weaponization of propaganda against not just militaries but civilian populations as well.[39]

Social media were not useful for just spreading propaganda; the Islamic State used it for a variety of operational purposes. First, the sheer volume of material it put out helped the group dominate and suppress other extremist groups online, ensuring that its message was the one both the curious and committed saw first. Online Islamic State operatives could then reach out to those who seemed receptive to their message to convince them to travel to the so-called caliphate.[40] In some cases this included directly facilitating travel.

Social media platforms like Ask.FM were used to spread "guides" on how individuals in the West could travel to Syria or support the cause from home. Individuals in Syria could provide advice on everything from what to pack and how much money to take, to how to avoid suspicion and best routes to travel. The group also hijacked trending topics in order to garner attention for itself. As noted in chapter 5, Islamic State supporters on Twitter used the Halifax Security Forum's hashtag (#HIS2014) to circulate a propaganda video featuring a British captive and sent direct messages to the forum's participants in 2014.[41] In this sense, social media went beyond radicalizing propaganda, facilitating mobilization as well. These efforts made real contributions to its efforts on the ground and to the overall strategy of blending battlespaces.

RUSSIA

From a Western perspective, the most serious threat of hybrid warfare comes from Russia, especially after the invasion of Crimea in 2014. Importantly, as Ofer Fridman notes, the Russian notion of hybrid warfare is different from what is typically used in the West. Whereas the latter thinks of hybrid warfare in terms of operational tactics and the hybridization of different military means, tactics, and technologies, the former takes a view of what they call *gibridnaya voyna* that is aimed more at society. This includes a wider appreciation of non-military means, an emphasis on trying to destroy an enemy indirectly from within rather than through direct physical confrontation, and emphasizes information warfare.[42]

In the West, Russia's hybrid warfare is often described as the "Gerasimov Doctrine," named after the Russian chief of the General Staff, Valery Gerasimov, who described his country's approach in a 2013 article titled "The Value of Science in Prediction."[43] Scholars (including Mark Galeotti, who coined the term "Gerasimov Doctrine") argue that this is an exaggeration. Many of the ideas that Gerasimov outlines were already decades old, and his article is best understood as a description of Russian methods rather than a new "doctrine" per se.[44] Nevertheless, Gerasimov's article made clear the extent to which Russian military officials emphasized the use of non-military means in conventional conflicts.

As we saw in chapter 5, Russia has been engaging in modern hybrid operations since the mid-2000s: the use of cyber warfare against Estonia in 2007 and Georgia in 2008, much of which was aimed at generating a psychological blow, falls into this category. One key lesson that Putin appears to have learned is that cyberattacks must hit a certain threshold in their impact before eliciting an international response.[45] As noted above, it was not until Russia invaded Crimea and commenced its ongoing hostile actions in Eastern Ukraine that the concept of hybrid warfare gained a much wider audience.

Yet, despite everything that came before, Russian efforts in Ukraine appear to have taken Western countries by surprise. Essentially, Russia was able to annex Crimea as well as occupy the eastern parts of Ukraine by using tools and tactics cloaked in ambiguity. This made it extremely difficult to mount an effective campaign to counter Russia's actions. Putin was able to get away with his aggression against Ukraine without consequence, even if it was widely known Russia was the source.[46] In particular, much has been made of what the Ukrainians called "little green men," Russian special operations forces in unmarked uniforms who seized government buildings and key infrastructure targets and armed the separatist militia.[47] This was complemented by a series of cyberattacks that began as limited incidents but grew in strength, such as the 2015 "Black Energy" cyberattack that targeted the Ukrainian power grid and the 2017 NotPetya attack that, as discussed in chapter 5, had devastating consequences far beyond that country's borders. The cyber campaign was relentless: in a two-month period in 2016 alone, Ukraine experienced 6,500 cyberattacks, although many appear to have been intended to harass rather than cause serious damage.[48]

These efforts were supported by a wide-ranging disinformation campaign that aimed to change or at least distort the narrative about Ukraine, essentially targeting the truth. There were three main prongs to this information campaign. The first involved the use of Russia's media networks, especially RT (formerly known as Russia Today) to push out stories that claimed Ukrainian brutality against Russian-speaking civilians and pushed conspiracy theories and lies that linked stories of Ukrainian aggression to the United States. These stories, which often included doctored photos and videos, targeted not only Russian-speakers at home and in the Ukraine, but also in the Baltic states who might one day be the objects of further Russian efforts.[49]

Second, a tidal wave of propaganda was unleashed on Ukrainian social media in 2014, including via VKontakte (now banned in Ukraine), Twitter, and YouTube. Online forums used to discuss the conflict were flooded with off-topic posts and inflammatory messages meant to disrupt communication.[50] As Russian investigative journalists Andrei Soldatov and Irina Borogan observed, these Russian social media trolls did not come from nowhere – they were directed by Russian "troll farms" that comprised individuals paid over 25,000 roubles (approximately $900 per month) to attack online spaces where issues related to the Ukraine might be discussed.[51] "In the 2000s they were used inside Russia against liberal and independent media bloggers. Now this army, hundreds of people, was directed outside."[52]

The "troll farms" that Soldatov and Borogan were writing about in 2015 became known as the "Internet Research Agency." This organization, funded by Russian oligarchs, was established around 2013 to help assert the Kremlin's control over the internet and away from digital activists.[53] Run out of an office in Olgino in St. Petersburg, dozens of workers were employed to write blog content or inflammatory content on the web. Emboldened by the success of its efforts against the Ukraine, the Kremlin began to direct operations against Western media outlets with trolls that overwhelmed content moderators in the United Kingdom, France, and Italy. This was the third prong of the Kremlin's disinformation campaign. More importantly, these efforts moved beyond comment boards and towards disrupting Western democracies, beginning as early as 2014.

Polarized Like-Minded Communities

A second phenomenon that played a role in the rise of online clandestine foreign influence is like-minded communities driven by social media, often described as "echo chambers" or "filter bubbles,"[54] which have polarized and contributed to an online tribalism that can be exploited by hostile foreign state and non-state actors. There is not the space to fully address the complex sociological aspects of this issue, which can be described as "homophily" (love of the same),[55] "selective exposure,"[56] or "preference bubbles,"[57] where people constantly feed on and seek more of what they like in the virtual world. Here two issues contribute to this phenomenon that should be highlighted for the purpose of this chapter. First, the rise of curated newsfeeds driven by personal preference and algorithms that provide users with content designed to keep them online and engaged. Social science research has shown that while individuals have an incentive to seek information that better informs them, they tend to prefer what confirms their "priors" or pre-existing beliefs.[58] Not only can people seek out and find information that suits their tastes, social media platforms like Twitter, Youtube, and Facebook are engineered to cater to the tastes and predispositions of users.

Second, not only do individuals prefer consuming content they agree with, they are far more likely to share it with others. Even these others are automatically filtered, however. Facebook friend networks tend to be ideologically segregated. The friend set of individuals who provide a political affiliation on Facebook comprised only 18–20 per cent of those with differing opinions. As such, individuals who get much of their news from Facebook receive it from persons who already share their beliefs, confirming their world view.[59]

These developments are important, as over half of social medial users rely on social media to get their news (although studies suggest that in 2016 only 12–14 per cent of adults used it as their primary source).[60] If individuals exist in reality-distorting bubbles, sending and receiving news that does not challenge their beliefs, they are likely to receive a skewed view of local and world events. In some cases, this has led to such bizarre groups as the "flat-earthers" who deny the earth is round. In other cases, the consequences could be dangerous – "anti-vaxxers," who believe that vaccines cause autism, despite overwhelming scientific evidence that disputes their claims. Sadly, the outbreak of measles in several Western countries has followed the rise of anti-vaccination propaganda online.

It is not only that the content is spread among the like-minded, it is that the quality of this content is often very poor. While much of this content is often described as "fake news," it is perhaps better described as "junk news," which researchers at the Oxford Internet Institute describe as "news sources that deliberately publish misleading, deceptive or incorrect information purporting to be real news about politics, economics or culture. This content includes ideologically extreme, hyper-partisan or conspiratorial news and information, as well as various forms of propaganda."[61] Although the content is not often about politics, when it is, the levels of engagement evident within the material has been described by researchers as superficial and emotionally driven, rather than substantive and rational.[62] Nevertheless, junk news content is very popular. A study that compared the sharing of stories deemed "false" and "true" on Twitter found that "falsehood diffused significantly farther, faster, deeper and more broadly than the truth in all categories of information, and the effects were more pronounced for false political news than for false news about terrorism, natural disasters, science, urban legends or financial information."[63]

It is hard to identify why junk news has been so successful in attracting attention, but research points to several possible factors. First, as discussed above, algorithms and like-minded groups that are eager to provide information to individuals interested in confirming what they already think is one factor. Second, the dire financial state of many (if not most) newsrooms means they are ill-equipped to counter falsehoods, as fewer resources are devoted to fact-checking.[64] Worse, in order to generate advertising revenue, they may even be incentivized to create content that consumers are more likely to click on – often described as clickbait. These are stories that are not designed primarily to convey factually accurate information, but to provoke an emotional response that will increase the likelihood, intensity, and duration of engagement with the content.[65] Similarly, researchers of the falsehood study cited above have hypothesized that false stories tended to be more "novel" and provoke strong emotional reactions, whereas true stories inspired "sadness, joy and trust."[66] In this way, junk news is designed to appeal to the human impulse to engage with and share what we think is true and interesting about the world.

Finally, junk news may perform well, relative to mainstream audiences, because there is simply so much of it. Junk news is generated from a number of sources. First, researchers Hunt Allcott and Matthew Gentzkow suggest that, on occasion, genuinely satirical articles have been interpreted as legitimate news stories when viewed out of context.[67] A second and more common source is sites that print intentionally fabricated and misleading articles. This may be done to generate revenue through sensationalized clickbait headlines. Famously, it was discovered in 2016 that much of the popular junk news aimed at the United States was coming from teenagers in a small town in Macedonia looking to make money.[68] Alternatively, it may be done to serve partisan or ideological ends and to help a particular political campaign. As the barriers to entry to produce junk news are low – it simply requires individuals to semi-plagiarize outlandish claims and conspiracy theories on a large scale – it should not be surprising that it is seen as a money-maker.[69]

Other forms of sharable online content in like-minded communities include memes. Memes are material that represents an idea, behaviour, style, or usage that spreads from person to person within a culture, and these days on social media. They often come in the form of easily sharable pictures and short moving graphics called "GIFs," virtually guaranteeing that anyone who has been on social media has seen one. Memes are designed to quickly relay a joke (often an in-joke), ironic point, or political message. They can easily become "meta," that is, memes that have evolved to replicate other viral content that is circulating online.

In most cases, memes are harmless fun: the well-known LOLCats phenomenon often features funny pictures of cats with bold text in "lolspeak" – a made-up cat-grammar – such as "I can haz cheezburger?"[70] In other cases, memes can be used to convey shorthand nods to racist ideas and in-jokes. Perhaps the most notorious example of this was Pepe the Frog, taken up by the alt-right and far-right supporters. Pepe is highly adaptable and can be redrawn to represent or reference Donald Trump, members of the alt-right movement, Harambe,[71] the pope, or internet culture itself. In 2019 he became a symbol of democratic resistance in Hong Kong.[72] Unfortunately, in the West, Pepe is often portrayed in racist and anti-Semitic forms, such as a persecuted Jew, victim of the Holocaust, Nazi soldier, Adolf Hitler, or a member of the Ku Klux Klan.[73] While this will be discussed further below, the key takeaway is that, like junk news, extremist and ideological memes have been used to further polarize like-minded communities.[74]

The rise of like-minded communities online and the spread of memes and junk news has contributed to two related changes. First, the creation of agents primed, willing, and able to share content that confirms their world view, whether the information is true, false, or offensive. Second, as the truthfulness of information has become less relevant, greater importance has been placed on "winning" rather than being proven correct.[75] In this case, winning is simply about dominating the discourse through reproduction and spreading of a certain narrative rather than proving its accuracy. And, as noted above, given our human instinct to share what we agree to with a network of like-minded people, this is not hard to accomplish.

An example of this phenomenon in Canada occurred in April 2018, when a CBC journalist tweeted two contradictory pieces of information following the Toronto van attack (briefly discussed in chapter 1). In the first, the journalist tweeted that the attacker looked "angry" and "Middle Eastern," and the second as "white" (which was correct). However, the erroneous tweet was picked up and retweeted many thousands of times more than the tweet with the correct information. In effect, a small group of Twitter users were able to propagate false information many more times than the accurate account, garnering a "win" for their preferred view.[76]

THE ALT-RIGHT AND DISINFORMATION

No group has mastered the spread of disinformation and junk news more than the alt-right. The far-right was discussed in chapters 1 and 2 as a growing violent extremist threat in Canada, but it is worth briefly revisiting the manifestation of the online alt-right as it relates to discussions of disinformation. Although there have been several definitions of the term, Angela Nagle provides a useful summary: "The alt-right is, to varying degrees, preoccupied with IQ, European demographic and civilizational decline, cultural decadence, cultural Marxism, anti-egalitarianism and Islamification but most importantly, as the name suggests, with creating an alternative to the right-wing conservative establishment, who they dismiss as 'cuckservatives' for their soft Christian passivity and for metaphorically cuckholding their womenfolk/nation/race to the non-white foreign invader."[77]

As Nagle notes, the alt-right made its online debut through lengthy treaties on obscure blogs. However, for their ideas to spread and connect to the mainstream, they had to make a connection to "the image- and humor-based culture of the irreverent meme factory of 4chan and later 8chan [image-based bulletin boards with few to no limits of what users may publish] that gave the alt-right its youthful energy, with its transgression and hacker tactics."[78] Through circles of in-jokes and responses to responses, these like-minded communities are able to evade direct interpretation and judgment through tricks and layers of metatextual self-awareness and irony, signalling their own communities while baffling others.[79] These groups can still be effective propagators. As researchers Alice Marwick and Rebecca Lewis note, far-right groups have mastered the techniques used by 4chan/8chan to "attention hack," or increase the visibility of their ideas through the use of social media, as well as by targeting journalists, bloggers, and influencers in an effort to spread content.[80]

For the alt-right, these tactics have proven useful. In seeking to bring about the political change they desire, they have harnessed like-minded communities with a view to bringing about cultural change. Alt-right activists and their sympathizers have been able to produce, promote, and spread content in volumes that frequently surpass engagements from traditional media sources, thus muddying the information environment. (As noted in chapter 1, many of these alt-right content producers are Canadian, including Faith Goldy, Gavin McInnes, and Laura Southern.) Researchers at the Oxford Internet Institute argue that coordinated efforts to distribute "fake news" stories contributed to increased polarization and cynicism that influenced traditional media, observing that the *New York Times* and *Washington Post* covered alt-right conspiracy theories about Hillary Clinton far more than Trump's actual ties to Russia or the allegations of sexual assault made against him.[81]

In summary, social media has facilitated the rise of like-minded communities primed to share content that confirms their pre-existing beliefs, whether it is true or false. This content is emotionally rewarding to people, reassuring rather than challenging – it strengthens priors and helps individuals avoid the cognitive dissonance they might encounter if confronted with information that challenges their beliefs.[82] Moreover, in these communities it is more important to be seen as winning than to be seen as correct. This may be accomplished by amplifying the group's ideas and preferences while suppressing alternative narratives. Groups will flood social media sites, overwhelming different views with their own content. With a plentiful trove of clickbait junk news, the result is a system where the truth has been devalued and falsehoods skew actual news coverage. In this way, the alt-right has increasingly mirrored the tactics of authoritarian states in the way they try to amplify and suppress information online.[83]

This is not exactly what digital-evangelists had planned. As Angela Nagle notes, while some once spoke of the "wisdom of crowds" or the idea of an upcoming network society where old practices would be replaced by swarms, the "hive-mind," and citizen journalism, the opposite appears to have taken place. Fuelled by clickbait populism that targets like-minded communities, the views of experts can be attacked and suppressed using viral content originating from obscure corners of the internet.[84]

Practice Makes Perfect

A series of successful campaigns allowed Russia to experiment and hone its disinformation techniques before directing its online activities against the West. In March 2014 Twitter accounts with links to Russia began promoting a petition on the WhiteHouse.gov website calling for the United States to give Alaska back to Russia. In a few days, it was able to gather more than 39,000 signatures online.[85] The bots involved in this campaign were closely tied to ones pushing out propaganda on the Syrian war that reflected Russia's foreign policy priorities.[86] After this incident, the Kremlin sought to promote conspiracy theories, amplify divisive narratives, and sow confusion about the news to suit its agenda. These early steps took advantage of a free and open Western internet as well as social media platforms with lax regulations about what could be said on their platforms. Unleashing the Internet Research Agency on a host of like-minded communities, these efforts produced tangible results and real-world consequences.

Promoting Conspiracy Theories

One of Russia's first salvos was a campaign that used RT videos on Youtube. In the first instance, content was produced to go viral and attract users.[87] Many of these videos featured live footage of natural disasters, animal videos, and accidents. Others were aimed at spreading conspiracy theories that reflected Russian views or, at the very least, would be damaging to the West. These included videos suggesting the West, and particularly the United States, was behind much of the world's political violence and plots linking migration to the "Islamization" of the Western world. In addition, RT columns on their website frequently promoted stories about the Illuminati, as well as anti-Semitic and anti-Western conspiracies.[88]

Russian-linked social media accounts also began amplifying conspiracy theories that were already emerging in the dark corners of the internet. Others were planted. In 2014 several dozen Russian troll accounts began tweeting that there had been an explosion at a chemical plant in Louisiana. Some even attributed the fabricated attack to the Islamic State. Attempts were made to alter photographs and create fake news accounts to make the effort more convincing. In December of that year, many of the same Twitter accounts used to spread the fake Columbia Chemicals incident began to post about an outbreak of Ebola in Atlanta. This attempt was accompanied by a YouTube video that appeared to show hazmat-suited workers transporting individuals from the Atlanta airport. The same day, different Russian accounts began tweeting that an unarmed Black woman had been shot to death by police, accompanied by a blurry video.[89]

The most infamous of the pre-2016 conspiracy theories that Russia amplified was the notion that a military exercise run by U.S. Special Operations Command called Jade Helm 15 was part of a secret plan to establish martial law and round up political dissidents in Texas. Promoted by a series of bloggers, personalities, and conspiratorial websites such as Infowars, Russian accounts began a campaign to amplify the Jade Helm conspiracy.[90] Eventually, the idea that there was a secret government plot to take over Texas became so popular that several hundred protestors showed up to shout down a U.S. Army officer giving a briefing of the event, and Texas Governor Greg Abbott deployed the Texas National Guard to monitor the U.S. military exercise to ensure there was no annexation taking place.[91] This was possibly the first success Russia had in helping to translate conspiracy theories into real-life actions in the United States.

Amplifying Division

When not promoting conspiracy theories, RT videos foment division and create confusion, doubt, and mistrust. A 2014 report of Russia's disinformation campaign found that it was amplifying far-left anti-globalists, far-right nationalist party leaders, and Julian Assange in a wide range of videos. These videos attracted audiences by broadcasting anti-U.S. and anti-Western themes and messages as well as the conspiracy videos discussed above. They also frequently featured questionable experts promoting conspiracy theories and outright racist ideas. In some cases, Holocaust deniers were presented as human rights activists and neo-Nazis as Middle East analysts. As the report's authors Peter Pomerantsev and Michael Weiss note, "Validating this approach is the idea, frequently articulated by senior management at RT, that there is no such thing as 'objective truth.' This concept is quickly stretched to mean that any opinion, however bizarre, has the same weight as others."[92] In challenging the truth, RT could present guests and "experts" with extremist views, amplifying their arguments without ever really facing any consequences for doing so.

Sowing Confusion

On 17 July 2014, Malaysia Airlines Flight MH17, flying from Amsterdam to Kuala Lumpur, was shot down while flying over Eastern Ukraine, killing all 298 persons on board. Just four months after the outbreak of the hybrid war between Russia and Ukraine, suspicion quickly turned to parties in the conflict as responsible for the blast. As evidence mounted that pro-Russia separatists were responsible, Russian outlets began a media blitz suggesting that Ukrainian rebels were responsible for the tragedy. When those efforts failed, the Kremlin offered bogus-alternative explanations. By June 2019 an EU-sponsored effort detected over 120 pro-Kremlin disinformation cases on MH17, including the idea that the victims were individuals who were already dead, suggesting MH17 was actually MH370 (a flight that had disappeared over the Indian Ocean in March 2014). And where those excuses were not accepted, pro-Kremlin accounts turned to accusing others of Russophobia and counter-accusations.[93]

Importantly, while these narratives were pushed by pro-Kremlin media outlets, everyday individuals appear to have played a considerable role in amplifying them on social media. Researchers in Denmark who examined pro-Kremlin tweets on MH17 speculate that audiences may have been attracted to the hyper-sensationalist headlines used to spread disinformation, reflecting earlier research findings (noted above) that falsehoods tend to spread faster and farther than true news stories. They also suggest that anti-globalist and anti-EU social media users attracted to the Kremlin's self-presentation as a challenge to global and EU-elites may simply have been attracted to the political message and wanted to spread it further.[94] Pomerantsev and Weiss argue that, by 2015, RT videos were increasingly finding salience with conspiracy-minded groups and individuals in Europe, suggesting that the Kremlin's goal of making critical, reality-based discourse difficult on certain issues might be succeeding.[95]

While scholars still dispute the overall impact of these efforts on the politics of the West, there is evidence that Moscow's efforts had an effect. A study by researchers at Harvard (which is sceptical of the "Russian bot" narrative overall), found that the alt-right conspiracy website Infowars was the eighth-most-tweeted site in the 2016 U.S. right-wing media ecosystem, and it regularly republished RT content.[96] We can actually trace this process in action with reference to at least one prominent conspiracy theory. A 2019 investigation by reporter Michael Isikoff found that the Russian Foreign Intelligence

Service (Sluzhba Vneshney Razvedki, or SVR) wrote a "brief" linking the tragic murder of a junior Democratic Party staffer, Seth Rich to Hillary Clinton. This "brief" appeared on a website linked to Russian propaganda that was then picked up by RT and Sputnik, which were, of course, immediately amplified by Internet Research Agency accounts. The conspiracy then found its way into the alt-right media ecosystem and eventually to Fox News.[97] Here we see how Russia was able to get its divisive stories to a large audience, one already primed to believe conspiracy theories.

So What Happened?

Whatever the truth about its efforts, it seems likely that Russia concluded that it achieved certain political ends through its disinformation efforts. Former U.S. military officer and FBI special agent Clint Watts argues that the Jade Helm exercise revealed to the Russians "just how easy social media influence could be with segments of the American public."[98] Former Director of the Central Intelligence Agency and National Security Agency Michael Hayden has said that he believes that the lesson Russia took from Jade Helm was that they could go "big time": "At that point, I think they made the decision, 'We're going to play in the electoral process.'"[99] Soon thereafter, "fluent in American trolling culture,"[100] Russia took its honed social media techniques and directed them towards the Brexit vote in the United Kingdom and the 2016 U.S. presidential election.

Before continuing further, an additional note on human agency is important. There is overwhelming evidence that prior to the 2016 election, Russia was sowing conspiracy theories in the West, amplifying division and creating confusion in order to muddy the waters of truth on issues that were detrimental to its interests. We know that many individuals were attracted to these narratives and brought them into polarized communities where they were shared. In some cases, like Jade Helm, there appear to have been real-world consequences to their amplification campaigns. And RT has become a popular outlet for news on YouTube. All of these are facts that can be observed, studied, and evaluated.

Nevertheless, there are questions that are more difficult to answer. The first is, What is more effective in spreading disinformation: automated sources (such as "bots" and algorithms) or people? The literature is split on the issue, with some scholars arguing that automated content plays a greater role in spreading junk news[101] – the kind that is often weaponized by pro-Kremlin accounts. Others, who trace patterns of online traffic and disinformation, argue that it is spread mostly through human choices, not algorithms.[102] Also in the mix are "cyborg" social media accounts – semi-automated, but with human input, often used to amplify messaging. While there is no clear answer to this question, it is important to avoid simplistic technological determinism in formulating our answers and appreciate the confluence of factors that came together in 2016 to produce shocking results in the West – of which Russian efforts were a part, but not the sole cause.

Deciphering these patterns is important for policymakers looking to protect and promote democratic institutions. Knowing the cause of the problem is necessary to help design programs that counter disinformation techniques. For national security agencies, the most important takeaway is that adversarial states, especially Russia, are using both in an effort to disrupt the online spaces where important political issues are discussed using clandestine foreign influence activities.

Second, while it is possible to trace who spreads Russian information, the rationale for doing so is not always clear. So far this chapter has cited reasons why this might be the case: individuals appear to be attracted to and engage with sensational headlines and information that confirms their world views more than other forms of information. But what attracts an individual online to a pro-Kremlin talking point or conspiracy theory is not well understood. Individuals have agency – they can make up their own minds about what they believe – and encountering a few tweets is not going to fundamentally change someone's world view. Therefore, we cannot automatically assume what the effect of Russian disinformation on the general public is, other than noting that it often appears to be popular among certain groups, particularly right-wing and far-right individuals who are statistically more likely to engage with it.[103]

And yet, for national security agencies the impact of the messaging is not as important as the fact it is taking place; it is the attempt, not the effect that is their mandate. National security and intelligence agencies are not equipped (and it is not clear that they should be) to measure the effect of ideas on society. They do, however, have a mandate to monitor the clandestine activities of foreign actors who have malicious intent against Canadian democratic institutions. That mandate starts when an attempt to engage in clandestine foreign influence is detected – not when it succeeds.

It is important to understand all this in the wake of the 2016 U.S. presidential election. Russian trolls did not elect Trump President of the United States – Americans did. But we know that Russians tried to effect this outcome and that is a problem.

Lessons from 2016

We now understand how Russia engaged in online clandestine foreign influence operations in 2016. Polarized like-minded communities became the perfect target for Russia, who had developed its information warfare techniques during its hybrid campaign in Ukraine and then tested them out on unsuspecting Americans in 2014 and 2015. This set the scene for an unprecedented disinformation operation that, according to the Mueller Report, evolved from an attempt to undermine the U.S. electoral system generally to one that aimed to promote Donald Trump and disparage Hillary Clinton.[104]

Importantly, the online operations were not the only way Russia tried to interfere in the U.S. election. The Mueller Report identifies three main ways influence operations were engaged in. First, the online campaign discussed throughout this chapter. Second, the targeted hacking and dumping operations against Clinton and the Democratic National Committee. Finally, multiple efforts to influence the Trump campaign and those around it. So what are the implications of the Mueller Report's findings for other countries?

Online

We have established that Russia had already begun to engage in a large clandestine foreign influence operation online by 2016. We now know this operation was called the Translator Project and that by July 2016 eighty individuals had been hired to conduct operations on social media platforms. This was part of a larger interference operation funded by a series of layered businesses owned by Russian oligarch Yevgeniy Viktorovich Prigozhin, referred to as Project Lakhta.[105] The result was a series of Facebook and Twitter postings and advertisements that reached hundreds of millions of users, including some that were quoted by news organizations.

Andrew Weisburd, Clint Watts, and J.M. Berger contend that the overall disinformation campaign by Russia has goals very similar to those the Soviet Union aimed to accomplish during the Cold War:

- Undermine citizen confidence in democratic governance;
- Foment and exacerbate divisive political fractures;
- Erode trust between citizens and elected officials and democratic institutions;
- Popularize Russian policy agendas within foreign populations;
- Create general distrust or confusion over information sources by blurring the lines between fact and fiction[106]

This assessment is similar to the Mueller Report's conclusion that the fake Facebook pages and accounts were on specifically divisive issues that emphasized hyper-patriotism, anti-immigration, Black social justice issues, and religious groups.[107] Some of these themes targeted like-minded groups, including those fuelled by far-right grievances and conspiracy theories, and would also appeal to the anti-globalist Left who equally despised Hillary Clinton. These include political (rampant voter fraud, election rigging, and political corruption), financial (instability and imminent market crashes), social issues (natural resources, migration, and police issues), and global calamity (nuclear war, world government conspiracy theories).[108]

Importantly, Weisburd, Watts, and Berger provide a framework for how disinformation campaigns work in the digital age. Whereas Soviet agents had placed stories in left-leaning newspapers during the Cold War, the Kremlin could now exploit a social media ecosystem that it had been cultivating for years. In this way, information travelled from "black" or covert sources – Russian online hecklers who could share and promote narratives – to "grey" sites that laundered covert narratives, placing them on conspiracy-oriented websites, news aggregators, and data-dump websites, and "white" or overt sites, such as Russia's state-owned media sites like RT that could pick up and publish the conspiracies from the grey sites.[109]

Hacking

A second feature of Russia's 2016 efforts to intervene in the U.S. election was hacking operations that targeted the Clinton campaign. As discussed in chapter 5, it is not uncommon for adversarial states to engage in cyber-espionage against political candidates – states often want to know what the policies of the candidates are, as well as the internal discussions a political party may be having. In engaging in cyber-espionage in 2016, however, Russia did not seek to gain information for themselves, but to (selectively) put it on display for the world, with a view to embarrassing a specific candidate or political party.

Russia had engaged in similar behaviour before, intercepting the phone calls of Ukrainian politicians and even U.S. officials and selectively releasing them to compromise and intimidate them.[110] However, the series of attacks on the DNC by Russian military intelligence ("Fancy Bear," the name given to a Russian espionage group associated with the GRU) were unprecedented in the West and devastating for the Clinton campaign. The GRU acquired hundreds of thousands of documents and shared them using the Russian online personas "DCLeaks" and "Guccifer 2.0," and through the willing and eager document dumping site, Wikileaks. Naturally, the release of the emails was promoted by pro-Kremlin bots, to like-minded communities, especially ones that were stridently in opposition to Clinton and were primed to believe conspiracy theories about her.

When "Online" Is "Offline"

The third important lesson to take away from Russia's clandestine foreign influence campaign is the fact that much of what appeared to be "online" involved "offline" tactics. First, it is important to note that a human intelligence operation was mounted in order to research salient political issues that could be targeted and where to target them. The Internet Research Agency sent two employees, Anna Bogacheva and Aleksandra Krylova, to the United States to gather intelligence to inform the social media operations they were planning. They travelled across the United States to gather information. According to a federal indictment, Bogacheva and Krylova spoke with an American affiliated with a "Texas-based grassroots organization" and learned "that they should focus their activities on 'purple states like Colorado, Virginia and Florida.'" From this point, Internet Research Agency personnel began to commonly refer to "targeting purple states" in directing their efforts.[111]

The second way that "online" spilled into "offline" was efforts made by the Internet Research Agency to turn internet outrage into real-life protests and confrontations. Internet Research Agency staff used stolen identities, including birthdates and social security numbers, and fake identification (such as driver's licences) to open PayPal accounts they could use to make purchases, including online advertisements. These fake and fraudulent personas were also used to communicate with unwitting Americans, volunteers, and Trump campaign supporters for a variety of reasons. Fake personas encouraged Trump supporters to (unwittingly) spread Internet Research Agency propaganda, encourage minority groups not to vote or to vote for third-party candidates, and – incredibly – to stage political rallies in the United States. This included several rallies in Florida, New York, Pennsylvania, Texas, and Washington, DC (and several after the election in New York and North Carolina).[112] In May 2016 the Internet Research Agency organized two opposing rallies in Houston, Texas – one against the "Islamification of Texas" and the other to "Save Islamic Knowledge," probably in the hope of sparking real-world confrontation.[113] Importantly, the Internet Research Agency would directly contact Americans and pay for many aspects of the rally, including paying Americans for their efforts. In one case the Internet Research Agency requested that an American build a cage on a flatbed truck and that another wear a costume portraying Clinton in a prison uniform.[114]

Here we see that sophisticated online clandestine influence operations do not depend on just being able to run a convincing network of social media bots. The Russian operation was effective because it understood the online environment prior to 2016, experimented with it, and – importantly – used human intelligence and real-world interactions to influence individuals in ways they felt would disrupt the U.S. election. As such, we should expect any such future campaigns of this magnitude to be complemented by human intelligence efforts.

The Future of Online Clandestine Foreign Influence

As the above section makes clear, Russian efforts can be categorized as a powerful mix of online and hacking operations supported by human intelligence gathering. Understanding this broad framework is important for anticipating how Russia is likely to interfere in other states, including Canada. While these campaigns may look different from the 2016 U.S. election, which was unprecedented in its scale and unique in its success, it is clear that other countries have been the victim of broadly similar efforts. Russia interfered in the 2016 Brexit campaign, supporting the pro-Leave side via social media messaging.[115] The Kremlin also targeted the 2017 French election with its now-familiar toolkit: attacks against presidential candidate Macron on Russian-state media, a serious social media disinformation campaign, and, reportedly, a barrage of 2,000 to 3,000 attempts to hack into the servers of political parties. In addition, the far-right Front Nationale, which shares many of the Kremlin's views, took money from a Russian bank to fund its campaign.[116]

A study of political social media bots in the 2017 German elections found a lower rate of sharing misinformation and automated activity relative to other countries.[117] Nevertheless, there have been clear cases of Russian foreign influence. In January 2016 anti-refugee sentiment was stoked by Russian-controlled media when they covered the story of a thirteen-year-old Russian-German girl who claimed she had been raped by Middle Eastern men. Although German authorities quickly realized the story was fake, it was fanned by Russian propaganda, leading to protests. It was even used by Russian Foreign Minister Sergei Lavrov to allege that the German state was involved in a cover-up.[118] It is also believed that Russia may have been behind a successful hack of the German parliament (Bundestag) in December 2017, although any information taken does not appear to have been released at the time of publication.[119]

In 2019 the *New York Times* revealed the extent to which Russia had been using online and offline clandestine foreign influence operations to bolster Sweden's far-right nationalist and anti-immigration movement. This included paying immigrant youth to "make trouble" in front of cameras for "news" footage. Russia had also helped to nurture a far-right digital ecosystem in Sweden that included closed Facebook groups and far-right junk news sites (responsible for up to 85 per cent of all junk election news in Sweden) that frequently were among the top ten media sites in that country. Investigations of web traffic found, however, that many of the sites had been bolstered by a global network of far-right outlets from outside of Sweden. The benefit of the links is that they help to bolster the Google ranking of the sites, making it more likely that Swedes will find them if they search for issues such as "immigration and crime."[120] While it is difficult to translate these efforts into electoral success, the far-right Sweden Democrats received 18 per cent of the vote in 2018 and they have had success in local elections.

Given the relatively low costs of these operations and their perceived successes, we can assume that they will continue. Even the threat of these operations is enough to be a distraction and generate controversy. As clandestine foreign influence is difficult to prevent, it is likely that Russia (and other countries learning from its experience) will continue to engage in these operations. So what does this mean for a country like Canada?

The Future of Foreign Influence and Implications for Canada

Canada too has been the target of some of these methods, but not (yet) to the same to degree as other Western countries. A 2017 report by the Communications Security Establishment (CSE) found that any attempt to meddle in the 2015 campaign were limited to "low-sophistication cyber threat activity" carried out by hacktivists and cybercriminals, all of which were covered in the Canadian media.[121] Nevertheless, in an updated version of that report in 2019, the CSE stated that it was "very likely" that the 2019 Canadian federal election would be targeted by adversarial state actors, but it was "improbable" that this would look like the 2016 U.S. election. Instead, attempts to meddle were anticipated to look like campaigns in other Western democracies.[122]

Although Russia is likely using the same broad framework of online influence and hacking supported by human intelligence operations in Canada, its specific approach appears to be different from what happened in the 2016 U.S. election. After all, it is not clear that such a campaign would be able to produce similar results in a country like Canada. As some scholars have argued, "Different political systems coming from different historical trajectories and institutional traditions will likely exhibit different effects of the same basic technological affordances."[123] Moreover, countries with a history of placing trust in media outlets (Canada and Germany, for example) may be more resilient against information operations than countries with more dysfunctional media ecosystems.[124]

Fortunately, on the basis of publicly available information, it seems that Canada has not suffered a *major* incident of online clandestine foreign influence at any of its federal or provincial elections between 2016 and 2019. In April 2019 it was reported that servers of political parties in Canada were already being hacked by foreign adversaries who may simply have been curious about their operations, or who might have been engaging in the early stages of a DNC-style attack.[125] In July 2019 it was reported that CSIS was aware of limited ongoing overt and covert attempts to meddle in the 2019 election, although they added that such measures included a broad range of activities.¹²⁶ If Russia, or another country, gained information, they did not make it public.

Nevertheless, an overview of recent online clandestine foreign influence activities targeting Canada, and how they are evolving, makes it clear we are not immune from this threat, even if it may be manifesting differently so far. This includes online disinformation campaigns targeting Canadian institutions, especially the Canadian Armed Forces (CAF), a campaign to discredit politicians, preliminary attempts to amplify divisive issues as seen in other countries, and the targeting of ethnic groups in Canada with propaganda and disinformation.

TARGETING CANADIAN INSTITUTIONS/CAF

Even before 2019 it was clear that Russia was targeting Canada for overt and covert foreign influence operations. Upon arriving in Latvia to lead a NATO mission in June 2017, Canadian troops were met with negative stories propagated by Russian media outlets. They included stories describing Canadian troops as homosexuals and linking them to Russell Williams, a former colonel in the Canadian Air Force convicted of the sexual assaults and murders of several women. Other anti-Canadian "fake news" included reports that Latvians were unhappy about the deployment and that Canadian troops would be walking around the capital, Riga, with guns, creating a public safety threat.¹²⁷ Later, disinformation focused on the idea of Canadians being bad guests who stayed in luxury apartments (at the behest of local taxpayers), littered extensively, and were fixated on buying beer.¹²⁸

In addition, Russia has targeted Canadian troops in Ukraine at least twice, suggesting that troops had been killed by Russian-backed separatist forces. In September 2016 a website linked to a separatist leader in Ukraine reported that eleven Canadians were killed.¹²⁹ In May 2018 stories began to circulate on Russian social media accounts that three Canadian soldiers in Ukraine were killed by a landmine. In this case, the rumour is reported to have spread when the false news was translated into English and then came to the attention of Western media outlets. The Department of National Defence was forced to issue a denial.¹³⁰

Inside Canada, RT covers issues of interest to Canadians and is happy to report political scandals that emphasize narratives about Western government corruption, as seen in other countries. In January 2019 a popular Russian TV host began his show by suggesting that Canada's Ukrainian diaspora (portrayed as the descendants of nationalists and fascists) runs Canada's foreign policy.[131]

TARGETING POLITICIANS

In 2017 Russia tried to target Foreign Minister Chrystia Freeland by passing (publicly available) information to Canadian journalists that her grandfather worked for a nationalist Ukrainian newspaper under the control of the Nazis during the Second World War.[132] When Canada expelled four Russian intelligence officers posing as diplomats in March 2018 (in solidarity with the United Kingdom for the chemical weapons attack in Salisbury) they cited this incident as an example of interference as a partial justification for the expulsion.[133] Almost immediately several journalists and commentators complained that this was not disinformation, but the truth; Freeland's grandfather had been a Nazi collaborator.[134] Nevertheless, from a national security perspective, the methods employed by Russian "diplomats" to amplify this story have the hallmarks of a clandestine foreign influence campaign: approaching journalists with juicy stories about political rivals, narratives that emphasize the fact that the other "side" is just as bad (in this case linking Ukraine to Nazis) and then watching "useful idiots" spin the story into one where Freeland was "lying about her Nazi past" when there is no evidence she ever lied about it.[135]

AMPLIFYING DIVISION

Finally, investigations into the use of social media by adversarial states for influence operations have revealed preliminary Russian attempts to influence Canadians, particularly on pipelines and immigration – although, relative to other countries, Canada still represents a very small portion of the overall effort.[136] It does indicate, though, that clandestine foreign influence was a genuine threat in the 2019 federal election.

Importantly, it would be wrong to assume that Russia is the only country that engages in these activities. In the wake of the diplomatic dispute between Canada and Saudi Arabia in August 2018, a wave of poorly written tweets from pro–Saudi Arabia accounts spread junk news about Canada and targeted the Canadian media as well as commentators on foreign affairs. In addition, preliminary research reveals that there have been some very limited efforts by Venezuela and Iran to engage in social media campaigns.[137] In May 2019 a network of Facebook pages created in Iran between April 2018 and March 2019 was shut down. Although the Facebook pages seem to have been targeting U.S. and Israeli politics, it is proof that Iran is refining its disinformation efforts – much of which seems to have been aimed at creating convincing fake pages for politicians.[138]

In all three of these cases, the social media efforts were unsophisticated, relative to Russian efforts. In particular, a Saudi-linked tweet that showed an airplane that appeared to be flying menacingly towards the CN Tower in Toronto seems to have only reminded its audience that a few Saudi citizens were deeply involved in the 9/11 attacks. Shortly thereafter the group responsible for the tweet was forced to apologize.[139]

Additionally, as noted in the last chapter, government documents reveal that it is concerned about clandestine foreign influence operations that will target the Chinese and Indian diasporas in Canada, likely using social media as a part of these efforts. While concerns have been raised over the use of WeChat for political organizing, there are indications the government is concerned over the targeting of the Canadian South Asian community with political propaganda or disinformation through instant messaging software, especially WhatsApp.[140] The extent to which this activity may be coordinated by a state like India is not clear. WhatsApp is an important communication tool in South Asia, and large amounts of disinformation on the platform may simply be the result of sharing by large networks of well-meaning friends and family members. However, the Canadian government appears to be concerned that these messaging services could be used to undermine provisions of the *Canada Elections Act* "to facilitate the potential for voter coercion or foreign interference."[141] However, the private and encrypted nature of WhatsApp means that it is extremely hard to follow and/or counter. This suggests a potential evolution in the nature of online clandestine foreign influence that could be used across many different groups and networks of friends and family in future elections, beyond ethnic communities.

All of this suggests that despite the lack of a major attempt to influence Canadian elections, government officials and the public should still be concerned about this issue. First the nature of the social media accounts suggests that other countries are trying to learn from Russia's example by targeting hot-button issues. Second, although the efforts of countries other than Russia have been of lower sophistication, they have can develop and improve, meaning that Canada, as well as other Western countries, may soon be dealing with a variety of hostile actors and not just one.

Canada's Policy Response

Warned by its own national security community, Canada has taken steps to address the problem. Following the 2017 Charlevoix G7 summit meeting, Canada established a G7 "Rapid Reaction Mechanism" (RRM) headquartered at Global Affairs Canada. The RRM will engage in threat analysis and work to find opportunities for coordination among G7 countries.[142] In addition, Canada has been a major player in the "Christchurch Call" to counter terrorist and extremist content online. Although the initiative is mostly aimed at tackling the problem of far-right extremism, it could also deny extremist content to adversarial states who seek to weaponize it in order to achieve political ends.[143]

Internally, Canada has taken steps that will also help to counter disinformation. These include drafting legislation that will give national security agencies the ability to help defend Canadian critical infrastructure in the private sector through Bill C-59. While CSE had been able to protect Elections Canada, the ability to protect designated critical infrastructure means that they can also assist with protecting election information in the hands of the private sector by working with telecommunications companies.

A second major step has been the creation of a plan to contend with a serious incident of clandestine foreign influence during the election period. This is a key step in countering clandestine foreign influence, given the difficulties experienced by the U.S. government when it realized there was a serious ongoing effort to influence the election and did not know how to respond.[144]

In January 2019 the Canadian government created a Critical Election Incident Public Protocol – a series of steps that can be taken if there is a major incident that compromises election security. This includes the creation of a panel of neutral, high-level civil servants (from Public Safety, Global Affairs Canada, the national security and intelligence advisor, the deputy attorney general, and the clerk of the Privy Council) who can make decisions on how to proceed should a range of incidents occur. While little is known about the protocol itself (to avoid alerting adversaries on how it works), it is said to envision a range of scenarios and solutions that the panel could take. This includes provisions for "informing candidates, organizations or election officials if they have been the known target of an attack; briefing the group of senior public servants at the heart of the Protocol; informing the Prime Minister and other party leaders (or their designates) that a public announcement is planned; and notifying the public."[145]

Conclusion

Considering what has occurred in other countries, will the steps taken by the Canadian government be enough? Canada has had the dubious advantage of watching other states go through sustained attempts to influence their democratic institutions. Sadly, we have benefited from their experience and our institutions are therefore better prepared for foreign influence operations.

And yet the constantly evolution of this threat is a significant challenge. Some limited steps have been taken by social media companies to deal with the problem and to change the algorithms for how information feeds flow. Unfortunately, these often backfire. A study of the impact of Facebook's attempt to improve the quality of discussions on its platforms found that it resulted in amplifying articles on emotional or divisive topics such as abortion, religion, and guns, and politics continues to dominate discussions. In addition, the study found that the Facebook content that generates most comment is often linked to junk news sites, and the most frequent "reaction" emoji to political stories was "angry."[146]

This issue is likely to get worse before it gets better for three reasons. First, regardless of the measurable impact, the evidence suggests that states believe relatively low-cost clandestine foreign influence operations give a good return on investment. In this sense, although there may not be a scholarly consensus about the impact of Russian efforts, Russia and other countries believe they work. As such, it should not be surprising that in the wake of the 2018 Salisbury chemical weapon attack, RT and other Russian-linked outfits attempted to "flood" the information zone with stories to frame the incident, or at least spread doubt about the truth. Researchers have detected over 130 Russian-generated narratives about the attack that often compete and contradict each other; they hypothesize that this ambitious attempt to create confusion and spread disinformation serves as a "crisis management" tool.[147] In this sense, so long as states believe it is useful, online clandestine foreign influence operations will continue.

Second, as noted above, more actors are getting into the business of clandestine foreign influence. While only some are able to engage in foreign influence in a sophisticated way, likely their capacity will grow by developing and refining their efforts, observing the actions of other successful states, or by employing proxies to engage in online clandestine foreign influence for them. For example, we already know that Russia has used its troll armies to support Syrian President Bashir al-Assad to use disinformation about his brutal tactics and to discredit humanitarian workers. Other states may look to find private or state-owned proxies they can recruit for similar purposes.

Third, with developments in computer technology, it is likely that disinformation will be harder to track: it will look and feel more authentic than what is currently available. Worse, with developments in AI technologies, it may be possible to generate or manipulate video in real time in order to put out disinformation about current events as fast as – or faster than – real media outlets can.

Known as "deep fakes," these are convincing fake audio and video that appear to be saying or doing things they have not done.[148] This technology will be used to exacerbate all of the threat-related activity discussed in this chapter, making it harder for everyone to know what the truth is, and that can be extremely detrimental in a crisis.

For the moment, Canadians have the power to choose whether clandestine foreign influence is successful. Russia and other countries may try to influence our politics, but ultimately it is up to us to determine how we behave online, including what views we seek out and what information we seek to share. In this sense, the solution to these problems may be less technical and more in the realm of critical thinking. Clandestine foreign influence is not a new phenomenon – but the speed and scale of the problem is. Canadians will have to adjust to the new reality with empathy and knowledge about the national security threats they face. Armed with a critical awareness, we stand a much better chance.

Conclusion

Being an intelligence analyst can sometimes feel like dipping in and out of an endless stream of information. You arrive at work, placing your electronics in a secure lock-box, pass through security, and, after inputting a series of passwords, you open a portal to a number of databases to be combed through, looking to find tiny pieces of information that will build up to a bigger picture of the threats Canada faces.

The reality is far from Hollywood – many of the portals of information behind layered security look a lot more like they belong on a 1980s Apple II than a state-of-the-art computer. Rather than providing direct answers, queries of the information stream can pull up hundreds or thousands of documents that must be read and sorted before an answer can be prepared for the policymaker or official who has requested your response by the end of the day. And in sorting through the information, there are few programs allowed that will help you with organizing your response – for security reasons, software requests can take years to get approved. Often an analyst's best friend is a pencil and an Excel sheet. Most rooms are without windows, the fluorescent lights somehow manage to be both too bright and not bright enough, and the coffee is bad.

Intelligence analysts can be a grumpy lot – many feel misunderstood, under-appreciated, and anxious. In most national security organizations in Canada, they have few career prospects – to be promoted often requires entering into a management stream, if there are any job openings, and if they can be promoted at all. And yet many analysts spend their professional lives working in this environment. Far removed from James Bond, as "subject matter experts" (or SMEs) they are expected to understand their file in order to help intelligence collectors, officials, and policymakers make better decisions. When a crisis arises, they know they will be among the first that others turn to for help making sense of what is going on.

Working as an analyst, I enjoyed entering through the intelligence porthole every day to see what information had been collected, what our allies had found, and what products other Canadian and foreign agencies had been working on. As someone who had been an academic, building expertise on a file was both intimidating and very rewarding. And there was tremendous satisfaction in putting together my own assessments or working on projects with a team – even if the approval process felt cumbersome.

But one of the most frustrating things about being an analyst was the feeling that no one outside of my building really understood what national security agencies in Canada do and why. Often, I would watch the House or Senate hearings with intelligence officials for whom I had been asked to contribute information for briefing binders. But the questions being asked were either badly informed or overly politicized. Watching the live-stream on my computer, it was clear that the politicians who are supposed to be holding the government accountable on national security either had an extremely limited understanding of the main issues or not enough interest to ask informed questions. It made for cringe-worthy watching.

At the same time, I watched as national security agencies stumbled in their responses to the 2013 Snowden leaks. Suddenly organizations used to operating away from the limelight were forced to account for their activities as new demands for privacy rights in a digital age were put forward. The agencies had been so quiet for so long they struggled to communicate to a public that is often ignorant of their work and the importance of it. Would Canadians believe that every one of their emails was not being scooped up if, for so long, national security agencies had let TV shows and the movies define their public image?

This is the context in which I made the decision to write this book as I transitioned out of government. I was determined to at least try to explain to Canadians what a national security threat is, why the government cares about them, and why they should too. While I want Canadians to continue to have faith in their national security and intelligence community, I also want them to demand more transparency from the agencies themselves, and better accountability from review bodies as well as MPs and Senators. I believe that with recent legislation and initiatives the government has taken some right steps in this direction, but there is more work to be done.

The combination of a better understanding of the threats to Canada and more transparency is necessary for combating the issues discussed in this book: a widened understanding of national security threats that is grounded in empathy, not panic. Often threat-actors target our sense of understanding and compassion, seeking to create fear and a sense of helplessness, and to amplify division to achieve their goals. Violent extremists seek to create terror in communities to intimidate others not to speak against them. Countries use geoeconomic strategies such as boycotts and bans to threaten markets and force concessions. Foreign influence campaigns threaten physical, material, or emotional harm to persons in Canada, and disinformation campaigns seek to amplify division on emotional topics like refugees, natural resources, and policing. If threat-actors have one thing in common, it is that they want to play on emotions to achieve their ends. While combating these threats takes the resources of a state, it is my hope that improved knowledge of the threat environment Canada faces can help create empathy, and this, in itself, can be useful.

The Future of National Security Threats to Canada

When I began formulating the book, the main national security threat to Canada was widely considered to be Al Qaida and Islamic State–inspired extremism, particularly the threat of foreign fighters. As I write this conclusion, the news is full of stories of white supremacists and far-right extremists targeting Jews, Mexicans, Blacks, and

Muslims and violent misogynist extremists targeting women. These incidents and other global events are often distorted through concerted disinformation campaigns by states and like-minded communities who are targeting trust in our democratic systems. And several reports indicate that after losing its caliphate, the Islamic State is already making a comeback.[1] The threat picture Canada faces has seldom been so challenging, or evolved so quickly.

In this sense, it is a bit of a mug's game to predict the future of national security threats in Canada. Nevertheless, we can identify drivers that will have an impact on the threats discussed in this book and how Canadian national security and intelligence agencies operate. This includes technology, trust, and the future world order.

Technology

From violent extremists shifting to encrypted apps, to states engaging in a wide range of cyber-operations, to the use of social media to control, intimidate, or misinform sections of the public in clandestine foreign influence operations, the opportunities and challenges of new technologies have a clear impact on national security. The role of technology in the national security enterprise as both an opportunity and challenge has been a constant theme of this book. It is almost certain that new and evolving technologies will have an important impact on all of the issues discussed in this book in the future. For the purpose of this conclusion, three will be highlighted here.

ARTIFICIAL INTELLIGENCE

Today it is not uncommon to hear all sorts of advertisements and promises from companies saying they are using "AI" and "machine learning" to generate faster, better, and cheaper results for their customers. But what they are discussing is often in the range of powerful algorithms and machine learning – not the futuristic machines long promised by science fiction. The difference here is between what is called *narrow artificial intelligence*, which addresses specific application areas such as playing strategic games, language translation, self-driving vehicles, and image recognition, and *artificial gen-*

eral intelligence (AGI), a speculative future AI system that exhibits behaviour that seems at least as advanced as a human's abilities across a full range of tasks.[2]

Powerful AI systems that will be able to think and/or act like humans, or mimic something close to it, will almost certainly have an impact on national security. Already, narrow AI is being used to help fight off some cyberattacks targeting Government of Canada systems. It is possible that AI could be used to help find patterns in unstructured data, assisting with labour-intensive tasks such as satellite imagery and intelligence analysis.[3] Additionally, AI could be used to discover irregularities that help find threats in real time.

But AI is also likely to create many challenges for national security. Using photos and videos already online, AI will be able to create "deep fakes," realistic video in real or near-to-real time that can be used to spread disinformation or pollute the information environment, making it difficult to know what to believe. If undertaken during a natural disaster or a crisis, such efforts could have deadly results. While AI is being used to help defend and defeat certain cyberattacks already, it will also be used to counter these efforts. This will increase the speed of cyber threats in the future, potentially creating a vicious cycle.[4]

QUANTUM COMPUTING

Without going into specific scientific details, the development of quantum computing will produce machines that can process information at an order of magnitude faster than the most powerful machines currently on the planet.[5] The good news is that quantum computing will allow humanity to discover new patterns and address difficult challenges through being able to process many different problems at the same time. The bad news is that this means current forms of encryption, which depend on tough math problems (the multiplication of two prime numbers) will be easily solved by quantum computing. This means that encryption as we know it will be broken.

Currently, governments around the world depend upon encryption to keep their communications safe. The advantage for states that develop quantum computing early is that they will be able to read the encrypted communication of other countries. Moreover, as the CSE notes, threat-actors "could collect encrypted sensitive information today, and hold onto it in order to decrypt it when quantum computing matures in 10 to 20 years. Information with a lifespan of more than 10 years could still be at risk of decryption."[6]

The solution to the threat of quantum computing breaking encryption is to develop encryption that can withstand the efforts of powerful computers trying to solve the problems upon which current encryption is based. The development of quantum-resistant cryptography (QRC) or post-quantum cryptography (PQC) is still preliminary, however, and much more research needs to be done as states race to develop quantum computing and quantum-resistant protection for their information.

MANAGING DATA

While technology will allow national security agencies to gather larger amounts of data, being able to usefully sift through them to find the answers to questions being asked will become a greater challenge. As noted at the beginning of this conclusion, simple queries in basic systems already turn up hundreds of results that can take hours to be sorted through; national security agencies are struggling with the amount of data they need to process. However, these issues are also getting exponentially bigger. The "big data" problem is not just about large datasets, but also "data velocity," that is the speed at which new data are generated, and the variety of data being generated.[7] The future challenge for intelligence agencies already confronted with marrying together fragmented data is that they will have to do so in far more complex ways. While algorithms, automation, and AI will play a role in how these data can be used and exploited, it will be just as important to understand the limits of these processes and what they can do to enhance intelligence analysis and operations.

Data: Privacy, Lawful Access, and the Private Sector

While discussions about technology centre upon the limits of what is possible, they raise a separate series of ethical and political questions of what states should be allowed to do. As discussed in chapter 7, some states are already using AI, machine learning, and data analytics to produce a bigger and more capable surveillance state. The use of these technologies by China to suppress the Uighurs in Xinjiang is a prime example of how national security agencies can create a dystopian nightmare.[8] It is likely that these activities will spread to other countries around the world; already China is finding many customers for its surveillance technology.[9]

There is no shortage of writing that can be done to address the question of balancing privacy rights with national security.[10] It is therefore difficult to do justice to this topic in the space of a conclusion. At the same time, it is important to at least acknowledge the issue and the challenging questions it gives rise to, if only because they will play a central role in the operations of national security agencies in the future: How should Western countries respond to a world where individuals leave digital trails of data as they go through their everyday lives using online devices, but where they also have expectations that this information will be used ethically? Should it be used at all? Or, as discussed in chapter 2, the "going dark" question: Should states be able to mandate a "back door" into encrypted applications so that law enforcement agencies can follow terrorists, spies, and criminals as they engage in threat-related and/or criminal activity – even if it weakens encryption for the rest of us? Are we better off having weak privacy laws if it means we can capture those who engage in harmful activities such as child exploitation and terrorism? Or does it put us too much at risk of becoming a surveillance state where tools that were meant to protect the public are instead used to monitor it in ways that many believe go too far? While Western politicians and policymakers continue to wrap their heads around what even constitutes "data," it is unlikely that answering any of these questions will get easier. We have yet to truly grapple with what constitutes privacy in a digital age.

THE PRIVATE SECTOR

A frequently overlooked sector in this debate is the private sector, with its ability to collect vast amounts of data. The number of information points a credit card company, internet search engine, or social media platform is able to collect on a person outweighs the privacy protections available to those in the West.[11] Should national security agencies be able to access this information for their investigations? And what happens when actors seek to use this information to target individuals or groups? These were the key questions asked in the Cambridge Analytica scandal, where it was found that a private company was harvesting and using personal data to micro-target people in ways that at least tried to make them more likely to vote in a particular way. Among 87 million individuals who had their Facebook information "improperly shared," 622,161 were Canadians.[12] However, Canadians are not affected by these companies only: Canadian companies, like AggregateIQ, are actively involved in using data for micro-targeting and found themselves questioned for their role in the Cambridge Analytical scandal.[13]

SOCIAL MEDIA

Another set of pressing questions can be raised about social media. Democracies value freedom of expression, but countries like Canada also criminalize hate speech and incitement to violence. If, as seems increasingly likely, like-minded communities are being targeted in an attempt to influence political events and social attitudes by threat-actors, does the government have a responsibility to regulate speech online? Should it regulate a "duty of care" for social media companies who have been reluctant to take on online harms?[14] Does free speech extend to hordes of automated and "cyborg" bots used to manipulate trending algorithms? Are social media companies doing enough to enforce their own terms and conditions?

Governments and national security agencies have been worried about online extremist content for decades. Much was made of the fact that Al Qaida was using (poorly) locked internet forums to spread their ideas.[15] Yet developments discussed in chapter 7 suggest that today image-based forums and social media platforms are playing a role in disinformation campaigns and far-right extremist violence. In response to the March 2019 attack against a mosque in New Zealand, live-streamed on the internet, Western governments (with the notable exception of the United States) have come together under the "Christchurch Call," "an action plan that commits government and tech companies to a range of measures, including developing tools to prevent the upload of terrorist and violent extremist content; countering the roots of violent extremism; increasing transparency around the removal and detection of content, and reviewing how companies' algorithms direct users to violent extremist content."[16] How we actually achieve this is another story. Social media platforms have had success in eliminating Al Qaida and Islamic State propaganda from the internet, forcing these groups onto encrypted messenger apps, like Telegram. While this continues to be a problem (as noted in the "going dark" discussion), the aggressive takedown has effectively shrunk the social media presence of these groups, though they remain online.[17]

Taking down far-right extremist material is a far greater challenge. First, the scale of the problem is different – there is far more interest and content available. A 2017 survey by firms researching violent extremism found that over a three-month period in the United States there were 35,000 searches for information to join Al Qaida– or ISIS-inspired groups, and 312,000 searches for information to join far-right and neo-Nazi organizations.[18] In the aftermath of the Christchurch shooter's attack, Facebook deleted 1.5 million attempts to re-upload the live-footage video of the massacre in just twenty-four hours.[19]

Second, far-right content is harder to detect and delete. As early as 2016, Facebook, Google, Microsoft, and Twitter joined together to find a way to share "hashes" – database of unique digital fingerprints – to more quickly delete extremist content.[20] Recently, the same companies pledged to support the Christchurch Call as well.[21] While algorithms can be trained to delete known images, the far-right's ability to quickly adapt their social media messaging makes this difficult. As discussed in chapter 7, the content being produced evolves very quickly, with meme layered upon meme to create self-referential "meta" images. Using coded words, languages, and metatextual self-awareness and irony, to send signals to their own communities, detecting and deleting these messages is extremely challenging for companies trying to train algorithms.

Should Canada enact strict penalties against social media content, such as the laws in Australia that can impose significant fines and possibly jail social media executives if they fail to rapidly remove extremist content online in a timely manner?[22] Should Canada keep an American approach, which largely leaves these decisions in the hands of the private sector? Or should it try to define its own legislation/regulatory approach, working with other like-minded countries to do so? Or is this issue too dangerous to legislate at all?

AGILE LEGAL REGIMES
In the wake of data breaches, social media fears and scandals, and details about how information was used in the 2016 U.S. presidential election, there has been an understandable outcry over privacy. It has become clear that simply regulating the government's use of information is no longer enough to protect Canadians. As the House of Commons Standing Committee on Access to Information, Privacy and Ethics observed in its investigation of these issues in light of the Cambridge Analytical Scandal, it has "brought to light issues relating to mass data harvesting, the use of data for nefarious purposes, and the threats and challenges these questionable methods can create for democracies around the world. The evidence that the Committee has heard so far gives rise to grave concerns that the Canadian democratic and electoral process is similarly vulnerable to improper acquisition and manipulation of personal data."[23] In other words, Canada is not well prepared to confront the challenges of mass-data harvesting on social media as threats to its democratic institutions. Although the Trudeau government made some changes in the *Elections Modernization Act* (2018) on political advertising on social media, the broader issue remains largely untouched by law. The furthest the government has gone is the introduction of a "digital charter" and a discussion of proposals to modernize the *Personal Information Protection and Electronic Documents Act*.[24] While analysts suggest that this regime would bring Canada close to the European Union's General Data Protection Law (GPDR),[25] it is not clear that this is enough: such laws do not protect the data that are most precious to tech firms, the inferred data produced by algorithms and used by advertisers.[26]

Moreover, as hinted at already, are these really issues we want national security and intelligence agencies to be involved with in the first place? In debating how Facebook uses our personal data, it does feel that we have come some way from worrying about foreign fighters headed to the Islamic State or Somalia. On the one hand, answering these questions is more than just answering an ethical dilemma. If Canadians do not trust online or internet services – or that their data will be respected by the government and/or private sector – it will harm the development of the online economy overall. Trust is crucial to realizing our potential online future. And as the standing committee found, there is real potential harm to our democracy.

On the other hand, how exactly do we want the intelligence community to be involved in crafting a solution to these issues – if at all? There is a clear nexus with national security if foreign actors are using online data and social media platforms to attack our democracy. But national security agencies are also interested parties in privacy and controlling access to information. If there is a threat, how should such an interested party engage?

Herein lies the challenge of many future national security questions, that they lie at the fringes of where one would expect the Canadian intelligence community to be. The future of national security in Canada, whether it is online trust, foreign investment, or critical infrastructure, will lie with these agencies having to find ways to work with non-traditional partners, such as Heritage Canada and Innovation Science and Economic Development in order to solve key challenges that have migrated to areas never envisioned in the early 1980s. In doing so, they will have to be subjected to oversight and review by well-staffed, competent bodies.

Trust

Will Canadians trust the enhanced review and oversight of the national security and intelligence community that has begun to take shape since 2017? Surveys suggest that overall Canadians have higher levels of trust in their government and institutions (like the media) than in other Western countries, especially the United States.[27] Moreover, surveys indicate that public confidence in national security agencies is relatively high. A 2017 survey found that 73 per cent of Canadians trust the CSE to act ethically in fulfilling its mandate.[28] A similar survey in 2018 found that 69 per cent of Canadians believe the mission of

CSIS is "very important" and 24 per cent "somewhat important." Of those surveyed, 84 per cent expressed at least some confidence in the Service, although only 64 per cent expressed only "some" confidence.[29]

This level of confidence is important for the intelligence community to operate. If Canadians do not feel that they can come forward with information, national security investigations will be jeopardized. At the same time, studies have revealed some important caveats. First, the majority of Canadians could not name either core intelligence collection agency when prompted. Only 30 per cent of Canadians could name CSIS and a shocking 3 per cent could name the CSE. When given the names, only 59 per cent recognized CSIS (33 per cent in Quebec) and 37 per cent recognized CSE.[30] Canadians may trust their national security institutions, but it seems clear they do not really know who they are. Is this a foundation for real trust?

Importantly, in both surveys, it was found that the Canadian public want more transparency from national security organizations.[31] This is something that the national security and intelligence community has been historically bad at in comparison to other Western countries. The only community-wide report is the *Public Report on the Terrorist Threat* – which excludes any reporting on espionage or foreign influence. In a welcome move, the Canadian Centre for Cyber Security[32] and the National Security and Intelligence Committee of Parliamentarians (NSICOP)[33] have started issuing public reports that provide basic but useful assessments of the threats Canada faces. But Canadians have far less information on their national security and intelligence services relative to other countries. In addition, although these organizations have taken great strides in their public outreach, too often the default response to a media inquiry is to give standard pre-approved lines or not comment at all.

NATIONAL SECURITY REPORTING IN THE MEDIA

There are other reasons Canadians may not be knowledgeable about or interested in the intelligence community. Although this book has argued that the threat environment has never been so fluid or complex, there are fewer journalists dedicated to national security issues in Canada than there have been in the past. National security issues, laws, and procedures are difficult to understand, and operations are dragged out over time. Given demands and pressures on newsrooms with increasingly anaemic resources (both material and personnel), it is likely that few reporters are given the opportunity to develop the expertise of many of their predecessors.

These developments are unfortunate: as my citations attest, this book would not have been possible without the dedicated work of reporters covering national security issues. Given an intelligence community that is still reluctant to speak to the media, pressures on newsrooms and reporters, and the speed at which events take place, a decline in the amount and often the quality of national security coverage is inevitable. What effect will this have on understanding and trust?

Informed, balanced reporting is important for accurate information when controversies arise, and there have been several in recent years: from allegations of racist and sexist abuse in Toronto,[34] to allegations that CSIS is spying on the environmental community,[35] through to outrage over revelations the Service was collecting, searching, and storing data without the legal grounds to do so.[36] Having well-informed reporters to explain the details of these issues to the public is vital to the public interest. Without context, the result can be a disaster. Infamously, when former National Security and Intelligence Advisor Daniel Jean tried to speak to the media off the record, about the threat of clandestine foreign influence from India in the wake of Prime Minister Justin Trudeau's visit there, reporters were quick to throw him under the metaphorical bus – many simply refused to believe him.[37] While there can be a reasonable debate over Jean's actions, the fact that the nation's highest national security official was said to be engaging in a conspiracy theory speaks volumes for the state of the relationship between many media outlets and security and intelligence agencies. Unfortunately, these kinds of incidents have a reinforcing effect, causing intelligence agencies to stay further away from the media and giving the media cause for further frustration and mistrust.

International Order

Perhaps one of the reasons Canadians are unfamiliar with their national security institutions is that they generally feel safe. As noted in the introduction of this book, Canada is well defended by natural borders with a relatively benign neighbour to our south. As such, Canadians can feel sheltered from the world in our "peaceable kingdom." So why bother thinking about national security if all of the problems are "over there"? Successive Canadian governments have refused to create an external human intelligence service or a "Canadian CIA," mostly because there has been no demand for one either from the public or inside the federal bureaucracy.

But the circumstances Canada finds itself in are no longer certain. There are reasons to believe the world is in for dramatic shifts in the international order that has kept us safe for decades, whether it is due to the aftershocks of the COVID-19 pandemic, or the result of climate change on global security and the Arctic. Moreover, with China on the rise and Russia attempting to re-envision its place in the world, the guarantors of security no longer seem as stable as they once were.

TRUMPISM

Perhaps the biggest risk to Canada's security is "Trumpism," a populist movement reflecting the candidacy and now presidency of Donald Trump that, when it comes to international affairs, is based on the principles of isolationism and political and economic nationalism that has little use for alliances. Trumpism sees little worth in the liberal values that have characterized U.S. Presidents since the Second World War: the promotion of free trade, human rights, and multilateralism. Instead, these institutions are seen as keeping America weak, preventing the United States from attaining its full potential. It is not just the United States that has seen the rise of "Trumpism" either. There are echoes of it throughout the West, including Brexit Britain and far-right populist movements throughout Europe that have seen recent electoral victories.

Unfortunately for Canada, our safety and security hinges on things that Trump and others of his ilk appear to abhor. Our economy thrives because of free trade, and we have a general interest in stable countries that grow when they protect the human rights of all of their citizens. Our security is guaranteed through the North Atlantic Treaty Organization (NATO), arguably the most successful military alliance in the world. Trump not only frequently bashes all of these institutions, regularly threatening to leave the NATO alliance, he has shown a marked openness to work with illiberal rulers like Putin and totalitarians such as North Korea's Kim Jong Un, seemingly rewarding their aggressive behaviour with receptions and lavish ceremonies.

Although Trump lost the 2020 election, it is not at all clear that the forces that support him and brought him into power will go away anytime soon. It is very possible that Trumpism as a phenomenon will survive Trump himself as enough Americans grow tired of the costs of global leadership, even if it brings them advantages. As Canada's then Minister of Foreign Affairs Chrystia Freeland noted in the House of Commons a day before the Liberal government announced its new defence strategy in June 2017, "Many of the voters in last year's presidential election cast their ballots, animated in part by a desire to shrug off the burden of world leadership. To say this is not controversial: it is simply a fact.... The fact that our friend and ally has come to question the very worth of its mantle of global leadership, puts into sharper focus the need for the rest of us to set our own clear and sovereign course."[38] Indeed, the basis of Freeland's remarkable speech was that, absent U.S. leadership and in light of the challenges wrought by populism and illiberalism, Canada will have to find its own way in the world. She argued this will require a stronger foreign and defence policy and for Canada to work with like-minded countries to preserve what remains of the international order.

Nowhere in her speech did Freeland suggest that Canada needed a more robust security and intelligence apparatus, or foreign intelligence. And yet it is hard to see how Canada will be able to navigate this more uncertain world without exactly that. If our two major intelligence allies, Britain and the United States, are turning inward, will Canada still have access to the information it needs to make decisions about national security? If the answer is no, how will we cope?

The Road Ahead

This book has been designed to explain national security threats to Canadians, not to provide policy advice to government. Yet it is important to address the policy implications that come out of the common themes of this book. To be brief, this section will examine four: ensuring new accountability mechanisms work, enhancing transparency, bringing the traditional security and intelligence community into dialogue with non-traditional partners, and a broader effort toward "Canadianizing" national security.[39]

Making New Institutions Work

Between 2017 and 2019 Canada went through the most important evolution to our national security architecture since 1984. A priority for the government must be that the new legislative powers and oversight and review bodies work well and are strengthened over time. This means ensuring that they are fully staffed and have an adequate budget. Departments and agencies that are being subject to regular review of their security and intelligence work should be given resources and treated with some degree of patience as they start the process of compliance.

Enhancing Transparency

A second major step should be enhancing transparency. Already there have been some recent positive steps taken. The new review bodies noted in the above section will provide accountability to the public in the form of reports. Public Safety has recently developed a National Security Transparency Commitment, which highlights six principles in information transparency (information about what the government does), executive transparency (explaining the legal structures of national security and how decisions are made), and policy transparency (to engage the public in conversations about the strategic issues affecting national security).[40] In July 2019 the government also announced the creation of an "advisory group on national security transparency" comprising experts who can advise the Minister of Public Safety on ways to implement the National Security Transparency Commitment.[41]

All of this is a good start for promoting transparency, but the government should go further, providing regular updates and briefings to MPs and Senators on national security threats. While MPs do not have security clearance, there are ways to provide information using open-source reporting. As well, it might be a way to better demystify the intelligence world to provide the basis of better accountability in Parliament. Moreover, as argued by NSICOP in its 2019 annual report, it is vital that officials in provinces and municipalities are also regularly briefed, and given security clearance if necessary.[42]

National security agencies should also try to improve their outreach to media organizations, which would make it easier for new reporters to grasp the fundamentals of national security. Building relationships with the media over time is not nefarious or clandestine. It is a way to provide background, context, and information when complex stories arise. National security agencies should not attempt to control what journalists write or say, but they can at least do a better job of providing their side of the story. This does mean they will need to be more forthright with Canadians when answering questions, even when doing so is deeply uncomfortable. If nothing else, the national security and intelligence community can look at what it has done over the previous three decades and ask itself if its media strategy has really worked.

New Government Partnerships

Throughout this book we have seen ways that new and evolving national security threats are challenging the very idea of what a national security threat is. To what extent is the economy a national security issue? Should CSIS monitor online forums? What is the impact of disinformation pushed by foreign adversaries on trust? All of these questions touch on national security issues, but national security agencies may not be best equipped to deal with them. Indeed, as noted above, complex threats mean that traditional security agencies like CSIS and CSE are going to have to work with non-traditional security agencies like Heritage Canada and Elections Canada.

This is, of course, easier said than done. National security agencies have a mandate to look at threats, and other government departments are responsible for wider policy issues. There is considerable room for disagreement between these two perspectives: while CSIS may worry about opaque objectives behind foreign investment, ISED may see the opportunity to promote growth and jobs. Given that there are few central agencies or formalized opportunities to reconcile these differences, finding a compromise may prove difficult.

Nevertheless, the idea that intelligence collection agencies can sit (literally) removed from "downtown" (short form for the rest of government) on a pile of information, providing a threat assessment or briefing here and there is outdated and ineffective. National security and intelligence agencies are having to learn to make themselves relevant and part of the conversation. Part of this lesson-drawing includes listening to and understanding a wide variety of perspectives and policy interests downtown.

Canadianizing National Security

If there is a solution that has been a constant throughout this book, it is that Canada is far better off when it works with its allies in finding solutions for problems. Whether it is combating the threat of foreign fighters, propaganda, and threats to democratic institutions, or cybersecurity issues, working with our partners means that our voice is amplified, and plans of actions will be stronger. Multilateral collaboration allows Canada to share what it knows, help others, and, in turn, learn from their experiences. But crucially, security simply requires international cooperation: transnational threats cannot be dealt with when policies stop at our nation's borders.

Importantly, this means that Canada should step up its efforts in promoting global security. For decades Canada has been a net consumer of intelligence: we take in far more than we give back, especially with our closest partners. Enhancing our contributions means increasing our own capacity. While there does not seem to be an appetite for creating an entirely new foreign intelligence service, finding ways to enhance or increase foreign intelligence collection, either through altering CSIS's mandate or establishing a body within a department like Global Affairs, would mean doing more for our closest allies.[43] Given international uncertainties, being able to prioritize Canadian intelligence requirements rather than depending on what our allies choose to give us would possibly help policymakers make decisions. This approach to intelligence is not without risks – intelligence gathering is inherently risky – but it feels long overdue.

Conclusion

Canadians are fortunate – we are safe from the problems that plague many of the world's countries. Despite our political differences, we enjoy stable governments and live in relative prosperity. Most Canadians go to bed at night without fear of chaos, or political or social upheaval. If national security is one of many government priorities but not the most pressing, it is to our good fortune as Canadians.

Nevertheless, this book has made the argument that threats to Canadian national security are real. As we go about our day-to-day lives, their impact is often invisible: the radicalizer quietly targeting youth after school, the internet forums and chat rooms that promote hate and disinformation, the pressure placed on new Canadians to refrain from speaking their minds by foreign entities, and the cyber-espionage stealing the future away one terabyte of data at a time. This is far removed from the antics of James Bond's enemies or dramatic violent extremist attacks. And it is out of sight and out of mind for most Canadians.

As this book has emphasized, the answer to these problems is not to get angry or frightened. Threat-actors often succeed when they make Canadians feel fear. What is necessary is for Canadians to responsibly widen their understanding of national security threats so that they may be more empathetic towards those affected. Through this understanding, we can take the critical steps towards meeting the complex and ever-evolving challenges of the twenty-first century.

Appendix: The Canadian National Security and Intelligence Community

Today, virtually every department in the Government of Canada has some sort of role to play in national security or a need for intelligence. While many people may first think of organizations like the Canadian Security Intelligence Service (CSIS) or the Communications Security Establishment (CSE) when it comes to national security, departments such as finance and agriculture depend on intelligence to perform their jobs and make informed decisions. However, to keep things manageable, this appendix will briefly outline the roles and responsibilities of the "core" agencies and departments of the national security and intelligence community in Canada, defined by function: central agencies, policy advice, collection and enforcement agencies, prosecution, and review.[1]

Centre of Government

Prime Minister's Office (PMO)

The PMO is a central agency of government that provides political advice to the Prime Minister and Cabinet. It is the only office staffed by political appointees and not neutral civil servants. Each PMO is arranged according to the Prime Minister's preferences so there is no set structure to how the office interacts with the intelligence community. While the PMO cannot task intelligence collectors, security-cleared personnel have access to intelligence products and briefings and may ask questions in line with their files to support the work of the Prime Minister.

Privy Council Office (PCO)

PCO is a central agency of government that provides non-partisan advice to Cabinet and helps to execute the policy decisions. The head of PCO is the Clerk of the Privy Council who is also the principal public service advisor to the Prime Minister. Although PCO coordinates policy in the entire government, it has specialized national security functions. In particular, it is home to the National Security and Intelligence Advisor (NSIA), who provides non-political advice to the Prime Minister and coordinates the work of the security and intelligence community. In addition, there are three secretariats within PCO: Security and Intelligence (PCO S&I) provides advice and manages urgent operational files, the Intelligence Assessment Secretariat (PCO IAS) provides assessments and coordinates assessment bodies across the intelligence community, and the Foreign and Defence Policy Secretariat (PCO FDP) provides advice on those issues. PCO staff often brief the prime minister and staff on security and intelligence issues.

Policy

Public Safety Canada (PSC)

PSC (also known as Public Safety and Emergency Preparedness Canada) was created in 2003 to ensure coordination across all federal departments and agencies responsible for national security and the safety of Canadians. While PSC assists in policy development and implementation, it is the lead department for several major national security and intelligence agencies, including CBSA, CSIS, and the RCMP. PSC is also the home for the Canada Centre for Community Engagement and the Prevention of Violence (CCCEPV or "Canada Centre"), which supports counter-violent extremism/counter-radicalization to violence programs across the country.

Collection Agencies

Canadian Security Intelligence Service (CSIS)

CSIS is Canada's primary domestic national security intelligence service. It focuses on threats to the security of Canada, making it more like the British Security Service/MI5 than the UK Secret Intelligence Service/MI6 or the American CIA. The main threats to Canada defined in the *Canadian Security and Intelligence Service Act* include espionage, foreign influence activity, violent extremism, and subversion – although the last has not been an area of investigation since at least 1986. At the direction of the Ministers of Foreign Affairs and Defence, the Service may collect information within Canada as relates to foreign states, a group of foreign states and/or non-Canadian persons/permanent residents. The Service is headed by a Director who is responsible to the Minister of Public Safety and Emergency Preparedness.

Communications Security Establishment (CSE)

The CSE is Canada's national cryptologic agency, making it similar to the American National Security Agency (NSA) and the UK Government Communications Headquarters (GCHQ). CSE has four mandates: collecting foreign intelligence through the global information infrastructure, protecting the information and communications of the Government of Canada, providing technical assistance to law enforcement in the performance of their lawful duties, and foreign cyber operations, including "active" (offensive) and defensive cyber operations. The last powers were granted under the *National Security Act* passed in 2019, which also gave the CSE its own statute, the *Communications Security Establishment Act*. CSE is under the Department of Defence Portfolio and is headed by a Chief who is responsible to the Minister of National Defence.

Enforcement Agencies

Canada Border Services Agency (CBSA)

CBSA is responsible for border protection and surveillance, immigration enforcement, and customs services in Canada. Although much of its work focuses on criminal investigations (arms, drugs, and human smuggling), it is also a key national security agency. CBSA collects information at the border and has an important role to play in detecting returning foreign fighters, "illegals" (spies as described in chapter 3), and violent extremists and their supporters trying to enter Canada. They also receive intelligence products and briefings from other national security agencies about the nature of the threats they are trying to prevent entering or leaving the country.

Royal Canadian Mounted Police (RCMP)

The RCMP is the federal police force of Canada and it also provides local and provincial policing services in many areas of Canada. The RCMP has a large mandate and covers a wide range of criminal activity, including national security offences, particularly terrorism, espionage, and cybercrime. While CSIS gathers intelligence on national security threats, the RCMP gathers evidence for national security prosecutions. The RCMP also has a role in protective policing, critical infrastructure protection, marine and air carrier security, and critical incident management. RCMP Headquarters also controls the Integrated National Security Enforcement Teams (INSETs) located throughout the country. INSETs are primarily focused on anti-terrorist investigations. They comprise representatives from the RCMP, but also other federal partners and agencies (like CSIS) and provincial and municipal police services.

Intelligence Analysis Bodies

Financial Transactions and Reports Analysis Centre of Canada (FINTRAC)

The Financial Transactions and Reports Analysis Centre of Canada (FINTRAC) is Canada's financial intelligence unit. Uniquely among intelligence agencies in Canada, it reports to the Minister of Finance. FINTRAC's mandate is to detect, prevent, and deter money laundering and counter-terrorism financing in line with Canadian law and its international obligations. FINTRAC's intelligence is based on mandatory and voluntary reporting by Canadian financial institutions. If assessed as meeting the threshold for disclosure, information will be passed on to law enforcement, amongst other partners, for further investigation.

Integrated Terrorism Assessment Centre (ITAC)

ITAC is an intelligence assessment body responsible for assessing terrorism threats to Canada and Canadian interests worldwide. Although housed physically within CSIS Headquarters in Ottawa, it is a separate body managed by its own Director, who is appointed by the National Security and Intelligence Advisor (NSIA) in consultation with the Director of CSIS. The Director of ITAC is responsible to the CSIS Director, as well as its Management Board, chaired by the NSIA and attended by the Deputy Ministers from participating organizations to review ITAC's performance. A large component of ITAC's analysts are secondees from across the federal government. However, it has increasingly hired its own analysts and managers in recent years. ITAC does not have its own collection capabilities but utilizes intelligence from other departments and agencies. Aside from writing terrorism assessments, ITAC is responsible for providing recommendations to the government on setting the National Terrorism Threat Level.

Prosecution

Department of Justice and the Public Prosecution Service of Canada

The Public Prosecution Service of Canada is in charge of prosecuting national security offences. The Department of Justice provides a range of services to national security agencies including in-house legal staff (all national security lawyers are Justice employees), providing legal advice on national security issues (including international law and human rights), and providing policy advice in the formulation of national security law and policy.

Other Government Departments

Department of National Defence (DND)

DND is responsible for the defence of Canada at home and abroad. To support its operations, it has a large intelligence apparatus through its Canadian Forces Intelligence Command (CFINTCOM). DND has the capability to collect both human and signals intelligence in support of its mandate to protect Canada. CFINTCOM also provides analysis and advice to the government through briefings and intelligence products. The Minister of Defence plays an important role in the authorization of certain intelligence activities for both CSIS (foreign intelligence collection within Canada) and the CSE (active and defensive cyber powers).

Global Affairs Canada (GAC)

GAC is Canada's department of foreign affairs. In this capacity, it manages diplomatic relations with other countries and international organizations, promotes international trade, and coordinates Canada's international development and humanitarian assistance. It also provides consular services to Canadians abroad. GAC does not collect intelligence, but it has a political reporting function known as the Global Security Reporting Program (GSRP) that provides information to Ottawa from abroad. In addition, it consumes intelligence analysis from other national security agencies and provides advice on international issues. The Minister of Foreign Affairs plays an important role in the authorization of certain intelligence activities for both CSIS (foreign intelligence collection within Canada) and the CSE (active cyber powers and consulted on the use of defensive cyber powers).

Oversight and Review Bodies

Intelligence Commissioner

The Intelligence Commissioner performs an independent quasi-judicial review of conclusions reached by Ministers when they issue certain ministerial authorizations for both the CSE and CSIS. This position was created by Bill C-59 and ensures the independent oversight of intelligence activities required by section 8 of the Canadian Charter of Rights and Freedoms (the right to be free from unreasonable search and seizure). For example, the Intelligence Commissioner has a role in reviewing the approved "datasets" that CSIS may collect and search.

National Security and Intelligence Committee of Parliamentarians (NSICOP)

NSICOP is a committee of Parliamentarians (not a parliamentary committee) with the mandate to review the legislative, regulatory, policy, administrative, and financial framework for national security and intelligence, the activity of any government department relating to national security or intelligence (unless it is a part of an ongoing operation or an investigation is deemed injurious to national security by the relevant Minister) or any matter relating to national security and intelligence referred to the committee. The committee is the first permanent review body made up of democratically elected representatives in Canada. To support the work of the MPs, NSICOP has a Director and Secretariat.

National Security and Intelligence Review Agency (NSIRA)

NSIRA is the agency tasked with assessing compliance of the national security and intelligence community with the laws of Canada. Unlike its predecessors, NSIRA has the power to review any activities performed by CSIS, the CSE, and any national security or intelligence-related activity carried out by federal departments and agencies. In this sense it is able to follow the way intelligence is used across the Canadian national security and intelligence committee. NSIRA comprises six part-time members and has its own secretariat to carry out its functions. NSIRA differs from NSICOP in that the former is concerned with compliance, the latter with efficacy – although this is by practice and not defined in any statute.

Notes

Preface

1. For the contrary view, see Andrew Potter, "We Are at War with COVID-19: We Need to Fight It like a War," *Globe and Mail*, 5 April 2020, https://www.theglobeandmail.com/opinion/article-we-are-at-war-with-covid-19-we-need-to-fight-it-like-a-war/.
2. On securitization, see Stefan Elbe, "Should HIV/AIDS Be Securitized? The Ethical Dilemmas of Linking HIV/AIDS and Security," *International Studies Quarterly* 28, no. 2 (2003): 78–111; Colin McInnes and Simon Rushton, "HIV/AIDS and Securitization Theory," *European Journal of International Relations* 19, no. 1 (2011): 119–44; Robert L. Ostergard Jr., "Politics in the Hot Zone: AIDS and National Security in Africa," *Third World Quarterly* 23, no. 2 (2002): 333–50. On the ethics of biosurveillance, see Sarah Davies, "Nowhere to Hide: Informal Disease Surveillance Networks Tracing State Behavior," *Global Change, Peace & Security* 24, no. 1 (2012): 95–107; Jeremy Youde, "Biosurveillance, Human Rights, and the Zombie Plague," *Global Change, Peace & Security* 24, no. 1 (2012): 83–93.
3. Evan Perez and David Shortell, "Man under Investigation for Plotting an Attack at a Hospital Believed to Be Treating Covid-19 Patients Was Killed during an FBI Investigation," CNN, 26 March 2020, https://www.cnn.com/2020/03/25/us/missouri-man-killed-fbi-investigation/index.html; Meagan Flynn, "Engineer Intentionally Crashes Train Near Hospital Ship Mercy, Believing in Weird Coronavirus Conspiracy, Feds Say," *Washington Post*, 2 April 2020, https://www.washingtonpost.com/nation/2020/04/02/train-derails-usns-mercy-coronavirus/.
4. David Brennan, "How Neo-Nazis Are Exploiting Coronavirus to Push Their Radical Agenda," *Newsweek*, 27 March 2020, https://www.newsweek.com

/how-neo-nazis-exploiting-coronavirus-push-radical-agenda-1494729; Hunter Walker and Jana Winter, "Federal Law Enforcement Document Reveals White Supremacists Discussed Using Coronavirus as a Bioweapon," Yahoo News, 22 March 2020, https://www.msn.com/en-us/news/us/federal-law-enforcement-document-reveals-white-supremacists-discussed-using-coronavirus-as-a-bioweapon/ar-BB11vT0H.

5 Bhinder Sajan and Kendra Manglone, "Hate crimes up 97% overall in Vancouver last year, anti-Asian hate crimes up 717%," CTV News, 18 February 2021, https://bc.ctvnews.ca/hate-crimes-up-97-overall-in-vancouver-last-year-anti-asian-hate-crimes-up-717-1.5314307.

6 Catharine Tunney, "Canada's Health Sector at Risk of Cyberattacks as COVID-19 Fear Spreads: CSE," CBC, 19 March 2020, https://www.cbc.ca/news/politics/health-covid-cyberattack-pandemic-1.5502968; Davey Winder, "Cyber Attacks against Hospitals Have 'Significantly Increased' as Hackers Seek to Maximize Profits," *Forbes*, 8 April 2020, https://www.forbes.com/sites/daveywinder/2020/04/08/cyber-attacks-against-hospitals-fighting-covid-19-confirmed-interpol-issues-purple-alert/#77b8be4c58bc.

7 DDoS attacks are explained in chapter 5.

8 Sara Morrison, "What We Know about the Health Department Website Cyberattack," Vox, 16 March 2020, https://www.vox.com/recode/2020/3/16/21181825/health-human-services-coronavirus-website-ddos-cyber-attack.

9 Raphael Satter, Jack Stubbs, and Christopher Bing, "Elite Hackers Target WHO as Coronavirus Cyberattacks Spike," Reuters, 23 March 2020, https://www.reuters.com/article/us-health-coronavirus-who-hack-exclusive/exclusive-elite-hackers-target-who-as-coronavirus-cyberattacks-spike-idUSKBN21A3BN.

10 Helen Warrell and Katrina Manson, "State-Backed Hackers Using Virus to Increase Spying, UK and US Warn," *Financial Times*, 8 April 2020, https://www.ft.com/content/37149106-eb16-4b4e-879b-2913b99da84f. The UK/US statement is available at the CISA, "UK and US Security Agencies Issue COVID-10 Cyber Threat Update," 8 April 2020, https://www.cisa.gov/news/2020/04/08/uk-and-us-security-agencies-issue-covid-19-cyber-threat-update.

11 CSE, "Cyber Threats to Canadian Health Organizations," 20 March 2020, https://www.cyber.gc.ca/en/alerts/cyber-threats-canadian-health-organizations; CSE, "Staying Cyber-Healthy during COVID-19," 8 April 2020, https://www.cyber.gc.ca/en/guidance/staying-cyber-healthy-during-covid-19.

12 Catharine Tunney, "Canada's Cyber Spies Taking Down Sites as Battle against COVID-19 Fraud Begins," CBC News, 23 March 2020, https://www.cbc.ca/news/politics/cse-disinformation-spoofing-1.5504619.
13 Reuters, "Dutch Telecommunications Towers Damaged by 5G Protestors: Telegraaf," 11 April 2020, https://www.reuters.com/article/us-netherlands-5g-sabotage/dutch-telecommunications-towers-damaged-by-5g-protestors-telegraaf-idUSKCN21T09P.
14 Bellemare, "Far-Right Groups May Try to Take Advantage of Pandemic."
15 William J. Broad, "Your 5G Phone Won't Hurt You. But Russia Wants You to Think Otherwise," *New York Times*, 12 May 2019, https://www.nytimes.com/2019/05/12/science/5g-phone-safety-health-russia.html.
16 Adam Rawnsley, "A Daily Beast Investigation Reveals Dozens of Russian Accounts Pushing Disinformation on Everything from Joe Biden to the Origin of the Novel Coronavirus," *Daily Beast*, 9 April 2020, https://www.thedailybeast.com/russian-trolls-hype-coronavirus-and-giuliani-conspiracies.
17 Steven Lee Myers, "China Spins Tale That the U.S. Army Started the Coronavirus Epidemic," *New York Times*, 17 March 2020, https://www.nytimes.com/2020/03/13/world/asia/coronavirus-china-conspiracy-theory.html.
18 Michael Wolfson, "What Happens after the Pandemic Curve Flattens?," *Globe and Mail*, 23 March 2020, https://www.theglobeandmail.com/opinion/article-what-happens-after-the-pandemic-curve-flattens/.
19 Wesley Wark, "Pandemic Gives Security and Intelligence Community an Urgent New Mission," *Policy Options*, 14 April 2020, https://policyoptions.irpp.org/magazines/april-2020/pandemic-gives-security-and-intelligence-community-an-urgent-new-mission/.
20 Sean Boynton, "Canadians Overwhelmingly Support Stronger Measures to Fight COVID-19, Ipsos Poll Suggests," Global News, 9 April 2020, https://globalnews.ca/news/6797614/coronavirus-canada-poll-measures/.
21 On the technical feasibility, see the comments of Christopher Parson in Murad Hemmadi and Caroline Mercer, "Trace Me on My Cellphone: The Different Ways Governments Are Using Phones to Fight COVID-19," Logic, 14 April 2020, https://thelogic.co/news/special-report/trace-me-on-my-cellphone-the-different-ways-governments-are-using-phones-to-fight-covid-19.
22 Jessica Davis, "Intelligence, Surveillance, and Ethics in a Pandemic," Just Security, 31 March 2020, https://www.justsecurity.org/69384/intelligence-surveillance-and-ethics-in-a-pandemic/; Andrew Roth, Stephanie Kirchgaessner, Daniel Boffey, Oliver Holmes, and Helen Davidson, "Growth in Surveillance May Be Hard to Scale Back after Pandemic,

Experts Say," *Guardian*, 14 April 2020, https://www.theguardian.com/world/2020/apr/14/growth-in-surveillance-may-be-hard-to-scale-back-after-coronavirus-pandemic-experts-say?CMP=share_btn_tw.

23 Office of the Director of National Intelligence, "Statement for the Record: Worldwide Threat Assessment of the US Intelligence Community," 29 January 2019, 23, https://www.dni.gov/files/ODNI/documents/2019-ATA-SFR---SSCI.pdf.

Introduction

1 The author has chosen to use "Islamic State," as it is the most widely recognized name for the group that has undergone many changes and names over time. This includes its origns as Jama'at al-Tawhid wal-Jihad in the 1990s, Al Qaida in Iraq (AQI), the Islamic State of Iraq (ISI), and the Islamic State of Iraq and Syria/the Islamic State of Iraq and the Levant (ISIS/ISIL). Officially, the Government of Canada refers to this organization as Daesh, a pejorative preferred by some to (rightly) avoid conflation with Islam. While the author is sympathetic with this later view, "Islamic State" continues to be widely used by most major media organizations and therefore was adopted for this book.
2 Craig Forcese, "Through a Glass Darkly: The Role and Review of 'National Security' Concepts in Canadian Law," *Alberta Law Review* 43, no. 4 (2006): 963–1000.
3 A search for "national security" at Termium, http://www.btb.termiumplus.gc.ca/.
4 Reg Whitaker, Gregory Kealy, and Andrew Parnaby, *The Secret Service: Political Policing in Canada from the Fenians to Fortress America* (Toronto: University of Toronto Press, 2013), 395.
5 One might include military operations as a part of this discussion. However, as this book is limiting its scope to those threat-related activities outlined in the *CSIS Act*, it will focus on national security operations within the domestic/criminal space. This becomes slightly more complex when discussing cyber-threats and clandestine foreign influence, as it may involve actors under the purview of the Department of Defence (especially the Communications Security Establishment) in Canada's response. However, as discussed below, there have already been several works published on the military's role and response to Canada's security threats.
6 The description of Canada as "the Peaceable Kingdom" comes from the title of an anthology edited by William Kilbourn, *Canada: A Guide to the Peaceable Kingdom* (Toronto: Macmillan of Canada, 1975). It was based on Northrop Frye's meditation on an eponymous painting by Edward Hicks.

William Kilbourn, "The Peaceable Kingdom Still," *Daedalus* 117, no. 4 (1988): 28.
7 Ana Douglas and Michael Izzo, "CANADA: America's Top Hat ... and 10 Other Jokes Americans Have Made about Our Neighbor to the North," *Business Insider*, 1 July 2012, http://www.businessinsider.com/canada-americas-top-hat-and-all-the-other-jokes-americans-have-made-about-our-neighbor-to-the-north-2012-6.
8 Karl Wolfgang Deutsch, *Political Community and the North Atlantic Area: International Organization in the Light of Historical Experience* (Princeton, NJ: Princeton University Press, 1957).
9 See, generally, Kim Richard Nossal, *Charlie Foxtrot: Fixing Defence Procurement in Canada* (Toronto: Dundurn, 2016).
10 Andrew B. Godefroy, *Defence and Discovery: Canada's Military Space Program, 1945–74* (Vancouver: UBCPress, 2012); J.L. Granatstein, *Who Killed the Canadian Military?* (Toronto: HarperCollins Publishers, 2004); Sean Maloney, *Learning to Love the Bomb: Canada's Nuclear Weapons during the Cold War* (Lincoln, NB: Potomac Books, 2007); Thomas Juneau, Philippe Lagassé, and Srdjan Vucetic, eds., *Canadian Defence Policy in Theory and Practice* (Basingstoke, UK: Palgrave Macmillan, 2019).
11 James G. Fergusson, *Canada and Ballistic Missile Defence, 1954–2009: Déjà Vu All Over Again* (Vancouver: UBCPress, 2010); Joseph T. Jockel, *Canada in NORAD: 1957–2007: A History* (Montreal and Kingston: McGill-Queen's University Press, 2007); Benjamin Zyla, *Sharing the Burden?: NATO and Its Second-Tier Powers* (Toronto: University of Toronto Press, 2014).
12 Jeffrey F. Collins, *Canada's Defence Procurement Woes* (forthcoming); Nossal, *Charlie Foxtrot*; Alan S. Williams, *Reinventing Canadian Defence Procurement: A View from the Inside* (Montreal and Kingston: McGill-Queen's University Press, 2006).
13 Colin McCullough, *Creating Canada's Peacekeeping Past* (Vancouver: UBCPress, 2017).
14 Janice Gross-Stein, *The Unexpected War: Canada In Kandahar* (Toronto: Penguin Canada, 2008); Stephen M. Saideman, *Adapting in the Dust: Lessons Learned from Canada's War in Afghanistan* (Toronto: University of Toronto Press, 2016); Jean-Christophe Boucher and Kim Richard Nossal, *The Politics of War: Canada's Afghanistan Mission, 2001–14* (Vancouver: UBCPress, 2018).
15 See, for example, David S. McDonough, ed., *Canada's National Security in the Post-9/11 World: Strategy, Interests, Threats* (Toronto: University of Toronto Press, 2012). Despite the title, the book only has one chapter on "homeland security," with most other chapters on traditional defence issues. Similarly, Elinor C. Sloan, *Security and Defence in the Terrorist Era*,

2nd ed. (Montreal and Kingston: McGill-Queen's University Press, 2010), focuses on defence policy and related issues.

16 For more on Canadian defence intelligence, see Thomas Juneau, "Department of National Defence," in *Top Secret Canada: Understanding the Canadian Intelligence and National Security Community*, ed. Stephanie Carvin, Thomas Juneau, and Craig Forcese (Toronto: University of Toronto Press, forthcoming). See also the report by the National Security and Intelligence Committee of Parliamentarians, *Special Report on the Collection, Use, Retention and Dissemination of Information on Canadians in the Context of the Department of National Defence and Canadian Armed Forces Defence Intelligence Activities*, tabled 12 March 2020, 7.

17 Fortunately, there is an increasing cadre of professors with real-world experience writing on intelligence and national security issues. Jessica Davis is a veteran and former analyst at CSIS and the Financial Transactions and Reports Analysis Centre. Davis's work has focused on women in terrorism and terrorism finance. See *Women in Modern Terrorism: From Liberation Wars to Global Jihad and the Islamic State* (Lanham, MD: Rowman & Littlefield, 2017). She has a forthcoming book on terrorism finance. Leah West is also a veteran and a former Department of Justice lawyer working on national security issues. She has a range of legal scholarly publications, including "The Problem of 'Relevance': Intelligence to Evidence Lessons from UK Terrorism Prosecutions," *Manitoba Law Journal* 41, no. 4 (2018): 57–112; and "Cyber Force: The International Legal Implications of the Communication Security Establishment's Expanded Mandate under Bill C-59," *Canadian Journal of Law & Technology* 16 (2019): 381–416. Thomas Juneau is a former intelligence analyst and Department of Defence employee. He and the author are currently involved in several research projects assessing the intelligence-policy nexus in Canada. Juneau has also edited a book on intelligence analysis. See *Strategic Analysis in Support of International Policy Making: Case Studies in Achieving Analytical Relevance* (Lanham, MD: Rowman & Littlefield, 2017). See also Michael Nesbitt, a former Department of Justice lawyer who worked for Global Affairs Canada and has written on national security issues, "An Empirical Study of Terrorism Charges and Terrorism Trials in Canada between September 2001 and September 2018," *Criminal Law Quarterly* 67, nos. 1 & 2 (2019): 95–139. Other writers include Phil Gurski, who has written several books on terrorism. See, for example, *The Threat from Within: Recognizing al Qaeda-Inspired Radicalization and Terrorism in the West* (Lanham, MD: Roman & Littlefield, 2015). Former CSIS Assistant Director of Intelligence Ray Boisvert, Andy Ellis, former Assistant Director of Operations, and Luc Portelance, the former President of the Canadian Border Services Agency,

and Deputy Director of Operations at CSIS, have engaged in public commentary, but all quickly found second careers in the public and private sectors.

18 J.L. Black and Martin Rudner, *The Gouzenko Affair: Canada and the Beginning of Cold War Counter-Espionage* (Newcastle, ON: Penumbra, 2006); J.L. Granatstein and David Stafford, *Spy Wars: Espionage in Canada from Gouzenko to Glasnost* (Toronto: Key Porter Books, 1990); Donald G. Mahar, *Shattered Illusions: KGB Cold War Espionage in Canada* (Lanham, MD: Roman & Littlefield, 2017).

19 J. Michael Cole, *Smokescreen: Canadian Security Intelligence after September 11, 2001* (Bloomington, IN: Iuniverse Publishing, 2008); Andrew Crosby and Jeffrey Monaghan, *Policing Indigenous Movements: Dissent and the Security State* (Black Point, NS: Fernwood Publishing, 2018); Mike Frost and Michel Gratton, *Spy World: Inside the Canadian and American Intelligence Establishments* (Toronto: Doubleday Canada, 1994); Andrew Mitrovica, *Covert Entry: Spies, Lies and Crimes inside Canada's Secret Service* (Toronto: Random House Canada, 2002).

20 Steve Hewitt, *Spying 101: The RCMP's Secret Activities at Canadian Universities, 1917–1997* (Toronto: University of Toronto Press, 2002); Gregory S. Kealey, *Spying on Canadians: The Royal Canadian Mounted Police Security Service and the Origins of the Long Cold War* (Toronto: University of Toronto Press, 2017); Christabelle Sethna and Steve Hewitt, *Just Watch Us: RCMP Surveillance of the Women's Liberation Movement in Cold War Canada* (Montreal and Kingston: McGill-Queen's University Press, 2018); Reg Whitaker and Steve Hewitt, *Canada and the Cold War* (Toronto: James Lorimer, 2003); Reg Whitaker and Gary Marcuse, *Cold War Canada: The Making of a National Insecurity State, 1945–1957* (Toronto: University of Toronto Press, 1996); Whitaker, Kealy, and Parnaby, *Secret Service*.

21 Frost and Gratton, *Spy World*; and Cole, *Smokescreen*, are examples of books by unhappy former employees.

22 Kim Bolan, *Loss of Faith: How the Air-India Bombers Got Away with Murder* (Toronto: McClelland & Stewart, 2005); Stewart Bell, *The Martyr's Oath: The Apprenticeship of a Homegrown Terrorist* (Mississauga, ON: John Wiley & Sons Canada, 2005); Bell, *Cold Terror: How Canada Nurtures and Exports Terrorism around the World* (Mississauga, ON: John Wiley & Sons Canada, 2007); Michelle Shephard, *Decade of Fear: Reporting from Terrorism's Grey Zone* (Vancouver: Douglas & McIntyre, 2011).

23 Christopher Andrew, *The Defence of the Realm: The Authorized History of MI5* (London: Penguin, 2009). Ironically, at time of writing, the UK signals intelligence agency, Government Communications Headquarters (GCHQ), had commissioned a Canadian, John Ferris, to write the official history

to be published in 2020. See John Ferris, *Behind the Enigma: The Authorised History of GCHQ, Britain's Secret Cyber-Intelligence Agency* (London: Bloomsbury Publishing, forthcoming).

24 At time of writing, the relationship of HTS to Al Qaida remains unclear. As of May 2018 the U.S. State Department describes HTS as an alias for Al Qaida's presence in Syria. However, those who follow the relationship between al Qaida and its current and former affiliates note there have been very public splits and spats between HTS and Al Qaida. Whether this is for show or a genuine parting of ways is unknown. However, this is a good example of the challenge that terrorism analysts and investigators face. See Thomas Joscelyn, "State Department Amends Terror Designation for al Nusrah Front," Foundation for the Defence of Democracies, 31 May 2018, https://www.longwarjournal.org/archives/2018/05/state-department-amends-terror-designation-for-al-nusrah-front.php. In April 2020, in the aftermath of this split, a group calling itself Hurras al-Din (Guardians of Religion Organization) has emerged as the al Qaida affiliate, ensuring the group still has a presence in the region and is widely viewed as posing a threat to Western interests. Aaron Y. Zelin, "Huras al-Din: The Overlooked al-Qaeda Group in Syria," Washington Institute, 24 September 2019, https://www.washingtoninstitute.org/policy-analysis/view/huras-al-din-the-overlooked-al-qaeda-group-in-syria.

25 In 2014 Justin Bourque, who subscribed to an anti-government ideology, shot and killed three RCMP officers and injured two more in New Brunswick. In January 2017 Alexandre Bissonnette shot and killed six individuals, injuring nineteen more, at a mosque in Quebec City. His trial revealed that Bissonnette consumed substantial amounts of anti-Islam and anti-Immigration media prior to his attack. In April 2018 Alek Minassian ran over ten individuals and injured sixteen more in a van attack in Toronto. Minassian professed allegiance to the "Incel" movement, a group of radically misogynistic individuals who blame society, especially women, for their failure to find sexual partners. These cases are described further in chapter 2.

26 Mack Lamoureux, "The Birth of Canada's Armed, Anti-Islamic 'Patriot' Group," Vice, 14 June 2017, https://www.vice.com/en_ca/article/new9wd/the-birth-of-canadas-armed-anti-islamic-patriot-group; Mack Lamoureux and Ben Makuch, "Atomwaffen, an American Neo-Nazi Terror Group, Is In Canada," Vice, 19 June 2018, https://www.vice.com/en_ca/article/a3a8ae/atomwaffen-an-american-neo-nazi-terror-group-is-in-canada.

27 Catherine Tunney, "CSIS Dealing with Right-Wing Extremism 'More and More,' Says Spy Chief," CBC News, 10 April 2019, https://www.cbc.ca/news/politics/csis-right-wing-white-supremacy-1.5092304.

28 Canadian Security Intelligence Service, *2018 CSIS Public Report*, June 2019, https://www.canada.ca/content/dam/csis-scrs/documents/publications/2018-PUBLIC_REPORT_ENGLISH_Digital.pdf.
29 Amar Amarasingam and Stephanie Carvin, "Defining Terrorism: Is It Time for a Change?," OpenCanada, 11 May 2018, https://www.opencanada.org/features/defining-terrorism-it-time-change/.
30 Nesbitt, "Empirical Study."
31 Amar Amarasingam and Stephanie Carvin, "ISIS Foreign Fighters: Their Return and Canadian Responses," in *Canada and the Middle East* (Toronto: University of Toronto Press, forthcoming).
32 See, generally, Public Policy Forum, *The Shattered Mirror: News, Democracy and Trust in the Digital Age*, January 2017, https://shatteredmirror.ca/.
33 Canadian Security Intelligence Service, "Who Said What: The Security Challenges of Modern Disinformation," February 2018, https://www.canada.ca/en/security-intelligence-service.html.
34 Canadian Civil Liberties Association, "Should the Snowden Revelations Matter to Canadians?," 9 February 2017.
35 Alex Boutilier, "CSIS Program Illegally Spied for a Decade, Judge Rules," *Toronto Star*, 3 November 2016, https://www.thestar.com/news/canada/2016/11/03/csis-illegally-kept-sensitive-data-about-people-for-a-decade-federal-court.html; Colin Freeze, "CSIS Not Being Forthcoming with Court, Federal Judge Says," *Globe and Mail*, 25 November 2013, https://www.theglobeandmail.com/news/national/csis-not-being-forthcoming-with-court-federal-judge-says/article15599674/.
36 Hill+Knowlton Strategies, *National Security Consultations: What We Learned Report*, May 2017, 4 and 13, https://www.publicsafety.gc.ca/cnt/rsrcs/pblctns/2017-nsc-wwlr/index-en.aspx.

1. Violent Extremism: The Canadian Context

1 Michael Friscolanti, "Uncovering a Killer: Addict, Drifter, Walking Contradiction," *Maclean's*, 30 October 2014, http://www.macleans.ca/news/canada/michael-zehaf-bibeau-addict-drifter-walking-contradiction/.
2 Friscolanti, "Uncovering a Killer."
3 See, for example, Kent Roach, "Why the Quebec City Mosque Shooting Was Terrorism," *Globe and Mail*, 19 April 2018, https://www.theglobeandmail.com/opinion/article-why-the-quebec-city-mosque-shooting-was-terrorism/; Michael Nesbit and Dana Hagg have engaged in empirical research on this question, finding that by early 2019, fifty-

three out of fifty-four of terrorism charges in Canada have been laid against individuals subscribing to al Qaida or Islamic State–inspired extremism. Far-right extremists have been charged with public order offences, but not terrorism charges. "Terrorism Prosecutions in Canada: Elucidating the Elements of the Offences," *Alberta Law Review* 57, no. 2 (2020): 595–648.
4 The full list of international treaties is found in section 83.01 (1) (a) of the Criminal Code of Canada. The international measures to suppress terrorism financing are discussed in chapter 2.
5 Kent Roach, *The 9/11 Effect: Comparative Counter-Terrorism* (Toronto: University of Toronto Press, 2011), 361.
6 Canada's current list of terrorist entities can be found on the Public Safety Canada website, "Currently Listed Entities," https://www.publicsafety.gc.ca/cnt/ntnl-scrt/cntr-trrrsm/lstd-ntts/crrnt-lstd-ntts-en.aspx. Thanks to Craig Forcese for helping me develop this section.
7 Reg Whitaker, G. Kealy, and A. Parnaby, *The Secret Service: Political Policing in Canada from the Fenians to Fortress America* (Toronto: University of Toronto Press, 2012), 19–59.
8 Bell, *Cold Terror*, 27; David Charters, "The (Un)Peaceable Kingdom? Terrorism and Canada before 9/11," *IRPP Policy Matters* 9, no. 4 (2008), http://irpp.org/wp-content/uploads/assets/research/security-and-democracy/the-unpeaceable-kingdom/pmvol9no4.pdf; Sam Mullins, "'Global Jihad': The Canadian Experience," *Terrorism and Political Violence* 25, no. 5 (2013): 734–76.
9 Charters, "(Un)Peaceable Kingdom," 8–14.
10 Charters, "(Un)Peaceable Kingdom," 16–17; Brian Stewart, "The October Crisis Reinterpreted," CBC News, 4 October 2010, https://www.cbc.ca/news/canada/the-october-crisis-reinterpreted-1.940346; Whitaker, Kealy, and Parnaby, *Secret Service*, 272–3.
11 Tony Addison and S.M. Murshed, "Transnational Terrorism as a Spillover of Domestic Disputes in Other Countries," *Defence and Peace Economics* 16, no. 2 (2005): 70.
12 Bell, *Cold Terror*, 31–2.
13 Charters, "(Un)Peaceable Kingdom," 18–19.
14 Bell, *Cold Terror*, 27–31; Charters, "(Un)Peaceable Kingdom," 19–20; Mary Janigan, "Assassination with a Vengeance," *Maclean's*, 6 September 1982, 12.
15 Charters, "(Un)Peaceable Kingdom," 19.
16 Maryam Razavy, "Sikh Militant Movements in Canada," *Terrorism and Political Violence* 18, no. 1 (2006): 80.

17 Renée Jeffery and Ian Hall, "Post-Conflict Justice in Divided Democracies: The 1984 Anti-Sikh Riots in India," *Third World Quarterly*, 2020. (Available online 5 February 2020).
18 Bell, *Cold Terror*, 27–45.
19 Stephanie Nolen and Wendy Stueck, "Does Canada Harbour Sikh Extremists?," *Globe and Mail*, 9 November 2012, http://www.theglobeandmail.com/news/world/does-canada-harbour-sikh-extremists/article5177449/; Razavy, "Sikh Militant Movements in Canada," 90. The issue of Sikh separatism in Canada re-emerged with the "Atwal Controversy" in early 2018 when an individual with historical ties to Sikh separatism appeared at an event with the Prime Minister and his wife in India. The extent to which Sikh separatism remains a concern in Canada was then fiercely debated in the media. For a critical perspective on the controversy, see Sandy Garossino, "The Truth behind the Story Engulfing Canada's Sikh Politicians," *National Observer*, 15 March 2018, https://www.nationalobserver.com/2018/03/15/opinion/truth-behind-story-engulfing-canadas-sikh-politicians.
20 Canadian Security Intelligence Service, *2018 CSIS Public Report*, 20; Public Safety Canada, *Public Report on the Terrorist Threat*, 3rd version, April 2019, 8, https://www.publicsafety.gc.ca/cnt/rsrcs/pblctns/pblc-rprt-trrrsm-thrt-cnd-2018/index-en.aspx.
21 In revising its report, the government stated, "The Government's communication of threats must be clear, concise, and cannot be perceived as maligning any groups. As we continue this review, it is apparent that in outlining a threat, it must be clearly linked to an ideology rather than a community." On the controversy, see Mia Rabson, "Terror Reports to Reference Ideology, Not Religions after 'Sikh Extremism' Criticism: Goodale," Global News, 12 April 2019, https://globalnews.ca/news/5162913/goodale-terror-report-language/.
22 U.S. Federal Bureau of Investigation, "Taming the Tamil Tigers from Here in the U.S.," January 2008, https://www.fbi.gov/news/stories/2008/january/tamil_tigers011008; Iain Overton and Henry Dodd, "A Short History of Suicide Bombing," Action on Armed Violence, 23 August 2013, https://aoav.org.uk/2013/a-short-history-of-suicide-bombings/.
23 Kate Pickert, "A Brief History of the Tamil Tigers," *Time*, 4 January 2009, http://content.time.com/time/world/article/0,8599,1869501,00.html.
24 See Bell, *Cold Terror*, 47–102; Human Rights Watch, *Funding the Final War: LTTE Intimidation and Extortion in the Tamil Diaspora*, 15 March 2006, https://www.hrw.org/report/2006/03/14/funding-final-war/ltte-intimidation-and-extortion-tamil-diaspora; John Thompson, "Hosting

Terrorism: The Liberation Tigers of Tamil Eelam in Canada," in *Terror in the Peaceable Kingtom: Understanding and Addressing Violent Extremism in Canada*, ed. Daveed Gartenstein-Ross and Senator Linda Frum, 31–45 (Washington DC: FDD, 2012). The issue of LTTE/WTM financing is discussed further in chapter 2. LTTE clandestine influence will be discussed in chapter 6.

25 The author is grateful for discussions with Amarnath Amarasingam on this point.

26 It is a challenge to navigate Tamil groups and political organizations in Canada. However, several politicians made high-profile visits with Tiger-affiliated groups. Then Finance Minister Paul Martin and Minister of International Cooperation Maria Minna attended a dinner hosted by the Federation of Associations of Canadian Tamils (FACT), in May 2000. FACT was an umbrella group for Tamil associations that was eventually take over by Tamil sympathizers. Bell, *Cold Terror*, 80–2. For this incident and FACT, see Amarnath Amarasingam, *Pain, Pride and Politics: Social Movement Activism and the Sri Lankan Tamil Diaspora in Canada* (Athens: University of Georgia Press, 2015), 85–9.

27 Charters, "(Un)Peaceable Kingdom," 20.

28 Alex P. Schmid, *Al-Qaeda's "Single Narrative" and Attempts to Develop Counter-Narratives: The State of Knowledge* (The Hague: International Centre for Counter-Terrorism, 2014), https://www.icct.nl/download/file/Schmid-Al-Qaeda%27s-Single-Narrative-and-Attempts-to-Develop-Counter-Narratives-January-2014.pdf.

29 For a survey, see Angel Rabasa, Peter Chalk, Kim Cragin, Sara A. Daly, Heather S. Gregg, Theodore W. Karasik, Kevin A. O'Brien, and William Rosenau, "South Asian Clusters," in *Beyond al-Qaeda Part 1: The Global Jihadist Movement*, 81–104 (Santa Monica, CA: RAND, 2006).

30 Mullins, "'Global Jihad,'" 735.

31 Bell, *Cold Terror*, 147–74; Mullins, "'Global Jihad,'" 735–6.

32 Bell, *Cold Terror*, 224–5. Mullins, "'Global Jihad,'" 735.

33 Mullins, "'Global Jihad,'" 737.

34 Bell, *Martyr's Oath*.

35 R v Khawaja, 2012 SCC 69, [2012] 3 SCR 555.

36 Manuel R. Torres Soriano, "Between the Pen and the Sword: The Global Islamic Media Front in the West," *Terrorism and Political Violence* 24, no. 5 (2012): 769–86, esp. 772–6.

37 Federal Bureau of Investigation, "Alleged Terrorist Charged with Conspiracy to Kill Americans in Iraq," 19 January 2011, https://archives.fbi.gov/archives/newyork/press-releases/2011/alleged-terrorist-charged-with-conspiracy-to-kill-americans-in-iraq; Tom Hays,

"Canadian Man Pleads Guilty to U.S. Terror Charges in Alleged Murder Conspiracy," CTV News (Associated Press), 6 March 2018.
38 Thomas Jocelyn, "Islamic State Facilitator Moved Recruits through Turkey, US Says," Long War Journal, 17 June 2017, https://www.longwarjournal.org/archives/2017/06/islamic-state-facilitator-moved-recruits-through-turkey-us-says.php.
39 Charlie Winter and Jade Parker, "Virtual Caliphate Rebooted: The Islamic State's Evolving Online Strategy," Lawfare, 7 January 2018, https://www.lawfareblog.com/virtual-caliphate-rebooted-islamic-states-evolving-online-strategy.
40 On the Toronto 18, see Michelle Shephard, "Toronto," in *Decade of Fear: Reporting from Terrorism's Grey Zone*, 103–36 (Vancouver: Douglas & McIntyre, 2011); Mitchell D. Silber, "Operation Osage (Canada 2006)," in *The al Qaeda Factor: Plots against the West*, 245–59 (Philadelphia: University of Pennsylvania Press, 2012).
41 See, generally, Shephard, "Toronto."
42 Robert Bostelaar, "Hiva Alizadeh Pleads Guilty to Terror Plot," *Ottawa Citizen*, 18 September 2014.
43 Chris Cobb, "Misbahuddin Ahmed Sentenced to 12 Years for Terrorism Crimes," *Ottawa Citizen*, 24 October 2014, http://ottawacitizen.com/news/local-news/misbahuddin-ahmed-sentenced-to-12-years-for-terrorism-crimes.
44 Jason Burke, *The New Threat: The Past, Present and Future of Islamic Militancy* (New York: New Press, 2015), 15–22. While Burke combines this ecosystem into three, lumping the main organizations with their affiliates, the author believes that the regional affiliates continue to have a large degree of autonomy as well as local grievances, which may drive their activities and interests and should be seen as separate.
45 On the Islamic State's apocalyptic thinking and reliance on prophesies as a recruitment tool, see William McCants, *The ISIS Apocalypse: The History, Strategy and Doomsday Vision of the Islamic State* (New York: St. Martin's, 2015).
46 Daniel Byman, "Where Will the Islamic State Go Next?," Lawfare, 22 June 2018, https://www.lawfareblog.com/where-will-islamic-state-go-next; Eric Schmitt, "ISIS May Be Waning, but Global Threats of Terrorism Continue to Spread," *New York Times*, 6 July 2018, https://www.nytimes.com/2018/07/06/world/middleeast/isis-global-terrorism.html?rref=collection/issuecollection/todays-new-york-times&action=click&contentCollection=todayspaper&region=rank&module=package&version=highlights&contentPlacement=2&pgtype=collection.

47 Stewart Bell, "Dealing with Foreign Fighters; Document Reveals RCMP Strategy for Possible 'Flood of Foreign Fighters' Returning to Syria," *National Post*, 27 October 2016.
48 Public Safety Canada, "2018 Public Report," 3.
49 Public Safety Canada, "2018 Public Report," 3.
50 Numbers provided to author by terrorism researcher and professor Amarnath Amarasingam, 4 April 2020.
51 Schmitt, "ISIS May Be Waning."
52 Byman, "Where Will the Islamic State Go Next?" Colin P. Clarke and Amarnath Amarasingam suggest that Islamic State fighters will break down into a "hard core" waiting for an "ISIS 2.0" or may seek to join other groups in the region, jihadis unable to return home who may seek the next zone of conflict and "returnees." See Colin P. Clarke and Amarnath Amarasingam, "Where Do ISIS Fighters Go When the Caliphate Falls?," *Atlantic*, 6 March 2017, https://www.theatlantic.com/international/archive/2017/03/isis-foreign-fighter-jihad-syria-iraq/518313/.
53 Brian H. Fishman, *The Master Plan: ISIS, al-Qaeda and the Jihadi Strategy for Final Victory* (New Haven, CT: Yale University Press, 2016), 102.
54 Rukmini Callimachi, "ISIS Spokesman Calls for Attacks on Arab Nations," *New York Times*, 22 April 2018, https://www.nytimes.com/2018/04/22/world/middleeast/isis-arabs-attacks.html.
55 Although Akhtar was originally charged with first-degree murder, evidence appears to have emerged suggesting that he was inspired by the Islamic State. What this evidence is and why police came to this conclusion was not clear at time of publication.
56 See, for example, Peter L. Bergen, *Manhunt: The Ten-Year Search for Bin Laden from 9/11 to Abbottabad* (Toronto: Anchor Canada, 2013), esp. "Epilogue: The Twilight of al-Qaeda," 250–61. To be fair, Bergen notes that there was the possibility that al Qaida could thrive in the chaos of the war in Syria and Yemen.
57 Jason Burke, "No Longer Does al-Qaida Grab the Headlines: That Might Be the Plan," *Guardian*, 4 August 2019, https://www.theguardian.com/commentisfree/2019/aug/04/no-longer-does-al-qaida-grab-headlines-that-might-be-plan.
58 Bruce Hoffmann, "Al-Qaeda's Resurrection," Council on Foreign Relations Expert Brief, 6 March 2018, https://www.cfr.org/expert-brief/al-qaedas-resurrection.
59 Catherine E. Shoichet and Josh Levs, "Al Qaeda Branch Claims Charlie Hebdo Attack Was Years in the Making," CNN, 21 January 2015, https://

www.cnn.com/2015/01/14/europe/charlie-hebdo-france-attacks/index.html; Hoffmann, "Al-Qaeda's Resurrection."

60 In 2018, Charles Lister estimates that HTS had 12,000 fighters, and Bruce Hoffmann estimates that al Qaida has 10,000–20,000 fighters. The latter includes HTS as al Qaida. See Hoffmann, "Al-Qaeda's Resurrection"; Charles Lister, "How al-Qa`ida Lost Control of Its Syrian Affiliate: The Inside Story," *CTC Sentinel* 11, no. 2 (2018): 1–9.

61 Lister, "How al-Qa`ida Lost Control," 8. Hoffmann sees the relationship between the two as strong, whereas Lister does not. Hoffmann, "Al-Qaeda's Resurrection."

62 Eric Schmitt, "U.S. Sees Rising Threat in the West from Qaeda Branch in Syria," *New York Times*, 29 September 2019, https://www.nytimes.com/2019/09/29/world/middleeast/syria-qaeda-terrorism.html; Aaron Y. Zelin, "Huras al-Din: The Overlooked al-Qaeda Group in Syria," Washington Institute, 24 September 2019, https://www.washingtoninstitute.org/policy-analysis/view/huras-al-din-the-overlooked-al-qaeda-group-in-syria.

63 Tore Refslund Hamming, "With the Islamic State in Decline, What's al-Qaeda's Next Move?," War on the Rocks, 27 April 2018, https://warontherocks.com/2018/04/with-islamic-state-in-decline-whats-al-qaedas-next-move/.

64 In January 2019 a youth in Kingston was arrested and charged with two terrorism offences: facilitation and counselling in relation to a bomb plot. These individuals appear to have been engaged in al Qaida or Islamic State–inspired extremism. However, there was insufficient detail available at time of publication to make a further assessment of this case. See Philip Ling, Catharine Tunney, and John Paul Tasker, "RCMP Charge Kingston, Ont., Youth with Terror-Related Offence after Security Probe," CBC News, 25 January 2019, https://www.cbc.ca/news/politics/rcmp-arrests-security-kingston-1.4992518.

65 Bruce Hoffmann, *Inside Terrorism*, 3rd ed. (New York: Columbia University Press, 2017), 14.

66 Hoffmann, *Inside Terrorism*, 17–18, 270. See also, generally, Dan Byman, *Deadly Connections: States That Sponsor Terrorism* (Cambridge: Cambridge University Press, 2005).

67 Byman, *Deadly Connections*, 11–15.

68 Department of Public Safety and Emergency Preparedness, "Currently Listed Entities: Lashkar-e-Tayyiba (LeT)," 15 February 2018, https://www.publicsafety.gc.ca/cnt/ntnl-scrt/cntr-trrrsm/lstd-ntts/crrnt-lstd-ntts-en.aspx#2037; Hoffmann, *Inside Terrorism*, 275.

69 Stephen Tankel, "Ten Years after Mumbai, the Group Responsible Is Deadlier Than Ever," War on the Rocks, 26 November 2018, https://warontherocks.com/2018/11/ten-years-after-mumbai-the-group-responsible-is-deadlier-than-ever/.
70 Silber, *Al Qaeda Factor*, 254; Bill Gillespie, "Accused in Toronto 18 Plot Pleads Guilty," CBC News, 26 February 2010, https://www.cbc.ca/news/canada/toronto/accused-in-toronto-18-plot-pleads-guilty-1.913929.
71 Stewart Bell, "U.S. Prosecutors Link Alleged Terror Cell to al-Qaeda: 'Army of the Righteous': Men Allegedly Spent a Week in Toronto Meeting with Suspects," *National Post*, 20 July 2006; Silber, *Al Qaeda Factor*, 254.
72 Jonathan Masters and Zachary Laub, "Hezbollah," Council on Foreign Relations, 3 January 2014, https://www.cfr.org/backgrounder/hezbollah.
73 BBC News, "Profile: Lebanon's Hezbollah Movement," 15 March 2016, https://www.bbc.com/news/world-middle-east-10814698.
74 Byman, *Deadly Connections*, 5.
75 BBC News, "Profile."
76 Federal Bureau of Investigation, "Hijacking of TWA Flight 847," n.d., https://www.fbi.gov/history/famous-cases/hijacking-of-twa-flight-847.
77 Chris Nuttall-Smith and Peter O'Neil, "Money and Hezbollah's Canadian Connections," *Vancouver Sun*, 23 January 2002.
78 Dan Chapman, "A Tobacco Road to Terror? Charlotte Men Accused of Aid to Hezbollah," *Atlanta Journal Constitution*, 2 May 2002; Matthew Levitt, "Hizballah's Canadian Procurement Network," in *Terror in the Peaceable Kingdom*, ed. Daveed Gartenstein-Ross and Linda Frum (Washington DC: FDD, 2012), 63.
79 Levitt, "Hizballah's Canadian Procurement Network," 63. More on Hezbollah's financing will be discussed in chapter 2.
80 Bell, *Cold Terror*, 103–6, 142–5.
81 Stewart Bell, "Canadian Wanted on Terrorism Charges in Bulgaria for Alleged Role in Hezbollah Bus Bombing," *National Post*, 22 January 2016, https://nationalpost.com/news/canada/canadian-wanted-on-terrorism-charges-in-bulgaria-for-alleged-role-in-hezbollah-bus-bombing.
82 Tu Than Ha, "Canadian Suspect, 25, Named in Bus Bombing," *Globe and Mail*, 26 July 2013; Adrian Humphreys, "Canadian Accused of Hezbollah Ties Could Be in Gaza Strip, Officials Say," *National Post*, 27 July 2013.
83 Barbara Perry and Ryan Scrivens, "Uneasy Alliances: A Look at the Right-Wing Extremist Movement in Canada," *Studies in Conflict and Terrorism* 39, no. 3 (2016): 821.
84 Perry and Scrivens, "Uneasy Alliances," 821.

85 Stanley Barrett, *Is God a Racist? The Right Wing in Canada* (Toronto: University of Toronto Press, 1987).
86 Richard B. Parent and James O. Eillis III, "Right-Wing Extremism in Canada," TSAS Working Paper Series no. 14-03, May 2014, 9–10.
87 Christine Sismondo, "The KKK Has a History in Canada, and It Can Return," *Maclean's*, 18 August 2017, https://www.macleans.ca/news/canada/the-kkk-has-a-history-in-canada-and-it-can-return/.
88 Samuel Tanner and Aurélie Campana, "The Process of Radicalization: Right-Wing Skinheads in Quebec," TSAS Working Paper Series 14-07, August 2014, 2.
89 Parent and Ellis, "Right-Wing Extremism," 13.
90 Parent and Ellis, "Right-Wing Extremism," 11.
91 Parent and Ellis, "Right Wing Extremism," 11.
92 Tim Bryan et al., "The Dangers of Porous Borders: The 'Trump Effect' in Canada," October 2018, https://www.researchgate.net/publication/330482179_The_Dangers_of_Porous_Borders_The_Trump_Effect_in_Canada_Journal_of_Hate_Studies. See also Barbara Perry and Ryan Scrivens, "Epilogue: The Trump Effect on Right-Wing Extremism in Canada," in Perry and Scrivens, *Right-Wing Extremism in Canada*. 143–72 (London: Palgrave Macmilllan, 2019).
93 Mack Lamoureux, "Canada Is Spending $300K on Research into Far-Right Extremism," Vice News, 7 March 2019, https://www.vice.com/en_ca/article/59xq7q/canada-is-investing-in-far-right-extremism-research.
94 Joseph Brean, "Canadian Founder Gavin McInnes Quits Proud Boys after FBI Labels It an 'Extremist Group with Ties to White Nationalism,'" *National Post*, 22 November 2018, https://nationalpost.com/news/canada/gavin-mcinnes-quits-proud-boys.
95 A more detailed history can be found in Perry and Scrivens, *Right-Wing Extremism in Canada*. See especially chapter 2, "Tracing the History of Right-Wing Extremism in Canada," 23–57.
96 Perry and Scrivens, *Right-Wing Extremism in Canada*, 27.
97 Mack Lamoureux, "Canada Adds Far-Right Groups to Terror Watch List for First Time," Vice News, 26 June 2019, https://www.vice.com/en_ca/article/8xz77k/canada-adds-far-right-groups-to-terror-watch-list-for-first-time.
98 La Meute members have gone on the record as describing themselves as far-right but not "extreme right." They argue that their group is not religious or homophobic but nationalist. However, the shared characteristics with other groups in this section, especially the idea that immigration is an existential threat, and Islamophobia, are clear. Jonathan Montpetit, "How Quebec's Largest Far-Right Group Tries to Win Friends,

Influence People," CBC News, 21 August 2017, https://www.cbc.ca/news/canada/montreal/quebec-la-meute-far-right-1.4255193.
99 Claire Loewen, "Counter-Protesters Swarm Far-Right La Meute Protest in Quebec City," *Montreal Gazette*, 3 May 2018, https://montrealgazette.com/news/local-news/hundreds-of-counter-protesters-swarm-far-right-la-meute-protest-in-quebec-city. On La Meute generally, see Brigitte Noël, "La Meute: The Illusions and Delusions of Quebec's 'Largest' Right-Wing Group," Vice, 6 January 2017, https://www.vice.com/en_ca/article/d7pmk7/la-meute-the-illusions-and-delusions-of-quebecs-largest-right-wing-group.
100 Mack Lamoureux, "In the End, a Quebec Far-Right Group's Biggest Enemy Was Themselves," Vice, 15 October 2018, https://www.vice.com/en_ca/article/d3nekz/in-the-end-la-muete-quebec-far-right-groups-biggest-enemy-was-themselves.
101 CBC News, "Police Investigating Clash inside Eaton Centre during Dyke March," 25 June 2019, https://www.cbc.ca/news/canada/toronto/eaton-centre-fight-1.5189651.
102 Raffy Boudjikanian, "Banned by Facebook, Shunned by Politicians, Soldiers of Odin Hold Event at Royal Canadian Legion Branch," CBC News, 2 May 2019, https://www.cbc.ca/news/canada/edmonton/soldiers-of-odin-legion-1.5119042; Mack Lamoureux, "Soldiers of Odin, Europe's Notorious Anti-Immigration Group, Beginning to Form Cells in Canada," Vice, 15 April 2016, https://www.vice.com/en/article/gqma9m/soldiers-of-odin-europes-notorious-anti-immigration-group-beginning-to-form-cells-in-canada.
103 Mack Lamoureux, "Far-Right Activists Targeted a Vegan Cafe Assuming Antifa Were There," Vice, 8 July 2019, https://www.vice.com/en_ca/article/xwn9ma/far-right-activists-targeted-a-vegan-cafe-assuming-antifa-were-there; Omar Mosleh, "Wolves of Odin Visit to Edmonton Mosque Prompts Police Investigation," *Toronto Star* (Edmonton), 25 January 2019, https://www.thestar.com/edmonton/2019/01/25/wolves-of-odin-visit-to-edmonton-mosque-prompts-police-investigation.html.
104 Mack Lamoureux, "Soldiers of Odin Edmonton Chapter Shuts Down, Rebrands as 'Canadian Infidels,'" Vice, 15 October 2018, https://www.vice.com/en_ca/article/xw9pwj/soldiers-of-odin-edmonton-chapter-shuts-down-rebrands-as-canadian-infidels.
105 Boudjikanian, "Banned by Facebook."
106 Mosleh, "Wolves of Odin."
107 Simon Coutu, "Canada's Newest Ultra-Nationalist Group Plans Show of Force," Vice, 7 September 2017, https://www.vice.com/en_ca/article/yww8ab/canadas-newest-ultra-nationalist-group-plans-show-of-force.

108 Caroline Orr, "Hate Groups Mix with Yellow Vests on 'Front Line' of Extremism in Canada," *National Observer*, 11 June 2019, https://www.nationalobserver.com/2019/06/11/news/hate-groups-mix-yellow-vests-front-line-extremism-canada.

109 Mack Lamoureux, "The Birth of Canada's Armed, Anti-Islamic 'Patriot' Group," Vice, 14 June 2017, https://www.vice.com/en_ca/article/new9wd/the-birth-of-canadas-armed-anti-islamic-patriot-group.

110 Mack Lamoureux and Ben Makuch, "Canadian Military Confirms Neo-Nazi Group Atomwaffen Was within Its Ranks," Vice, 28 May 2019, https://www.vice.com/en_ca/article/a3xndb/canadian-military-confirms-neo-nazi-group-atomwaffen-was-within-its-ranks.

111 Stewart Bell and Mercedes Stephenson, "Canadian Armed Forces Members Linked to Six Hate Groups: Internal Report," Global News, 27 May 2019, https://globalnews.ca/news/5322011/canadian-armed-forces-members-linked-to-six-hate-groups-internal-report/.

112 Ben Makuch, "Audio Recording Claims Neo-Nazi Terror Group Is Disbanding," Vice, 16 March 2020, https://www.vice.com/en_ca/article/qjdnam/audio-recording-claims-neo-nazi-terror-group-is-disbanding.

113 Nathan A. Sales, "Designation of the Russian Imperial Movement," U.S. Department of State, 6 April 2020, https://www.state.gov/designation-of-the-russian-imperial-movement/. The move is different from listing the group as a "foreign terrorist organization" but has a similar policy impact. See Charlie Savage, Adam Goldman, and Eric Schmitt, "U.S. Will Give Terrorist Label to White Supremacist Group for First Time," *New York Times*, 6 April 2020, https://www.nytimes.com/2020/04/06/us/politics/terrorist-label-white-supremacy-Russian-Imperial-Movement.html.

114 Jason Wilson, "Revealed: The True Identity of the Leader of an American Neo-Nazi Terror Group," *Guardian*, 24 January 2020, https://www.theguardian.com/world/2020/jan/23/revealed-the-true-identity-of-the-leader-of-americas-neo-nazi-terror-group.

115 Ryan Thorpe, "White Supremacist in Army Reserve," *Winnipeg Free Press*, 19 August 2019, https://www.winnipegfreepress.com/local/white-supremacist-in-army-reserve-553050082.html.

116 Ben Makuch and Mack Lamoureux, "Neo-Nazis Are Organizing Secretive Paramilitary Training across America," Vice, 20 November 2018, https://www.vice.com/en_us/article/a3mexp/neo-nazis-are-organizing-secretive-paramilitary-training-across-america.

117 Ben Makuch, "Experts Say Neo-Nazi 'Accelerationists' Discuss Taking Advantage of Coronavirus Crisis," Vice, 18 March 2020, https://www.vice.com/en_ca/article/pkcwgv/experts-say-neo-nazi-accelerationists-discuss-taking-advantage-of-coronavirus-crisis; Wilson, "Revealed: The True Identity."

118 Wilson, "Revealed: The True Identity."
119 James McCarten, "Patrik Mathews, Former Canadian Forces Reservist and Accused Neo-Nazi, Pleads Not Guilty to U.S. Weapons Charges," *Toronto Star*, 18 February 2020, https://www.thestar.com/news/canada/2020/02/18/patrik-mathews-former-canadian-forces-reservist-and-accused-neo-nazi-to-appear-in-court-in-maryland.html.
120 Alice Marwick and Rebecca Lewis, "Media Manipulation and Disinformation Online," *Data & Society*, 15 May 2017, 5–7, https://datasociety.net/output/media-manipulation-and-disinfo-online/.
121 For more on this, see the discussion on "like-minded groups" in chapter 7.
122 Shannon Carranco and Jon Milton, "Canada's New Far Right: A Trove of Private Chat Room Messages Reveals an Extremist Subculture," *Globe and Mail*, 29 April 2019, https://www.theglobeandmail.com/canada/article-canadas-new-far-right-a-trove-of-private-chat-room-messages-reveals/.
123 Jonathan Goldsbie and Graeme Gordon, "Faith Goldy Fired from the Rebel," Canadaland, 17 August 2017, http://www.canadalandshow.com/faith-goldy-gone-rebel/; Maya Oppenheim, "Lauren Southern: Far-Right Canadian Activist Detained in Calais and Banned from Entering UK," *Independent*, 13 March 2018, https://www.independent.co.uk/news/uk/home-news/lauren-southern-far-right-canada-racist-calais-detain-uk-ban-enter-visa-a8254116.html; Brooke Rolfe, "Far-Right Youtube Activist Has Her Australian Visa Rejected – the Day before She Was Scheduled to Arrive for 'Anti-Immigration Speaking Tour,'" *Daily Mail Australia*, 8 July 2018, http://www.dailymail.co.uk/news/article-5932185/Far-right-Youtube-activist-Australian-visa-rejected-hours-fly-out.html.
124 Martin Patriquin et al., "The Racist Podcaster Who Started a Neo-Nazi Coffee Company to Fund White Nationalism," Vice, 16 May 2018, https://www.vice.com/en_ca/article/59qb93/the-racist-podcaster-who-started-a-neo-nazi-coffee-company-to-fund-white-nationalism.
125 Kathleen Harris, "Facebook Bans Faith Goldy and 'Dangerous' Alt-Right Groups," CBC News, 8 April 2019, https://www.cbc.ca/news/politics/facebook-faith-goldy-ban-alt-right-1.5088827.
126 Richard B. Parent and James O. Ellis III, "The Future of Right-Wing Terrorism in Canada," TSAS Working Paper Series, 16-12, July 2016, 12.
127 Parent and Ellis, "Future of Right-Wing Terrorism," 15.
128 Parent and Ellis, "Future of Right-Wing Terrorism," 18.
129 Jana G. Pruden, "Police Killer Espoused Extremist Views Online; Raddatz Railed against Courts, Government," *Edmonton Journal*, 11 June 2015.
130 Parent and Ellis, "Future of Right-Wing Terrorism," 18; Perry and Scrivens, *Right-Wing Extremism*, 174 and 214.
131 CBC News, "Justin Bourque: Latest Revelations about Man Charged in Moncton Shooting," 5 June 2014, http://www.cbc.ca/news/canada

/new-brunswick/justin-bourque-latest-revelations-about-man-charged-in-moncton-shooting-1.2665900; Tamsin McMahon, Michael Friscolanti, and Martin Patriquin, "The Untold Story of Justin Bourque," *Maclean's*, 15 June 2014, https://www.macleans.ca/news/canada/untold-story-justin-bourque/.

132 Jeff Gruenewald, Steven Chermak, and Joshua D. Freilich, "Far-Right Lone Wolf Homicides in the United States," *Studies in Conflict & Terrorism* 36, no. 12 (2013): 1007.

133 Amy Dempsey, "'I Was Like, How Did He Get a Van?' Inside the Life of Alek Minassian, the Toronto Van Rampage Suspect No One Thought Capable of Murder," *Toronto Star*, 11 May 2018, https://www.thestar.com/news/gta/2018/05/11/i-was-like-how-did-he-get-a-van-inside-the-life-of-alek-minassian-the-toronto-van-rampage-suspect-no-one-thought-capable-of-murder.html.

134 BBC News, "Elliot Rodger: How Misogynist Killer Became 'Incel Hero,'" 26 April 2018, https://www.bbc.com/news/world-us-canada-43892189; Mack Lamoureux, "A Brief History of 'Incel,' the Misogynistic Group Allegedly Cited by Toronto Van Attacker," Vice, 24 April 2018, https://www.vice.com/en_ca/article/pax9kz/a-brief-history-of-incel-the-misogynistic-group-allegedly-cited-by-toronto-van-attacker.

135 Nicole Brockbank, "Alek Minassian Reveals Details of Toronto Van Attack in Video of Police Interview," CBC News, 27 September 2019, https://www.cbc.ca/news/canada/toronto/alek-minassian-police-interview-1.5298021.

136 Erik White, "Alexander Stavropoulos Pleads Guilty to Two Counts of Attempted Murder in Random Knife Attack," CBC News, 13 January 2020, https://www.cbc.ca/news/canada/sudbury/alexander-stavropoulos-sentencing-random-knife-attack-1.5398849.

137 Perry and Scrivens, "Uneasy Alliances," 826 and 830.

138 Perry and Scrivens, "Uneasy Alliances," 830.

139 Perry and Scrivens, "Uneasy Alliances," 823.

140 Adam Carter, "'Hateful' Protest at Hamilton Pride Event Condemned," CBC News, 15 June 2019, https://www.cbc.ca/news/canada/hamilton/hamilton-pride-festival-altercation-police-1.5177439.

141 CBC News, "Police Investigating Clash."

142 Andy Riga, "Quebec Mosque Killer Confided He Wished He Had Shot More People, Court Told," *Montreal Gazette*, 17 April 2018, http://montrealgazette.com/news/local-news/quebec-mosque-shooter-alexandre-bissonnette-trawled-trumps-twitter-feed.

143 Josh K. Elliott, "New Zealand Shooter Covered Weapons with Names of Canada's Alexandre Bissonnette, Other Killers," Global News, 18 March

2019, https://globalnews.ca/news/5059136/christchurch-shooter-guns-names-new-zealand/.
144 Weiyi Cai and Simone Landon, "Attacks by White Extremists Are Growing. So Are Their Connections," *New York Times*, 3 April 2019, https://www.nytimes.com/interactive/2019/04/03/world/white-extremist-terrorism-christchurch.html?mtrref=www.google.ca&assetType=REGIWALL.
145 Robert Evans, "The El Paso Shooting and the Gamification of Terror," 4 August 2019, Bellingcat, https://www.bellingcat.com/news/americas/2019/08/04/the-el-paso-shooting-and-the-gamification-of-terror/.
146 Perry and Scrivens, "Uneasy Alliances," 831–3.
147 Perry and Scrivens, "Uneasy Alliances," 829.
148 Security Intelligence Review Committee, *SIRC Annual Report 2017–2018: Building for Tomorrow: The Future of Security Intelligence Accountability in Canada* (Ottawa: Public Works and Government Services Canada, 2018), http://www.sirc-csars.gc.ca/anrran/2017-2018/index-eng.html.
149 SIRC, *Annual Report 2017–2018*.
150 CSIS, *2018 CSIS Public Report*, 23.
151 CSIS, *2019 CSIS Public Report*, 11.
152 Jill Sanborn, "Confronting the Rise in Anti-Semitic Domestic Terrorism," statement before the House Committee on Homeland Security, Subcommittee on Intelligence and Counterterrorism, 26 February 2020, https://www.fbi.gov/news/testimony/confronting-the-rise-in-anti-semitic-domestic-terrorism.
153 Jennifer Varriale Carson, "Left-Wing Terrorism: From Anarchists to the Radical Environmental Movement and Back," in *The Handbook of the Criminology of Terrorism*, ed. Gary LaFree and Joshua D. Freilich, 310–22 (Chichester: John Wiley & Sons, 2017).
154 Brent L. Smith and Kathryn D. Morgan, "Terrorists Right and Left: Empirical Issues in Profiling American Terrorists," *Studies in Conflict and Terrorism* 17, no. 1 (1994): 44–50.
155 Jeffrey Monaghan and Kevin Walby, "Surveillance of Environmental Movements in Canada: Critical Infrastructure Protection and the Petro-Security Apparatus," *Contemporary Justice Review* 20, no. 1 (2017): 51–70.
156 Craig Proulx, "Colonizing Surveillance: Canada Constructs an Indigenous Terror Threat," *Anthropologica* 56, no. 1 (2014): 83–100.
157 Jeffrey Ian Ross and Ted Robert Gurr, "Why Terrorism Subsides: A Comparative Study of Canada and the United States," *Comparative Politics* 21, no. 4 (1989): 405–26.
158 Lorne Slotnick, "Group Lays Claim Litton Bombing," *Globe and Mail*, 21 October 1982.

159 Gordon Hak, *The Left in British Columbia: A History of Struggle* (Vancouver: Ronsdale, 2013), 158–9.
160 Stéphane Leman-Langlois and Jean-Paul Brodeur, "Terrorism Old and New: Counterterrorism in Canada," *Police Practice and Research* 6, no. 2 (2005): 128; Zuhair Kashmeri, "Five Charged in B.C. over Litton Bombing," *Globe and Mail*, 21 January 1983.
161 Leman-Langlois and Brodeur, "Terrorism Old and New," 128.
162 Walter Laqueur, "Post-modern Terrorism," *Foreign Affairs* 75, no. 5 (1996): 25.
163 Terrine Friday, "Explosion in Quebec Linked to G20 Violence, Professor Says," *National Post*, 3 July 2010.
164 Nora T. Lamontagne and Justin Ling, "Inside Canada's Five-Year-Long Anti-Terror Investigation of a Group of Quebec Communists," Vice, 19 March 2015, https://www.vice.com/en_ca/article/4w7kvq/inside-canadas-five-year-long-anti-terror-investigation-of-a-group-of-young-communists-235.
165 Andrew Seymour, "Man Charged in Firebombing Denied Bail," *Ottawa Citizen*, 29 June 2010.
166 Brent Wittmeier, "Pipeline Bomber Wiebo Ludwig Dies," *Star Phoenix*, 10 April 2012. Importantly, Ludwig does not fit into any convenient political category. While he may have been acting out of environmental concern, he also subscribed to a very conservative set of religious and social views. Paul Joosse, "Leaderless Resistance and Ideological Inclusion: The Case of the Earth Liberation Front," *Terrorism and Political Violence* 19 (2007): 362–3.
167 Carson, "Left-Wing Terrorism."
168 Jennifer Varriale Carson, Gary LaFree, and Laura Dugan, "Terrorist and Non-Terrorist Criminal Attacks by Radical Environmental and Animal Rights Groups in the United States, 1970–2007," *Terrorism and Political Violence* 24, no. 2 (2012): 316.
169 Carson, "Left-Wing Terrorism," 319; Steven Chermak and Jeffrey A. Gruenewald, "Laying a Foundation for the Criminological Examination of Right-Wing, Left-Wing and al Qaeda-Inspired Extremism in the United States," *Terrorism and Political Violence* 27, no. 1 (2015): 133–59.
170 Ideas in this section are discussed in Amarasingam and Carvin, "Defining Terrorism."
171 Amarasingam and Carvin, "Defining Terrorism"; Mike Blanchfield, "Conservative MP Questions Whether Rail Blockades Constitute Terrorism," CTV News, 27 February 2020, https://www.ctvnews.ca/politics/conservative-mp-questions-whether-rail-blockades-constitute-terrorism-1.4830220.

172 Omar Mosleh, "Canada Adds Extremist Neo-Nazi Groups with Alberta History to List of Terrorist Entities for First Time," *Toronto Star* (Edmonton), 26 June 2019, https://www.thestar.com/edmonton/2019/06/26/canada-adds-extremist-neo-nazi-groups-with-alberta-history-to-list-of-terrorist-entities-for-first-time.html.

2. Violent Extremist Threats in Canada Today

1 Kim Willsher, "Trial of Paris Attacks Suspect Salah Abdeslam Opens in Belgium," *Guardian*, 5 February 2018, https://www.theguardian.com/world/2018/feb/05/paris-attacks-suspect-salah-abdeslam-goes-on-trial-in-belgium.
2 Based on a survey of "Threat Environment" reports issued by the CSIS since 2001.
3 CBC News, "Montreal, Toronto Flights Targeted in Alleged British Bomb Plot," 3 April 2008, https://www.cbc.ca/news/world/montreal-toronto-flights-targeted-in-alleged-british-bomb-plot-1.747225.
4 Silber, *Al Qaeda Factor*, 47. See also Dominic Cascian, "Liquid Bomb Plot: What Happened," BBC News, 7 September 2009, http://news.bbc.co.uk/2/hi/uk_news/8242479.stm.
5 Stewart Bell, "Canada Was on Osama Bin Laden's Hit List: Intelligence Report," *National Post*, 6 January 2013, http://nationalpost.com/news/canada/canada-was-on-osama-bin-ladens-hit-list-intelligence-report.
6 Query done through the Canadian Incident Database, 8 July 2018, http://extremism.ca/.
7 Luke Harding and Rosie Cowan, "Pakistan Militants Linked to London Attacks," *Guardian*, 19 July 2005, https://www.theguardian.com/uk/2005/jul/19/july7.pakistan.
8 William K. Raushbaum, "Terror Suspect Is Charged with Plot to Use Bombs," *New York Times*, 24 September 2009, https://www.nytimes.com/2009/09/25/nyregion/25terror.html.
9 Canadian Press, "FBI Agent Who Helped Nab Via Rail Plotters Worries Sleeper Soldier in U.S. May Have Gotten Away," CBC News, 22 October 2017, https://www.cbc.ca/news/canada/toronto/fbi-agent-via-rail-american-1.4366571; Mark Hosenball, "Canada Train Plot Suspect Traveled to Iran – U.S. Officials," 25 April 2013, https://www.reuters.com/article/canada-suspect-iran-travel-idINDEE93O0F120130425.
10 Scott Shane, "The Enduring Influence of Anwar al-Awlaki in the Age of the Islamic State," *CTC Sentinel* 9, no. 7 (2016), https://ctc.usma.edu

/the-enduring-influence-of-anwar-al-awlaki-in-the-age-of-the-islamic-state/.

11 Rukmini Callimachi, "Not 'Lone Wolves' After All: How ISIS Guides World's Terror Plots from Afar," *New York Times*, 4 February 2017, https://www.nytimes.com/2017/02/04/world/asia/isis-messaging-app-terror-plot.html.

12 Stewart Bell and Brian Hill, "He Plotted to Bomb Times Square for ISIS. Records Show He's Mentally Ill. Is He a Terrorist?," Global News, 20 June 2018, https://globalnews.ca/news/4274935/canadian-isis-plot-new-york/.

13 There is some debate as to what we should call these individuals. "Lone wolf" is often used, but within counterterrorism circles it is often felt that this term glamourizes terrorist activity. On the term "lone wolf" see Jason Burke, "The Myth of the 'Lone Wolf' Terrorist," *Guardian*, 30 March 2017, https://www.theguardian.com/news/2017/mar/30/myth-lone-wolf-terrorist?CMP=Share_iOSApp_Other. This book will use "lone actor." For a typology, see Raffaello Pantucci, "A Typology of Lone Wolves: Preliminary Analysis of Lone Islamist Terrorists," International Centre for the Study of Radicalization and Political Violence, March 2011, https://icsr.info/wp-content/uploads/2011/04/1302002992ICSRPaper_ATypologyofLoneWolves_Pantucci.pdf.

14 Sam Mullins, "Lone-Actor vs. Remote-Controlled Jihadi Terrorism: Rethinking the Threat to the West," War on the Rocks, 20 April 2017, https://warontherocks.com/2017/04/lone-actor-vs-remote-controlled-jihadi-terrorism-rethinking-the-threat-to-the-west/. See also Daniel L. Byman, "How to Hunt a Lone Wolf: Countering Terrorists Who Act on Their Own," Brookings, 14 February 2017, https://www.brookings.edu/opinions/how-to-hunt-a-lone-wolf-countering-terrorists-who-act-on-their-own/?utm_medium=social&utm_source=twitter&utm_campaign=fp; Pantucci, "Typology of Lone Wolves."

15 Stewart Bell, "Mental Health System Failed Quebec Man Who Became Infatuated with ISIS and Killed a Soldier: Coroner," *National Post*, 5 May 2017, http://nationalpost.com/news/canada/martin-couture-rouleau-quebec-coroners-report; Paul Cherry, "Coroner: Martin Couture-Rouleau's Father Was 'Desperate' to Find Help for Son," *Montreal Gazette*, 5 May 2017, http://montrealgazette.com/news/local-news/provincial-coroner-issues-long-awaited-report-on-death-of-martin-couture-rouleau.

16 There is conflicted open-source reporting on whether or not Zehaf-Bibeau suffered from poor mental health. Zehaf-Bibeau was known

to exhibit erratic behaviour and his mother was of the view that he suffered from poor mental health. However, the RCMP has said on at least two occasions that there is no evidence that Zehaf-Bibeau suffered from any mental health problems. On this issue see Jim Bronskill, "Safety Minister Says 'Explosive Cocktail' of Ideology, Addiction, Mental Illness Led to Ottawa Shooting," iPolitics, 4 November 2014, https://ipolitics.ca/2014/11/04/safety-minister-says-explosive-cocktail-of-ideology-addiction-mental-illness-led-to-ottawa-shooting/; Canadian Press, "Mental Breakdown Not Key Factor in Parliament Hill Shooting, RCMP Boss Says," CBC, 15 January 2016, http://www.cbc.ca/news/canada/ottawa/zehaf-bibeau-paulsen-key-factor-1.3406181; Postmedia News, "Ottawa Shooting by Michael Zehaf-Bibeau was 'Last Desperate Act' of a Mentally Ill Person, His Mother Writes," *National Post*, 25 October 2014, http://nationalpost.com/news/canada/michael-zehaf-bibeau-mother-says-killing-was-last-desperate-act-of-a-mentally-ill-person.

17 Michael Friscolanti, "Uncovering a Killer: Addict, Drifter, Walking Contradiction," *Maclean's*, 30 October 2014, https://www.macleans.ca/news/canada/michael-zehaf-bibeau-addict-drifter-walking-contradiction/.

18 Amarnath Amarasingam, "What Aaron Told Me: An Expert on Extremism Shares His Conversations with the Terror Suspect," *National Post*, 11 August 2016, https://nationalpost.com/news/canada/what-aaron-told-me-an-expert-on-extremism-shares-his-conversations-with-the-terror-suspect; Alex Migdal, Kat Eschner, and Andrea Woo, "Who Was Aaron Driver? The Latest Updates about the Man Killed after Standoff in Strathroy," *Globe and Mail*, 11 August 2016, https://www.theglobeandmail.com/news/national/who-is-aaron-driver-what-we-know-so-far-about-the-man-killed-by-rcmp-instrathroy/article31374573/.

19 CBC News, "Man Charged with 5 Counts of Attempted Murder for Edmonton Attacks," 2 October 2017, https://www.cbc.ca/news/canada/edmonton/terrorism-charges-edmonton-attacks-1.4316450.

20 Karen Bartko, "Man Charged in Edmonton U-Haul Rampage Will Go to Trial," Global News, 14 March 2018, https://globalnews.ca/news/4082449/abdulahi-hasan-sharif-court-march-14/.

21 Caley Ramsay, "Edmonton Terror Attacks: Who Is Accused Abdulahi Sharif?," Global News, 2 October 2018, https://globalnews.ca/news/3780356/edmonton-terror-attacks-who-is-accused-abdulahi-sharif/. In addition, as discussed in chapter 1, Saad Akhtar allegedly murdered a woman with a knife in Toronto in what police believe was a violent

extremist attack motivated by the Islamic State, although much remains unknown about the case. As such it was not listed in this chapter.

22 Riga, "Quebec Mosque Killer Confided He Wished He Had Shot More People."

23 In some cases, we know that individuals were encouraged to do so. For example, in April 2015 Aaron Driver was known to have been in contact with radicalized individuals in the year leading up to his attack. In April 2015 he was described as in "fairly consistent" contact with another radicalized youth in the United Kingdom who was later arrested for his role in a plot in Australia. In May 2015 he was in contact with Elton Simpson hours before Simpson is killed 4 May 2015 in Texas, after opening fire outside a controversial contest for cartoons depicting the Prophet Muhammad. (The nature of the contact is unknown, as it was encrypted.) Canadian Press, "TIMELINE: Aaron Driver's History of Radicalization," CBC News, 11 August 2016, https://www.cbc.ca/news/canada/aaron-driver-timeline-1.3717169. However, this was over a year before his attack. Driver was arrested in June 2015 and unable to use the internet as a part of his peacebond conditions until shortly before his attack. As such, while it is reasonable to conclude these interactions may have played a role in his radicalized mindset, the extent to which they were important to his decision to mobilize is unknown.

24 Bart Schuurman, et al. "Lone Actor Terrorist Attack Planning and Preparation: A Data-Driven Analysis," *Psychiatry and Behavioral Science* 63, no. 4 (2018): 1191.

25 Michael Petrou, *Renegades: Canadians in the Spanish Civil War* (Vancouver: UBCPress, 2008).

26 See, generally, Bell, *Cold Terror*, esp. 23–145; Stewart Bell, "The Recruit: How Did This Girl Go from Toronto to a Terrorist Training Camp in Iraq?," *National Post*, 23 September 2006. The MeK is no longer listed as a terrorist entity.

27 Stewart Bell, "Canadian Appears in Terror Group's Propaganda Video Two Years after Being Killed in Somalia," *National Post*, 8 January 2015, https://nationalpost.com/news/canadian-appears-in-terror-groups-propaganda-video-two-years-after-being-killed-in-somolia.

28 Stewart Bell, "Canadian Wanted on Terrorism Charges in Bulgaria for Alleged Role in Hezbollah Bus Bombing," *National Post*, 22 January 2016, https://nationalpost.com/news/canada/canadian-wanted-on-terrorism-charges-in-bulgaria-for-alleged-role-in-hezbollah-bus-bombing.

29 Nahlah Ayed, "Xristos Katsiroubas, Canadian in Algeria Gas Plant Attack, Attempted Suicide Bombing," CBC News, 16 January 2014,

https://www.cbc.ca/news/world/xristos-katsiroubas-canadian-in-algeria-gas-plant-attack-attempted-suicide-bombing-1.2497150.

30 Public Safety Canada, "2018 Public Report on the Terrorist Threat to Canada," December 2018, https://www.publicsafety.gc.ca/cnt/rsrcs/pblctns/pblc-rprt-trrrsm-thrt-cnd-2018/index-en.aspx.

31 Maria Abi-Habib and Joe Parkinson, "How Jihadists Slip through Europe's Dragnet and into Syria," *Wall Street Journal*, 22 February 2015, https://www.wsj.com/articles/how-jihadists-slip-through-europes-dragnet-and-into-syria-1424653670.

32 Lorne Dawson and Amarnath Amarasingam, "Talking to Foreign Fighters: Insights into the Motivations for Hijrah to Syria and Iraq," *Studies in Conflict and Terrorism* 40, no. 3 (2017): 199.

33 McCants, *ISIS Apocolypse*.

34 Dawson and Amarasingam, "Talking to Foreign Fighters," 199–205.

35 Burke, *New Threat*, 105–6.

36 Lorenzo Vidino, Francesco Marone, and Eva Entenmann, *Fear Thy Neighbour: Radicalization and Jihadist Attacks in the West* (Milan: Italian Institute for International Political Studies (ISPI), 2017, 61.

37 Thomas Hegghammer and Petter Nesser, "Assessing the Islamic State's Commitment to Attacking the West," *Perspectives on Terrorism* 9, no. 4 (2015), http://www.terrorismanalysts.com/pt/index.php/pot/article/view/440/html.

38 For example, research suggests that some violent extremist groups may be misusing web archive services in order to maintain public access to material that has been taken down by web administrators or authorities. See Savvas Zannettou, Jeremy Blackburn, Emiliano De Cristofaro, Michael Sirivianos, and Gianluca Stringhini, "Understanding Web Archiving Services and Their (Mis)Use on Social Media," *Proceedings of the 12th International AAAI Conference on Web and Social Media (ICWSM 2018)*, 9 April 2018, https://arxiv.org/abs/1801.10396v2.

39 In November 2009 the RCMP arrested twenty-nine persons for their involvement in a massive counterfeiting ring in Ontario and Quebec that produced fake identification documents such as passports, driver's licences, and health cards. Times and Transcript, "Forged Passport Ring Quashed; Police Say No Terror Links to Sophisticated Ring," 26 November 2009, C5. There were no links to terrorism found, although there was no knowing where the documents ended up. Since 2009, new security measures have been added to Canadian passports. See Government of Canada, "Features of the Passport," 7 March 2018, https://www.canada.ca/en/immigration-refugees-citizenship/services/canadian-passports/about/passport-features.html.

40 It is believed that Dirie was killed in Syria circa 2013. CBC News, "'Toronto 18' Member Ali Mohamed Dirie Reportedly Died in Syria," 26 September 2013, https://www.cbc.ca/news/world/toronto-18-member-ali-mohamed-dirie-reportedly-died-in-syria-1.1868119.

41 Stewart Bell and Tristan Hopper, "B.C. Man Who Went to Syria Becomes the First Charged with Terrorism under New Canadian Law," *National Post*, 23 July 2014, https://nationalpost.com/news/canada/rcmp-charge-b-c-man-who-went-to-syria-with-terrorism-the-first-such-official-allegation-in-the-sprawling-conflict.

42 The 2017 *Public Report on the Terrorist Threat* claims that "those numbers have remained relatively stable over the past two years, as it has become more difficult for extremists to successfully leave or return to Canada."

43 See, for example, Tim Hume, "Far-Right Extremists Have Been Using Ukraine's War as a Training Ground: They're Returning Home," Vice, 31 July 2019, https://www.vice.com/en_us/article/vb95ma/far-right-extremists-have-been-using-ukraines-civil-war-as-a-training-ground-theyre-returning-home; Jeff Seldin, "White Supremacists Lead New Wave of Foreign Fighters," Voice of America, 30 September 2019, https://www.voanews.com/usa/white-supremacists-lead-new-wave-foreign-fighters.

44 Soufan Center, "White Supremacy Extremism: The Transnational Rise of the Violent White Supremacist Movement," September 2019, https://thesoufancenter.org/wp-content/uploads/2019/09/Report-by-The-Soufan-Center-White-Supremacy-Extremism-The-Transnational-Rise-of-The-Violent-White-Supremacist-Movement.pdf, p. 28.

45 Further facilitation provisions in 83.19 reiterate much of what is in 83.3, as well as 83.191, which outlaws travel to facilitate a terrorist act.

46 Timothy Holman, "'Gonna Get Myself Connected': The Role of Facilitation in Foreign Fighter Mobilizations," *Perspectives on Terrorism* 10, no. 2 (2016): 7–8.

47 Holman, "Gonna Get Myself Connected," 17.

48 Stewart Bell, "How RCMP Officers Tracked Three Canadian Girls in Egypt before They Could Join ISIS in Syria," *National Post*, 15 April 2015, https://nationalpost.com/news/canada/how-rcmp-tracked-canadian-girls-in-egypt-before-they-could-join-isis-in-syria.

49 Stewart Bell, *Cold Terror*, 107.

50 The most prominent of these being the United Nations Convention against Illicit Traffic in Narcotic Drugs and Psychotropic Substances (1988), also known as the Vienna Convention, as well as the United Nations Convention against Transnational Organized Crime, also known as the Palermo Convention (2000), although it did not enter into force until 2003. For a more detailed discussion of these and other measures,

see Nicholas Ryder, *The Financial War on Terrorism: A Review of Counter-Terrorist Financing Strategies since 2001* (Abingdon, UK: Routledge, 2015), 32–40.
51 Financial Action Task Force, "About," http://www.fatf-gafi.org/about/; see also the discussion in Ryder, *Financial War on Terrorism*, 43–6.
52 This treaty was adopted by UN General Assembly Resolution 109 in December 1999.
53 UNSCR 1373 (2001). See also the discussion in Ryder, *Financial War on Terrorism*, 7–8.
54 Ryder, *Financial War on Terrorism*, 56–61.
55 See the discussion in Roach, *9/11 Effect*, 384–5.
56 Roach, *9/11 Effect*, 382–4; David Berman and Christina Pellegrini, "Canada Given Lukewarm Grade on Anti-Money Laundering Efforts," *Globe and Mail*, 15 September 2016, https://www.theglobeandmail.com/report-on-business/canada-given-lukewarm-grade-on-anti-money-laundering-efforts/article31892936/.
57 Standing Committee on Finance, *Terrorist Financing in Canada and Abroad: Needed Fedreal Actions*, June 2015, https://www.ourcommons.ca/Content/Committee/412/FINA/Reports/RP8048561/finarp13/finarp13-e.pdf.
58 Canadian Security Intelligence Service, "Mobilization to Violence (Terrorism) Research: Key Findings," February 2018, https://www.canada.ca/content/dam/csis-scrs/documents/publications/IMV_-_Terrorism-Research-Key-findings-eng.pdf.
59 HCI vigorously defends itself from any allegations that it supports terrorist activity. It broke off contact with Khadr after he was arrested for allegedly financing a terror attack in Egypt. HCI has unsuccessfully sued the government of Canada for cutting off financial support, given concerns about its activities. After CSIS twice claimed in 2005 that Khadr worked closely with Al Qaida in Afghanistan while he was Director, HCI complained to CSIS's watchdog, the Security and Intelligence Review Committee (SIRC), in 2005. In 2007 SIRC agreed the complaint had merit, finding that there was insufficient information to support CSIS's claim. See Bell, *Cold Terror*, 197; Stewart Bell, "Khadr Killed in Gunfight: Report," *National Post*, 14 October 2003; Jim Bronskill and Rick Mofina, "Ottawa Charity Denies Role in al-Qaeda: U.S. Treasury Department Wants Operation's Assets Frozen," *Ottawa Citizen*, 13 October 2001; Jim Bronskill, "Charity Wrongly Linked to al-Qaeda Awaits Apology; Khadr Was a Volunteer Regional Director," *Globe and Mail*, 6 November 2007; Jeff Sallot, "CSIS Reports on Charity Must Be Kept Secret: Ottawa National Security Cited in Court Documents Responding to Lawsuit," *Globe and Mail*, 10 June 1999.

60 Bell, *Cold Terror*, 11, 41.
61 Les Whittington, "Hezbollah Added to Terror Blacklist," *Toronto Star*, 11 December 2002.
62 Amarasingam, *Pain, Pride and Politics*, 82–3.
63 Amarasingam, *Pain, Pride and Politics*, 88; Stewart Bell, "RCMP's Tamil Probe Extended," *National Post*, 27 April 2007; Bell, *Cold Terror*, 59–71; Human Rights Watch, *Funding the Final War*.
64 Tania Mehta, "Police Seize Fake Magic Bullets, Kylie Jenner Makeup among $2.5M Worth of Counterfeit Goods," CBC News, 9 December 2016, https://www.cbc.ca/news/canada/toronto/police-seize-fake-magic-bullets-kylie-jenner-makeup-among-2-5m-worth-of-counterfeit-goods-1.3889278.
65 Catherine McIntyre, "Why Canada Is a Haven for Knock-off Goods," *Maclean's*, 4 April 2007, https://www.macleans.ca/economy/why-canada-is-a-haven-for-knock-off-goods/.
66 Dave Todd, "Miami Trial of Canadian Businessmen Likely to Reveal Details of IRA Fundraising," *Ottawa Citizen*, 22 April 1993.
67 Bell, *Cold Terror*, 118–19.
68 Chris Thompson, "Suspects Linked to Terror: Three Windsor Men Allegedly Acted as Couriers for Multimillion-Dollar Ring That Funded Hezbollah," *Windsor Star*, 30 March 2006; Trevor Wilhelm, "Local Trio Key to Smuggling Ring: Illegal Smokes Operation Helped Send Funds to Hezbollah," *Windsor Star*, 6 October 2006.
69 Bell, *Cold Terror*, 147–74.
70 Paul Koring, "Suspect in Terrorist Plot a Petty Crook, Court Hears," *Globe and Mail*, 29 June 2001; Benjamin Weiser, with Craig Pyes, "U.S., in Pursuit of Bomb Plot, Indicts Man Held in Canada," *New York Times*, 19 January 2000, https://www.nytimes.com/2000/01/19/nyregion/us-in-pursuit-of-bomb-plot-indicts-man-held-in-canada.html.
71 Catherine Solyom, "Montreal Teen Robbed for ISIS, Crown Argues; Terror Trial," *National Post*, 18 September 2005.
72 Catherine Solyom, "Bail Hearing for Terror Suspect on Friday," *Ottawa Citizen*, 15 March 2016.
73 Home Office (UK), "Counter-Terrorism and Security Bill," November 2014. https://assets.publishing.service.gov.uk/government/uploads/system/uploads/attachment_data/file/540539/CTS_Bill_-_Factsheet_9_-_Kidnap_and_Ransom.pdf.
74 Marc Sageman, "The Stagnation in Terrorism Research," *Terrorism and Political Violence* 26 (2014): 565–80.
75 For example, on psychology, see John Horgan, *The Psychology of Terrorism* (London: Routledge, 2005); on political/social factors, see Mia Bloom,

Dying to Kill: The Allure of Suicide Terror (New York: Columbia University Press, 2005); on behavioural factors, see Paul Gill, *Lone-Actor Terrorists: A Behavioural Analysis* (London: Routledge, 2015).

76 Amarnath Amarasingam and Lorne L. Dawson, "I Left to Be Closer to Allah: Learning about Foreign Fighters from Family and Friends," Institute for Strategic Dialogue, 2018, 5, http://www.isdglobal.org/wp-content/uploads/2018/05/Families_Report.pdf.

77 On charismatic leadership, see David C. Hofmann and Lorne L. Dawson, "The Neglected Role of Charismatic Authority in the Study of Terrorist Groups and Radicalization," *Studies in Conflict and Terrorism* 37, no. 4 (2014): 348–68.

78 Bell, *Martyr's Oath*, 49–50; Terence McKenna, "Passport to Terror," CBC News, October 2004, http://www.cbc.ca/news2/background/jabarah/.

79 Pantucci, "Typology of Lone Wolves," 24–9.

80 Marc Sageman, *Understanding Terror Networks* (Philadelphia: University of Pennsylvania Press, 2004), 135.

81 Willem Koomen and Joop van der Pligt, *The Psychology of Radicalization and Terrorism* (London: Routledge, 2015), 174–6.

82 Nazim Baksh and Devin Heroux, "Key Member of Calgary Jihadist Cluster Revealed for 1st Time," CBC News, 30 March 2017, http://www.cbc.ca/news/canada/calgary/calgary-canada-jihad-terrorism-waseem-youcef-damian-clairmont-iraq-1.4046574.

83 See Maura Conway, "Determining the Role of the Internet in Violent Extremism and Terrorism: Six Suggestions for Progressing Research," *Studies in Conflict & Terrorism* 40, no. 1 (2013): 77–98; Gill, *Lone-Actor Terrorists*, esp. "Chapter 5: The Role of the Internet," 86–102; Kooman and van der Pligt, *Psychology of Radicalization and Terrorism*, 182–85. Peter R. Neumann, "Options and Strategies for Countering Online Radicalization in the United States," *Studies in Conflict & Terrorism* 36, no. 6 (2013): 431–59.

84 Neumann, "Options and Strategies," 436.

85 Kooman and van der Pligt, *Psychology of Radicalization and Terrorism*, 183. The role of these like-minded communities in the spread of misinformation and "junk news" is discussed further in chapter 7.

86 Gill, *Lone-Actor Terrorism*, 89.

87 Jennifer Williams, Alex Ward, Jen Kirby, and Amanda Sakuma, "Christchurch Mosque Shooting: What We Know So Far," Vox, 18 March 2019, https://www.vox.com/world/2019/3/14/18266624/christchurch-mosque-shooting-new-zealand-gunman-what-we-know.

88 For example, the Canada Center for Community Engagement and the Prevention of Violence housed within Public Safety Canada, which coordinates many countering violent extremism programing. Some of the more prominent CVE programs in Canada are the Center for the Prevention of Radicalization Leading to Violence in Montreal and the ReDirect program in Calgary.
89 Craig Forcese and Kent Roach, "Criminalizing Terrorist Babble: Canada's Dubious New Terrorist Speech Crime," *Alberta Law Review* 53, no. 1 (2015): 35–84.
90 Forcese and Roach, "Criminalizing Terrorist Babble," 67–9.
91 Canadian Civil Liberties Association, "The Terrorist Speech Offence and Bill C-59," 12 September 2017, https://ccla.org/terrorist-speech-bill-c-59; Craig Forcese and Kent Roach, "A Report Card on the National Security Bill," *Policy Options*, 22 June 2017, http://policyoptions.irpp.org/magazines/june-2017/a-report-card-on-the-national-security-bill/.
92 Roach, *9/11 Effect*, 424.
93 Craig Forcese and Kent Roach, *False Security: The Radicalization of Canadian Anti-Terrorism* (Toronto: Irwin Law, 2015), 66–9.
94 Gill, *Lone-Actor Terrorists*, 53 (table 3.3).
95 Canadian Security Intelligence Service, "——— of the Indicators of Mobilization to Violence Project: Mobilization Specifics for Minors and Young Adults," IMV 2016-17/01, 12 May 2016. Full name unavailable. Access to Information and Privacy request data via Amarnath Amarasingam.
96 See, for example, Marc Sageman, *Leaderless Jihad: Terror Networks in the Twenty-First Century* (Philadelphia: University of Pennsylvania Press, 2008), 62–5.
97 Emily Corner and Paul Gill, "A False Dichotomy? Mental Illness and Lone-Actor Terrorism," *Law and Human Behaviour* 39, no. 1 (2015): 23; Gill, *Lone-Actor Terrorists*, 103–6; Koomen and Van Der Pligt, *Psychology of Radicalization*, 93–4.
98 Corner and Gill, "False Dichotomy," 31; Gill, *Lone-Actor Terrorists*, 106.
99 Corner and Gill, "False Dichotomy," 31.
100 Canadian Security Intelligence Service, *2018 CSIS Public Report*, 10 and 20.
101 Zachary K. Goldman, Ellie Maruyama, Elizabeth Rosenberg, Edoardo Saravalle, and Julia Solomon-Strauss, *Terrorist Use of Virtual Currencies: Containing the Potential Threat* (Washington DC: Centre for New American Security, May 2017), https://s3.amazonaws.com/files.cnas.org/documents/CNASReport-TerroristFinancing-Final.pdf?mtime=20170502033819.

3. Espionage

1. Colin Freeze and Jane Taber, "'So Dead Inside': How the Mounties Cracked Jeffrey Delisle," *Globe and Mail*, 26 March 2017, https://www.theglobeandmail.com/news/politics/so-dead-inside-how-the-mounties-cracked-jeffrey-delisle/article4630144/.
2. At time of writing, Ortis's trial is still pending, and it may take years. As the case remains under a publication ban, little is publicly known and it will therefore not be discussed in detail here. Thanks to Leah West and Jessica Davis for advising the author on what we know about this case in April 2020.
3. Definition modified from Jan Goldman, *Words of Intelligence: An Intelligence Professional's Lexicon for Domestic and Foreign Threats*, 2nd ed. (Lanham, MD: Scarecrow, 2011), 110.
4. Communications Security Establishment, "Foreign Signals Intelligence," 22 June 2017, https://www.cse-cst.gc.ca/en/inside-interieur/signals-renseignement.
5. Mark M. Lowenthal, *Intelligence: From Secrets to Policy*, 7th ed. (London: Sage, 2017), 221.
6. Lowenthal, *Intelligence*, 222.
7. Frederick L. Wettering, "Counterintelligence: The Broken Triad," in *Secret Intelligence: A Reader*, ed. Christopher Andrew, Richard J. Aldrich, and Wesley K. Wark (London: Routledge, 2009), 282.
8. Whitaker, Kealy, and Parnaby, *Secret Service*, 56–9.
9. Whitaker, Kealy, and Parnaby, *Secret Service*, 99.
10. See Don Munton, "Our Men in Havana: Canadian Foreign Intelligence Operations in Castro's Cuba," *International Journal* 70, no. 1 (2015): 23–9; Bill Warden, *Diplomat, Dissident, Spook: A Candian Diplomat's Chronicles through the Cold War and Beyond* (Victoria, BC: Tellwell, 2017). However, as this book focuses on threats to Canada and not Canadian foreign intelligence collection, these events are not discussed.
11. For some recent academic articles highlighting aspects of this debate, see Barry Cooper, *CFIS: A Foreign Intelligence Service for Canada* (Calgary: Canadian Defence & Foreign Affairs Institute, 2007); Stuart Farson and Nancy Teeple, "Increasing Canada's Foreign Intelligence Capability: Is It a Dead Issue?," *Intelligence and National Security* 30, no. 1 (2014): 47–76; Paul Robinson, "The Viability of a Canadian Foreign Intelligence Service," *International Journal* 64, no. 3 (2009): 703–16.
12. Munton, "Our Men in Havana," 23.
13. Conservative Party of Canada, *Stand Up for Canada: Conservative Party of Canada Federal Election Platform*, 2006, 26.

14 Colin Freeze, "RCMP, CSIS See No Significant Support for Operations from Federal Budget," *Globe and Mail*, 23 March 2016, https://www.theglobeandmail.com/news/politics/rcmp-csis-see-no-significant-support-for-operations-from-federal-budget/article29374887; David Ljunggren, "Canada Security Services Struggle with Extremist Threat Resources Gap," Reuters, 31 October 2014, http://ca.reuters.com/article/domesticNews/idCAKBN0IK1Y020141031.

15 For more information on the CSE, see Bill Robinson, "Communications Security Establishment," and Thomas Juneau, "Department of Defence," in *Top Secret Canada: Understanding the Canadian Intelligence and National Security Community*, ed. Stephanie Carvin, Thomas Juneau, and Craig Forcese (Toronto: University of Toronto Press, forthcoming).

16 Cited in *National Security and Intelligence Committee of Parliamentarians Annual Report 2018*, 9 April 2019, 64, http://www.nsicop-cpsnr.ca/reports/rp-2019-04-09/intro-en.html. The report cites the Joint Doctrine Branch Canadian Forces Warfare Centre, *Canadian Forces Joint Publication (CFJP) 2.1 Intelligence Operations*, August 2017.

17 A useful summary of DND intelligence activities can be found in *National Security and Intelligence Committee of Parliamentarians Annual Report 2018*, 61–96. This was followed up with a "Special Report" on the use of DND collection of information on Canadians. See NSICOP, *Special Report on the Collection, Use, Retention and Dissemination of Information on Canadians in the Context of the Department of National Defence and Canadian Armed Forces Defence Intelligence Activities*, 20 August 2019, https://www.nsicop-cpsnr.ca/reports/rp-2020-03-12-sr/intro-en.html.

18 David E. Hoffman, *The Billion Dollar Spy: A True Story of Cold War Espionage and Betrayal* (New York: Anchor Books, 2015), 130–1.

19 Hoffman, *Billion Dollar Spy*, 130.

20 Among many sources of this tale, see Amy Knight, *How the Cold War Began: The Gouzenko Affair and the Hunt for Soviet Spies* (Toronto: McClelland & Stewart, 2005), esp. chapter 1, "The Defection," 14–43.

21 Whitaker and Marcuse, *Cold War Canada*, 33–4.

22 Knight, *How the Cold War Began*, 148–9.

23 Mahar, *Shattered Illusions*, 56; Martin Rudner, "Introduction" in Black and Rudner, *Gouzenko Affair*, 9.

24 Whitaker, Kealy, and Parnaby, *Secret Service*, 226–7. Aleksei P. Makarov, "Living with the KGB and GRU: A 'Clean' Diplomat Recalls His Experiences inside Soviet Embassies," in Black and Rudner, *Gouzenko Affair*, 152 and 176.

25 Whitaker, Kealy, and Parnaby, *Secret Service*, 221 2.

26 Whitaker, Kealy, and Parnaby, *Secret Service*, 220–1.

27 Mahar, *Shattered Illusions*, 54. KGB stands for Komitet Gosudarstvennoy Bezopasnosti, usually translated as the "Committee for State Security." The KGB was the civilian foreign intelligence and domestic security agency of the Soviet Union, though its tasks were weighted more towards the latter than the former. Johnathan Haslam, *Near and Distant Neighbours: A New History of Soviet Intelligence* (New York: Farrar, Straus and Giroux, 2015), xv.
28 Whitaker, Kealy, and Parnaby, *Secret Service*, 233.
29 Granatstein and Stafford, *Spy Wars*, 119.
30 Christopher Andrew and Oleg Gordievsky, *KGB: The Inside Story of Its Foreign Operations from Lenin to Gorbachev* (New York: HarperCollins Publishers, 1990), 445. Whitaker, Kealy, and Parnaby speculate that Hambleton missed his wartime espionage activities, where he fought with the French resistance behind enemy lines. Granatstein and Stafford also argue that Hambleton was "captive of a fantasy world of spying" and addicted to espionage. *Spy Wars*, 165–9.
31 Whitaker, Kealy, and Parnaby, *Secret Service*, 241. See also Granatstein and Stafford, *Spy Wars*, "Chapter 8: The Fantasist and the Film Maker," 151–86.
32 Whitaker, Kealy, and Parnaby, *Secret Service*, 241.
33 Whitaker, Kealy, and Parnaby, *Secret Service*, 232. See also *Globe and Mail*, "Featherstone Trial Told of Locker Find," 6 April 1967, 43.
34 Whitaker, Kealy, and Parnaby, *Secret Service*, 237–8.
35 Mahar, *Shattered Illusions*, 54–6.
36 Whitaker, Kealy, and Parnaby, *Secret Service*, 239.
37 Makarov, "Living with the KGB and GRU," 152.
38 GRU is the Russian acronym of Glavnoye Razvedyvatelnoye Upravlenie, or "Main Intelligence Directorate." This is the Soviet/Russain military intelligence agency. Although the name was formally changed to "Main Directorate" (GU) in 2010, it is still commonly referred to as the "GRU."
39 There are differing accounts of how Soviet agents were discovered. Whitaker, Kealy, and Parnaby argue that the Soviet intelligence agents were "well schooled in counter-surveillance tactics" and that the RCMP relied on bugging, analysis, and technology. Makarov, a former Soviet diplomat on the inside, argues that it was mostly KGB/GRU incompetence. It would not be surprising if both factors came into play. Whitaker, Kealy, and Parnaby, *Secret Service*, 230–1; Marakov, "Living with the KGB and GRU," 154.
40 Whitaker, Kealy, and Parnaby, *Secret Service*, 232.
41 Whitaker, Kealy, and Parnaby, *Secret Service*, 227.
42 Christopher Andrew and Vasili Mitrokhin, *The Sword and the Sheild: The Mitrokhin Archive and the Secret History of the KGB* (New York: Basic Books, 1999), 408.

43 Andrew and Mitrokhin, *Sword and the Shield*, 408.
44 Haslam, *Near and Distant Neighbours*, 195.
45 Brik was assumed to have paid the normal price for betraying the USSR – death – but for some reason he was spared this fate. He served his sentence and was released. Eventually making contact with the the UK embassy, he was exfiltrated back to Canada with the help of CSIS as the Cold War came to an end in 1992. The entire story is told in Mahar, *Shattered Illusions*.
46 Granatstein and Stafford, *Spy Wars*, 135.
47 Ludek Zemenek was known to the Czech government as Dalibar Valoushek, and some literature (Andrew and Mitrokhin) refers to him by that name. See also Ronald J. Ostrow, "Saved $300,000 during U.S. Stay: Former KGB Agent Wants to Go Home with His Cash," *Los Angeles Times*, 2 November 1986, http://articles.latimes.com/print/1986-11-02/news/mn-15763_1_kgb-agents
48 Andrew and Mitrokhin, *Sword and the Shield*, 191–2; and Granatstein and Stafford, *Spy Wars*, 158–78.
49 Andrew and Mitrokhin, *Sword and the Shield*, 197.
50 William M. Carley, "How the FBI Broke Spy Case That Baffled Agency for 30 Years," *Wall Street Journal*, 21 November 1996. See also Andrew and Mitrokhin, *Sword and the Shield*, 193–4.
51 Andrew and Mitrokhin, *Sword and the Shield*, 195–6.
52 *Report of the Royal Commission on Security (Abridged)*, June 1969, p. 59, para. 161, http://publications.gc.ca/collections/collection_2014/bcp-pco/Z1-1966-5-eng.pdf.
53 Sarah Boesveld, "Government Infiltrated by Spies, CSIS Boss Says," *Globe and Mail*, 22 June 2010, https://www.theglobeandmail.com/news/politics/government-infiltrated-by-spies-csis-boss-says/article4392618/. The remark set off a political firestorm, which will be discussed in chapter 6 on foreign-influenced activities.
54 Standing Committee on Public Safety and National Security, *Report on Canadian Security Intelligence Service Director Richard Fadden's Remarks Regarding Alleged Foreign Influence of Canadian Politicians*, March 2011, http://www.ourcommons.ca/DocumentViewer/en/40-3/SECU/report-8. Chinese espionage in Canada will be discussed in chapter 4. But the particularly sore point was the allegation that Canadian politicians were the target of foreign influence campaigns. Clandestine foreign influence will be discussed in chapter 6. Of note, the National Security and Intelligence Committee of Parliamentarians cited Fadden's 2010 comments, suggesting that he was correct. See *National Security and Intelligence Committee of Parliamentarians Annual Report 2018*, 27.
55 Senate Standing Committee on Security and National Defence, 7 March 2016. CSIS Director Michel Coulombe spoke about the collection against

China in Canada in response to a question by Senator Colin Kenny. https://sencanada.ca/en/Content/SEN/Committee/421/secd/02ev-52409-e.

56 For example, see NSICOP, *Annual Report 2018*, 26. The CSE identified Russia as a cyber threat in the Netherlands and United States in the context of discussing cyber threats to Canada in 2017. See CSE, *Cyber Threats to Canada's Democratic Process*, 2017, https://cyber.gc.ca/sites/default/files/publications/cse-cyber-threat-assessment-e.pdf. In addition, it named Russia as a threat against Canada in its 2018 National Cyber Threat Assessment. See CSE, "National Cyber Threat Assessment, 2018," https://cyber.gc.ca/sites/default/files/publications/national-cyber-threat-assessment-2018-e_1.pdf. Canada's attribution of cyber attacks is discussed in detail in chapter 5.

57 Stewart Bell, "Ottawa Company Barred from National Security Work after Alleged Contact with Indian Intelligence," Global News, 30 January 2020, https://globalnews.ca/news/6478679/ottawa-company-contact-indian-intelligence/.

58 Nomi Morris, "The New Spy Wars," *Maclean's*, 2 September 1996; Nick Pron and Phinjo Gombu, "Glimpse into the World of Spies," *Toronto Star*, 1 June 1996. Of note, Yelena/Elena Olshanskaya separated from Dmitry Olshanskiy before they were caught and married a doctor, Peter Miller. Ten years later Elena Miller tried to sue the Canadian government to be let back into the country permanently, but her case was dismissed. Marina Jiménez, "Russian Spy Sues Ottawa for Being Left Out in the Cold," *Globe and Mail*, 4 October 2006; and Jiménez, "Ex-Spy Loses Lawsuit over Canada's Refusal to Let Her Return," *Globe and Mail*, 22 December 2006.

59 Michael Friscolanti, "The Russian Spies Who Raised Us," *Maclean's*, 10 August 2017, http://www.macleans.ca/the-russian-spies-who-raised-us/; Shaun Walker, "The Day We Discovered Our Parents Were Russian Spies," *Guardian*, 7 May 2016, https://www.theguardian.com/world/2016/may/07/discovered-our-parents-were-russian-spies-tim-alex-foley.

60 Friscolanti, 'Russian Spies."

61 Canada (Minister of Citizenship and Immigration) v Vavilov 2019 SCC 65. The author is grateful to Craig Forcese for help in interpreting this decision.

62 Paul Cherry, "Details Emerge in Spy Case: Suspect Had Three Canadian Passports," *Colgary Herald*, 22 November 2006; Nelson Wyatt, "'Hampel' a Spy, Agent Says," *Toronto Star*, 29 November 2006.

63 Whitakerr, Kealy, and Parnaby, *Secret Service*, 460. The use of security certificates for counterterrorism is briefly discussed in chapter 2.

64 Colin Freeze, "Transcript of RCMP Interrogation of Jeffrey Delisle," *Globe and Mail*, 22 October 2012, https://www.theglobeandmail.com

/news/national/transcript-of-rcmp-interrogation-of-jeffrey-delisle/article4630151/.
65 CBC News, "Navy Spy Sold Secrets to Russia for $3K a Month," 10 October 2017, http://www.cbc.ca/news/canada/nova-scotia/navy-spy-sold-secrets-to-russia-for-3k-a-month-1.1148431.
66 Steven Chase, Colin Freeze, and Oliver Moore, "Inside Trinity, the Secretive Halifax Facility Where an Alleged Spy Last Worked." *Globe and Mail*, 27 January 2017, https://www.theglobeandmail.com/news/politics/inside-trinity-the-secretive-halifax-facility-where-an-alleged-spy-last-worked/article533865/.
67 CBC News, "Navy Spy Delisle's Ex-Wife Recalls 'Good Guy' Gone Wrong," 10 January 2013, http://www.cbc.ca/news/canada/navy-spy-delisle-s-ex-wife-recalls-good-guy-gone-wrong-1.1343417.
68 Brian Stewart, "Was Canada's Delisle Spying for the Russian Mob?," CBC News, 7 February 2013, http://www.cbc.ca/news/world/brian-stewart-was-canada-s-delisle-spying-for-the-russian-mob-1.1351173.
69 Alison Auld, "Navy Spy Who Sold Secrets to Russia Apologizes for Pain He Caused," CTV Atlantic, 1 February 2013, http://atlantic.ctvnews.ca/navy-spy-who-sold-secrets-to-russia-apologizes-for-pain-he-caused-1.1138861?playVideo=.
70 Canadian Security Intelligence Service, "Canadian Security Intelligence Service (CSIS) Injury Assessment Report Provided for RCMP Project Stoique," 22 February 2012, https://www.scribd.com/document/119816468/CSIS-Injury-Assessment.
71 The *Act* was later renamed the *Security of Canadian Information Sharing Act* under Bill C-51 in 2015 and the Security of *Canadian Information Disclosure Act* under Bill C-59 in 2018.
72 Steven Chase, Oliver Moore, and Tamara Baluja, "Ottawa Expels Russian Diplomats in Wake of Charges against Canadian," *Globe and Mail*, 19 January 2012, https://www.theglobeandmail.com/news/politics/ottawa-expels-russian-diplomats-in-wake-of-charges-against-canadian/article1359125/.
73 Government of Canada, Termium Plus Data Bank. This definition can also be found on the NATOTerm website: https://nso.nato.int/natoterm/content/nato/pages/home.html?lg=en.
74 Reg Whitaker and Steve Hewitt, "The Security Panel: Nerve Centre of Ottawa's Cold War," in *Canada and the Cold War*, 23–4.
75 Whitaker, Kealy, and Parnaby, *Secret Service*, 224. It is not clear why the project came to an end – whether the project "exhausted itself" or other priorities such as Quebec separatism and/or international terrorism took precedence in RCMP operations. See also Jim Bronskill, "Operation Feather Bed: RCMP's Fruitless Cold War Mole Hunt Zeroed

In on Key Diplomats," *Huffington Post*, 22 March 2012, http://www.huffingtonpost.ca/2012/03/22/operation-feather-bed-rcmp_n_1371814.html; Whitaker and Hewitt, "Operation Feather Bed," in *Canada and the Cold War*, 207–9.

76 Jim Bronskill, "For Three Decades, Mounties Spied on NDP Leader Douglas: Files Are Declassified," *Montreal Gazette*, 18 December 2006; Whitaker, Kealy, and Parnaby, *Secret Service*, 336.
77 Whitaker, Kealy, and Parnaby, *Secret Service*, 348–9.
78 Whitaker, Kealy, and Parnaby, *Secret Service*, 307–9.
79 Whitaker, Kealy, and Parnaby, *Secret Service*, 242.
80 Steve Hewitt, "Reforming the Canadian Security State: The Royal Canadian Mounted Police Security Service and the 'Key Sectors' Program," *Intelligence and National Security* 17, no. 4 (2002): 165–84. The program was halted in 1977, the same time as the MacDonald Commission.
81 Whitaker and Hewitt, "John Watkins," in *Cold War Canada*, 157–9.
82 Whitaker, Kealy, and Parnaby, *Secret Service*, 211–17; Whitaker and Hewitt, "E. Herbert Norman: The Man Who Might Have Been," in *Cold War Canada*, 79–82. Donald Barry argues that while no definitive proof emerged about Norman, he confounded the case against himself by not being honest about his past and his past associations with communism. Barry's argument also suggests that the Department of External Affairs had an interest in determining Norman was not guilty and may not have been as objective in their assessment as they wanted the RCMP to believe. Barry, "Cleared or Covered Up? The Department of External Affairs Investigations of Herbert Norman, 1950–52," *International Journal* 66, no. 1 (2011): 147–69.
83 Cited in Whitaker, Kealy, and Parnaby, *Secret Service*, 347.
84 The disruption powers, which fall under section 12 of the *CSIS Act*, were in section 42 of Bill C-51. The most prominent criticism of the legislation as then written can be found in Forcese and Roach, *False Security*.
85 Whitaker, Kealy, and Parnaby, *Secret Service*, 229–30.
86 Whitaker, Kealy, and Parnaby, *Secret Service*, 239.
87 Whitaker, Kealy, and Parnaby, *Secret Service*, 257–8.
88 NSCIOP, *Annual Review 2019*, 3–54.

4. The Economy and National Security

1 Bert Hill, "Where Nortel's Troubles Began," *Ottawa Citizen*, 16 January 2013, http://www.ottawacitizen.com/business/where+nortel+troubles+began/7823499/story.html.

2 Jamie Sturgeon, "Nortel Executives Found Not Guilty on All Counts of Fraud," *Financial Post*, 14 January 2013, https://business.financialpost.com/technology/nortel-executives-found-not-guilty-on-all-counts.
3 Siobhan Gorman, "Chinese Hackers Suspected in Long-Term Nortel Breach," *Wall Street Journal*, 14 February 2012, https://www.wsj.com/articles/SB10001424052970203363504577187502201577054. Some of these accusations were recently explored in Tom Blackwell, "Did Huawei Bring Down Nortel? Corporate Espionage, Theft, and the Parallel Rise and Fall of Two Telecom Giants," *National Post*, 24 February 2020, https://nationalpost.com/news/exclusive-did-huawei-bring-down-nortel-corporate-espionage-theft-and-the-parallel-rise-and-fall-of-two-telecom-giants.
4 Gorman, "Chinese Hackers Suspected."
5 David Pugliese, "The Mystery of the Listening Devices at DND's Nortel Campus," *Ottawa Citizen*, 18 October 2016, http://ottawacitizen.com/news/national/defence-watch/the-mystery-of-the-listening-devices-at-dnds-nortel-campus.
6 Whitaker, Kealy, and Parnaby, *Secret Service*, 226.
7 Lowenthal, *Intelligence*, 420. See also Andrea McIntosh, "Spying Game: Industrial Espionage," *Gazette*, 14 June 1993; Naomi Morris, "The New Spy Wars," *Maclean's*, 2 September 1996.
8 Mark Gollom, "Brazil-Canada Espionage: Which Countries Are We Spying On?," CBC News, 9 October 2013, http://www.cbc.ca/news/canada/brazil-canada-espionage-which-countries-are-we-spying-on-1.1930522.
9 McIntosh, "Spying Game."
10 CBC News, "CSIS Comments Anger Chinese Community," 24 June 2010, http://www.cbc.ca/news/canada/british-columbia/csis-comments-anger-chinese-community-1.919518. Standing Committee on Public Safety and National Security, *Report on Canadian Security Intelligence Service Director Richard Fadden's Remarks*. Of note, the National Security and Intelligence Committee of Parliamentarians cited Fadden's 2010 comments, suggesting that he was correct. See *National Security and Intelligence Committee of Parliamentarians Annual Report 2018*, 27.
11 Treasury Board of Canada Secretariat, "Statement by the Chief Information Officer for the Government of Canada," 29 July 2014.
12 Michel Coulombe, Testimony to the Senate Standing Committee on National Seecurity and Defence, 7 March 2016, https://sencanada.ca/en/Content/Sen/committee/421/secd/52409-e.
13 Jim Bronskill, "Russia, China Are Out to Steal Canada's Secrets, Spy Agency Warns," *Toronto Star*, 21 November 2016, https://www.thestar

.com/news/canada/2016/11/21/russia-china-are-out-to-steal-canadas-secrets-spy-agency-warns.html.
14. National Security and Intelligence Committee of Parliamentarians, *National Security and Intelligence Committee of Parliamentarians Annual Report 2018*, 26–7.
15. See James R. Clapper, "Worldwide Threat Assessment of the US Intelligence Community," 26 February 2015, https://www.dni.gov/files/documents/Unclassified_2015_ATA_SFR_-_SASC_FINAL.pdf; See also the "Worldwide Threat Assessment of the US Intelligence Community," 9 February 2016, https://www.dni.gov/files/documents/SASC_Unclassified_2016_ATA_SFR_FINAL.pdf.
16. United States Department of Justice, "U.S. Charges Five Chinese Military Hackers for Cyber Espionage against U.S. Corporations and a Labor Organization for Commercial Advantage," 19 May 2014, https://www.justice.gov/opa/pr/us-charges-five-chinese-military-hackers-cyber-espionage-against-us-corporations-and-labor. See also Shane Harris, "Exclusive: Inside the FBI's Fight against Chinese Cyber-Espionage," 27 May 2014, Foreign Policy, http://foreignpolicy.com/2014/05/27/exclusive-inside-the-fbis-fight-against-chinese-cyber-espionage/; Robert D. Blackwill and Jennifer M. Harris, *War by Other Means: Geoeconomics and Statecraft* (Cambridge, MA: Belknap/Harvard University Press, 2016), 59–65.
17. Matthew Braga, "Canada 'Remiss' in Approach to Cyber Attacks: Stolen Information State-Run Chinese Hacking Pervasive: Report," *Financial Post*, 20 February 2013 Ian MacLeod, "Cyber Hack Targeted Potash Industry," *Edmonton Journal*, 29 October 2011.
18. Mandiant, *APT1: Exposing One of China's Cyber Espionage Units*, February 2013, https://www.fireeye.com/content/dam/fireeye-www/services/pdfs/mandiant-apt1-report.pdf.
19. CSIS, *2014–2016 Public Report*, https://www.canada.ca/en/security-intelligence-service/corporate/publications/public-report-2014-2016.html.
20. Mahnoor Yawar, "Vancouver Businessman Sentenced to Jail for Stealing U.S. Military Data," *Globe and Mail*, 14 July 2016.
21. Matt Bunn and Scott D. Sagan, "Introduction: Inside the Insider Threat," in *Insider Threats*, ed. Matt Bunn and Scott D. Sagan (Ithaca, NY: Cornell University Press, 2016), 3.
22. Bunn and Sagan, "Introduction," 4.
23. Bunn and Sagan, "Introduction," 4.
24. Canadian Press, "Canadian Scientists Perplexed Why Researcher Would Try to Smuggle Readily Available Pathogen to China," *National Post*, 4

April 2013, http://nationalpost.com/news/canada/canadian-scientists-perplexed-why-researcher-would-try-to-smuggle-readily-available-pathogen-to-china/wcm/bcf3bcb6-9a0a-4517-9ac4-f2d6f746c63f.

25 Nathan Vanderklippe, "Chinese View Canadian Naval Spy Charges with Amusement, Skepticism," *Globe and Mail*, 2 December 2013, https://www.theglobeandmail.com/news/national/some-in-china-question-arrest-of-canadian-charged-with-trying-to-pass-on-naval-secrets/article15712338/.

26 FBI, "Six Chinese Nationals Indicted for Conspiring to Steal Trade Secrets from U.S. Seed Companies," 19 December 2013, https://archives.fbi.gov/archives/omaha/press-releases/2013/six-chinese-nationals-indicted-for-conspiring-to-steal-trade-secrets-from-u.s.-seed-companies.

27 At time of writing, no charges have been laid. Karen Pauls, "Chinese Researcher Escorted from Infectious Disease Lab amid RCMP Investigation," CBC News, 5 July 2019, https://www.cbc.ca/news/canada/manitoba/chinese-researcher-escorted-from-national-microbiology-lab-amidst-rcmp-investigation-1.5211567; and Paauls, "University Severs Ties with Two Researchers Who Were Escorted out of National Microbiology Lab Social Sharing," CBC News, 15 July 2019, https://www.cbc.ca/news/canada/manitoba/lab-researcher-rcmp-national-microbiology-lab-1.5212851.

28 Blackwill and Harris, *War by Other Means*, 1.

29 William J. Norris, *Chinese Economic Statecraft: Commercial Actors, Grand Strategy and State Control* (Ithaca, NY: Cornell University Press, 2016), 13–14.

30 Blackwill and Harris, *War by Other Means*, chapter 2, "Geoeconomics and the International System," 33–48.

31 Blackwill and Harris, *War by Other Means*, esp. chapter 6, "U.S. Foreign Policy and Geoeconomics in Historical Context," 152–78.

32 Thomas J. Christensen, *The China Challenge: Shaping the Choices of a Rising Power* (New York: W.W. Norton, 2016), 4-8. Insights in this section presented by the author to the Public Policy Forum's Consultative Forum on China. See Stephanie Carvin, "A Mouse Sleeping Next to a Dragon: New Twitches and Grunts," *Public Policy Forum*, September 2017, https://medium.com/ppf-consultative-forum-on-china/a-mouse-sleeping-next-to-a-dragon-new-twitches-and-grunts-970f2c225b55.

33 Christensen, *China Challenge*, 108–12.

34 Canadian Security Intelligence Service, *China and the Age of Strategic Rivalry: Highlights from an Academic Outreach Workshop*, May 2018, 108, https://www.canada.ca/content/dam/csis-scrs/documents/publications/CSIS-Academic-Outreach-China-report-May-2018-en.pdf.

35 It is also not clear that China has actually changed its policies, despite dropping the name "Made in China 2025." See Emily Crawford, "Made in China 2025: The Industrial Plan That China Doesn't Want Anyone Talking About," PBSFrontline, 7 May 2019, https://www.pbs.org/wgbh/frontline/article/made-in-china-2025-the-industrial-plan-that-china-doesnt-want-anyone-talking-about/; James McBride and Andrew Chatzky, "Is 'Made in China 2025' a Threat to Global Trade?," Council on Foreign Relations, 13 May 2019, https://www.cfr.org/backgrounder/made-china-2025-threat-global-trade; Lingling Wei and Bob Davis, "China Prepares Policy to Increase Access for Foreign Companies," *Wall Street Journal*, 12 December 2018, https://www.wsj.com/articles/china-is-preparing-to-increase-access-for-foreign-companies-11544622331?mod=hp_lead_pos4. For a more sympathetic take, see Johnsen Romero and Paul Evans, "Ignoring the Circumstances That Compel Chinese Policymaking Is Unproductive: Canada Should Do Its Homework on What Led to Made in China 2025," *Policy Options*, 28 May 2019, https://policyoptions.irpp.org/magazines/may-2019/why-canada-should-better-understand-made-in-china-2025/.
36 Blackwill and Harris, *War by Other Means*, 56.
37 Babacar Dione and Cara Anna, "Chinese Leader Arrives for Africa Visit as US Interest Wanes," *Financial Post*, 21 July 2018, https://financialpost.com/pmn/business-pmn/chinese-leader-arrives-for-africa-visit-as-us-interest-wanes.
38 Wenjie Chen and Roger Nord, "A Rebalancing Act for China and Africa," International Monetary Fund, Washington, DC, 2017, 2, https://www.imf.org/~/media/Files/Publications/DP/2017/44711-afrdp.ashx.
39 Jyhjong Hwang, Deborah Brautigam, and Janet Eom, "How Chinese Money Is Transforming Africa: It's Not What You Think," *China-Africa Research Initiative, Johns Hopkins University School of Advanced Studies* 11 (2016): 3.
40 On the opportunities, see Chen and Nord, "Rebalancing Act"; and Hwang, Brautigam, and Eom, "How Chinese Money Is Transforming Africa." On "debtbook diplomacy," see Sam Parker and Gabrielle Chefitz, *Debtbook Diplomacy: China's Strategic Leveraging of Its Newfound Economic Influence and the Consequences for U.S. Foreign Policy* (Cambridge, MA: Harvard Kennedy School, Belfer Centre for Science and International Affairs, May 2018), https://www.belfercenter.org/sites/default/files/files/publication/Debtbook%20Diplomacy%20PDF.pdf
41 Parker and Chefitz, *Debtbook Diplomacy*, 1.
42 Ann Hui, "What's Really behind China's Decision to Restrict Canola: Science or Politics?," *Globe and Mail*, 30 August 2016, https://www

.theglobeandmail.com/news/national/whats-really-behind-chinas-decision-to-restrict-canola-science-or-politics/article31625635/.

43 Stephen Chase, "'Since the End of December We Have Not Sold a Single Vessel': Canadian Farmers Continue to Struggle with China's Ban on Exports," *Globe and Mail*, 4 August 2019, https://www.theglobeandmail.com/politics/article-the-chinese-ban-on-canadian-agricultural-exports-is-increasingly/.

44 Rosa Saba, "What Is Ractopamine and Why Did China Shut Down Canadian Meat Exports over It?," *Toronto Star*, 26 June 2019, https://www.thestar.com/calgary/2019/06/26/what-is-ractopamine-and-why-did-china-shut-down-canadian-meat-exports-over-it.html.

45 Blackwill and Harris, *War by Other Means*, 109.

46 David Mulroney, *Middle Power, Middle Kingdom: What Canadians Need to Know about China in the 21st Century* (Toronto: Allen Lane, 2015), 110–11.

47 Aileen McCabe, "University of Calgary Becomes Latest to Receive Cold Shoulder," *Vancouver Sun*, 6 February 2010. The "delisting" lasted for one academic year, ending in 2011. *Maclean's*, "UCalgary Regains Accreditation in China," 4 April 2011, https://www.macleans.ca/education/uniandcollege/ucalgary-regains-accreditation-in-china/.

48 U.S. Department of Justice, "Chinese Telecommunications Conglomerate Huawei and Huawei CFO Wanzhou Meng Charged with Financial Fraud," 28 January 2019, https://www.justice.gov/opa/pr/chinese-telecommunications-conglomerate-huawei-and-huawei-cfo-wanzhou-meng-charged-financial.

49 Lu Shaye, "China's Ambassador: Why the Double Standard on Justice for Canadians, Chinese?," Hill Times, 9 January 2019, https://www.hilltimes.com/2019/01/09/double-standard-justice-canadians-chinese/182367.

50 Margaret McCuaig-Johnston, "McCuaig-Johnston: Canada Must Take Stronger Action against China to Free Our 'Detainees,'" *Ottawa Citizen*, 8 April 2918, https://ottawacitizen.com/opinion/columnists/mccuaig-canada-must-take-stronger-action-against-china-to-free-our-detainees.

51 Robert Fife, "After Arrest and Isolation, China Seizes Kovrig's Reading Glasses," *Globe and Mail*, 2 July 2019, https://www.theglobeandmail.com/politics/article-china-escalates-pressure-on-detainee-issue-with-seizure-of-michael/.

52 Chris Buckley, "China Sentences a Canadian, Robert Lloyd Schellenberg, to Death," *New York Times*, 14 January 2019, https://www.nytimes.com/2019/01/14/world/asia/china-canada-schellenberg-retrial.html.

53 BBC News, "China Sentences Second Canadian to Death," 30 April 2019, https://www.bbc.com/news/world-asia-china-48104607#:~:text=A%20

court%20in%20China%20has,were%20also%20sentenced%20on%20 Tuesday.
54 Jessica Murphy, "Kevin and Julia Garratt on Their Experience as Detainees in China," BBC News, 29 January 2019, https://www.bbc.com/news/world-us-canada-46981048; Nathan Vanderklippe, "Canadian Couple Recounts 'Survival Story' of Their Detention in China," 28 November 2018, https://www.theglobeandmail.com/world/article-canadian-couple-recounts-survival-story-of-their-detention-in-china/.
55 Associated Press, "B.C. Man Su Bin Pleads Guilty to Stealing U.S. Military Secrets," CBC News, 24 March 2016, https://www.cbc.ca/news/canada/british-columbia/b-c-man-su-bin-pleads-guilty-to-stealing-u-s-military-secrets-1.3505571.
56 Mark MacKinnon, "Ottawa, China Trade Deal to Protect Investors: Harper; Looking to Correct 'Significant Imbalance,' Prime Minister Urges Beijing to Grant Canadian Businesses Greater Access to Key Sectors," *Globe and Mail*, 10 September 2012.
57 Canadian Security Intelligence Service, *China in an Age of Strategic Rivalry*, 109.
58 Comments made by Margaret McCuaig-Johnston, *Opportunities and Challenge in China's Innovation System*, Public Policy Forum, December 2017.
59 Canadian Security Intelligence Service, *China in an Age of Strategic Rivalry*, 108.
60 Canadian Security Intelligence Service, *China in an Age of Strategic Rivalry*, 110.
61 Christine Negroni, "China Market Challenges Plane Makers," *International Herald Tribune*, 14 Many 2012; Toh Han Shih, "Dilemma for the Foreign Firms Who Must Help Rivals," *South China Morning Post*, 4 January 2010.
62 Mulroney, *Middle Power*, 42.
63 Nathan Vanderklippe and Nicolas van Praet, "How China Built a Global Rail Behemoth That's Leaving Western Train Makers Behind," *Globe and Mail*, 9 June 2017, https://www.theglobeandmail.com/report-on-business/international-business/how-china-built-a-global-rail-behemoth-thats-leaving-western-train-makers-behind/article35272833/.
64 European Union Chamber of Commerce in China, "China Manufacturing 2025: Putting Industrial Policy Ahead of Market Forces," 2017, 31.
65 Wade Shepard, "China Hits Record High M&A Investments in Western Firms," *Forbes*, 10 September 2016, https://www.forbes.com/sites/wadeshepard/2016/09/10/from-made-in-china-to-owned-by-china-chinese-enterprises-buying-up-western-companies-at-record-pace/#20be55a5d879.

66 Pricewaterhouse Coopers, *State-Owned Enterprises: Catalysts for Public Value Creation?*, April 2015, 8, https://www.pwc.com/gx/en/psrc/publications/assets/pwc-state-owned-enterprise-psrc.pdf.
67 Duanjie Chen, "China's State-Owned Enterprises: How Much Do We Know? From CNOOC to Its Siblings," *University of Calgary School of Public Policy Research Papers* 6, no. 19 (2013): 3.
68 *Economist*, "Fixing China Inc," 30 August 2014, https://www.economist.com/news/china/21614240-reform-state-companies-back-agenda-fixing-china-inc.
69 OECD, *State-Owned Enterprises as Global Competitors: A Challenge or an Opportunity?*, 8 December 2016, 21, http://www.oecd.org/corporate/state-owned-enterprises-as-global-competitors-9789264262096-en.htm.
70 Pricewaterhouse Coopers, *State-Owned Enterprises*, 8.
71 Pricewaterhouse Coopers, *State-Owned Enterprises*, 8.
72 OECD, *State-Owned Enterprises*, 13.
73 OECD, *State-Owned Enterprises*, 21.
74 Duanjie Chen, "China's State-Owned Enterprises: How Much Do We Know? From CNOOC to Its Siblings?," *University of Calgary School of Public Policy Research Papers* 6, no. 19 (2013): 3, https://www.policyschool.ca/wp-content/uploads/2016/03/chinas-soes-chen.pdf.
75 Norris, *Chinese Economic Statecraft*, 71.
76 Norris, *Chinese Economic Statecraft*, 71.
77 *Economist*, "Fixing China Inc."
78 Norris, *Chinese Economic Statecraft*, 72.
79 Minxi Pei, *China's Crony Capitalism: The Dynamics of Regime Decay* (Cambridge, MA: Harvard University Press, 2016), 30.
80 Pei, *China's Crony Capitalism*, 180–1.
81 Pei, *China's Crony Capitalism*, 117.
82 Pei, *China's Crony Capitalism*, 152–3.
83 Pei, *China's Crony Capitalism*, 151–5.
84 Pei, *China's Crony Capitalism*, 181.
85 *Economist*, "Reform of China's Ailing State-Owned Firms Is Emboldening Them," 22 July 2017, https://www.economist.com/news/finance-and-economics/21725293-outperformed-private-firms-they-are-no-longer-shrinking-share-overall.
86 *Economist*, "Reform of China's Ailing State-Owned Firms."
87 *Economist*, "A Whimper, Not a Bang," 17 September 2015, https://www.economist.com/news/business/21665065-chinas-plan-reform-its-troubled-state-firms-fails-impress-whimper-not-bang.
88 Yuen Pau Woo, "Chinese Lessons: State-Owned Enterprises and the Regulation of Foreign Investment in Canada," *China Economic Journal* 7, no. 1 (2014): 21.

89 Margaret Cornish, *Behaviour of Chinese SOEs: Implications for Investment and Cooperation in Canada,* Canadian Council of Chief Executives and the Canadian International Council, February 2012, 7, https://thecic.org/research-publications/reports/behaviour-of-chinese-soes-implications-for-investment-and-cooperation-in-canada; Steven Globerman, "A Policy Perspective on Outward Foreign Direct Investment by Chinese State-Owned Enterprises," *Frontiers of Economics in China* 11, no. 4 (2016): 546.
90 Woo, "Chinese Lessons," 35.
91 Globerman, "Policy Perspective," 542.
92 Globerman, "Policy Perspective," 543.
93 Woo, "Chinese Lessons," 34.
94 Norris, *Chinese Economic Statecraft*, 27–8.
95 *Economist*, "Fixing China Inc"; and *Economist*, "A Whimper, Not a Bang."
96 *Economist*, "Reform of China's Ailing State-Owned Firms."
97 *Economist*, "Reform of China's Ailing State-Owned Firms"; and Caroline Freund and Dario Sidhu, "WP 17-3: Global Competition and the Rise of China," Peterson Institute for International Economics, February 2017, https://piie.com/publications/working-papers/global-competition-and-rise-china
98 Economist. "Reform of China's Ailing State-Owned Firms."
99 Jennifer Hughes, "China's Communist Party Writes Itself into Company Law," *Financial Times*, 14 August 2017, https://www.ft.com/content/a4b28218-80db-11e7-94e2-c5b903247afd.
100 Hughes, "China's Communist Party."
101 *Economist*, "Reform of China's Ailing State-Owned Firms."
102 Freund and Sidhu, "Global Competition," 16.
103 Caroline Freund, "Why China Isn't Ready Yet to Lead Globalization," Peterson Institute for International Economics, 24 July 2017, https://piie.com/blogs/china-economic-watch/why-china-isnt-ready-yet-lead-globalization.
104 Dorothy Denning, "How the Chinese Cyberthreat Has Evolved," *Scientific American*, 7 October 2017, https://www.scientificamerican.com/article/how-the-chinese-cyberthreat-has-evolved/.
105 Woo, "Chinese Lessons," 35.
106 Woo, "Chinese Lessons," 27.
107 Woo, "Chinese Lessons," 28.
108 For a description and a brief analysis of the 2009 changes, see Subrata Bhattacharjee, "National Security with a Canadian Twist: The Investment Canada Act and the New National Security Review Test," *Transnational Corporations Review* 1, no. 4 (2009): 12–19.
109 Norris, *Chinese Economic Statecraft*, 76; Kelly Cryderman, "Canada's Future Linked to Foreign Investment," *Calgary Herald*, 5 January 2013.

110 Nathan Vanderklippe, "Nexen Deal Comes Back to Haunt CNOOC," *Globe and Mail*, 3 December 2013, https://www.theglobeandmail.com/report-on-business/international-business/asian-pacific-business/nexen-acquisition-hurting-cnoocs-performance/article15742860/.

111 Nathan Vanderklippe, Shawn McCarthy, and Jacquie McNish, "Harper Draws a Line in the Oil Sands," *Globe and Mail*, 9 December 2012, https://www.theglobeandmail.com/globe-investor/harper-draws-a-line-in-the-oil-sands/article6143202/.

112 Industry Canada (now Innovation, Science and Economic Development Canada), "Statement Regarding Investment by Foreign State-Owned Enterprises," 7 December 2012, http://www.ic.gc.ca/eic/site/ica-lic.nsf/eng/lk81147.html.

113 Patrick Brown, "FIPA Agreement with China: What's Really in it for Canada?," CBC News, 19 September 2014, https://www.cbc.ca/news/canada/fipa-agreement-with-china-what-s-really-in-it-for-canada-1.2770159.

114 A good summary of the debate over Huawei's obligation to the Chinese government may be found in Yuan Yang, "Is Huawei Compelled by Chinese Law to Help with Espionage?," *Financial Times*, 5 March 2019, https://www.ft.com/content/282f8ca0-3be6-11e9-b72b-2c7f526ca5d0. For a description of the law, see CSIS, "China's Intelligence Law and the Country's Future Intelligence Competitions," in *China and the Age of Strategic Rivalry*, 83–91.

115 National Cyber Security Centre (UK), "Ciaran Martin's CyberSec Speech in Brussels," 20 February 2019, https://www.ncsc.gov.uk/news/ciaran-martins-cybersec-speech-brussels.

116 U.S. Department of Homeland Security, "Recommended Practice: Improving Industrial Control System Cybersecurity with Defense-in-Depth Strategies," September 2016, 2, https://www.us-cert.gov/sites/default/files/recommended_practices/NCCIC_ICS-CERT_Defense_in_Depth_2016_S508C.pdf.

117 Sean Silcoff, Robert Fife, Steven Chase, and Christine Dobby, "How Canadian Money and Research Are Helping China Become a Global Telecom Superpower," *Globe and Mail*, 26 May 2019, https://www.theglobeandmail.com/canada/article-how-canadian-money-and-research-are-helping-china-become-a-global/.

118 CBC Spark, "What's the Real Danger of Relying on Huawei's 5G Technology?," 24 February 2019, https://www.cbc.ca/radio/spark/spark-427-1.5024321/what-s-the-real-danger-of-relying-on-huawei-s-5g-technology-1.5024324.

119 Catharine Tunney, "Huawei Hit with Security Questions as It Unveils High-Speed Rural Internet Project," CBC News, 22 July 2019, https://www.cbc.ca/news/politics/huawei-north-high-speed-1.5220354.

120 Canadian Security Intelligence Service, *Public Report 2010–2011*, 2012, 19, https://www.canada.ca/content/dam/csis-scrs/documents/publications/2010-2011PublicReport_English.pdf.
121 William A. Galston, "Second Thoughts on Trade with China," *Wall Street Journal*, 8 August 2017, https://www.wsj.com/articles/second-thoughts-on-trade-with-china-1502234236.
122 Mulroney, *Middle Power, Middle Kingdom*, 54.
123 Mulroney, *Middle Power, Middle Kingdom*, 68–9.

5. Cybersecurity

1 Canadian Security Intelligence Service, "Remarks by Director David Vigneault at the Economic Club of Canada," 4 December 2018, https://www.canada.ca/en/security-intelligence-service/news/2018/12/remarks-by-director-david-vigneault-at-the-economic-club-of-canada.html.
2 Ben Makuch, "Ottawa's Cyberspies Confirm Iranian Hackers Targeted Canadian Systems," Vice, 23 March 2018, https://news.vice.com/en_ca/article/paxpy7/ottawas-cyberspies-confirm-iranian-hackers-targeted-canadian-systems.
3 Thomas Rid, *Rise of the Machines: A Cybernetic History* (New York: W.W. Norton, 2016).
4 James R. Clapper, Marcel Lettre, and Michael S. Rogers, "Joint Statement for the Record to the Senate Armed Services Committee Foreign Cyber Threats to the United States," 5 January 2017, https://www.armed-services.senate.gov/imo/media/doc/Clapper-Lettre-Rogers_01-05-16.pdf.
5 On "cyber-proxies," see Tim Maurer, *Cyber Mercenaries: The State, Hackers and Power* (Cambridge: Cambridge University Press, 2018).
6 Warnings of cyber-9/11 have been made by U.S. officials since at least 2003 and continue. See, for example, Sue Cant, "'Cyber 9/11 Risk Warning," *Age*, 22 April 2003; Veronica Stracqualursi, "US Intelligence Chief: 'The Warning Lights Are Blinking Red Again' on Cyberattacks," CNN.com, 14 July 2018, https://www.cnn.com/2018/07/14/politics/director-of-national-intelligence-dan-coats-cyberattacks-russia/index.html.
7 Modified definition from P.W. Singer and Allan Friedman, *Cybersecurity and Cyberwar: What Everyone Needs to Know* (Oxford: Oford University Press, 2014), 43 and 297; Raef Meeuwisse, *Cybersecurity for Beginners*, 2nd ed. (London: Cybersimplicity, 2017), 25.

8 Canadian Centre for Cyber Security, *An Introduction to the Cyber Threat Environment*, 6 December 2018, 6, https://www.cyber.gc.ca/en/guidance/introduction-cyber-threat-environment.
9 Paul Wood, "10th Anniversary of the Anna Kournikova Virus," Symantec, 10 February 2011, https://www.symantec.com/connect/blogs/10th-anniversary-anna-kournikova-virus.
10 Timothy B. Lee, "How a Grad Student Trying to Build the First Botnet Brought the Internet to Its Knees," *Washington Post*, 1 November 2013, https://www.washingtonpost.com/news/the-switch/wp/2013/11/01/how-a-grad-student-trying-to-build-the-first-botnet-brought-the-internet-to-its-knees/?utm_term=.d5fe70aaeb44; Fred Kaplan, *Dark Territory: The Secret History of Cyber War* (New York: Simon & Schuster, 2016), 60.
11 Symantec, "What Is a Trojan? Is it a Virus or Is It Malware?," https://us.norton.com/internetsecurity-malware-what-is-a-trojan.html.
12 Lillian Ablon and Timothy Bogart, *Zero Days, Thousands of Nights: The Life and Times of Zero-Day Vulnerabilities and Their Exploits* (Santa Monica: RAND, 2017).
13 Ablon and Bogart, *Zero Days*, x.
14 Canadian Centre for Cyber Security, *Introduction*, 9.
15 Karl Grindal, "Operation Buckshot Yankee," in *A Fierce Domain: Conflict in Cyberspace, 1986 to 2012*, ed. Jason Healey, 205–11 (Arlington, VA: Cyber Conflict Studies Association, 2013); Singer and Friedman, *Cybersecurity and Cyberwar*, 40.
16 Grindal, "Operation Buckshot Yankee," 207–8; Kaplan, *Dark Territory*, 181–2.
17 Meeuwisse, *Cybersecurity*, 183.
18 Canadian Centre for Cyber Security, "National Cyber Threat Assessment 2018," 2 and 22–5.
19 There are several accounts of the Stuxnet virus. See Kaplan, *Dark Territory*, 206–11; Chris Morton, "Stuxnet, Flame and Duqu: The OLYMPIC GAMES," in *A Fierce Domain: Conflict in Cyberspace, 1986 to 2012*, ed. Jason Healey, 212–31 (Arlington, VA: Cyber Conflict Studies Association, 2013); Adam Segal, *The Hacked World Order: How Nations Fight, Trade, Maneuver and Manipulate in the Digital Age* (New York: Public Affairs, 2017), 2–5; Singer and Friedman, *Cybersecurity and Cyberwar*, 114–18.
20 Kaplan, *Dark Territory*, 213; Lucas Kello, *The Virtual Weapon and International Order* (New Haven, CT: Yale University Press, 2017), 170–3; Kim Zetter, "Wiper Malware That Hit Iran Left Possible Clues of Its Origins," *Wired*, 29 August 2012, https://www.wired.com/2012/08/wiper-possible-origins/.
21 Singer and Friedman, *Cybersecurity and Cyberwar*, 118.

22 Kaplan, *Dark Territory*, 210; Singer and Friedman, *Cybersecurity and Cyberwar*, 114–18.
23 Kaplan, *Dark* Territory, 213; Maurer, *Cyber Mercenaries*, 82–3; Morton, "Stuxnet, Flame and Duqu," 229.
24 Maurer, *Cyber Mercenaries*, 82.
25 Maurer, *Cyber Mercenaries*, 84–8.
26 Maurer, *Cyber* Mercenaries, 50–2, 132–3; Segal, *Hacked World Order*, 57–7.
27 Gordon Corera, "How France's TV5 Was Almost Destroyed by 'Russian Hackers,'" BBC.com, 10 October 2016, https://www.bbc.com/news/technology-37590375.
28 Kaplan, *Dark Territory*, 270; Maurer, *Cyber* Mercenaries, 51; Segal, *Hacked World Order*, 60.
29 CTV News, "Cyberattack Takes Down CSIS Website," 29 June 2015, https://www.ctvnews.ca/canada/cyberattack-takes-down-csis-website-1.2446727.
30 Andreas Schmidt, "The Estonian Cyberattacks," in *A Fierce Domain: Conflict in Cyberspace, 1986 to 2012*, ed. Jason Healey, 174–93 (Arlington, VA: Cyber Conflict Studies Association, 2013); Kaplan, *Dark Territory*, 162–3; Segal, *Hacked World Order*, 67–77; Brandon Valeriano, Benjamin Jensen, and Ryan C. Maness, *Cyber Strategy: The Evolving Character of Power and Coercion* (Oxford: Oxford University Press, 2018), 124–7.
31 Andreas Hagen, "The Russo-Georgian War 2008," in *A Fierce Domain: Conflict in Cyberspace, 1986 to 2012*, ed. Jason Healey, 194–204 (Arlington, VA: Cyber Conflict Studies Association, 2013); Kaplan, *Dark Territory*, 164–6; Maurer, *Cyber Mercenaries*, 101–2; Segal, *Hacked World Order*, 74–7.
32 Segal, *Hacked World Order*, 77–83. More on hybrid warfare will be discussed in chapter 7.
33 Maurer, *Cyber Mercenaries*, ix–x, 98–100.
34 Garrett M. Graff, "How a Dorm Room *Minecraft* Scam Brought Down the Internet," *Wired*, 13 December 2017, https://www.wired.com/story/mirai-botnet-minecraft-scam-brought-down-the-internet/.
35 Brian Krebs, "Mirai Botnet Authors Avoid Jail Time," Krebs on Security, 19 September 2018, https://krebsonsecurity.com/2018/09/mirai-botnet-authors-avoid-jail-time/.
36 Brian Krebs, "KrebsOnSecurity Hit with Record DDoS," Krebs on Security, 21 September 2016, https://krebsonsecurity.com/2016/09/krebsonsecurity-hit-with-record-ddos/.
37 Dan Goodin, "Meet dark_nexus, Quite Possibly the Most Potent IoT Botnet Ever," *Ars Technica*, 9 April 2020, https://arstechnica.com/information-technology/2020/04/meet-dark_nexus-quite-possibly-the-most-potent-iot-botnet-ever/. The story refers to a report on the

botnet: Bitdefender, "New dark_nexus IoT Botnet Puts Others to Shame," April 2020, https://www.bitdefender.com/files/News/CaseStudies/study/319/Bitdefender-PR-Whitepaper-DarkNexus-creat4349-en-EN-interactive.pdf?clickid=1newORyPnxyORZ9wUx0Mo38VUkixAPRhW0e-Sk0&irgwc=1&MPid=10078&cid=aff%7Cc%7CIR.

38 Singer and Freidman, *Cybersecurity and Cyberwar*, 96–7.
39 Jose Pagliery, "ISIS Is Attacking the U.S. Energy Grid (and Failing)," CNN, 16 October 2015, https://money.cnn.com/2015/10/15/technology/isis-energy-grid/index.html.
40 Associated Press, "Hacker Who Gave Isis 'Hitlist' of US Targets Jailed for 20 Years," *Guardian*, 24 September 2016, https://www.theguardian.com/world/2016/sep/24/hacker-who-gave-isis-hitlist-of-us-targets-jailed-for-20-years; Maurer, *Cyber Mercenaries*, 163.
41 Maurer, *Cyber-Mercenaries*, 11.
42 Segal, *Hacked World Order*, 18.
43 Christopher Reynolds, "Purported Daesh Target List Contains 150 Canadian Names," *Toronto Star*, 16 June 2016.
44 Jane Taber, "The Three Most Important Discussions at the Halifax International Security Forum," *Globe and Mail*, 23 November 2014, https://www.theglobeandmail.com/news/politics/the-three-most-important-discussions-at-the-halifax-international-security-forum/article21718099/.
45 Laith Alkhouri and Alex Kassirer, "Tech for Jihad: Dissecting Jihadists' Digital Toolbox," Flashpoint, July 2016, https://www.flashpoint-intel.com/wp-content/uploads/2016/08/TechForJihad.pdf.
46 There have been several successful prosecutions of individuals in the United States who have used Bitcoin to support the Islamic State. There is also evidence that terrorists in the Gaza Strip have used virtual currencies to fund their operations. Nevertheless, the use of cryptocurrencies by terrorist groups remains limited by the availability of technological and financial infrastructure in many areas of the world where such groups operate (the Horn of Africa, Afghanistan, Syria, etc.). In this sense, the use of cryptocurrency appears to be small-scale, mostly potential, rather than actualized. See European Parliament, *Virtual Currencies and Terrorist Financing: Assessing the Risks and Evaluating the Responses*, May 2018, http://www.europarl.europa.eu/RegData/etudes/STUD/2018/604970/IPOL_STU(2018)604970_EN.pdf. Zachary K. Goldman, Ellie Maruyama, Elizabeth Rosenberg, Edoardo Saravalle, and Julia Solomon-Strauss, *Terrorist Use of Virtual Currencies: Containing the Potential Threat* (Washington, DC: Centre for New American Security, May 2017), https://www.cnas.org/publications/reports/terrorist-use-of-virtual-currencies;

Ankit Panda, "Cryptocurrencies and National Security," Council on Foreign Relations, 28 February 2018, https://www.cfr.org/backgrounder/cryptocurrencies-and-national-security.

47 Kesha Hannam, "An American Woman Used Bitcoin to Send Money to Islamic State," *Forbes*, 15 December 2017, http://fortune.com/2017/12/15/women-islamic-state-bitcoin/.

48 Michael Edison Hayden, "White Supremacists Are Investing in a Cryptocurrency That Promises to Be Completely Untraceable," *Newsweek*, 27 March 2018, https://www.newsweek.com/white-supremacists-cryptocurrency-monero-bitcoin-861104.

49 Singer and Friedman, *Cybersecurity and Cyberwar*, 99–103.

50 W.J. Hennigan, "Islamic State's Deadly Drone Operation Is Faltering, but U.S. Commanders See Broader Danger ahead," *Los Angeles Times*, 28 September 2017, http://www.latimes.com/world/la-fg-isis-drones-20170928-story.html.

51 Mia Bloom and Chelsea Daymon, "Assessing the Future Threat: ISIS's Virtual Caliphate," *Orbis* 62, no. 3 (2018): 372–88; Mina Hamblet, "The Islamic State's Virtual Caliphate," *Middle East Quarterly* 24, no. 4 (2017): 1-8; Charlie Winter and Jade Parker, "Virtual Caliphate Rebooted: The Islamic State's Evolving Online Strategy," Lawfare, 7 January 2018, https://www.lawfareblog.com/virtual-caliphate-rebooted-islamic-states-evolving-online-strategy.

52 Henry Ridgwell, "Huge Decline in ISIS Propaganda Mirrors Losses on Battlefield," Voice of America, 1 December 2017, https://www.voanews.com/a/isis-propaganda-declies-mirrors-losses-on-battlefield/4144838.html; Charlie Winter, "Inside the Collapse of Islamic State's Propaganda Machine," *Wired*, 20 December 2017, https://www.wired.co.uk/article/isis-islamic-state-propaganda-content-strategy.

53 Maurer, *Cyber Mercenaries*, xi.

54 Maurer, *Cyber Mercenaries*, 84–8.

55 Maurer, *Cyber Mercenaries*, 20–1.

56 Maurer, *Cyber Mercenaries*, 97–103. Maurer notes that there is some debate on whether or not some of these activities (such as the attacks against Georgia in 2008) are better thought of as *orchestration* rather than *sanctioning*. However, he notes there is no proof of direct Kremlin involvement in these attacks, although the Russian government certainly benefited from it (101).

57 Maurer, *Cyber Mercenaries*, 89–90.

58 Maurer, *Cyber Mercenaries*, 107–19.

59 Maurer, *Cyber Mercenaries*, 83. Cylance, *#OperationCleaver*, 2015, https://www.cylance.com/content/dam/cylance/pages/operation-cleaver/Cylance_Operation_Cleaver_Report.pdf.

60 Nicole Perlroth, "Hackers in China Attacked The Times for Last 4 Months," *New York Times*, 30 January 3013, https://www.nytimes.com/2013/01/31/technology/chinese-hackers-infiltrate-new-york-times-computers.html.

61 Symantec, "Advanced Persistent Threats: A Symantec Perspective," 2011, 1, http://index-of.es/Varios/b-advanced_persistent_threats_WP_21215957.en-us.pdf.

62 Cybersecurity firm Symantec describes four phases: incursion, discovery, capture, and exfiltration. Fireye lists six: entry, discovery, reinforcement (establishing additional points of compromise), gathering data, exfiltration, and cover-up of the operation (with ongoing compromise). Although it is broken up into separate steps, both companies are effectively describing the same process. See Fireye, "The Six Steps of and APT Attack," n.d., https://www.fireeye.com/current-threats/anatomy-of-a-cyber-attack.html; Symantec, "Advanced Persistent Threats," 2–6.

63 Meeuwisse, *Cybersecurity for Beginners*, 179; Singer and Friedman, *Cybersecurity and Cyberwar*, 55–60.

64 Mandiant, "APT1."

65 FireEye, "APT1," https://www.fireeye.com/current-threats/apt-groups.html#apt1; Mandiant, "APT1," 3.

66 FireEye, "Advanced Persistent Threat Groups: Who's Who of Cyber Threat Actors," https://www.fireeye.com/current-threats/apt-groups.html.

67 Alex Boutilier, "Hackers Target Federal Government Networks an Average of 474 Million Times Per Day, Memo Shows," *Toronto Star*, 17 October 2018, https://www.thestar.com/politics/federal/2018/10/17/hackers-target-federal-government-networks-an-average-of-474-million-times-per-day-memo-shows.html.

68 Public Safety Canada, "Horizontal Evaluation of Canada's Cyber Security Strategy," 29 September 2017, 17, https://www.publicsafety.gc.ca/cnt/rsrcs/pblctns/vltn-cnd-scrt-strtg/vltn-cnd-scrt-strtg-en.pdf.

69 Greg Weston, "Foreign Hackers Attack Canadian Government," CBC News, 16 February 2011, https://www.cbc.ca/news/politics/foreign-hackers-attack-canadian-government-1.982618.

70 Colin Freeze, "China Hack Cost Ottawa 'Hundreds of Millions,' Documents Show," *Globe and Mail*, 30 March 2017, https://www.theglobeandmail.com/news/national/federal-documents-say-2014-china-hack-cost-hundreds-of-millions-of-dollars/article34485219/.

71 Canadian Centre for Cyber Security, "National Cyber Threat Assessment," 3.

72 Public Safety Canada, *National Cyber Security Strategy: Canada's Vision for Security and Prosperity in the Digital Age*, 12 June 2018, 34, https://www

.publicsafety.gc.ca/cnt/rsrcs/pblctns/ntnl-cbr-scrt-strtg/ntnl-cbr-scrt-strtg-en.pdf.
73 Jamie Bartlett, *The Dark Net: Inside the Digital Underworld* (Brooklyn, NY: Melville House Publishing, 2015). See esp. "On the Road," 135–65.
74 Modified definition based on Meeuwisse, *Cybersecurity*, 198.
75 Maurer, *Cyber Mercenaries*, 132–3. Foreign locations may also help obscure attribution. Tim Maurer observes that in recent years Thailand and Vietnam have become hotspots for cyber-criminals, with individuals or groups of hackers from North Korea, Eastern Europe, Russia, Belarus, and Ukraine, etc., conducting their operations from those places.
76 White House, "Press Briefing on the Attribution of the WannaCry Malware Attack to North Korea," 19 December 2017, https://www.whitehouse.gov/briefings-statements/press-briefing-on-the-attribution-of-the-wannacry-malware-attack-to-north-korea-121917/.
77 Segal, *Hacked World Order*, 88–9.
78 Segal, *Hacked World Order*, 88.
79 CTV News, "Wasaga Beach Pays Ransom Following Computer System Hacking," 24 July 2018, https://barrie.ctvnews.ca/wasaga-beach-pays-ransom-following-computer-system-hacking-1.4026570.
80 Government of Canada, *Equality + Growth: A Strong Middle Class* (Budget 2018), 27 February 2018, 203–4, https://www.budget.gc.ca/2018/docs/plan/budget-2018-en.pdf.
81 Howard Solomon, "New RCMP Cyber Co-ordination Unit Won't Be Fully Operational until 2023," IT World Canada, 5 April 2019, https://www.itworldcanada.com/article/new-rcmp-cyber-co-ordination-unit-wont-be-fully-operational-until-2023/416561.
82 Andy Greenberg, "The Untold Story of NotPetya, the Most Devastating Cyberattack in History," *Wired*, 22 August 2018, https://www.wired.com/story/notpetya-cyberattack-ukraine-russia-code-crashed-the-world/; Mark Landler and Scott Shane, "U.S. Condemns Russia for Cyberattack, Showing Split in Stance on Putin," *New York Times*, 15 February 2018, https://www.nytimes.com/2018/02/15/us/politics/russia-cyberattack.html.
83 Greenberg, "Untold Story of NotPetya."
84 The FSB stands for Federal'naya Sluzhba Bezopasnosti or Federal Security Service.
85 Michael Lista, "The Hacker King," *Toronto Life*, 2 January 2018, https://torontolife.com/city/crime/kid-made-millions-hacking-emails-fbi-took/.
86 United States of America v Dimitry Dokuchaev, et al. 28 February 2017, https://www.justice.gov/opa/press-release/file/948201/download.
87 Standing Senate Committee on Banking, Trade and Commerce, *cyber.assualt: It Should Keep You Up at Night*, October 2018, https://sencanada

.ca/content/sen/committee/421/BANC/reports/BANC_Report
_FINAL_e.pdf.
88 Data were compiled with the assistance of three research assistants between 2016 and 2018: Lucas Brydges, James Murray, and Mireille Seguin. Result were discovered searching Lexis Nexis using "cyber attack," "cyber espionage," "computer hacking," "hacking," and "computer virus."
89 Calce has since become a cybersecurity consultant. Andy Riga, "Mafiaboy Grows Up: Computer Hacking Taught Him How to Protect Companies," *Montreal Gazette*, 13 June 2016, https://montrealgazette.com/news/local-news/mafiaboy-grows-up-computer-hacking-taught-him-how-to-protect-companies.
90 See Federal Court of Canada, In the Matter of an Application by X For Warrants Pursuant to Section 12 and 21 of the *CSIS Act*, R. S. C. 1985, C. C-23 and in the Presence of the Attorney General and Amici and in the Matter of X Threat-Related Activities, 4 October 2016, https://decisions.fct-cf.gc.ca/fc-cf/decisions/en/item/212832/index.do.
91 The 2001 *Anti-Terrorism Act* made the first mention of CSE's mandate and legislative powers in Canadian law. These formally authorized the CSE to engage in three broad areas of activity: acquiring foreign intelligence; providing advice, guidance, and services to protect electronic information and infrastructures of importance to the Government of Canada; and providing technical and operational assistance to federal law enforcement and security agencies in the performance of their lawful duties. See Department of Justice, "About the Anti-Terrorism Act," last modified 26 July 2017, https://www.justice.gc.ca/eng/cj-jp/ns-sn/act-loi.html.
92 *Communications Security Establishment Act*, s. 18.
93 Two of the most prominent critics of the Harper Government's C-51, Craig Forcese and Kent Roach, have supported C-59 in this way. See Craig Forcese and Kent Roach, "The Roses and the Thorns of Canada's New National Security Bill," *Maclean's*, 20 June 2017, https://www.macleans.ca/politics/ottawa/the-roses-and-thorns-of-canadas-new-national-security-bill/; Forcese and Roach, "A Report Card on the National Security Bill," *Policy Options*, 22 June 2017, http://policyoptions.irpp.org/magazines/june-2017/a-report-card-on-the-national-security-bill/. The author has also publicly supported C-59 in this way. See Kent Roach, Stephanie Carvin, and Craig Forcese, "We Need Real, Honest Debate on Bill C-59," *Globe and Mail*, 4 December 2017, https://www.theglobeandmail.com/opinion/we-need-real-honest-debate-on-bill-c-59/article37175837/.

94 Christopher Parsons, Lex Gill, Tamir Israel, Bill Robinson, and Ronald Deibert, *Analysis of the Communications Security Establishment Act and Related Provisions in Bill C-59 (An Act Respecting National Security Matters), First Reading (December 18, 2017)*, December 2017, https://citizenlab.ca/wp-content/uploads/2017/12/C-59-Analysis-1.0.pdf; British Columbia Civil Liberties Association, "Nine Things You Need to Know about Bill C-59," 22 January 2018, https://bccla.org/2018/01/nine-things-need-know-bill-c-59/.
95 Canadian Security Establishment, "Canadian Centre for Cyber Security," October 2018, 16, https://www.cse-cst.gc.ca/en/backgrounder-fiche-information. The website of the CCSC is available at https://cyber.gc.ca/en/.
96 Canadian Security Establishment, "Canadian Centre for Cyber Security," October 2018, 16.
97 The findings of the 2016 cyber consultation may be found online: Nielsen, *Cyber Review Consultations Report*, 17 January, https://www.publicsafety.gc.ca/cnt/rsrcs/pblctns/2017-cybr-rvw-cnslttns-rprt/2017-cybr-rvw-cnslttns-rprt-en.pdf.
98 Department of National Defence, *Strong, Secure, Engaged: Canada's Defence Policy*, June 2017, http://publications.gc.ca/collections/collection_2017/mdn-dnd/D2-386-2017-eng.pdf.
99 Department of National Defence, *Strong, Secure, Engaged*, 72.
100 Department of National Defence, *Strong, Secure, Engaged*, 55.
101 Public Safety Canada, *National Cyber Security Strategy: Canada's Vision for Security and Prosperity in the Digital Age*, June 2018, https://www.publicsafety.gc.ca/cnt/rsrcs/pblctns/ntnl-cbr-scrt-strtg/index-en.aspx.
102 Public Safety Canada, *National Cyber Security Strategy*, 17.
103 FireEye, "Redline Drawn: China Recalculates Its Use of Cyber Espionage," 2016, https://www.fireeye.com/content/dam/fireeye-www/current-threats/pdfs/rpt-china-espionage.pdf.
104 FireEye, *Facing Forward: Cyber Security in 2019 and Beyond*, 2018, 21, https://content.fireeye.com/predictions/rpt-security-predictions-2019.
105 Alyza Sebenius and Nico Grant, "China Violating Cyber Agreement with U.S., NSA Official Says," Bloomberg, 8 November 2018, https://www.bloomberg.com/news/articles/2018-11-08/china-violating-cyber-agreement-with-u-s-nsa-official-says.
106 Treasury Board of Canada Secretariat, "Statement by the Chief Information Officer for the Government of Canada," 29 July 2014.
107 Ben Makuch and Justin Ling, "Iranian Hackers Infiltrated a Canadian Government System," Vice, 9 July 2015, https://news.vice.com/en_us/article/pa4dxm/iranian-hackers-infiltrated-a-canadian-government-system.

108 Steven Chase, "Canada, Western Allies Rebuke Russia over Alleged Global Hacking Campaign," *Globe and Mail*, 4 October 2018, https://www.theglobeandmail.com/politics/article-canada-western-allies-rebuke-russia-over-alleged-global-hacking/. See also the G7 statement, "Charlevoix Commitment on Defending Democracy from Foreign Threats," 1 January 2019, https://www.international.gc.ca/world-monde/international_relations-relations_internationales/g7/documents/2018-06-09-defending_democracy-defense_democratie.aspx?lang=eng.

109 Chase, "Canada, Western Allies." See Canada's statement: Global Affairs Canada, "Canada Identifies Malicious Cyber-Activity by Russia," 4 October 2018, https://www.canada.ca/en/global-affairs/news/2018/10/canada-identifies-malicious-cyber-activity-by-russia.html.

110 MSPs are companies that provide information management services to other clients. Jim Bronskill, "Canada among Targets of Alleged Chinese Hacking Campaign," Canadian Press via CBC News, 20 December 2018, https://www.cbc.ca/news/politics/canada-among-china-hacking-victims-1.4954608; see Canada's statement: Communications Security Establishment, "Canada and Allies Identify China as Responsible for Cyber-Compromise," 20 December 2018, https://cse-cst.gc.ca/en/media/media-2018-12-20.

111 Makuch, "Ottawa's Cyberspies."

112 See the G7 communiqué, "Charlevoix Commitment on Defending Democracy from Foreign Threats," 9 June 2018, https://www.international.gc.ca/world-monde/international_relations-relations_internationales/g7/documents/2018-06-09-defending_democracy-defense_democratie.aspx?lang=eng.

113 FireEye, "APT19," https://www.fireeye.com/current-threats/apt-groups.html#apt19.

114 Communications Security Establishment, "Quantum Computing Security Issues for Public Key Cryptography," May 2017, https://cyber.gc.ca/en/guidance/quantum-computing-security-issues-public-key-cryptography-itse00017.

115 *Economist*, "Quantum Computers Will Break the Encryption That Protects the Internet," 20 October 2018, https://www.economist.com/science-and-technology/2018/10/20/quantum-computers-will-break-the-encryption-that-protects-the-internet.

116 Lily Hay Newman, "Australia's Encryption-Busting Law Could Impact Global Privacy," *Wired*, 7 December 2018, https://www.wired.com/story/australia-encryption-law-global-impact/.

6. Clandestine Foreign Influence

1 Tom Blackwell, "Uyghur Activist Who Sparked Chinese-Student Protest at McMaster Worried about Message Targeting Her Son," *Montreal Gazette*, 16 February 2019, https://montrealgazette.com/news/uyghur-activist-who-sparked-chinese-student-protest-at-mcmaster-worried-about-message-targeting-her-son/wcm/2d875d41-5a26-4e90-ba29-da7b3f7fde1b.
2 Elsa Kania and Peter Wood, "Major Themes in China's 2019 National Defense White Paper," *China Brief* 19, no. 14, 31 July 2019, https://jamestown.org/program/major-themes-in-chinas-2019-national-defense-white-paper/.
3 On the surveillance and repression of the Uighur minority in China, see Chris Buckley and Paul Mozur, "How China Uses High-Tech Surveillance to Subdue Minorities," *New York Times*, 22 May 2019, https://www.nytimes.com/2019/05/22/world/asia/china-surveillance-xinjiang.html; Isobel Cockerell, "Inside China's Massive Surveillance Operation," *Wired*, 9 May 2019, https://www.wired.com/story/inside-chinas-massive-surveillance-operation/.
4 Blackwell, "Uyghur Activist."
5 CBC News, "'China Is Your Daddy': Backlash against Tibetan Student's Election Prompts Questions about Foreign Influence," 14 February 2019, https://www.cbc.ca/news/canada/toronto/china-tibet-student-election-1.5019648.
6 Levon Sevunts, "Chinese Officials Pressured Concordia University to Cancel Event with Uighur Activist," CBC News, 27 March 2019, https://www.cbc.ca/news/canada/montreal/chinese-officials-concordia-university-cancel-event-with-uighur-activist-1.5074423.
7 CSIS, "The CSIS Mandate," *Backgrounder #1*, rev. February 2005. This is also the definition used by the National Security and Intelligence Committee of Parliamentarians (NSICOP) in their review of clandestine foreign influence. See NSICOP, *Annual Report 2019*, August 2019, 55–110, https://www.nsicop-cpsnr.ca/reports/rp-2020-03-12-ar/annual_report_2019_public_en.pdf.
8 NSICOP, *Annual Report*, 55.
9 Craig Forcese and Leah West, "Interference," in *National Security Law*, 2nd ed. (Toronto: Irwin Law, forthcoming).
10 Forcese and West, "Interference." For example, in a show of solidarity with the United Kingdom in the wake of the chemical attack against UK residents in March 2018, over twenty mainly Western states "PNG'ed" dozens of Russian diplomats. (Canada expelled four diplomats and

denied credentials to another three.) See Kathleen Harris, "Canada to Expel 4 Russian Diplomats, Reject Credentials of 3 More," CBC News, 26 March 2018, https://www.cbc.ca/news/politics/canada-russia-diplomats-sanctions-1.4593062.

11 While this may seem somewhat obvious, it arose as an issue in July 2018 when the Federal Court ruled that while CSIS can spy on a foreign power, they could not lift territorial restrictions on their surveillance operations. In other words, if a foreign individual was engaging in clandestine influence against a country from within but not against Canada, there was no clear mandate to get a warrant to spy on what the clandestine influencer was doing. The case is complicated, but a good summary of the issues can be found in Craig Forcese, "Oh, What Tangled Webs the CSIS Act Weaves: The Federal Court's Latest Decision on CSIS's Foreign Intelligence Mandate," National Security Law (blog), 19 July 2018, http://craigforcese.squarespace.com/national-security-law-blog/2018/7/19/oh-what-tangled-webs-the-csis-act-weaves-the-federal-courts.html. See also Colin Freeze, "Federal Appeals Court Upholds Ruling Blocking CSIS from Conducting Certain Forms of Spying on Foreign States," *Globe and Mail*, 19 November 2018, https://www.theglobeandmail.com/canada/article-federal-appeals-court-upholds-ruling-blocking-csis-from-conducting/.

12 Harold D. Lasswell, "The Strategy of Soviet Propaganda," *Proceedings of the Academy of Political Science: The Defense of the Free World* 24, no. 2 (1951): 66–78.

13 Dennis Kux, "Soviet Active Measures and Disinformation: Overview and Assessment," *Parameters* 15, no. 4 (1985): 19–20.

14 Richard H. Shultz and Roy Godson, *Dezinformatsia: The Strategy of Soviet Disinformation* (New York: Berkley Books, 1986), 2.

15 Kux, "Soviet Active Measures," 19.

16 Shultz and Godson, *Dezinformatsia*, 44.

17 Johnathan Haslam, *Near and Distant Neighbours: A New History of Soviet Intelligence* (New York: Farrar, Straus and Giroux, 2015), 9–10.

18 Haslam, *Near and Distant Neighbours*, 28–32.

19 Kux, "Soviet Active Measures," 20.

20 Halsam, *Near and Distant Neighbours*, 50–3.

21 Kux, "Soviet Active Measures," 21–2; and Shultz and Godson, *Dezinformatsia*, 106–30. For a critical but sympathetic overview, see Günter Wernicke, "The Communist-Led World Peace Council and the Western Peace Movements: The Fetters of Bipolarity and Some Attempts to Break Them in the Fifties and Early Sixties," *Peace and Change* 23, no. 3 (1998): 265–311; and Wernicke, "The Unity of Peace and Socialism? The World

Peace Council on a Cold War Tightrope between the Peace Struggle and Intrasystemic Communist Conflicts," *Peace and Change* 26, no. 3 (2001): 332–52.

22 Jennifer Anderson, *Propaganda and Persuasion: The Cold War and the Canadian-Soviet Friendship Society* (Winnipeg: University of Manitoba Press, 2017), 153; Whitaker and Hewitt, *Canada and the Cold War*, 103–6.
23 Whitaker and Hewitt, *Canada and the Cold War*, 103–6.
24 Anderson, *Propaganda and Persuasion*, 9.
25 Anderson, *Propaganda and Persuasion*, 11.
26 Anderson, *Propaganda and Persuasion*, 52.
27 Robert Grimes, "Russian Fake News Is Not New: Soviet Aids Propaganda Cost Countless Lives," *Guardian*, 14 June 2017, https://www.theguardian.com/science/blog/2017/jun/14/russian-fake-news-is-not-new-soviet-aids-propaganda-cost-countless-lives; Reuters, "Soviets Accused of AIDS 'Mischief' Moscow Planting Stories Blaming Disease on U.S., Experts Say," *Toronto Star*, 28 April 1987.
28 *Baltimore Sun*, "Scientist Believes AIDS Began in Bio-Warfare Lab," in *Montreal Gazette*, 16 February 1992.
29 Kux, "Soviet Active Measures," 23–5.
30 Grant Robertson, "The Department of Meddling," *Globe and Mail*, 28 December 2017, https://www.theglobeandmail.com/news/investigations/department-meddling-canada-russia-influence-campaign/article37432974/.
31 Anderson, *Propaganda and Persuasion*, 82–3.
32 Anderson, *Propaganda and Persuasion*, 83–4.
33 Kux, "Soviet Active Measures," 22.
34 Whitaker and Hewitt, *Canada and the Cold War*, 32.
35 Whitaker and Hewitt, *Canada and the Cold War*, 32–3.
36 Mahar, *Shattered Illusions*, 54–5.
37 Anderson, *Propaganda and Persuasion*, 9.
38 Bell, *Cold Terror*, 61.
39 Amarasingam, *Pain, Pride and Politics*, 82–9.
40 Bell, *Cold Terror*, 60 and 65–6; Human Rights Watch, *Funding the Final War*.
41 Bell, *Cold Terror*, 61; Human Rights Watch, *Funding the Final War*; John La, "Forced Remittances in Canada's Tamil Enclaves," *Peace Review* 16, no. 3 (2004): 381; Steven Seligman, "Explaining Canadian Foreign Policy toward Sri Lanka under the Harper Government," *International Journal* 7, no. 2 (2016): 256.
42 Bell, *Cold Terror*, 72–5.
43 Human Rights Watch, *Funding the Final War*.
44 Human Rights Watch, *Funding the Final War*.

45 Human Rights Watch, *Funding the Final War*.
46 Amarasingam, *Pain, Pride and Politics*, 85.
47 Amarasingam, *Pain, Pride and* Politics, 88; Bell, *Cold Terror*, 62–3; Human Rights Watch, *Funding the Final War*.
48 La, "Forced Remittances," 383.
49 Peter Chalk, "Liberation Tigers of Tamil Eelam's (LTTE) International Organization and Operations: A Preliminary Analysis," commentary no. 77, Canadian Security Intelligence Service, 17 March 2000.
50 Chalk, "Liberation Tigers."
51 Chalk, "Liberation Tigers."
52 Bell, *Cold Terror*, 50–2, 61.
53 Amarasingam, *Pain, Pride and Politics*, 88–9; Bell, *Cold Terror*, 80–2; Seligman, "Explaining Canadian Foreign Policy toward Sri Lanka," 256.
54 On the politics of this terrorism listing and how the Harper government managed its relationship with Sri Lanka and the Canadian Tamil diaspora, see Seligman, "Explaining Canadian Foreign Policy towards Sri Lanka."
55 Nevertheless, political conversations and mobilization within the community remains challenging and difficult. Amarasingam, *Pain, Pride and Politics*, 89–94.
56 Jeremiah Goulka, Lydia Hansell, Elizabeth Wilke, and Judith Larson, *The Mujahedin-e Khalq in Iraq: A Policy Conundrum* (Santa Monica: RAND Corporation, 2009), sponsored by the American Department of Defense (Office of the Secretary of Defense); Human Rights Watch, "No Exit: Human Rights Abuses inside the MKO Camps," May 2005, https://www.hrw.org/legacy/backgrounder/mena/iran0505/iran0505.pdf; Michael Rubin, "The Mojahedin e-Khalq Aren't America's Friends," *National Interest*, 28 March 2019, https://nationalinterest.org/blog/middle-east-watch/mojahedin-e-khalq-arent-americas-friends-49547.
57 Jonathan Masters, "Mujahadeen-e-Khalq (MEK)," Council on Foreign Relations, 28 July 2014, https://www.cfr.org/backgrounder/mujahadeen-e-khalq-mek.
58 Bell, "Recruit." The MeK was delisted in several Western countries, including Canada in 2012, following an extensive lobbying campaign. See Masters, "Mujahadeen-e-Khalq."
59 Stewart Bell, "Canada a Cash Conduit for Terrorists, Report Says," *Star Phoenix*, 5 October 2006; Gary Dimmock, "Saddam's Fighters Active in Canada: Money Collected Nationwide," *Calgary Herald*, 12 March 2003.
60 Stewart Bell, "CSIS Visits B.C. Tory MP after Rally for Iran: Agents Accuse Exile Group of Terrorism," *National Post*, 15 April 2004. The group, no longer listed but still controversial, continues to successfully lobby

current and former Canadian politicians. In 2018 several Liberal and Conservative MPs, including former Prime Minister Stephen Harper, spoke at an MEK event in France in July 2018. CBC, *The Current*, "Stephen Harper Criticized for Speaking at 'Free Iran' Event hosted by Dissident Group Social Sharing," 4 July 2018, https://www.cbc.ca/radio/thecurrent/the-current-for-july-4-2018-1.4732996/stephen-harper-criticized-for-speaking-at-free-iran-event-hosted-by-dissident-group-1.4733009.

61 Goulka et al., *Mujahedin-e Khalq*, 4 and 68–7; Human Rights Watch, "No Exit," 2.

62 Sikh separatism was discussed in chapter 1. See also Bell, *Cold Terror*, esp. chapter 1, "Spillover," 23–45.

63 National Security and Intelligence Committee of Parliamentarians, *Special Report into the Allegations Associated with Prime Minister Trudeau's Official Visit to India in February 2018*, 13 December 2018, 4, http://www.nsicop-cpsnr.ca/reports/rp-2018-12-03/SpecialReport-en.pdf.

64 Bryan Johnson, "Canadian Sikhs Linked to Impending Violence in India, Source Warns," *Globe and Mail*, 13 August 1987; Zuhair Kashmeri, "Sikh Separatist Movement in Canada Target of Indian Spy Game, Sources Say," *Globe and Mail*, 28 November 1985; *Toronto Star*, "Indian Official Says Diplomats Who Went Home Are 'Not Ppies,'" 28 March 1987

65 Kashmeri, "Sikh Separatist Movement."

66 See, for example, Mark Kennedy, "Harper Backs Sikh Political Rights in Canada; PM Won't 'Interfere' with Separatists' Freedom of Speech, but Assures India of Support for Unity," *Vancouver Sun*, 9 November 2012; *Toronto Sun*, "Trudeau Must Not Duck Canada's Sikh Extremism," 17 February 2018. Also discussed in NSICOP, *Special Report*, 4.

67 NSICOP, *Special Report*, 8.

68 Lee Berthiaume, "Officials Warned China, India Could Use Communities in Canada to Advance Agendas," *National Post*, 12 July 2019, https://nationalpost.com/news/politics/officials-warned-china-india-could-use-communities-in-canada-to-advance-agendas; Catharine Tunney, "Federal Government Warning of Voter Coercion, Foreign Election Interference through Private Messaging Services," CBC News, 9 February 2020, https://www.cbc.ca/news/politics/voter-coercion-foreign-interference-private-message-1.5451504.

69 See Public Safety Canada, *2018 Public Report on the Terrorist Threat to Canada*, 3rd rev., April 2019, 8, https://www.publicsafety.gc.ca/cnt/rsrcs/pblctns/pblc-rprt-trrrsm-thrt-cnd-2018/pblc-rprt-trrrsm-thrt-cnd-2018-en.pdf. (It is worth noting that the original mention of "Sikh extremism" was removed after pressure from the Sikh community. Mia

Rabson, "Terror Reports to Reference Ideology, Not Religions after 'Sikh Extremism' Criticism: Goodale," Global News, 12 April 2019, https://globalnews.ca/news/5162913/goodale-terror-report-language/).

70 Anne-Marie Brady, "Magic Weapons: China's Political Influence Activities under Xi Jinping," Wilson Centre, 18 September 2017, 4, https://www.wilsoncenter.org/article/magic-weapons-chinas-political-influence-activities-under-xi-jinping; Hoover Institution, *Chinese Influence & American Interests: Promoting Constructive Vigilance*, 2018, 3 and 31, https://www.hoover.org/sites/default/files/research/docs/chineseinfluence_americaninterests_fullreport_web.pdf.

71 Hoover Institution, *Chinese Influence*, 132.

72 Hoover Institution, *Chinese Influence*, 138.

73 Ray Wang and Gerry Groot, "Who Represents? Xi Jinping's Grand United Front Work, Legitimation, Participation and Consultative Democracy," *Journal of Contemporary China* 27, no. 112 (2118): 571–5.

74 Brady, "Magic Weapons," 3.

75 Brady, "Magic Weapons," 3.

76 Research by the Hoover Institution argues that the focus of UFW "target almost exclusively the Chinese diaspora", *Chinese Influence*, 138. Others argue that the UFW has a broader social purpose in the West, softening opinions about issues such as SOE investment in natural resources and technology. See Tom Blackwell, "How China Uses Shadowy United Front as a 'Magic Weapon' to Try to Extend Its Influence in Canada," *National Post*, 28 January 2019; and Brady, "Magic Weapons," 5.

77 Alexander Bowe, "China's Overseas United Front Work: Background and Implications for the United States," U.S.-China Economic and Security Review Commission Staff Report, 24 August 2018, 5–6, https://www.uscc.gov/sites/default/files/Research/China%27s%20Overseas%20United%20Front%20Work%20-%20Background%20and%20Implications%20for%20US_final_0.pdf; Brady, "Magic Weapons," 1.

78 Bowe, "China's Overseas United Front Work," 9–10; Hoover Institution, *Chinese Influence*, 14.

79 Tom Blackwell, "Activists Say New Canadian Group Supporting China's Control of Tibet Is a Front for Beijing," *National Post*, 24 April 2019, https://nationalpost.com/news/activists-say-new-canadian-group-supporting-chinas-control-of-tibet-is-a-front-for-beijing; J. Michael Cole, "Pro-Beijing Tibetan Group Hints at China's Influence Operations in Canada," MacDonald-Laurier Institute, 26 April 2019, https://www.macdonaldlaurier.ca/pro-beijing-tibetan-group-hints-chinas-influence-operations-canada-j-michael-cole-inside-policy/; Xiao Xu, "Trudeau Welcome Letter to Group Promoting Tibet-China Unity Is Fake, PMO

Says," *Globe and Mail*, 24 April 2019, https://www.theglobeandmail.com/canada/article-pmo-says-letter-congratulating-a-group-advocating-tibetan-unity-with/.
80 Bowe, "China's Overseas United Front Work," 10–12; Hoover, *Chinese Influence*, 43–4; Jonathan Manthorpe, *Claws of the Panda: Beijing's Campaign of Influence and Intimidation in Canada* (Toronto: Cormorant Books, 2019), 188–9. See also NSICOP, *Annual Report*, 70-1.
81 Gary Shih, "Angry over Campus Speech by Uighur activist, McMaster University Students Contact Chinese Consulate, Film presentation," *Hamilton Spectator*, 15 February 2019, https://www.thespec.com/news-story/9177855-angry-over-campus-speech-by-uighur-activist-mcmaster-university-students-contact-chinese-consulate-film-presentation/; Gerry Shih and Emily Rauhala, "Angry over Campus Speech by Uighur Activist, Chinese Students in Canada Contact Their Consulate, Film Presentation," *Washington Post*, 14 February 2019, https://www.washingtonpost.com/world/angry-over-campus-speech-by-uighur-activist-students-in-canada-contact-chinese-consulate-film-presentation/2019/02/14/a442fbe4-306d-11e9-ac6c-14eea99d5e24_story.html?utm_term=.5e6b3ab6e5d1.
82 Manthorpe, *Claws of the Panda*, 50.
83 Zak Vescera, "Local Chinese Groups Take Out Pro-Communist Party Ads Amidst Hong Kong Protests," *Vancouver Sun*, 26 June 2019, https://vancouversun.com/news/local-news/local-chinese-groups-take-out-pro-communist-party-ads-amidst-hong-kong-protests.
84 Tom Blackwell, "Open Letter from Chinese-Canadian Groups Boosts Hong Kong Government, Blasts Protesters," *National Post*, 9 July 2019, https://nationalpost.com/news/open-letter-from-chinese-canadian-groups-boosts-hong-kong-government-blasts-protesters.
85 Brady, "Magic Weapons," 5; Hoover Institute, *Chinese Influence*, 81.
86 Koh Gui Qing and John Shiffman, "Beijing's Covert Radio Network Airs China-Friendly News across Washington, and the World," Reuters, 2 November 2015, https://www.reuters.com/investigates/special-report/china-radio/.
87 Steven Jiang, "Beijing Has a New Propaganda Weapon: Voice of China," CNN, 21 March 2018, https://money.cnn.com/2018/03/21/media/voice-of-china-propaganda-broadcaster/index.html; *Economist*, "Nation Shall Preach Xi unto Nation: China Is Spending Billions on Its Foreign Language Media," 14 June 2018, https://www.economist.com/china/2018/06/14/china-is-spending-billions-on-its-foreign-language-media.
88 Manthorpe, *Claws of the Panada*, 171–2; Hoover Institution, *Chinese Influence*, 83.

89 Stephen Chase, "Ottawa Defends Chinese-Media Visa Denials," *Globe and Mail*, 13 August 2018.
90 Dan Levin, "Chinese-Canadians Fear China's Rising Clout Is Muzzling Them," *New York Times*, 27 August 2016, https://www.nytimes.com/2016/08/28/world/americas/chinese-canadians-china-speech.html.
91 Hoover Institution, *Chinese Influence*, 86–8; Duzhe, "How China's Government Is Attempting to Control Chinese Media in America"; Manthorpe, *Claws of the Panda*, 170.
92 Brady, "Magic Weapons"; Levin, "Chinese-Canadians Fear"; NSICOP, *Annual Report 2019*, 68.
93 Levin, "Chinese-Canadians Fear"; Manthorpe, *Claws of the Panda*, 171.
94 Canadaland, "Is the Canadian-Chinese Press Controlled by Beijing?," 26 June 2016, https://www.canadalandshow.com/podcast/canadian-chinese-press-controlled-beijing/; Levin, "Chinese-Canadians Fear."
95 Simon Denyer, "Gap Apologizes to China over Map on T-Shirt That Omits Taiwan, South China Sea," *Washington Post*, 15 May 2018, https://www.washingtonpost.com/news/worldviews/wp/2018/05/15/u-s-retailer-gap-apologizes-to-china-over-map-on-t-shirt-that-omits-taiwan-south-china-sea/?utm_term=.63b9de91310b.
96 Ross Marowits, "Air Canada Bows to Pressure, Listing Capital of Taiwan as Part of China," *Toronto Star*, 15 May 2018, https://www.thestar.com/business/2018/05/15/air-canada-bows-to-pressure-listing-capital-of-taiwan-as-part-of-china.html.
97 Brady, "Magic Weapons," 4–5; Manthorpe, *Claws of the Panda*, 13; NSCIOP, *Annual Report 2019*, 62.
98 The Canadian Coalition on Human Rights in Canada, *Harassment and Intimidation of Individuals in Canada Working on China-Related Activism*, 3 April 2017, 2. Report on file with author. For media coverage of this report, see Tom Blackwell, "The Long Arm of China; Report Details Covert Campaign in Canada against Dissidents – and Their Families," *National Post*, 6 January 2018.
99 Canadian Coalition, *Harassment and Intimidation*, 5. See also Geoffrey Alexander et al., "Familiar Feeling: A Malware Campaign Targeting the Tibetan Diaspora Resurfaces," Citizen Lab, 8 August 2018, https://citizenlab.ca/2018/08/familiar-feeling-a-malware-campaign-targeting-the-tibetan-diaspora-resurfaces/.
100 Adam Carter, "Activist Accuses Chinese Government of Meddling after McMaster Speech Disrupted," CBC News, 15 February 2019, https://www.cbc.ca/news/canada/hamilton/mcmaster-university-china-1.5021406.
101 Canadian Coalition, *Harassment and Intimidation*, 7.

102 Catherine Porter, "Even in Canada, a Dissident Feels the Long Reach of China's Fury," *New York Times*, 2 April 2019.
103 Canadian Coalition, *Harassment and Intimidation*, 6–7.
104 Mike Blanchfield, "From Influence to Interference: Canada Should Be Wary Chinese Pressure Tactics," *Ottawa Citizen*, 9 December 2017; Canadian Coalition, *Harassment and Intimidation*, 8–10; Manthorpe, *Claws of the Panda*, 15–16, 185.
105 Manthorpe, *Claws of the Panda*, 28–9.
106 Nathan Vanderklippe, "China Targeting Overseas Uyghur Students," *Globe and Mail*, 30 October 2017; *Globe and Mail*, "For Uyghur Diaspora, There Is No Escape," 13 August 2018.
107 Mulroney, *Middle Power, Middle Kingdom*, 110–11.
108 Mulroney, *Middle Power, Middle Kingdom*, 111.
109 Marie Danielle-Smith, "China Again Tries to Influence Campus Event: Concordia," *National Post*, 29 March 2019.
110 Brady, "Magic Weapons," 8 and 18; Hoover, *Chinese Influence*, 4; Human Rights Watch, "China: Government Threats to Academic Freedom Abroad," 21 March 2019, https://www.hrw.org/news/2019/03/21/china-government-threats-academic-freedom-abroad; Manthorpe, *Claws of the Panda*, 188–9; NSICOP, *Annual Report 2019*, 71.
111 Human Rights Watch, "China."
112 Bowe, "China's Overseas United Front Work," 12; Hoover, *Chinese Influence*, 41; Manthorpe, *Claws of the Panda*, 192–3.
113 Bowe, "China's Overseas United Front Work," 12.
114 Janet French, "While Canada's Relationship with China Grows Tense, Edmonton Public Schools Renews Deal with Confucius Institute," *Edmonton Journal*, 31 January 2019, https://edmontonjournal.com/news/local-news/while-canadas-relationship-with-china-grows-tense-edmonton-public-schools-renews-deal-with-confucius-institute.
115 Hoover, *Chinese Influence*, 41; Manthorpe, *Claws of the Panda*, 194.
116 Hoover, *Chinese Influence*, 41.
117 Hoover, *Chinese Influence*, 42. Hanban is a Chinese abbreviation for "The National Office Leadership Group for the International Promotion of the Chinese Language."
118 Manthorpe, *Claws of the Panda*, 197.
119 Hoover, *Chinese Influence*, 42; Manthorpe, *Claws of the Panda*, 197–9.
120 James Bradshaw and Colin Freeze, "McMaster Closing Confucius Institute over Hiring Issues," *Globe and Mail*, 7 February 2013, https://www.theglobeandmail.com/news/national/education/mcmaster-closing-confucius-institute-over-hiring-issues/article8372894/.
121 Shane Fowler, "Education Minister Pulling Plug on Chinese Education Program in Schools," CBC News, 21 February 2019, https://www.cbc

.ca/news/canada/new-brunswick/education-mnister-pulling-plug-confucius-institute-new-brunswick-1.5028098; Manthorpe, *Claws of the Panda*, 199; Austin Ramzy, "Toronto School District Cancels Plans for Confucius Institute," *New York Times* (Sinosphere Blog), 30 October 2014, https://sinosphere.blogs.nytimes.com/2014/10/30/toronto-school-district-cancels-plans-for-confucius-institute/.

122 National Security and Intelligence Committee of Parliamentarians, *Annual Report 2018*, 27; Jeff Lee And Jonathan Fowlie, "CSIS Chief Backs Down on Claim of Foreign Influence on Politicians; Remarks Unleash Criticism from All Levels of Government," *Vancouver Sun*, 24 January 2010; Standing Committee on Public Safety and National Security, *Report on Canadian Security Intelligence Service Director Richard Fadden's Remarks*.

123 Cited from Manthorpe, *Claws of the Panda*, 249.

124 James Kynge, Lucy Hornby, and Jamil Anderlini, "Inside China's Secret 'Magic Weapon' for Worldwide Influence," *Financial Times*, 26 October 2017, https://www.ft.com/content/fb2b3934-b004-11e7-beba-5521c713abf4.

125 NSCIOP, *Annual Report 2019*, 64.

126 Robert Fife, Steven Chase, and Xiao Xu, "Beijing Foots Bill for Canadian Senators, MPs to visit China," *Globe and Mail*, 1 December 2017, https://www.theglobeandmail.com/news/politics/beijing-foots-bill-for-visits-to-china-by-canadian-senators-mps/article37162592/; Robert Fife and Steven Chase, "Majority of Canadians Oppose Parliamentarians Accepting Free Trips: Poll," *Globe and Mail*, 8 January 2018, https://www.theglobeandmail.com/news/politics/majority-of-canadians-oppose-parliamentarians-accepting-free-trips-poll/article37521224/; Stephen Chase and Robert Fife, "Conservative MP Bob Saroya Took Trip to China Paid For by Communist Party," *Globe and Mail*, 3 May 2018, https://www.theglobeandmail.com/politics/article-conservative-mp-bob-saroya-took-trip-to-china-paid-for-by-communist/.

127 See also Ashley Wadhwani, "B.C. Mayor Criticizes School Trustees Ahead of Paid Trip to China," *Hope Standard* (Port Coquitlam), 17 January 2019, https://www.hopestandard.com/news/b-c-mayor-criticizes-school-trustees-ahead-of-paid-trip-to-china/.

128 Manthorpe, *Claws of the Panda*, 263–4; NSICOP, *Annual Report 2018*, 27; Guadalupe Pardo, Robert Fife, and Stephen Chase, "Trudeau Attended Cash-for-Access Fundraiser with Chinese Billionaires," 22 November 2016, https://www.theglobeandmail.com/news/politics/trudeau-attended-cash-for-access-fundraiser-with-chinese-billionaires/article32971362/.

129 See, for example, Clive Hamilton, *Silent Invasion: China's Influence in Australia* (Melbourne: Hardy Grant Books, 2018), esp. chapter 4, "Dark Money," 55–92.

130 On Australia's "lax" political donation laws and the problem of "dark money" in politics, see Lindy Edwards, "The Truth about Political Donations: There Is So Much We Don't Know," Conversation, 1 February 2018, https://theconversation.com/the-truth-about-political-donations-there-is-so-much-we-dont-know-91003. But recognizing the problem (and under pressure from the public), the Australian Parliament passed a "foreign donations bill" to restrict how much money foreign governments and SOEs can donate to political parties. Yee-Fui Ng, "The Foreign Donations Bill Will Soon Be Law: What Will It Do, and Why Is It Needed?," Conversation, 27 November 2018, https://theconversation.com/the-foreign-donations-bill-will-soon-be-law-what-will-it-do-and-why-is-it-needed-107095. Canadian law allows only Canadians and permanent residents to make political donations, in 2018 legislation (Bill C-76 was passed to ban advocacy groups from ever using money from foreign entities to conduct partisan campaigns).

131 Berthiaume, "Officials Warned China, India"; Manthorpe, *Claws of the Panda*, 253–4.

132 Cited in Berthiaume, "Officials Warned China, India."

133 Blanchfield, "From Influence to Interference ."

134 Manthorpe, *Claws of the Panda*, 256; Jenny Peng and Joanna Chiu, "Vancouver Society at Centre of Vote-Buying Allegations Has Ties to Chinese Government," *Toronto Star*, 16 October 2018, https://www.thestar.com/vancouver/2018/10/16/vancouver-society-at-centre-of-vote-buying-allegations-has-ties-to-chinese-government.html.

135 Agence France-Presse, "More Than 20 Ambassadors Condemn China's Treatment of Uighurs in Xinjiang," *Guardian*, 11 July 2019, https://www.theguardian.com/world/2019/jul/11/more-than-20-ambassadors-condemn-chinas-treatment-of-uighurs-in-xinjiang.

136 NSCIOP, *Annual Report 2019*, 104.

137 NSCIOP, *Annual Report 2019*, 109.

138 Government of Australia, "National Counter Foreign Influence Coordinator," last updated 29 August 2019, https://www.homeaffairs.gov.au/about-us/our-portfolios/national-security/countering-foreign-interference/cfi-coordinator.

7. Disinformation and Threats to Democratic Institutions

1 @realdonaldtrump, 25 July 2016, https://twitter.com/realDonaldTrump/status/757538729170964481?s=20.

2 See, for example, the Netflix documentary *The Great Hack* (2019).

3 Yochai Benkler, Robert Faris, and Hal Roberts, *Network Propaganda: Manipulation, Disinformation, and Radicalization in American Politics* (Oxford: Oxford University Press, 2018), 43; Yochai Benkler, Robert Faris, Hal Roberts, and Ethan Zuckerman, "Study: Breitbart-Led Right-Wing Media Ecosystem Altered Broader Media Agenda," *Columbia Journalism Review*, March 2017, https://www.cjr.org/analysis/breitbart-media-trump-harvard-study.php.
4 Alexander Lanoszka, "Disinformation in International Politics," *European Journal of International Security* 4, no. 2 (2019): 227–48.
5 For an overview, see P.W. Singer and Emerson T. Brooking, *Like War: The Weaponization of Social Media* (New York: Houghton Mifflin Harcourt, 2018), esp. 24–52; Thomas Rid, *Rise of the Machines: A Cybernetic History* (New York: W.W. Norton, 2016), esp. 294–339.
6 Taylor Owen, *Disruptive Power: The Crisis of the State in the Digital Age* (Oxford: Oxford University Press, 2015), 9.
7 Arjun Kharpal, "Google Has Been Accused of Working with China. Here's What They've Been Doing There," CNBC, 17 July 2019, https://www.cnbc.com/2019/07/17/google-china-what-businesses-the-search-giant-has-in-the-country.html.
8 Bethany Allen-Ebrahimian, "The Man Who Nailed Jello to the Wall," Foreign Policy, 29 June 2016, https://foreignpolicy.com/2016/06/29/the-man-who-nailed-jello-to-the-wall-lu-wei-china-internet-czar-learns-how-to-tame-the-web/.
9 Freedom House, "Freedom on the Net 2018: The Rise of Digital Authoritarianism," 2018, 6, https://freedomhouse.org/report/freedom-net/2018/rise-digital-authoritarianism.
10 Freedom House, "Freedom on the Net 2018," 7.
11 Andrei Soldatov and Irina Borogan, *The Red Web: The Struggle between Russia's Digital Dictators and the New Online Revolutionaries* (New York: Public Affairs, 2015), 281–5.
12 Soldatov and Borogan, *Red Web*, x.
13 Soldatov and Borogan, *Red Web*, esp. chapter 15, 291–309.
14 Freedom House, "Freedom on the Net 2018," 15.
15 Chinese efforts to control the narrative were discussed in chapter 6. On Russian state control of the media under Putin, see William J. Dobson, *The Dictator's Learning Curve: Inside the Global Battle for Democracy* (New York: Doubleday, 2012), 17–18, 44–5; Arkady Ostrovsky, *The Invention of Russia: From Gorbachev's Freedom to Putin's War* (New York: Viking, 2015); Soldatov and Borogan, *Red Web*, 101–21.
16 BBC News, "Russian Soldiers Face Ban on Selfies and Blog Posts," 5 October 2017, https://www.bbc.com/news/world-europe-41510592.

17 Bellingcat Investigation Team, "Full Report: Skripal Poisoning Suspect Dr. Alexander Mishkin, Hero of Russia," Bellingcat, 9 October 2018, https://www.bellingcat.com/news/uk-and-europe/2018/10/09/full-report-skripal-poisoning-suspect-dr-alexander-mishkin-hero-russia/.
18 Owen, *Disruptive Power*, 191–2.
19 Freedom House, "Freedom on the Net 2018," 1–2.
20 Freedom House, "Freedom on the Net 2018," 9.
21 Freedom House, "Freedom on the Net 2018," 10.
22 James J. Coyle, "Russia Has Complete Information Dominance in Ukraine," Atlantic Council, 12 May 2015, https://www.atlanticcouncil.org/blogs/ukrainealert/russia-has-complete-informational-dominance-in-ukraine; Soldatov and Borogan, *Red Web*, 279, and 287–9.
23 A discussion of Russian attempts to influence the 2016 U.S. election is available in the *Report on the Investigation into Russian Interference in the 2016 Presidential Election* – also known as the Mueller Report. The version used for this chapter is *The Mueller Report: Presented with Related Materials by the Washington Post* (New York: Scribner, 2019). Books on the subject include Angela Nagel, *Kill All Normies: Online Culture Wars from 4Chan and Tumblr to Trump and the Alt-Right* (Winchester, UK: Zero Books, 2017); David Sanger, *The Perfect Weapon: War, Sabotage and Fear in the Cyber Age* (New York: Crown, 2018), esp. 152–239; P.W. Singer and Emerson T. Brooking, *LikeWar: The Weaponization of Social Media* (Boston: Houghton Mifflin Harcourt, 2018); Clint Watts, *Messing with the Enemy: Surviving in a Social Media World of Hackers, Terrorists, Russians and Fake News* (New York: Harper, 2018).
24 Frank G. Hoffman, *Conflict in the 21st Century: The Rise of Hybrid Wars* (Arlington, VA: Potomac Institute for Policy Studies, December 2007), 29, https://potomacinstitute.org/reports/19-reports/1163-conflict-in-the-21st-century-the-rise-of-hybrid-wars; Guillaume Lasconjarias and Jeffrey A. Larsen, "Introduction: A New Way of Warfare," in *NATO's Response to Hybrid Threats*, ed. Guillaume Lasconjarias and Jeffrey A. Larsen, NATO Defense College Forum Paper 24, 2015; Ralph D. Thiele, "Crisis in Ukraine: The Emergence of Hybrid Warfare," Institut für Strategie Politik Sicherheits-und Wirtschaftsberatung Strategy Series: Focus on Defense and International Security, no. 347, May 2015, https://www.files.ethz.ch/isn/190792/347_Thiele_RINSA.pdf.
25 Max Boot, "Chapter One: The Changing Character of Conflict – Countering Hybrid Warfare," *Armed Conflict Survey* 1, no. 1 (2015): 11–19; Élie Tenenbaum, "Hybrid Warfare in the Strategic Spectrum: An Historical Assessment," in *NATO's Response to Hybrid Threats*, ed. Guillaume Lasconjarias and Jeffrey A. Larsen, NATO Defense College

Forum Paper 24, 2015; Robert Wilkie, "Hybrid Warfare: Something Old, Not Something New," *Air & Space Power Journal* (Winter 2009): 13–17; Williamson Murray and Peter R. Mansoor, eds., *Hybrid Warfare: Fighting Complex Opponents from the Ancient World to the Present* (Cambridge: Cambridge University Press, 2012); James K. Wither, "Making Sense of Hybrid Warfare," *Connections: The Quarterly Journal* 15, no. 2 (2016): 73–87.

26 Lawrence Freedman, *The Future of War: A History* (New York: Public Affairs, 2017); Neil Chuka and Jean François Born, "Hybrid Warfare: Implications for CAF Force Development," Defence Research and Development Canada Scientific Report DRCD-RDDC-2014-R43, August 2014, http://pubs.drdc-rddc.gc.ca/BASIS/pcandid/www/engpub/DDW?W%3DSYSNUM=800375.

27 Dan G. Cox, Thomas Bruscino, and Alex Ryan, "Why Hybrid Warfare Is Tactics Not Strategy: A Rejoinder to 'Future Threats and Strategic Thinking,'" *Infinity Journal* 2, no. 2 (2012): 25–9; Michael Koffman and Matthew Rojansky, "Kennan Cable No. 7: A Closer Look at Russia's 'Hybrid War,'" Wilson Centre, April 2015, https://www.wilsoncenter.org/publication/kennan-cable-no7-closer-look-russias-hybrid-war; Andrew Monaghan, "The 'War' in Russia's Hybrid Warfare," *Parameters* 45, no. 5 (2015–16: 66–74.

28 For a useful anaylsis of the concept of hybrid warfare, see Ofer Fridman, *Russian Hybrid Warfare: Resurgence and Politicisation* (Oxford: Oxford University Press, 2018).

29 Hoffman, *Conflict in the 21st Century*, 29.

30 Lasconjarias and Larsen, "Introduction," 3.

31 Wilkie, "Hybrid Warfare," 14.

32 Chuka and Born, *Hybrid Warfare*, 2.

33 Tenenbaum, "Hybrid Warfare in the Strategic Spectrum."

34 Frank G. Hoffman, "Hybrid vs. Compound War: The Janus Choice of Modern War: Defining Today's Multifaceted Conflict," *Armed Forces Journal*, 1 October 2009, 1–2.

35 See, for example, Andrea Beccaro, "Modern Irregular Warfare: The ISIS Case Study," *Small Wars and Insurgencies* 29, no. 2 (2018): 207–28; Andreas Jacobs and Guillaume Lasconjarias, "NATO's Hybrid Flanks: Handling Unconventional Warfare in the South and the East," in *NATO's Response to Hybrid Threats*, ed. Guillaume Lasconjarias and Jeffrey A. Larsen, 257–6, NATO Defense College Forum Paper 24, 2015; Lasconjarias and Larsen, "Introduction," 3; Scott Jasper and Scott Moreland, "The Islamic State Is a Hybrid Threat: Why Does That Matter?," *Small Wars Journal*, 1 December 2014, https://smallwarsjournal.com/jrnl/art/the-islamic-state-is-a-hybrid-threat-why-does-that-matter; Clint Watts does not use the

concept "hybrid warfare" to describe the Islamic State's media efforts, but for a description of their online tactics, see *Messing with the Enemy*, 42–8. Additionally, see the discussion in Singer and Brooking, *LikeWar*, 150–4, 212–14.

36 Jacobs and Lasconjarias, "NATO's Hybrid Flanks," 264. There are various claims about the size of the Islamic State's forces at its peak. American figures often cite up to 100,000 fighters. Liz Sly and Louisa Loveluck, "The 'Caliphate' Is No More. But the Islamic State Isn't Finished Yet," *Washington Post*, 23 March 2019, https://www.washingtonpost.com/world/the-islamic-states-caliphate-has-been-defeated-us-backed-forces-say/2019/03/23/04263d74-36f8-11e9-8375-e3dcf6b68558_story.html?utm_term=.b65fb5843c48. For a discussion of estimates, see Daveed Gartenstein-Ross, "How Many Fighters Does the Islamic State Really Have?," War on the Rocks, 9 February 2015, https://warontherocks.com/2015/02/how-many-fighters-does-the-islamic-state-really-have/.

37 Singer and Brooking, *LikeWar*, 152–3.

38 Charlie Winter, *Media Jihad: The Islamic State's Doctrine for Information Warfare* (London: International Centre for the Study of Radicalization, 2017), 8, https://icsr.info/wp-content/uploads/2017/02/ICSR-Report-Media-Jihad-The-Islamic-State%E2%80%99s-Doctrine-for-Information-Warfare.pdf.

39 Winter, *Media Jihad*, 15–18.

40 See, for example, discussions of online recruitment in Elizabeth Pearson and Emily Winterbotham, "Women, Gender and Daesh Radicalisation," *RUSI Journal* 162, no. 3 (2017) 60–72.

41 CTV Atlantic, "ISIL Targets Security Forum through Social Media," 22 November 2014, https://atlantic.ctvnews.ca/isil-targets-security-forum-through-social-media-1.2114981.

42 Fridman, *Russian Hybrid Warfare*, 96–7.

43 Valery Gerasimov, "The Value of Science in Prediction," *Military-Industrial Kurier*, 27 February 2013, trans. Mark Galeotti, *In Moscow's Shadows*, 6 July 2014, https://inmoscowsshadows.wordpress.com/2014/07/06/the-gerasimov-doctrine-and-russian-non-linear-war/.

44 Fridman, *Russian Hybrid Warfare*, 142; Mark Galeotti, "The Mythical 'Gerasimov Doctrine' and the Language of Threat," *Critical Studies on Security*, 27 February 2018; Galeotti, "I'm Sorry for Creating the 'Gerasimov Doctrine,'" Foreign Policy, 5 March 2018, https://foreignpolicy.com/2018/03/05/im-sorry-for-creating-the-gerasimov-doctrine/.

45 Adam Segal, *The Hacked World Order: How Nations Fight, Trade, Maneuver and Manipulate in the Digital Age* (New York: Public Affairs, 2017), 79.

46 Sanger, *Perfect Weapon*, 158–9.
47 Wither, "Making Sense of Hybrid Warfare," 81.
48 Sanger, *Perfect Weapon*, 168–9.
49 Singer and Brooking, *LikeWar*, 203–6; Soldatov and Borogan, *Red Web*, 284.
50 Soldatov and Borogan, *Red Web*, 280–1.
51 Soldatov and Borogan, *Red Web*, 280–5.
52 Soldatov and Borogan, *Red Web*, 281.
53 Adrian Chen, "The Agency," *New York Times*, 2 June 2015, https://www.nytimes.com/2015/06/07/magazine/the-agency.html; *Economist*, "How to Be a Dadaist Troll: Inside the Internet Research Agency's Lie Machine," 22 February 2018, https://www.economist.com/briefing/2018/02/22/inside-the-internet-research-agencys-lie-machine; *Mueller Report*, 14.
54 Eli Pariser, *The Filter Bubble: What the Internet Is Hiding from You* (London: Penguin Books, 2011); Cass R. Sunstein, *Republic.com* (Princeton, NJ: Princeton University Press, 2001).
55 Singer and Brooking, *LikeWar*, 123.
56 Samantha Bradshaw and Phillip N. Howard, "Why Does Junk News Spread so Quickly across Social Media? Algorithms, Advertising, and Exposure in Public Life," Knight Foundation/Oxford Internet Institute, 29 January 2018, https://www.oii.ox.ac.uk/blog/why-does-junk-news-spread-so-quickly-across-social-media-2/.
57 Watts, *Messing with the Enemy*, 216.
58 Hunt Allcott and Matthew Gentzkow, "Social Media and Fake News in the 2016 Election," *Journal of Economic Perspectives* 31, no. 2 (2017): 218.
59 Allcott and Gentzkow, "Social Media," 221; Eytan Bakshy, Solomon Messing, and Lada A. Adamic, "Exposure to Ideologically Diverse News and Opinion on Facebook," *Science* 348 (2015): 1130–2.
60 Allcott and Genzkow, "Social Media," 212; Bradshaw and Howard, "Why Does Junk News," 4.
61 Dimitra (Mimie) Liotsiou, Bencce Kollanyi, and Philip N. Howard, "The Junk News Aggregator: Examining Junk News Posted on Facebook, Starting with the 2018 US Midterm Elections," 17 April 2019, https://arxiv.org/abs/1901.07920.
62 Bradshaw and Howard, "Why Does Junk News," 5.
63 Soroush Vosoughi, Deb Roy, and Sinan Aral, "The Spread of True and False News Online," *Science* 356 (2018): 1146.
64 Joshua A. Tucker, Yannis Theocharis, Margaret E. Roberts, and Pablo Barberá, "From Liberation to Turmoil: Social Media and Democracy," *Journal of Democracy* 28, no. 4 (2017): 52.
65 Bradshaw and Howard, "Why Does Junk News," 11.
66 Vosoughi, Roy, and Aral, "Spread of True and False," 1146.

67 Allcott and Gentzkow, "Social Media," 217.
68 Simon Oxenham, "'I Was a Macedonian Fake News Writer,'" BBC Future, 29 May 2019, http://www.bbc.com/future/story/20190528-i-was-a-macedonian-fake-news-writer.
69 Allcott and Gentzkow, "Social Media," 221.
70 In case this actually needs referencing, see the website I Can Has Cheezburger, https://icanhas.cheezburger.com/lolcats
71 Harambe was a gorilla killed in a Cincinnati zoo to protect a three-year-old boy who had fallen in his enclosure that became an obsession of certain circles of the internet. This is a good example of how memes can cross each other, adapt, and go "meta" – a meme within a meme.
72 Emma Grey Ellis, "Pepe the Frog Means Something Different in Hong Kong – Right?," *Wired*, 23 August 2019, https://www.wired.com/story/pepe-the-frog-meme-hong-kong/.
73 Anti-Defamation League, "Pepe the Frog," https://www.adl.org/education/references/hate-symbols/pepe-the-frog.
74 See the discussion of memes and Pepe in Singer and Brookings, *LikeWar*, 186–93.
75 Watts, *Messing with the Enemy*, 226.
76 Chris Meserole, "How Misinformation Spreads on Social Media – And What to Do about It," Brookings, 9 May 2018, https://www.brookings.edu/blog/order-from-chaos/2018/05/09/how-misinformation-spreads-on-social-media-and-what-to-do-about-it/.
77 Nagle, *Kill All Normies*, 12.
78 Nagle, *Kill All Normies*, 13.
79 Nagle, *Kill All Normies*, 31.
80 Marwick and Lewis, "Media Manipulation and Disinformation Online."
81 Bradshaw and Howard, "Why Does Junk News," 7.
82 Bradshaw and Howard, "Why Does Junk News," 14.
83 Tucker et al., "From Liberation," 52–3.
84 Nagle, *Kill All Normies*, 3; Watts, *Messing with the Enemy*, 217–20.
85 Watts, *Messing with the Enemy*, 82.
86 See Clint Watt's testimony to the U.S. Senate's Intelligence Committee, "Disinformation: A Primer In Russian Active Measures and Influence Campaigns," 30 March 2017, https://www.intelligence.senate.gov/sites/default/files/documents/os-cwatts-033017.pdf
87 Singer and Brookings, *LikeWar*, 108.
88 Adam Holland, "Russia Today Has an Illuminati Correspondent. Really," *Daily Beast*, 14 April 2017, https://www.thedailybeast.com/russia-today-has-an-illuminati-correspondent-really.
89 Chen, "Agency."

90 Watts, *Messing with the Enemy*, 92. Cassandra Pollock and Alex Samuels, "Hysteria over Jade Helm Exercise in Texas was Fueled by Russians, Former CIA Director Says," *Texas Tribune*, 3 May 2018, https://www.texastribune.org/2018/05/03/hysteria-over-jade-helm-exercise-texas-was-fueled-russians-former-cia-/.
91 Watts, *Messing with the Enemy*, 91–2.
92 Peter Pomerantsev and Michael Weiss, *The Menace of Unreality: How the Kremlin Weaponizes Information, Culture and Money*, Institute for Modern Russia/The Interpreter, November 2014, 15, https://www.stratcomcoe.org/peter-pomerantsev-michael-weiss-menace-unreality-how-kremlin-weaponizes-information-culture-and.
93 EU vs Disinfo, "Renewed Focus on MH17," 20 June 2019, https://euvsdisinfo.eu/renewed-focus-on-mh-17/.
94 Yevgeniy Golovchenko, Mareike Hartmann, and Rebecca Alder-Nissen, "State, Media and Civil Society in the Information Warfare over Ukraine: Citizen Curators of Digital Disinformation," *International Affairs* 94, no. 5 (2018): 992–3.
95 Pomerantsev and Weiss, *Menace of Unreality*, 15.
96 Benkler, Faris, and Roberts, *Network Propaganda*, 244.
97 Michael Isikoff, "Exclusive: The True Origins of the Seth Rich Conspiracy Theory: A Yahoo News Investigation," Yahoo News, 9 July 2019, https://news.yahoo.com/exclusive-the-true-origins-of-the-seth-rich-conspiracy-a-yahoo-news-investigation-100000831.html.
98 Watts, *Messing with the Enemy*, 92.
99 Cited from Pollock and Samuels, "Hysteria over Jade Helm."
100 Nicholas Thompson and Issie Lapowsky, "How Russian Trolls Used Meme Warfare to Divide America," *Wired*, 17 December 2018, https://www.wired.com/story/russia-ira-propaganda-senate-report/.
101 Bradshaw and Howard, "Why Does Junk News Spread," 10–11; Samuel C. Woolley and Philip N. Howard, "Political Communication, Computational Propaganda, and Autonomous Agents," *International Journal of Communication* 10 (2016): 4882–90.
102 Benkler et al., "Study: Breitbart-Led Right-Wing Media"; Vosoughi, Roy, and Aral, "Spread of True and False News"; Bakshy, Messing, and Adamic, "Exposure to Ideologically Diverse News."
103 H. Allcott and M. Gentzkow, "Social Media and Fake News in the 2016 Election," *Journal of Economic Perspectives* 31, no. 2 (2017): 224; Nahema Marchal, Lisa-Maria Neudert, Bence Kollanyi, and Philip N. Howard, "Polarization, Partisanship and Junk News Consumption on Social Media during the 2018 US Midterm Elections," COMPROP Data Memo 2018.5 (Oxford Internet Institute), 1 November 2018, http://comprop.oii.ox.ac

.uk/research/midterms2018/; Craig Silverman and Jeremy Singer-Vine, "Most Americans Who See Fake News Believe It, New Survey Said," Buzzfeed News, 6 December 2018, https://www.buzzfeednews.com /article/craigsilverman/fake-news-survey.
104 *Mueller Report*, 4.
105 See the indictment, United States of America v Internet Research Agency and Others, United States District Court for the District of Columbia, 16 February 2018, 6, https://www.justice.gov/file/1035477/download.
106 Andrew Weisburd, Clint Watts, and J.M. Berger, "Trolling for Trump: How Russia Is trying to Destroy Our Democracy," War on the Rocks, 6 November 2018, https://warontherocks.com/2016/11/trolling-for -trump-how-russia-is-trying-to-destroy-our-democracy/.
107 *Mueller Report*, p. 25.
108 Weisburd, Watts, and Berger, "Trolling for Trump."
109 Weisburd, Watts, and Berger, "Trolling for Trump."
110 Soldatov and Borogan, *Red Web*, 287–8.
111 See the indictment, United States of America v Internet Research Agency and Others, 13.
112 United States of America v Internet Research Agency and Others, 16–23.
113 Claire Allbright, "A Russian Facebook Page Organized a Protest in Texas. A Different Russian Page Launched the Counterprotest," *Texas Tribune*, 1 November 2017, https://www.texastribune.org/2017/11/01/russian -facebook-page-organized-protest-texas-different-russian-page-l/.
114 United States of America v Internet Research Agency and Others, 23.
115 Committee on Foreign Relations United States Senate (Minority Staff Report), *Putin's Asymmetric Assault on Democracy in Russia and Europe: Implications for U.S. National Security*, 10 January 2018, 16–20, https:// www.foreign.senate.gov/imo/media/doc/FinalRR.pdf; Karla Adam and William Booth, "Rising Alarm in Britain over Russian Meddling in Brexit Vote," *Washington Post*, 17 November 2017, https://www.washingtonpost .com/world/europe/rising-alarm-in-britain-over-russian-meddling-in -brexit-vote/2017/11/17/2e987a30-cb34-11e7-b506-8a10ed11ecf5_story .html?utm_term=.64716fd9296a.
116 Committee on Foreign Relations, *Putin's Asymmetric Assault*, 121–5.
117 Lisa-Maria N. Neudert, "Computational Propaganda in Germany: A Cautionary Tale," Computational Proaganda Research Project, Oxford Internet Institute, working paper 2017.7, 2017, http://blogs.oii.ox.ac .uk/politicalbots/wp-content/uploads/sites/89/2017/06/Comprop -Germany.pdf.
118 Damien McGuinness, "Russia Steps into Berlin 'Rape' Storm Claiming German Cover-Up," BBC News, 27 January 2016, https://www.bbc.com /news/blogs-eu-35413134.

119 BBC News, "Fancy Bear: Germany Investigates Cyber-Attack 'by Russians,'" 28 February 2018, https://www.bbc.com/news/world-middle-east-43232520.
120 Jo Becker, "The Global Machine behind the Rise of Far-Right Nationalism," *New York Times*, 10 August 2019, https://www.nytimes.com/2019/08/10/world/europe/sweden-immigration-nationalism.html.
121 Communications Security Establishment, *Cyber Threats to Canada's Democratic Process*, July 2017, 33, https://cyber.gc.ca/sites/default/files/publications/cse-cyber-threat-assessment-e.pdf.
122 Communications Security Establishment, *2019 Update: Cyber Threats to Canada's Democratic Procese*, April 2019, 5.
123 Benkler, Faris, and Roberts, *Network Propaganda*, 8.
124 Benkler, Faris, and Roberts, *Network Propaganda*, 267–8. Canadians have relatively stronger trust in traditional media than their American counterparts. For a survey of Canadian attitudes towards the media, see Taylor Owen et al., *Digital Democracy Project: Research Memo #1 Media, Knowledge and Misinformation* (Toronto: Public Policy Forum, August 2019), https://ppforum.ca/wp-content/uploads/2019/08/DDP-Research-Memo-1-Aug2019.pdf.
125 Alex Boutilier, Marco Chown Oved, Craig Silverman, and Jane Lytvynenko, "Canadian Political Parties Already Targeted by Foreign Hacking, Electronic Spy Agency Says," *Toronto Star*, 8 April 2019, https://www.thestar.com/politics/federal/2019/04/08/canadian-political-parties-already-targeted-by-foreign-hacking-electronic-spy-agency-says.html.
126 Alex Boutilier, Craig Silverman, and Jane Lytvynenko, "Canadians Are Being Targeted by Foreign Influence Campaigns, CSIS Says," *Toronto Star*, 2 July 2019, https://www.thestar.com/politics/federal/2019/07/02/canadas-voters-being-targeted-by-foreign-influence-campaigns-spy-agency-says.html.
127 Chris Brown, "Anti-Canada Propaganda Greets Troops in Latvia," CBC News, 16 June 2017, https://www.cbc.ca/news/world/latvia-propaganda-1.4162612.
128 Tom Blackwell, "Russian Fake-News Campaign against Canadian Troops in Latvia Includes Propaganda about Litter, Luxury Apartments," *National Post*, 17 November 2017, https://nationalpost.com/news/canada/russian-fake-news-campaign-against-canadian-troops-in-latvia-includes-propaganda-about-litter-luxury-apartments.
129 Ben Makuch, "Pro-Russian News Once Claimed 11 Canadian Commandos Died in Ukraine. That Didn't Happen," Vice, 5 June 2018, https://news.vice.com/en_ca/article/ywe5bk/pro-russian-news-once-claimed-11-canadian-commandos-died-in-ukraine-that-didnt-happen.

130 CTV News, "Feds Deny Russian Rumours That 3 Canadian Soldiers Were Killed in Ukraine," 18 May 2018, https://www.ctvnews.ca/politics/feds-deny-russian-rumours-that-3-canadian-soldiers-were-killed-in-ukraine-1.3936488.
131 Chris Brown, "Top Russian News Host Takes Aim at Ukrainian Canadians," CBC News, 17 January 2019, https://www.cbc.ca/news/world/top-russian-news-host-takes-aim-at-ukrainian-canadians-1.4980859.
132 Justin Ling, "Canada's Foreign Minister Warns of Russian Destabilization Efforts — and She Might Be a Target," Vice, 6 March 2017, https://news.vice.com/en_ca/article/8xmyna/canadas-foreign-minister-warns-of-russian-destabilization-efforts-and-she-might-be-a-target.
133 Stephen Chase, "Trudeau Links Russian Diplomats' Ouster with Smear Campaign Aimed at Freeland," *Globe and Mail*, 4 April 2018.
134 David Pugliese, "Chrystia Freeland's Granddad Was Indeed a Nazi Collaborator – So Much for Russian Disinformation," *Ottawa Citizen*, 8 March 2017, https://ottawacitizen.com/news/national/defence-watch/chrystia-freelands-granddad-was-indeed-a-nazi-collaborator-so-much-for-russian-disinformation; Thomas Walkom, "Why Did Canada Expel Four Russian Diplomats? Because They Told the Truth," *Toronto Star*, 5 April 2018, https://www.thestar.com/opinion/star-columnists/2018/04/05/why-did-canada-expel-four-russian-diplomats-because-they-told-the-truth.html.
135 Terry Glavin, "How Russia's Attack on Freeland Got Traction in Canada," *Maclean's*, 14 March 2017, https://www.macleans.ca/politics/how-russias-attack-on-freeland-got-traction-in-canada/.
136 Roberto Rocha and Jeff Yates, "Twitter Trolls Stoked Debates about Immigrants and Pipelines in Canada, Data Show," CBC News, 12 February 2019, https://www.cbc.ca/news/canada/twitter-troll-pipeline-immigrant-russia-iran-1.5014750.
137 Rocha and Yates, "Twitter Trolls."
138 Lily Hay Newman, "Facebook Removes a Fresh Batch of Innovative, Iran-Linked Fake Accounts," *Wired*, 28 May 2019, https://www.wired.com/story/iran-linked-fake-accounts-facebook-twitter/.
139 Ashifa Kassam, "Saudi Group Posts Photo of Plane about to Hit Toronto's CN Tower amid Canada Spat," *Guardian*, 8 August 2018, https://www.theguardian.com/world/2018/aug/07/saudi-arabia-canada-toronto-cn-tower-9-11-photo-apology; Ryan Patrick Jones, "Saudi Arabian Group Apologizes for Posting Image Appearing to Threaten Canada with 9/11-Style Attack," CBC News, 6 August 2018, https://www.cbc.ca/news/canada/toronto/saudi-arabian-group-apologizes-for-posting-image-appearing-to-threaten-canada-with-9-11-style-attack-1.4775509.

140 Ahmar Khan, "'It's a Huge Problem': WhatsApp Takes Action after Spread of Dangerous Coronavirus Lies," Yahoo Canada News, 2 April 2020, https://ca.news.yahoo.com/its-a-huge-problem-whats-app-being-used-to-spread-deadly-lies-about-coronavirus-205920988.html; Catharine Tunney, "Federal Government Warning of Voter Coercion, Foreign Election Interference through Private Messaging Services," CBC News, 9 February 2020, https://www.cbc.ca/news/politics/voter-coercion-foreign-interference-private-message-1.5451504.
141 Tunney, "Federal Government Warning."
142 Democratic Institutions (Canada), "G7 Rapid Response Mechanism," 30 January 2019, https://www.canada.ca/en/democratic-institutions/news/2019/01/g7-rapid-response-mechanism.html.
143 Prime Minister's Office, "Canada Joins Christchurch Call to Action to Eliminate Terrorist and Violent Extremist Content Online," 15 May 2019, https://pm.gc.ca/en/news/news-releases/2019/05/15/canada-joins-christchurch-call-action-eliminate-terrorist-and-violent.
144 Greg Miller, *The Apprentice: Trump, Russia and the Subversion of American Democracy* (New York: Custom House, 2018), 161–8.
145 Democratic Institutions (Canada), "Critical Election Incident Public Protocol," last updated 9 July 2019, https://www.canada.ca/en/democratic-institutions/services/protecting-democracy/critical-election-incident-public-protocol.html; Democratic Institutions (Canada), "Cabinet Directive on the Critical Election Incident Public Protocol," last updated 9 July 2019, https://www.canada.ca/en/democratic-institutions/services/protecting-democracy/critical-election-incident-public-protocol/cabinet.html.
146 Laura Hazard Owen, "One Year In, Facebook's Big Algorithm Change Has Spurred an Angry, Fox News–Dominated – and Very Engaged! – News Feed," NiemanLab, 15 March 2019, https://www.niemanlab.org/2019/03/one-year-in-facebooks-big-algorithm-change-has-spurred-an-angry-fox-news-dominated-and-very-engaged-news-feed/.
147 Gordon Ramsay and Sam Robertshaw, "Weaponising News: RT, Sputnik and Targeted Disinformation," Policy Institute, King's College London, January 2019, https://www.kcl.ac.uk/policy-institute/research-analysis/weaponising-news.
148 Robert Chesney and Danielle Keats Citron, "Deep Fakes: A Looming Challenge for Privacy, Democracy, and National Security," *California Law Review* 107 (2019): 1753–1820.

Conclusion

1 Jeff Seldin, "Islamic State Working to Make US Military's Fears Come True," Voice of America, 10 August 2019, https://www.voanews.com/usa/islamic-state-working-make-us-militarys-fears-come-true.

2 Executive Office of the President, National Science and Technology Council Committee on Technology, *Preparing for the Future of Artificial Intelligence*, October 2016, 7, https://obamawhitehouse.archives.gov/sites/default/files/whitehouse_files/microsites/ostp/NSTC/preparing_for_the_future_of_ai.pdf.

3 Greg Allen and Taniel Chan, *Artificial Intelligence and National Security* (Cambridge, MA: Belfer Center for Science and International Affairs, 2017), https://www.belfercenter.org/sites/default/files/files/publication/AI%20NatSec%20-%20final.pdf.

4 Allen and Chan, *Artificial Intelligence*; Robert Chesney and Danielle Keats Citron, "Deep Fakes: A Looming Challenge for Privacy, Democracy, and National Security," *California Law Review* 107 (2019): 1753–1820.

5 A useful and brief overview can be found at the Institute for Quantum Computing at the University of Waterloo, "Quantum Computing 101," https://uwaterloo.ca/institute-for-quantum-computing/quantum-computing-101#What-is-quantum-computing. See also Michele Mosca and Bill Munson, "The Quantum Threat to Cyber Security," in *Governing Cyberspace during a Crisis in Trust: An Essay Series on the Economic Potential — and Vulnerability — of Transformative Technologies and Cyber Eecurity*, ed. Aaron Shull, 60–3 (Waterloo, ON: Centre for International Governance and Innovation, 2019), https://www.cigionline.org/sites/default/files/documents/Cyber%20Series%20Web.pdf.

6 Communications Security Establishment, "Quantum Computing Security Issues for Public Key Cryptography," May 2017, https://cyber.gc.ca/sites/default/files/publications/itse-00-017-eng.pdf.

7 Damien Van Puyvelde, Stephen Coulthart, and M. Shahriar Hossain, "Beyond the Buzzword: Big Data and National Security Decision-Making," *International Affairs* 93, no. 6 (2017): 1401.

8 Paul Monzur, "One Month, 500,000 Face Scans: How China Is Using A.I. to Profile a Minority," *New York Times*, 14 April 2019, https://www.nytimes.com/2019/04/14/technology/china-surveillance-artificial-intelligence-racial-profiling.html.

9 Paul Mozur, Jonah M. Kessel, and Melissa Chan, "Made in China, Exported to the World: The Surveillance State," *New York Times*, 24 April 2019, https://www.nytimes.com/2019/04/24/technology/ecuador-surveillance-cameras-police-government.html.

10 See, for example, R.K. Lippert, K. Walby, I. Warren, and D. Palmer, *National Security, Surveillance and Terror: Canada and Australia in Comparative Perspective* (Basingstoke, UK: Palgrave Macmillan, 2016).

11 Cameron F. Kerry, "Why Protecting Privacy Is a Losing Game Today – and How to Change the Game," Brookings Institute, 12 July 2018, https://

www.brookings.edu/research/why-protecting-privacy-is-a-losing-game-today-and-how-to-change-the-game/.

12 Alex Boutilier and Sabrina Nanji, "More Than 600,000 Canadians Caught in Facebook Data Scandal," *Toronto Star*, 4 April 2018, https://www.thestar.com/news/canada/2018/04/04/more-than-600000-canadians-caught-in-facebook-data-scandal.html.

13 Aaron Wherry, "Canadian Company Linked to Data Scandal Pushes Back at Whistleblower's Claims," CBC News, 24 April 2019, https://www.cbc.ca/news/politics/aggregate-iq-mps-cambridge-wylie-brexit-1.4633388.

14 HM Government (UK), *Online Harms White Paper*, April 2019, https://assets.publishing.service.gov.uk/government/uploads/system/uploads/attachment_data/file/793360/Online_Harms_White_Paper.pdf.

15 Aaron Y. Zelin, "The State of Global Jihad Online: A Qualitative, Quantitative, and Cross-Lingual Analysis," New America Foundation, January 2013, https://www.washingtoninstitute.org/uploads/Documents/opeds/Zelin20130201-NewAmericaFoundation.pdf.

16 Jacinda Ardern, "Christchurch Call to Eliminate Terrorist and Violent Extremist Online Content Adopted," 16 May 2019, https://www.beehive.govt.nz/release/christchurch-call-eliminate-terrorist-and-violent-extremist-online-content-adopted.

17 Joby Warrick, "In Fight against ISIS's Propaganda Machine, Raids and Online Trench Warfare," *Washington Post*, 18 August 2018, https://www.washingtonpost.com/world/national-security/in-fight-against-isiss-propaganda-machine-raids-and-online-trench-warfare/2018/08/19/379d4da4-9f46-11e8-8e87-c869fe70a721_story.html.

18 Warrick, "In Fight against ISIS's Propaganda Machine."

19 Shibani Mahtani, "Facebook Removed 1.5 Million Videos of the Christchurch Attacks within 24 hours – and There Were Still Many More," *Washington Post*, 17 March 2019, https://www.washingtonpost.com/world/facebook-removed-15-million-videos-of-the-christchurch-attacks-within-24-hours--and-there-were-still-many-more/2019/03/17/fe3124b2-4898-11e9-b871-978e5c757325_story.html.

20 Olivia Solon, "Facebook, Twitter, Google and Microsoft Team Up to Tackle Extremist Content," *Guardian*, 6 December 2016, https://www.theguardian.com/technology/2016/dec/05/facebook-twitter-google-microsoft-terrorist-extremist-content.

21 Microsoft, "The Christchurch Call and Steps to Tackle Terrorist and Violent Extremist Content," 15 May 2019, https://blogs.microsoft.com/on-the-issues/2019/05/15/the-christchurch-call-and-steps-to-tackle-terrorist-and-violent-extremist-content/.

22 Damien Cave, "Australia Passes Law to Punish Social Media Companies for Violent Posts," *New York Times*, 3 April 2019, https://www.nytimes.com/2019/04/03/world/australia/social-media-law.html.
23 Standing Committee on Access to Information, Privacy and Ethics, *Addressing Digital Privacy Vulnerabilities and Potential Threats to Canada's Democratic Electoral Process*, 28 June 2018, https://www.ourcommons.ca/Content/Committee/421/ETHI/Reports/RP9932875/ethirp16/ethirp16-e.pdf.
24 Innovation, Science and Economic Development Canada, *Canada's Digital Charter: Trust in a Digital World*, 26 June 2019, https://www.ic.gc.ca/eic/site/062.nsf/eng/h_00108.html; and *Strengthening Privacy for the Digital Age*, 21 May 2019, https://www.ic.gc.ca/eic/site/062.nsf/eng/h_00107.html.
25 Howard Solomon, "Canada Announces Digital Charter, Promises Serious Fines to Business for Not Protecting Privacy," IT World Canada, 21 May 2019, https://www.itworldcanada.com/article/canada-announces-digital-charter-promises-serious-fines-to-business-for-not-protecting-privacy/418217.
26 Howard Yu, "GDPR Isn't Enough to Protect Us in an Age of Smart Algorithms," Conversation, 29 May 2018, http://theconversation.com/gdpr-isnt-enough-to-protect-us-in-an-age-of-smart-algorithms-97389.
27 Keith Neuman, "Canadians' Confidence in National Institutions Steady," *Policy Options*, 2 August 2018, https://policyoptions.irpp.org/magazines/august-2018/canadians-confidence-in-national-institutions-steady/; Owen et al., *Digital Democracy Project*.
28 EKOS Research Associates, "Attitudes towards the Communications Security Establishment Baseline Study," June 2017, http://epe.lac-bac.gc.ca/100/200/301/pwgsc-tpsgc/por-ef/communications_security_establishment/2017/128-16-e/summary/summary.pdf.
29 EKOS Research Associates, *Attitudes to the Canadian Security Intelligence Service (CSIS) – Baseline Study Final Report*, 12 June 2018, http://publications.gc.ca/collections/collection_2019/scrs-csis/PS74-8-1-2018-eng.pdf.
30 EKOS Research Associates, "Attitudes" (2017), *Attitudes* (2018).
31 EKOS Research Associates, "Attitudes" (2017), *Attitudes* (2018).
32 Canadian Centre for Cyber Security, "National Cyber Threat Assessment 2018."
33 NSICOP, *National Security and Intelligence Committee of Parliamentarians Annual Report 2018*.
34 Michelle Shephard, "CSIS Settles Multimillion-Dollar Lawsuit with Employees Who Claimed Workplace Islamophobia, Racism and Homophobia," *Toronto Star*, 14 December 2017.

35 Jim Bronskill, "'This Isn't about National Security': Civil Liberties Group Publishes CSIS Reports Related to Alleged Spying," Canadian Press (CBC News), 8 July 2019, https://www.cbc.ca/news/canada/british-columbia/csis-protesters-energy-documents-1.5203496
36 Boutilier, "CSIS Program Illegally Spied."
37 See, for example, David Akin, "ANALYSIS: How Justin Trudeau's India Trip Went from Bad to 'Bengal Bungle,'" Global News, 23 February 2018, https://globalnews.ca/news/4044543/david-akin-analysis-justin-trudeaus-bengal-bungle/; Brian Lilley, "Justin Trudeau Pushes Fake News, Punishes the Truth," 24 February 2018, http://brianlilley.com/justin-trudeau-pushes-fake-news-punishes-the-truth/.
38 *Maclean's*, "Chrystia Freeland on Canada's Foreign Policy: Full Speech," 6 June 2017, https://www.macleans.ca/politics/ottawa/chrystia-freeland-on-canadas-foreign-policy-full-speech/.
39 Research on bridging traditional security and intelligence agencies with non-traditional partners and "Canadianizing" intelligence comes out of findings from interviews with Thomas Juneau. This research is sponsored by the Social Sciences and Humanities Research Council as well as the Canadian Network for Terrorism, Security and Society and will be the focus of at least two future books on the intelligence community in Canada.
40 Public Safety Canada, "National Security Transparency Commitment," 2 July 2019, https://www.canada.ca/en/services/defence/nationalsecurity/national-security-transparency-commitment.html#s1.
41 Public Safety Canada, "The National Security Transparency Advisory Group (NS-TAG)," 2 July 2019, https://www.canada.ca/en/services/defence/nationalsecurity/national-security-transparency-commitment/national-security-transparency-advisory-group.html#s6.
42 NSICOP, *Annual Report 2019*, 109.
43 Of course, such measures would be difficult and complex. Foreign intelligence collection requires a legal and operational basis and mandate completely different from domestic-focused security intelligence. While not impossible, the addition of a foreign intelligence mandate to CSIS or GAC would have to be done very carefully.

Appendix

1 For more information on these departments and agencies, see Stephanie Carvin, Thomas Juneau, and Craig Forcese, *Top Secret Canada: Understanding the Canadian Intelligence and National Security Community* (Toronto: University of Toronto Press, forthcoming).

Select Bibliography

Ablon, L., and T. Bogart. *Zero Days, Thousands of Nights: The Life and Times of Zero-Day Vulnerabilities and Their Exploits.* Santa Monica, CA: RAND, 2017.

Addison, T., and S.M. Murshed. "Transnational Terrorism as a Spillover of Domestic Disputes in Other Countries." *Defence and Peace Economics* 16, no. 2 (2005): 69-82. https://doi.org/10.1080/10242690500070078.

Allcott, H., and M. Gentzkow. "Social Media and Fake News in the 2016 Election." *Journal of Economic Perspectives* 31, no. 2 (2017): 211–35. https://doi.org/10.1257/jep.31.2.211.

Amarasingam, A. *Pain, Pride and Politics: Social Movement Activism and the Sri Lankan Tamil Diaspora in Canada.* Athens: University of Georgia Press, 2015.

Amarasingam A., and L. Dawson. "I Left to Be Closer to Allah: Learning about Foreign Fighters from Family and Friends." Institute for Strategic Dialogue, 2018, 5 .http://www.isdglobal.org/wp-content/uploads/2018/05/Families_Report.pdf.

Anderson, J. *Propaganda and Persuasion: The Cold War and the Canadian-Soviet Friendship Society.* Winnipeg: University of Manitoba Press, 2017.

Andrew, C., and O. Gordievsky. *KGB: The Inside Story of Its Foreign Operations from Lenin to Gorbachev.* New York: HarperCollins Publishers, 1990.

Andrew, C., and V. Mitrokhin. *The Sword and the Shield: The Mitrokhin Archive and the Secret History of the KGB.* New York: Basic Books, 1999.

Bakshy, E., S. Messing, and L.A. Adamic. "Exposure to Ideologically Diverse News and Opinion on Facebook." *Science* 348, no. 3269 (2015): 1130–2. https://doi.org/10.1126/science.aaa1160. Medline:25953820.

Barry, D. "Cleared or Covered Up? The Department of External Affairs Investigations of Herbert Norman, 1950–52." *International Journal* 66, no. 1 (2011): 147–69. https://doi.org/10.1177/002070201106600110.

Bartlett, J. *The Dark Net: Inside the Digital Underworld*. Brooklyn, NY: Melville House Publishing, 2015.

Beccaro, A. "Modern Irregular Warfare: The ISIS Case Study." *Small Wars and Insurgencies* 29, no. 2 (2018): 207–28. https://doi.org/10.1080/09592318.2018.1433469.

Bell, S. *Cold Terror: How Canada Nurtures and Exports Terrorism around the World*. Mississauga, ON: John Wiley & Sons Canada, 2007.

– *The Martyr's Oath: The Apprenticeship of a Homegrown Terrorist*. Mississauga, ON: John Wiley & Sons Canada, 2005.

Benkler, Y., R. Faris, and H. Roberts. *Network Propaganda: Manipulation, Disinformation, and Radicalization in American Politics*. Oxford: Oxford University Press, 2018.

Benkler, Y., R. Faris, H. Roberts, and E. Zuckerman. "Study: Breitbart-Led Right-Wing Media Ecosystem Altered Broader Media Agenda." *Columbia Journalism Review*, March (2017), https://www.cjr.org/analysis/breitbart-media-trump-harvard-study.php.

Bhattacharjee, S. "National Security with a Canadian Twist: The Investment Canada Act and the New National Security Review Test." *Transnational Corporations Review* 1, no. 4 (2009): 12–19. https://doi.org/10.1080/19186444.2009.11658208.

Black, J.L., and M. Rudner. *The Gouzenko Affair: Canada and the Beginning of Cold War Counter-Espionage*. Newcastle, ON: Penumbra, 2006.

Blackwill, R., and J. Harris. *War by Other Means: Geoeconomics and Statecraft*. Cambridge, MA: Belknap/Harvard University Press, 2016.

Bloom, M. *Dying to Kill: The Allure of Suicide Terror*. New York: Columbia University Press, 2005.

Bloom, M. and C. Daymon. "Assessing the Future Threat: ISIS's Virtual Caliphate." *Orbis* 62, no. 3 (2018): 372–88. https://doi.org/10.1016/j.orbis.2018.05.007.

Bolan, K. *Loss of Faith: How the Air-India Bombers Got Away with Murder*. Toronto: McClelland & Stewart, 2005.

Brady, A. "Magic Weapons: China's Political Influence Activities under Xi Jinping." Wilson Centre, 18 September 2017. https://www.wilsoncenter.org/article/magic-weapons-chinas-political-influence-activities-under-xi-jinping.

Bryan, T., T. Mirrlees, B. Perry, and R. Scrivens. "The Dangers of Porous Borders: The 'Trump Effect' in Canada." *Journal of Hate Studies* 14 (2018): 53–75. https://www.researchgate.net/publication/330482179_The_Dangers_of_Porous_Borders_The_Trump_Effect_in_Canada_Journal_of_Hate_Studies.

Bunn, M., and S. Sagan. "Introduction: Inside the Insider Threat." In *Insider Threats*, edited by Matt Bunn and Scott D. Sagan, 1–9. Ithaca, NY: Cornell University Press, 2016.

Burke, J. *The New Threat: The Past, Present and Future of Islamic Militancy*. New York: New Press, 2015.
Byman, D. *Deadly Connections: States That Sponsor Terrorism*. Cambridge: Cambridge University Press, 2005.
Canadian Security Intelligence Service. *China and the Age of Strategic Rivalry: Highlights from an Academic Outreach Workshop*, 2018, 108. https://www.canada.ca/content/dam/csis-scrs/documents/publications/CSIS-Academic-Outreach-China-report-May-2018-en.pdf.
– "Mobilization to Violence (Terrorism) Research: Key Findings." February 2018. https://www.canada.ca/content/dam/csis-scrs/documents/publications/IMV_-_Terrorism-Research-Key-findings-eng.pdf.
– "Who Said What: The Security Challenges of Modern Disinformation," 2018. https://www.canada.ca/en/security-intelligence-service/corporate/publications/who-said-what-the-security-challenges-of-modern-disinformation.html.
Carson, J., G. LaFree, and L. Dugan, L. "Terrorist and Non-Terrorist Criminal Attacks by Radical Environmental and Animal Rights Groups in the United States, 1970–2007," *Terrorism and Political Violence* 24, no. 2 (2012): 295–319. https://doi.org/10.1080/09546553.2011.639416.
Carvin, S. "A Mouse Sleeping Next to a Dragon: New Twitches and Grunts." *Public Policy Forum*, December 2017. https://medium.com/ppf-consultative-forum-on-china/a-mouse-sleeping-next-to-a-dragon-new-twitches-and-grunts-970f2c225b55.
Carvin, S., T. Juneau, and C. Forcese. *Top Secret Canada: Understanding the Canadian Intelligence and National Security Community*, Toronto: University of Toronto Press, 2020.
Chalk, P. "Liberation Tigers of Tamil Eelam's (LTTE) International Organization and Operations – A Preliminary Analysis." Commentary 77, Canadian Security Intelligence Service, 2000.
Charters, D. "The (Un)Peaceable Kingdom? Terrorism and Canada before 9/11." *IRPP Policy Matters* 9, no. 4 (2008).
Chermak S., and J. Gruenewald. "Laying a Foundation for the Criminological Examination of Right-Wing, Left-Wing and Al Qaeda-Inspired Extremism in the United States." *Terrorism and Political Violence* 27, no. 1 (2015): 133–59. https://doi.org/10.1080/09546553.2014.975646.
Chesney, B., and D. Citron. "Deep Fakes: A Looming Challenge for Privacy, Democracy, and National Security." *California Law Review* 107 (2019): 1753–1820. https://doi.org/10.2139/ssrn.3213954.
Christensen, T. *The China Challenge: Shaping the Choices of a Rising Power*. New York: W.W. Norton, 2016.
Chuka, N. and J. Born. *Hybrid Warfare: Implications for CAF Force Development*. Defence Research and Development Canada Scientific Report DRCD-

RDDC-2014-R43, August 2014. https://apps.dtic.mil/dtic/tr/fulltext/u2/1017608.pdf.

Conway, M. "Determining the Role of the Internet in Violent Extremism and Terrorism: Six Suggestions for Progressing Research." *Studies in Conflict & Terrorism* 40, no. 1 (2013): 77–98. https://doi.org/10.1080/1057610x.2016.1157408.

Cooper, B. *CFIS: A Foreign Intelligence Service for Canada*. Calgary: Canadian Defence & Foreign Affairs Institute, 2007.

Corner, E., and P. Gill. "A False Dichotomy? Mental Illness and Lone-Actor Terrorism." *Law and Human Behaviour* 39, no. 1 (2015): 23–34. https://doi.org/10.1037/lhb0000102. Medline:25133916.

Cornish, M. "Behaviour of Chinese SOEs: Implications for Investment and Cooperation in Canada. Canadian Council of Chief Executives and the Canadian International Council," February 2012. https://thecic.org/research-publications/reports/behaviour-of-chinese-soes-implications-for-investment-and-cooperation-in-canada/.

Cox, D., T. Bruscino, and A. Ryan. "Why Hybrid Warfare Is Tactics Not Strategy: A Rejoinder to 'Future Threats and Strategic Thinking.'" *Infinity Journal* 2, no. 2 (2012): 25–9.

Davis, J. *Women in Modern Terrorism: From Liberation Wars to Global Jihad and the Islamic State*. Lanham, MD: Rowman & Littlefield, 2017.

Dawson L., and A. Amarasingam. "Talking to Foreign Fighters: Insights into the Motivations for *Hijrah* to Syria and Iraq." *Studies in Conflict and Terrorism* 40, no. 3 (2017): 191–210. https://doi.org/10.1080/1057610x.2016.1274216.

Dobson, W. *The Dictator's Learning Curve: Inside the Global Battle for Democracy*. New York: Doubleday, 2012.

Farson, S., and N. Teeple. "Increasing Canada's Foreign Intelligence Capability: Is It a Dead Issue?" *Intelligence and National Security* 30, no. 1 (2014): 47–76. https://doi.org/10.1080/02684527.2014.961243.

Fishman, B. *The Master Plan: ISIS, Al-Qaeda and the Jihadi Strategy for Final Victory*. New Haven, CT: Yale University Press, 2016.

Forcese, C. "Through a Glass Darkly: The Role and Review of 'National Security' Concepts in Canadian Law." *Alberta Law Review* 43, no. 4 (2006): 963–1000. https://doi.org/10.29173/alr396.

Forcese, C., and K. Roach. "Criminalizing Terrorist Babble: Canada's Dubious New Terrorist Speech Crime." *Alberta Law Review* 53, no. 1 (2015): 35–84.

– *False Security: The Radicalization of Canadian Anti-Terrorism*. Toronto: Irwin Law, 2015.

Forcese, C., and L. West. "Interference." In *National Security Law*, 2nd ed. Toronto: Irwin Law, forthcoming.

Freedman, L. *The Future of War: A History*. New York: Public Affairs, 2017.
Fridman, O. *Russian Hybrid Warfare: Resurgence and Politicisation*. Oxford: Oxford University Press, 2018.
Gartenstein-Ross, D., and L. Frum, eds. *Terror in the Peaceable Kingdom: Understanding and Addressing Violent Extremism in Canada*. Washington, DC: FDD, 2012.
Gill, P. *Lone-Actor Terrorists: A Behavioural Analysis*. London: Routledge, 2015.
Globerman, S. "A Policy Perspective on Outward Foreign Direct Investment by Chinese State-Owned Enterprises." *Frontiers of Economics in China* 11, no. 4 (2016): 537–47.
Golovchenko, Y., M. Hartmann, and R. Adler-Nissen. "State, Media and Civil Society in the Information Warfare over Ukraine: Citizen Curators of Digital Disinformation." *International Affairs* 94, no. 5 (2018): 975–94. https://doi.org/10.1093/ia/iiy148.
Granatstein, J.L., and D. Stafford. *Spy Wars: Espionage in Canada from Gouzenko to Glasnost*. Toronto: Key Porter Books, 1990.
Gurski, P. *The Threat from Within: Recognizing Al Qaeda-Inspired Radicalization and Terrorism in the West*. Lanham, MD: Roman & Littlefield, 2015.
Hamblet, M. "The Islamic State's Virtual Caliphate." *Middle East Quarterly* 24, no. 4 (2017): 1–8.
Hamilton, C. *Silent Invasion: China's Influence in Australia*. Melbourne: Hardy Grant Books, 2018.
Haslam, J. *Near and Distant Neighbours: A New History of Soviet Intelligence*. New York: Farrar, Straus and Giroux, 2015.
Healey, J., ed. *A Fierce Domain: Conflict in Cyberspace, 1986 to 2012*. Arlington, VA: Cyber Conflict Studies Association, 2013.
Hegghammer, T., and P. Nesser. "Assessing the Islamic State's Commitment to Attacking the West." *Perspectives on Terrorism* 9, no 4. (2015), http://www.terrorismanalysts.com/pt/index.php/pot/article/view/440/html.
Hewitt, S. "Reforming the Canadian Security State: The Royal Canadian Mounted Police Security Service and the 'Key Sectors' Program." *Intelligence and National Security* 17, no. 4 (2002): 165–84. https://doi.org/10.1080/02684520412331306680.
– *Spying 101: The RCMP's Secret Activities at Canadian Universities, 1917–1997*. Toronto: University of Toronto Press, 2002.
Hoffman, D.E. *The Billion Dollar Spy: A True Story of Cold War Espionage and Betrayal*. New York: Anchor Books, 2015.
Hoffman, F. "Conflict in the 21st Century: The Rise of Hybrid Wars." Arlington, MD: Potomac Institute for Policy Studies, December 2007. https://potomacinstitute.org/reports/19-reports/1163-conflict-in-the-21st-century-the-rise-of-hybrid-wars.

- "Hybrid vs. Compound War: The Janus Choice of Modern War: Defining Today's Multifaceted Conflict." *Armed Forces Journal* (October 2009): 1–2.
Hoffmann, B. *Inside Terrorism*. 3rd ed. New York: Columbia University Press, 2017.
Hofmann, D.C., and L. Dawson. "The Neglected Role of Charismatic Authority in the Study of Terrorist Groups and Radicalization." *Studies in Conflict and Terrorism* 37, no. 4 (2014): 348–68. https://doi.org/10.1080/1057610x.2014.879436.
Holman, T. "'Gonna Get Myself Connected': The Role of Facilitation in Foreign Fighter Mobilizations." *Perspectives on Terrorism* 10, no. 2 (2016): 2–23.
Hoover Institution. *Chinese Influence & American Interests: Promoting Constructive Vigilance*, 2018. https://www.hoover.org/sites/default/files/research/docs/chineseinfluence_americaninterests_fullreport_web.pdf.
Horgan, J. *The Psychology of Terrorism*. London: Routledge, 2005.
Human Rights Watch. "Funding the "Final War": LTTE Intimidation and Extortion in the Tamil Diaspora;" 15 March 2006. https://www.hrw.org/report/2006/03/14/funding-final-war/ltte-intimidation-and-extortion-tamil-diaspora.
Jeffery, R., and I. Hall. "Post-Conflict Justice in Divided Democracies: The 1984 Anti-Sikh Riots in India." *Third World Quarterly*, 41, no. 6 (2020): 994–1011.
Juneau, T., ed. *Strategic Analysis in Support of International Policy Making: Case Studies in Achieving Analytical Relevance*. Lanham, MD: Rowman & Littlefield, 2017.
Kaplan, F. *Dark Territory: The Secret History of Cyber War*. New York: Simon & Schuster, 2016.
Kello, L. *The Virtual Weapon and International Order*. New Haven, CT: Yale University Press, 2017.
Knight, A. *How the Cold War Began: The Gouzenko Affair and the Hunt for Soviet Spies*. Toronto: McClelland & Stewart, 2005.
Koomen, W., and J. van der Plight. *The Psychology of Radicalization and Terrorism*. London: Routledge, 2015.
Kux, D. "Soviet Active Measures and Disinformation: Overview and Assessment." *Parameters* 15, no. 4 (1985): 19–28.
La, J. "Forced Remittances in Canada's Tamil Enclaves." *Peace Review* 16, no. 3 (2004): 379–85. https://doi.org/10.1080/1040265042000278630.
Lanoszka, A. "Disinformation in International Politics." *European Journal of International Security* 4, no. 2 (2019): 227–48. https://doi.org/10.1017/eis.2019.6.
Lasconjarias, G., and J. Larsen, eds. "NATO's Response to Hybrid Threats." NATO Defense College Forum Paper 24, 2015.

Lippert, R., K. Walby, and I. Warren. *National Security, Surveillance and Terror: Canada and Australia in Comparative Perspective*. Basingstoke, UK: Palgrave Macmillan, 2016.

Lowenthal, M. *Intelligence: From Secrets to Policy*. 7th ed. London: Sage, 2017.

Mahar, D. *Shattered Illusions: KGB Cold War Espionage in Canada*. Lanham, MD: Roman & Littlefield, 2017.

Manthorpe, J. *Claws of the Panda: Beijing's Campaign of Influence and Intimidation in Canada*. Toronto: Cormorant Books, 2019.

Marchal, N., L. Neudert, B. Kollanyi, and P. Howard. "Polarization, Partisanship and Junk News Consumption on Social Media during the 2018 US Midterm Elections." COMPROP Data Memo 2018.5 (Oxford Internet Institute), 1 November 2018. http://comprop.oii.ox.ac.uk/research/midterms2018/.

Marwick, A., and R. Lewis, R. *Media Manipulation and Disinformation Online*. Data and Society Research Institute, 2017. https://datasociety.net/pubs/oh/DataAndSociety_MediaManipulationAndDisinformationOnline.pdf.

Maurer, T. *Cyber Mercenaries: The State, Hackers and Power*. Cambridge: Cambridge University Press, 2018.

McCants, W. *The ISIS Apocalypse:The History, Strategy and Doomsday Vision of the Islamic State*. New York: St. Martin's, 2015.

Meeuwisse, R. *Cybersecurity for Beginners*. 2nd ed. London: Cybersimplicity, 2017.

Monaghan, A. "The 'War' in Russia's Hybrid Warfare." *Parameters* 45, no. 5 (2015–16): 66–74.

Mullins, S. "'Global Jihad': The Canadian Experience." *Terrorism and Political Violence* 25, no. 5 (2013): 734–76. https://doi.org/10.1080/09546553.2012.693552.

Mulroney, D. *Middle Power, Middle Kingdom: What Canadians Need to Know about China in the 21st Century*. Toronto: Allen Lane, 2015.

Munton, D. "Our Men in Havana: Canadian Foreign Intelligence Operations in Castro's Cuba." *International Journal* 70, no. 1 (2015): 23–9. https://doi.org/10.1177/0020702014562592.

Murray, W., and P. Mansoor, eds. (2012) *Hybrid Warfare: Fighting Complex Opponents from the Ancient World to the Present*. Cambridge: Cambridge University Press, 2012.

Nagel, A. *Kill All Normies: Online Culture Wars from 4Chan and Tumblr to Trump and the Alt-Right*. Winchester: Zero Books, 2017.

Nesbitt, M. "An Empirical Study of Terrorism Charges and Terrorism Trials in Canada between September 2001 and September 2018." *Criminal Law Quarterly* 67, nos. 1 & 2 (2019): 95–139.

Nesbitt, M., and D. Hagg. "Terrorism Prosecutions in Canada: Elucidating the Elements of the Offences," *Alberta Law Review* 57, no. 3 (2020): 595–648. https://doi.org/10.29173/alr2590.

Neumann, P. "Options and Strategies for Countering Online Radicalization in the United States." *Studies in Conflict & Terrorism* 36, no. 6 (2013): 431–59. https://doi.org/10.1080/1057610x.2013.784568.

Norris, W. *Chinese Economic Statecraft: Commercial Actors, Grand Strategy and State Control*. Ithaca, NY: Cornell University Press, 2016.

Ostrovsky, A. *The Invention of Russia: From Gorbachev's Freedom to Putin's War*. New York: Viking, 2015.

Owen, T. *Disruptive Power: The Crisis of the State in the Digital Age*. Oxford: Oxford University Press, 2015.

Pantucci, R. "A Typology of Lone Wolves: Preliminary Analysis of Lone Islamist Terrorists." International Centre for the Study of Radicalization and Political Violence, March 2011. https://icsr.info/2011/04/05/a-typology-of-lone-wolves-preliminary-analysis-of-lone-islamist-terrorists/.

Parent R., and J. Eillis III. "Right-Wing Extremism in Canada." TSAS Working Paper Series no. 14-03, May 2014.

Pearson, E., and E. Winterbotham. "Women, Gender and Daesh Radicalisation." *RUSI Journal* 162, no. 3 (2017): 60–72. https://doi.org/10.1080/03071847.2017.1353251.

Pei, M. *China's Crony Capitalism: The Dynamics of Regime Decay*. Cambridge, MA: Harvard University Press, 2016.

Perry, B., and R. Scrivens. "Uneasy Alliances: A Look at the Right-Wing Extremist Movement in Canada." *Studies in Conflict and Terrorism* 39, no. 3 (2016): 819–41. https://doi.org/10.1080/1057610x.2016.1139375.

Perry, B., and R. Scrivens. *Right-Wing Extremism in Canada*. London: Palgrave Macmilllan, 2019.

Razavy, M. "Sikh Militant Movements in Canada." *Terrorism and Political Violence* 18, no. 1 (2006): 79–93. https://doi.org/10.1080/09546550500174913.

Rid, T. *Rise of the Machines: A Cybernetic History*. New York: W.W. Norton, 2016.

Roach, K. *The 9/11 Effect: Comparative Counter-Terrorism*. Toronto: University of Toronto Press, 2011.

Robinson, P. "The Viability of a Canadian Foreign Intelligence Service." *International Journal* 64, no. 3 (2009): 703–16.

Ryder, N. *The Financial War on Terrorism: A Review of Counter-Terrorist Financing Strategies since 2001*. Abingdon, UK: Routledge, 2015.

Sageman, M. *Leaderless Jihad: Terror Networks in the Twenty-First Century*. Philadelphia: University of Pennsylvania Press, 2008.

– "The Stagnation in Terrorism Research." *Terrorism and Political Violence* 26 (2014): 565–80. https://doi.org/10.1080/09546553.2014.895649.

- *Understanding Terror Networks*. Philadelphia: University of Pennsylvania Press, 2004.
Sanger, D. *The Perfect Weapon: War, Sabotage and Fear in the Cyber Age*. New York: Crown, 2018.
Schuurman, B., E. Bakker, P. Gill, and N. Bouhana. "Lone Actor Terrorist Attack Planning and Preparation: A Data-Driven Analysis." *Psychiatry and Behavioral Science* 63, no. 4 (2018): 1191–1200. https://doi.org/10.1111/1556-4029.13676. Medline:29059713.
Segal, A. *The Hacked World Order: How Nations Fight, Trade, Maneuver and Manipulate in the Digital Age*. New York: Public Affairs, 2017.
Seligman, S. "Explaining Canadian Foreign Policy toward Sri Lanka under the Harper Government." *International Journal* 7, no. 2 (2016): 249–65. https://doi.org/10.1177/0020702015609381.
Shephard, M. *Decade of Fear: Reporting from Terrorism's Grey Zone*. Vancouver: Douglas & McIntyre, 2011.
Shultz, R., and R. Godson. *Dezinformatsia: The Strategy of Soviet Disinformation*. New York: Berkley Books, 1986.
Silber, M. *The Al Qaeda Factor: Plots against the West*. Philadelphia: University of Pennsylvania Press, 2012.
Singer, P., and E. Brooking. *Like War: The Weaponization of Social Media*. New York: Houghton Mifflin Harcourt, 2018.
Singer, P., and A. Friedman. *Cybersecurity and Cyberwar: What Everyone Needs to Know*. Oxford: Oxford University Press, 2014.
Soldatov, A., and I. Borogan. *The Red Web: The Struggle between Russia's Digital Dictators and the New Online Revolutionaries*. New York: Public Affairs, 2015.
Soriano, M. "Between the Pen and the Sword: The Global Islamic Media Front in the West." *Terrorism and Political Violence* 24, no. 5 (2012): 769–86. https://doi.org/10.1080/09546553.2011.643934.
Tanner, S., and A. Campana. *The Process of Radicalization: Right-Wing Skinheads in Quebec*, TSAS Working Paper Series 14-07. August 2014.
Tucker, J., Y. Theocharis, M. Roberts, and P. Barberá. "From Liberation to Turmoil: Social Media and Democracy." *Journal of Democracy* 28, no. 4 (2017): 46–59.
Valeriano, B., B. Jensen, and R. Maness. *Cyber Strategy: The Evolving Character of Power and Coercion*. Oxford: Oxford University Press, 2018.
Van Puyvelde, D., S. Coulthart, and M. Hossain. "Beyond the Buzzword: Big Data and National Security Decision-Making." *International Affairs* 93, no. 6 (2017): 1397–1416. https://doi.org/10.1093/ia/iix184.
Wernicke, G. "The Communist-Led World Peace Council and the Western Peace Movements: The Fetters of Bipolarity and Some Attempts to Break Them in the Fifties and Early Sixties." *Peace and Change* 23, no. 3 (1998): 265–311. https://doi.org/10.1111/0149-0508.00087.

- "The Unity of Peace and Socialism? The World Peace Council on a Cold War Tightrope between the Peace Struggle and Intrasystemic Communist Conflicts." *Peace and Change* 26, no. (2001): 332–52. https://doi.org/10.1111/0149-0508.00197.
Vidino, L., F. Marone, and E. Entenmann. *Fear Thy Neighbour: Radicalization and Jihadist Attacks in the West*. Milan: Italian Institute for International Political Studies, 2017.
Warden, B. *Diplomat, Dissident, Spook: A Canadian Diplomat's Chronicles through the Cold War and Beyond*. Victoria, BC: Tellwell, 2017.
Watts, C. *Messing with the Enemy: Surviving in a Social Media World of Hackers, Terrorists, Russians and Fake News*. New York: Harper, 2018.
West, L. "Cyber Force: The International Legal Implications of the Communication Security Establishment's Expanded Mandate under Bill C-59." *Canadian Journal of Law & Technology* 16 (2019): 381–416.
Wettering, F. "Counterintelligence: The Broken Triad." In *Secret Intelligence: A Reader*, edited by C. Andrew, R.J. Aldrich, and W.K. Wark, 281–307. London: Routledge, 2009.
Whitaker, R., and S. Hewitt. *Canada and the Cold War*. Toronto: James Lorimer, 2003.
Whitaker, R., G. Kealy, and A. Parnaby. *The Secret Service: Political Policing in Canada from the Fenians to Fortress America*. Toronto: University of Toronto Press, 2013.
Whitaker, R., and G. Marcuse. *Cold War Canada:The Making of a National Insecurity State, 1945–1957*. Toronto: University of Toronto Press, 1996.
Wilkie, R. "Hybrid Warfare: Something Old, Not Something New." *Air & Space Power Journal* (Winter 2009): 13–17.
Winter, C. *Media Jihad: The Islamic State's Doctrine for Information Warfare*. London: International Centre for the Study of Radicalization, 2017. https://icsr.info/wp-content/uploads/2017/02/ICSR-Report-Media-Jihad-The-Islamic-State%E2%80%99s-Doctrine-for-Information-Warfare.pdf.
Wither, J. "Making Sense of Hybrid Warfare." *Connections: The Quarterly Journal* 15, no. 2 (2016): 73–87. https://doi.org/10.11610/connections.15.2.06.
Woo, Y. "Chinese Lessons: State Owned Enterprises and the Regulation of Foreign Investment in Canada." *China Economic Journal* 7, no. 1 (2014): 31–8. https://doi.org/10.1080/17538963.2013.874073.
Woolley, S., and P. Howard. "Political Communication, Computational Propaganda, and Autonomous Agents." *International Journal of Communication* 10 (2016): 4882–90.

Index

Abbott, Greg, 242
Abdulmutallab, Umar Farouk (the "Underwear Bomber"), 57
Abel, Rudolf (aka Vilyam Willie Fisher), 100
active insider, 122
"active measures" by Soviet Union, 190–1, 193
"advanced, persistent threats" (APTs), 165–6
adware, 150
Africa, and China's influence, 125–6
agencies (national security/intelligence agencies), xi, xiii–xiv, 82–3
agencies in Canada. *See* national security and intelligence community in Canada
AggregateIQ, 268
Ahmed, Misbahuddin, 28
Air Canada, and China, 207
Air India bombings, 23
Akhtar, Saad, 31
Al-Awlaki, Anwar, 58
algorithms, 264–5
Alizadeh, Hiva Mohammad, 28, 58

Allcott, Hunt, 237
Al Qaida: description and activities, 31–2, 296n24; expansion, 65–6; foreign-directed attacks in Canada, 57; as inspiration, 25–8; recruits, 65; targets, 66; as threat, 9, 31, 33; and violent extremism in Canada today, 29, 31–3
Al Qaida in the Arabian Peninsula (AQAP), 31
Al Qaida/Islamic State–inspired extremism, 25–6
Al Shabaab, 64
Altikat, Atilla, 23
alt-right: description, 238–9; and disinformation, 238–40, 243–4. *See also* far-right supporters
The Americans (TV show), 103
Anderson, Jennifer, 193
Andrew, Christopher, 100
Anna Kournikova Virus, 150
anti-government extremism, 43
anti-pipeline civil disobedience, 53
Anti-Terrorism Act (Bill C-36; 2001): creation, 19–20; financing offences, 72; first conviction, 27;

Anti-Terrorism Act (continued)
  mandate of CSE, 345n91;
  problems with, 52–3; and
  radicalization, 80
"anti-vaxxers," 235
Armenian extremist groups, 22–3
Armenian Secret Army for the
  Liberation of Armenia
  (ASALA), 23
artificial general intelligence (AGI),
  264–5
artificial intelligence (AI), 180, 264–5
Asia, and China's influence, 126
Associated Press hack, 160–1
"Atomwaffen," 40
attack planning and violent
  extremism in Canada: domestic
  attacks, 59; foreign-approved
  plots, 58–9; foreign-directed
  attacks, 56–7; lone actors, 59–63
Australia, 214, 218, 269, 358n130
authoritarian states, control of
  internet and digital technologies,
  225–8
Ayub, Fauzi, 35

Babar Khalsa, 74
Baratov, Karim, 164, 170–1
Barry, Donald, 328n82
"The Base" network, 40
Basij, 155
Bell¿ngcat site, 46–7, 226
Berger, J.M., 247–8
"berserking," 45
Bezrukov, Andrey (aka Don
  Heathfield), 103–4
Bill C-36 (2001). See *Anti-Terrorism Act*
Bill C-51 (2015), 91, 111
Bill C-59 (2017), 80, 92, 173–4, 256
biosurveillance, for pandemics,
  xi–xii

Bissonnette, Alexandre, 10, 46, 62
"Black Energy" cyberattack, 233
Blood and Honour, 38
Bogacheva, Anna, 249
Bombardier, in China, 130
border security in Canada, 81–2
Born, Jean François, 229
Borogan, Irina, 234
botnets and bots, 157, 159, 222–3,
  241, 245
Bourque, Justin, 19, 43–4
boycotts, by China, 127
Breivik, Anders, 45
Brik, Yevgeni Vladimirovich (aka
  David Soboloff), 99–100
Britain, and foreign-directed attacks
  in Canada, 56–7
Brunet, Gilles, 97, 109, 112
Bunn, Matt, 121, 122
business strategies theft, 119
Butina, Maria, 102
Byman, Daniel, 33

Calce, Michael, 172
Cambridge Analytica, 268, 270
Canada Border Services Agency
  (CBSA), role and responsibilities,
  284
Canada-China Foreign Investment
  Protection Agreement, 140
Canada Elections Act, 255
Canada-Wenzhou Friendship
  Society, 214
Canadian Armed Forces (CAF),
  disinformation campaign, 253–4
Canadian Association of University
  Teachers (CAUT), 211
Canadian Centre for Cyber Security,
  ix–x, 154, 168, 174–5, 272
Canadian Charter of Rights and
  Freedoms, 53, 79, 80

"Canadian extremist travellers" (CETS), 63. *See also* foreign fighters
Canadian Peace Congress, 192
Canadian Security Intelligence Service (CSIS or "the Service"): counter-intelligence activities, 92; and datasets, 173; on Delisle case, 105–6; "disruption" powers, 111, 113; and elections meddling, 252–3; and far-right extremism, 10, 47–8; on financing, 73; and foreign influence, 187, 212; industrial espionage, 117–18; intelligence collection, 91–2; intentions of extremists, 82; mandate, 5–6, 188, 349n11; role and responsibilities, 283; Sikh separatism, 24; on SOEs, 144; terminology changes, 48; trust in, 272. See also *CSIS Act*
Canadian Security Intelligence Service Act (*CSIS Act*), 5–6, 91–2, 110, 187, 188–9
Canadian-Soviet Friendship Society (CSFS), 193, 194–5
Carr, Sam, 95
charismatic leaders, and radicalization, 77
charities, and financing of violent extremism in Canada, 73–4
Charities Registration (Security Information) Act (2001), 72
Charlie Hebdo attack, 31, 74
Chen, Duanjie, 133
Cheng, Keding, 123
China: APTs, 166; control of internet and digital technologies, 225–6, 227; cybercrime in Canada, 178; cybersecurity laws and directives, 225–6; discrimination in business and retaliation, 125–31, 145; disinformation and COVID-19, x; dominance strategies, 125, 144–5; espionage (*see* China and espionage); foreign and trade policy, 125–7, 129; foreign influence (*see* China and foreign influence in person); and geoeconomics (*see* geoeconomics and China); and intellectual property (IP), 122–3, 131, 145, 176–7; investment strategies, 129–31; proxies for cyber-terrorism, 164; public accusation of cyberattacks, 119–20, 147–8; SOEs and companies (*see* state-owned enterprises [SOEs] in China); state-championed companies, 128, 140–3; threats to Canadians, 127–9; Uighurs' suppression, 183–4, 208–9, 210, 216, 217, 267
China and espionage: in Canada, 101–2; cyber-espionage, 120–1, 167, 176–7; economic espionage, 118; public accusation from Canada, 118–19
China and foreign influence in person: in community and institutions, 205; diaspora monitoring, 209–11; dissent silencing, 183–5, 204, 207–9; front groups, 204; media and newspapers, 189, 206–7, 215–16, 219; overview, 202–4, 215–16, 218–19; and political influence, 211–15, 325n54; and universities, 184, 204, 209–11
China Daily newspaper, 206
China Global Television Network (CGTN), 205, 206

China Radio International (CRI), 205, 206
Chinese Benevolent Association of Vancouver, 205
Chinese Communist Party (CCP), 124–5, 136–7, 202–3, 210
Chinese National Overseas Oil Corporation (CNOOC), 138–9
Chinese National Petroleum Corporation (CNPC), 138
Chinese Students and Scholars Associations (CSSAs), 204, 210
Chrétien, Jean, and government, 19–20
Christchurch (NZ) massacre perpetrator, 10, 46, 79, 268
"Christchurch Call," 268–9
Chuka, Neil, 229
"Church of the Creator," 37
Cirillo, Nathan, 17, 60
Citizenship Act, and spies, 103
clandestine foreign influence: online (*see* foreign influence [clandestine] and online); in person (*see* foreign influence [clandestine] and in-person)
clickbait, 236, 237, 240
climate change, xii–xiv
Clinton, Hillary, 221, 239, 244, 246, 248
Cold War: economic espionage, 117–18; espionage threats in Canada, 94–101; and foreign influence by Soviets, 190–5, 247, 248; and subversion, 108, 109; suspects in Canada, 108
Combat-18, 38, 54
Communications Security Establishment (CSE): cyber-espionage, 167; cyber-threats and COVID-19, x; and DND, 7; and elections, 252; and encryption, 181, 266; and Huawei, 142; industrial espionage, 117–18; intelligence collection and information assurance, 92–3; mandate, 92–3, 113, 345n91; powers, 174; role and responsibilities, 113, 283–4; trust in, 271. See also *Communications Security Establishment Act*
Communications Security Establishment Act (CSE Act), 92, 93, 173, 174
Communist Party of Canada (CPC), 195
Communists in Canada, 95–6, 97, 107–8, 192, 195
companies, 88, 89, 120–1, 207, 267–8. *See also* state-owned enterprises (SOEs) in China
Confucius Institutes, 210–11, 213, 217
Conservative Party. *See* Harper, Stephen, and government
conspiracy theories, x, 241–2, 243
Convention for the Suppression of Unlawful Acts against the Safety of Civil Aviation (1971), 19
Convention for the Suppression of Unlawful Seizure of Aircraft (1970), 19
Coulombe, Michel, 118–19
counterfeit goods sales, 74, 75
counter-intelligence (CI): activities and kinds, 90, 92; dark side, 106–10; and espionage, 89–90
Couture-Rouleau, Martin, 60, 68
COVID-19 pandemic: impact, xii; as national security threat, vii–viii, x–xi; security issues in, viii–x
"Creativity," 37

Crimea annexation, 233
Criminal Code: definition of terrorism, 20; facilitation of terrorist act, 70; financing of terrorism, 72; other terrorism aspects, 20–1; radicalization and speech, 80
Critical Election Incident Public Protocol, 257
critical infrastructure: cyberattacks and intrusions, 153–6, 159, 169; protection in Canada, 154, 174, 256
Cross, James, 22
Crown corporations in Canada, 132
cryptocurrencies, and cyber-terrorism, 161–2, 341n46
crypto-miners, 150
CSE. *See* Communications Security Establishment
CSIS. *See* Canadian Security Intelligence Service
CSIS Act. See *Canadian Security Intelligence Service Act*
Cubans, anti-Castro, 22
cyber and cyber realm: components, 149; concept and nature of, 148–9, 182; ethics in, 181–2; policy in Canada, 148, 173–9; proxies, 162–4, 180; as threat to national security, 148, 149, 181–2; understanding by Canadians, 179
cyberattacks and cyber-intrusions/incidents: attribution and response in Canada, 147–8, 178, 179; consequences, 154–5, 156, 158–9; and critical infrastructure, 153–6, 159, 169; DDoS attacks, 156–9, 163; description, 149–50; malware, 150–3, 154, 155–6, 158–9, 170; as national security threats, 147–8; public accusation of China, 119–20, 147–8; by specific countries, 155, 156, 180, 233; targets and trends in Canada, 172–3; and technical sophistication, 160; and terrorism, 159–64; types and examples, 150–9

cybercrime: in Canada, 169–70, 171–5, 178; description and examples, 164, 168–9, 170–1, 233
cyber-espionage: agreements, 176–9; and Canada, 167; cases and APTs, 165–6; against companies, 120–1; description and role, 164–5; and politics, 248
cybersecurity: and COVID-19 pandemic, ix–x; and diplomacy, 176–9; and future technologies, 180–1; and internet, 179–80, 182; laws in China, 225–6
cybersecurity in Canada: challenges and trends, 179–82; institutions, 169–70, 174–5; international component, 176–9; law and legislation, 173–4; and national security, 147–8, 173–4; new strategies and policies, 175–6; offensive (active) powers of CSE, 174; in telecommunications infrastructure, 141–3
Cyberspace Administration of China (CAC), 225
cyber-terrorism: proxies, 162–4; and violent extremism, 159–62
cyber-threats: and COVID-19 pandemic, ix–x; states and actors, 149, 155, 163

dark_nexus botnet, 159
data management, 261, 266

data mass-harvesting, 270
data privacy and access, 266–71
Dbouk, Mohammed, 35
DDoS attacks (distributed denial of service), 156–9, 163
"debtbook diplomacy," 126
"deep fakes," 259, 265
Delisle, Jeffrey Paul, 87, 104–6, 121
democracy, threats to, 11, 270–1
Democratic National Committee (DNC) hacking, 188, 248
Deng Xiaoping, 133
Department of Homeland Security (DHS; in United States), ix
Department of Justice (Canada), role and responsibilities, 286
Department of National Defence (Canada): cybersecurity, 175–6; and intelligence, 93–4; in Nortel Campus, 116; role and responsibilities, 7, 286
diaspora (monitoring) and foreign influence, 189, 195–6, 198, 200, 209–11, 214, 215
digital technologies and states, 224–5, 227–8. *See also* internet
diplomacy and diplomats, 98, 176–9
Direct Action group, 50
Dirie, Ali Mohammed, 69
Discord app, 41–2
disinformation: and alt-right, 238–40, 243–4; campaigns in Canada, 253–6; and conspiracy theories, 241–2, 243; and COVID-19, x–xi; to discredit United States by Soviet Union, 193–4; in election of 2016 in United States, 246, 247, 248; and elections, 223; and human agency, 244–5; impact on behaviour, 223; and "junk news," 236–7; and national security, 246; online by Russia, 222, 227–8, 240–4, 245; policy in Canada, 256–7; as propaganda in foreign influence, 193–5, 198–9, 205–6; on specific social media, 235, 240, 241, 247, 255, 257–8; tracking and "deep fakes," 258–9; on Ukraine by Russia, 233–4, 253
dissent silencing and foreign influence, 183–5, 197–8, 204, 207–9
domestic attacks in Canada, 59
Douglas, Tommy, 108
Driver, Aaron, 61, 315n24
Dyn registry service attack, 158

economic espionage: cyber-espionage, 120–1; description, 88, 89, 117; goals, 119–20; insider threats, 121–3; Nortel case, 115–16; public accusation from Canada, 118–19; as threat, 117–19, 123
"economic statecraft," 124. *See also* geoeconomics and China
Economist, and SOEs in China, 134, 136
economy and national security: and cybersecurity, 147; description and overview, 11, 116–17, 143–4, 146; economic espionage (*see* economic espionage); forced technology transfer, 130; geoeconomics, 124–31; and investment in Canada, 137–43; Nortel example, 115–16; as problem in Canada, 144–6
Edmund Burke Society, 36
El Bahnasawy, Abdulrahman, 58
election of 2016 in United States: meddling and foreign influence

by Russia, 11, 188, 221, 244, 246–50; right-wing aspects, 37–8, 223
elections: and disinformation, 223; foreign influence, 11, 213, 214, 218; meddling in Canada, 252–3, 254, 255–7; past examples of meddling, 250–1; protection in Canada, 256–7
Elections Canada, 256
Elections Modernization Act (2018), 270
empathy, as response to national security threats, xiv–xv, 4, 16, 263, 279
encryption and encrypted apps, 84–5, 181, 265–6; "back door" to, 84, 267
Endicott, James, 192
enforcement agencies in Canada, 284
environment, 51, 53
espionage: in Cold War in Canada, 94–101; and counter-intelligence, 89–90; and COVID-19 pandemic, ix–x; cyber-espionage (*see* cyber-espionage); defence intelligence in Canada, 93–4; Delisle case, 87, 104–6; description and background, 88, 89, 90, 164; economic (*see* economic espionage); foreign threats today in Canada, 101–2, 110; ideological motivation, 95–7; industrial espionage, 117–18; information assurance, 93; intelligence collection in Canada, 90–4; legal and illegal Soviet spies, 98–101, 102–4; for money, 97; partnerships of Canada, 90–1, 106; recent cases in Canada, 87–8, 103–6; review of activities, 111, 112–13; and subversion, 107–11; traditional form, 88–9, 94
Esseghaier, Chiheb, 58
Estonia, and DDoS attack, 157
ethics in cyber realm, 181–2
exploits, 151, 154, 170
export bans on Canadian products by China, 126–7

Facebook: and disinformation, 235, 247, 255, 257–8; and privacy, 268, 269
facilitation and facilitators, 70–1
Fadden, Richard, 101, 118, 212, 325n54
"fake news," 236–7, 238, 240, 253
family, and lone actors' intentions, 82–3
"Fancy Bear" group, 248
far-left extremism: description and characteristics, 48–9, 51; history in Canada, 49–51; as threat, 49, 50; and violent extremism in Canada today, 48–51
far-right extremism: in Canada, 36–7, 38–40, 47; and COVID-19 pandemic, viii; definition, 36; description and beliefs, 36, 45; internet and social media, 41–3; and national security in Canada, 45, 47–8, 54; online content detection and deletion, 268–9; rise in, 37–40; self-referencing and influence, 10, 44, 46–7; as threat, 9–10; violence mobilization, 45–6; and violent extremism in Canada today, 36–48
far-right supporters: and disinformation, 238–40, 243–4; influence from Russia, 251; and memes, 237–8

Featherstone, Bower, 97
Federal Bureau of Investigation (FBI), 48, 120, 171
federal government and departments: and cybercrime, 168; cyber-espionage, 167, 177; cyber policy and strategy, 173–9, 182; decisions for businesses, 144; and foreign influence campaigns online, 255–7; and national security in Canada, 110, 111, 114, 281–2, 286–7; policy recommendations, 275–9; protection of Canadians, 3–4; support to victims of foreign influence, 216–18; trust in, 271. *See also specific departments; specific prime ministers*
Federation of Associations of Canadian Tamils (FACT), 197, 199, 300n26
Ferizi, Ardit, 160, 161
finance and violent extremism in Canada: charities in, 73–4; criminal means, 74–5; fundraising, 71; international treaties, 71–2; kidnapping for ransom, 75–6; legitimate means, 73; prosecutions and prevention, 72–3, 74
Financial Action Task Force (FATF), 71, 72
Financial Times, 212–13
Financial Transactions and Reports Analysis Centre of Canada (FINTRAC), 72, 285
FireEye firm, 177
5G network in Canada, 141, 142–3
"Five Eyes" partners, 87
Flame (aka Wiper) virus, 154
Foley, Tracey (real name Elena Vavilova), 103–4

forced technology transfers by China, 130
Forcese, Craig, 4, 188
foreign-approved plots in violent extremism in Canada, 58–9
foreign-directed attacks in violent extremism in Canada, 56–7
foreign direct investment (FDI), and China, 125–6
foreign fighters (Canadian extremist travellers): description and activities, 63; detection, 68; estimates for Canada, 30, 64; joining groups abroad, 9, 63–6; prevention from leaving Canada, 66–7, 68, 69–70; radicalization, 77; return to Canada, 30, 67–8; as threat in Canada, 10, 30, 69–70
foreign influence (clandestine) and in-person: by China in Canada (*see* China and foreign influence in person); and COVID-19 pandemic, x–xi; and cyber activity, 171–3; definition in Canada, 187–8; description and understanding of, 185–7, 188–9; history in Canada, 185, 189–202; by India in Canada, 200–2, 214; by Iran in Canada, 199–200; in law and policy of Canada, 187–9; by LTTE in Canada, 195–9; as national security, 185, 187, 189; not hidden, 189, 213; by Soviets in Canada and Cold War, 190–5, 247, 248; and threats to persons, 189, 196, 197–8, 202, 207, 208, 216; today in Canada, 183–5, 202, 215–19; victims support, 216–18
foreign influence (clandestine) and online: in Canada, 252–7, 259; election of 2016 in United States, 188, 221, 244, 246–50; future

of, 250–3, 255–9; and hybrid
warfare, 228–34; and like-minded
communities, 234–40, 246; as mix
of online and human work, 249,
250; and national security, 223–4,
227–8, 246, 254; new actors, 255,
258; overview and impact, 221–2,
223; policy in Canada, 256–7; by
Russia (*see* Russia and foreign
influence online); and social media,
222–3, 234–5, 257–8; successes by
exploiting trends, 240–4
foreign investment. *See* investment
Foreign Investment Review Act (*FIRA*;
1974), 138
foreign policy, and geoeconomics,
125–7
4chan/8chan boards, 41, 239
France, and elections meddling, 250
Freedom House report, 227
Freeland, Chrystia, 254, 275
Freeman-on-the-Land, 43
free-speech, and radicalization in
Canada, 79–81
Fridman, Ofer, 232
Friedman, Allan, 155
Front de Libération du Québec
(FLQ), 3, 21–2, 49
front groups for foreign influence,
192–3, 196, 204
FSB and Centre for Information
Security (Russia), 171

G7 countries, and cybersecurity,
178–9
G7 "Rapid Reaction Mechanism"
(RRM), 256
Galeotti, Mark, 232
Gap Inc., and China, 207
Garratt, Kevin, and Julia, 129
General Data Protection Law
(GDPR), 270

Gentzkow, Matthew, 237
geoeconomics and China: China's
vision, 124–5, 143–5; description
and as tool, 124, 131, 143; foreign
and trade policy, 125–7; and
Huawei, 140–3; and investment,
129–31, 135–6, 137–9, 144–5; and
national security in Canada,
139–46; and state owned
enterprises (SOEs), 131–7, 143;
threats to Canadians, 127–9
Georgia, and DDoS attack,
157–8, 159
Gerasimov, Valery, 232
Germany, and elections meddling,
250–1
Global Affairs Canada (GAC), 176,
256, 286–7
Globe and Mail, message boards and
far-right extremism, 41–2
Godson, Roy, 191
Goldy, Faith, 42
Gouzenko, Igor, and classified
documents, 94–5, 96
"Great Firewall of China," 225
group polarization, and
radicalization, 77–8
"Guardians of Peace" hackers, 156

Habib, Ismael, 75
hackers and hacking: charges in
United States, 160; cyber-theft of
information, 120–1; and DDoS,
157; in election of 2016 in United
States, 188, 248; examples, 156,
165; and Nortel collapse, 115–16;
as problem, 179–80; as proxies for
cyber-terrorism, 164
Halifax Security Forum hashtag,
161, 231
Hambleton, Hugh, 96–7
Hampel, Paul William, 104

Hanban/Confucius Institute Headquarters, 211
Haouari, Mokhtar, 75
Harper, Stephen, and government: cybersecurity and cyber-espionage, 178; and Delisle case, 106; extremist travel from Canada, 64; intelligence agency creation, 91; SOEs of China, 139; and subversion, 111; terrorism speech offence, 80
hashtags, and cyber-terrorism, 161
Hassan, Hassan el Hajj, 35, 64
hate crimes, and COVID-19, viii
Hayat Tahrir al-Sham (HTS), 32, 296n24
Hayden, Michael, 244
Heathfield, Don (real name Andrey Bezrukov), 103–4
health intelligence, issues in, xi–xii
HIV/AIDS and disinformation, 194
Hizballah, 34–5, 74, 75, 230
Hoffman, Frank, 228–9, 230
Hongwei, Wang, 122–3
House of Commons Standing Committee on Access to Information, Privacy and Ethics, 270, 271
House of Commons Standing Committee on Finance (2015), 72–3
Huang, Qing Quentin, 122
Huawei technologies, 128, 140–3
Human Concern International (HCI), 73, 318n60
human resources, and information theft, 120, 122
Human Rights Watch, and foreign influence, 197–8, 210
human sources (HUMINT) in espionage, 89

Hurras al-Din (Guardians of Religion Organization), 32
hybrid warfare: concept and role, 228–30, 232, 233; and non-state actors, 230–2; and Russia, 232–4

illegal and legal Soviet spies, 98–101, 102–4
"Incel" (involuntary celibate) subculture, 44, 296n25
India, 102, 200–2, 214
industrial espionage, 117–18
information assurance, 93
information theft, and Nortel collapse, 115–16
Infowars website, 243
Initiative de Résistance Internationaliste (IRI), 50
insiders, definition and types, 121, 122
insider threats, 121–3, 152
Integrated Terrorism Assessment Centre (ITAC), role and responsibilities, 285
intellectual property (IP): acquisition by China, 131, 145; theft, 119, 122–3, 176–7
intelligence analysis bodies in Canada, 285
intelligence analysts, work and reality, 261–2
Intelligence Commissioner (Canada), role and responsibilities, 113, 287
International Convention against the Taking of Hostages (1979), 19
International Convention for the Suppression of the Financing of Terrorism (1999), 71, 72
internet: control by state, 225–7, 234; for cybercrime, 168; and

cybersecurity, 179–80, 182; DDoS attacks, 156–9; disruptive power, 224–5; and far-right extremism, 41–3; message boards and chatrooms, 41–2; and offline tactics, 249–50; podcasts, 42; and radicalization, 78–9; regulation of speech, 268–9; surveillance by authorities, 54. *See also* social media
"internet of things" and cybersecurity, 179–80
"Internet Research Agency" in Russia, 234, 241, 244, 249–50
"internet sovereignty," 227
investment: and geoeconomics of China, 129–31, 135–6, 137–9, 144–5; and national security in Canada, 137–43; policies in Canada, 137–8
Investment Canada Act (*ICA*; 1985), 138
Iran, 155, 180, 199–200, 255
Iranian nuclear program, 154
Irish Fenians, 21
'Isa, Faruq Khalil Muhammad, 27
Isikoff, Michael, 243–4
Islamic State (ISIS) and caliphate: cyber-terrorism, 160, 161–2; description and activities, 29–31; and extremist travel, 65, 66; facilitation, 70–1; foreign fighters returning, 30; hybrid warfare and social media, 230–2; as inspiration, 25–8; internet use, 27; Paris attack of 2015, 55; as threat, 9, 29, 33, 66; and violent extremism in Canada today, 29–31, 33
Islamic State–inspired extremism, 25–6

Jabarah, Mohammed Mansour, 27, 77
Jabhat al-Nusra (JN), 31–2
Jade Helm conspiracy, 241–2, 244
James, Jahmaal, 34
Japan, boycotts by China, 127
Jean, Daniel, 273
Johnson, David, 109
joint ventures in China, 129–30
"junk news," 236–7, 238, 240, 253
Jurman, Inga (aka Ingalore Moerke), 100
Justice Commandos of the Armenian Genocide (JCAG), 23

Kamel, Fateh, 26
Katsiroubas, Xristos, 64
Khadr, Ahmed Said, 26, 73, 318n60
Khan, Aabid, 34
Khawaja, Mohammad Momin, 27, 70
kidnapping for ransom (KFR), 75–6
kill lists, and cyber-terrorism, 161
Klassen, Ben, 37
Kneschke, Rudolf, 100
Kovrig, Michael, 128
Krebs, Brian, 158
Krylova, Aleksandra, 249
Ku Klux Klan, 36–7

La Meute, 38, 305n98
Lanoszka, Alexander, 223
Laporte, Pierre, 22
Larsen, Jeffrey A., 229
Lasconjarias, Guillaume, 229
Latvia, and CAF mission, 253
Lavrov, Sergei, 251
law and legislation: charges of terrorism in Canada, 10, 28, 52; and cybersecurity, 173–4, 225–6; and foreign influence in Canada, 187–9; and national security in Canada, 112–13, 270–1; and social

law and legislation (*continued*)
  media, 269–70; and subversion, 111; and term "national security," 4; and terrorism in Canada, 19–20, 52–3. *See also specific acts*
Lebanon War (2006), 230
legal and illegal Soviet spies, 98–101, 102–4
Lewis, Rebecca, 239
LGBT2Q persons, and violence, 45
Lhamo, Chemi, 184, 208
Liberal Party of Canada, political donations, 213
Liberation Tigers of Tamil Eelam or "Tamil Tigers" (LTTE), 24–5, 74, 195–9
lone-actor attacks: attack planning, 59–63; and connections, 59–60; description and targets, 45–6, 60; examples in Canada, 60–2; intent mentioned to family, 82–3; key points for Canada, 62–3; and mental health, 84; and national security in Canada, 54; and radicalization, 79
Lowenthal, Mark, 89–90
Ludwig, Wiebo, 51, 311n166

MacDonald Commission (1977), 108
machine learning, 264–5
Made in China 2025 strategy, 125
Mahar, Donald G., 97
Malaysia Airlines Flight MH17, 242–3
malware, 150–3, 154, 155–6, 158–9, 170
marginalized groups, seen as threats, xiv
Marwick, Alice, 239
Mathews, Patrik, 40
Maurer, Tim, 160, 162–3, 164
May, Alan Nunn, 95, 96

McCants, William, 65
McMaster University, and foreign influence by China, 183–4, 204, 211
"Media Operative, You Are a Mujahid, Too" (Islamic State), 231
Medlej, Ali, 64
memes, 237–8
Meng Wanzhou case, 126–8, 143, 147–8
mental health, and violent extremism, 83–4
message boards, 41–2
Minassian, Alek, 44, 78
Minecraft game, 158
Minister of Industry, and SOEs of China, 139–40
Ministry of State Security (China), 147–8
"Mirai" malware, 158–9
Mitrokhin, Vasili, 100
Mojahedin-e Khalq (People's Mujahedeen of Iran, or MEK), 199–200
Molody, Konon (aka Gordon Arnold Lonsdale), 99
money laundering, 71
Morris, William, 151
Morrison, James, 99–100
Morris Worm, 151
Mueller Report (United States), 246, 247, 360n23
Mulroney, Brian, and government, 138
Mulroney, David, 145, 209, 214

Nagle, Angela, 238–9, 240
Namouh, Said, 27, 58
narrow artificial intelligence, 264–5
National Cybercrime Coordination Unit (RCMP), 169–70, 174

National Cyber Security Strategy, 176
National Intelligence Coordination Centre (RCMP), 88
National Microbiology Lab (NML), 123
National Research Council, and cyber-espionage, 167, 178
national security: agencies, xi, xiii–xiv, 82–3; in Canada (*see* national security in Canada); concept and definition, 4–6; and COVID-19 as threat, vii–viii, x–xi; cyber as threat, 148, 149, 181–2; and cybercrime, 168–9; and data management, 261, 266; data privacy and access, 266–71; and defence issues, 6–7; and disinformation, 246; and economy (*see* economy and national security); future of, 264–70; mandate, 246; and quantum computing, 181; and radicalization, 79–80; and reporters, 8, 272–3; and social media, 268–70; and social trends, 11; and technology, 264–6; threats (*see* national security threats); understanding by public and politicians, 262–3, 276–7; writings on in Canada, 6–8
National Security and Intelligence Committee of Parliamentarians (NSICOP): briefings of officials, 276; and foreign influence, 187–8, 217–18; and institutional culture, 113; public accusation of espionage, 119; reports, 272; role and responsibilities, 112, 113, 287
national security and intelligence community in Canada:

challenges, 18; encryption and encrypted apps, 84–5; future of, 276, 277–8; institutional culture, 112, 113; knowledge of, 272; mandates, 5, 277; national security work, 271, 277–8, 283–4; outreach and media, 276; public understanding of, 8, 262, 263; radicalization and free speech, 80, 81; response to global issues, xiii, 278–9; and transnational terrorism, 28; transparency and issues, 11–12, 272, 276–7; trust in, 271–2
National Security and Intelligence Review Agency (NSIRA), role and responsibilities, 112–13, 288
national security in Canada: agencies' work in, 271, 277–8, 283–4; architecture of, 173–4, 276, 281–8; areas of violent extremist activities, 55–6; and cooperation, 278–9; cybersecurity and policy, 147–8, 173–4; and far-right extremism, 45, 47–8, 54; and federal government, 110, 111, 114, 281–2, 286–7; future of, 269–79; and institutional culture, 112, 113; intelligence analysts, 261–2; and investment by Chinese companies, 137–43; law and legislation, 112–13, 270–1; and media, 272–3, 277; oversight and review bodies, 112–13, 287–8; and trust, 271–3; understanding by public and politicians, 262, 263, 276–7; and world order, 273–5. *See also* national security and intelligence community in Canada
national security threats: and changing world, 8–12, 263–4,

national security threats (*continued*) 279; and civil liberties, 3; and cyberattacks, 147–8; reports in Canada, 272; securitization of issues, 15; understanding and empathy, xiv–xv, 4, 16, 263, 279; understanding by public, 179, 263, 277
National Security Transparency Commitment, 276
neo-Nazis in Canada, 37, 38, 40
newsfeeds on social media, 235, 236–7
New York Times, 46, 165, 206, 251
Nexen purchase, 138–9
Nielsen, Klaus, 122
Norman, E. Herbert, 109, 328n82
Nortel Campus, 116
Nortel collapse, and hackers, 115–16
Northern Neighbours, 195
North Korea, 156, 169
NotPetya ransomware/attack, 170, 233

oil sands, 138–40
Olshanskaya, Yelena/Elena (aka Laurie Lambert), 102
Olshanskiy, Dmitriy (aka Ian Lambert), 102
online activity. *See* internet
online foreign influence. *See* foreign influence (clandestine) and online
Operation Infektion, 194
Ortis, Cameron, 88
oversight and review bodies in national security in Canada, 112–13, 287–8
Owen, Taylor, 224–5
Oxford Internet Institute, 236, 239

pandemics: biosurveillance, xi–xii; as security issues, x–xi, xiii–xiv. *See also* COVID-19 pandemic

Paris attack (2015), 55
passive insider, 122
passports, 69, 101
Patriotic Europeans against the Islamization of the West (PEGIDA), 38–9
People's Daily, 206
Pepe the Frog, 237–8
Perry, Barbara, 36
Personal Information Protection and Electronic Documents Act, 270
personal information theft, 119, 120, 121
persona non grata (PNG), 98
Petrovich, Gennadiy (aka Peter Fischer), 100
phishing, 152, 166
podcasts, 42
political donations, 213–14, 358n130
political influence and foreign influence, 198–202, 211–15, 325n54
political parties, links for foreign influence, 195
politicians, 254, 262, 276–7
Pomerantsev, Peter, 242, 243
Pontecorvo, Bruno, 96
post-quantum cryptography (PQC), 266
Potash Corp., theft of information, 121
Prigozhin, Yevgeniy Viktorovich, 247
Prime Minister's Office (PMO), role and responsibilities, 281–2
privacy protection, 12, 181, 267–8
private sector, 88, 89, 120–1, 207, 267–8
Privy Council Office (PCO), role and responsibilities, 282
product bans, by China, 126–7
Project Feather Bed, 108

Project Lakhta, 247
propaganda for foreign influence, 193–5, 198–9, 205–6
proxies, 155, 162–4, 180, 258
public order threats, vs. national security, 47
Public Report (CSIS, 2018), 24
Public Report on the Terrorist Threat to Canada (PSC, 2018), 24, 272
Public Safety Canada (PSC): extremist travel from Canada, 64; and foreign fighters, 30; listed terrorist entities, 38; role and responsibilities, 282–3; Sikh separatism, 24; and transparency, 276
Putin, Vladimir, 226, 233

Qiu, Xiangguo, 123
quantum computing, 180–1, 265–6
quantum resistance cryptography (QRC), 181, 266
Qutb, Sayyid, 26

Raddatz, Norman Walter, 43
radical environmentalism, 51
radicalization to violent extremism in Canada: description and process, 76–7; and free speech, 79–81; hybrid means, 79; in person, 77–8, 79; online, 78–9
radical left. *See* far-left extremism
"RAHOWA" or "racial holy war," 37
ransomware, 168, 169, 170, 173
"Rapid Reaction Mechanism" (RRM), 256
Royal Canadian Mounted Police (RCMP): attack against, 19, 43–4; and cybercrime, 169–70, 174–5; and far-left extremism, 49; and financing of violent extremism in Canada, 72–3, 74;

and foreign influence, 193; institutional culture, 112; internal espionage case, 87–8; role and responsibilities in national security, 91, 112, 284; and subversion, 107, 108–9, 111
Red Scare, 89, 107, 110, 190
"remote controlled" plots and actors, 58–9, 60
reporters, on national security in Canada, 8, 272–3
Résistance Internationaliste (RI), 50
Ressam, Ahmed, 27, 75
returnees, 30, 67–8
Rich, Seth, 244
right-wing media, and election of 2016 in United States, 223
Roach, Kent, 81
Rodger, Elliot, 44
Roof, Dylann, 46, 62
Rose, Fred, 95
Royal Commission on National Development in the Arts, Letters and Sciences (Massey Commission), 190
Royal Commission on Security (the Mackenzie Commission), 101
RT (formerly Russia Today) network, 233–4, 241, 242, 243, 244, 254
Russia: APTs, 166; control of internet and digital technologies, 226–8, 234; cyberattacks and cybercrime, 156, 170, 171, 178, 233; cyber-espionage, 248; cybersecurity laws, 226; DDoS attacks, 157–8, 159; and Delisle case, 87; espionage in Canada and United States, 87, 102–5; foreign influence (*see* Russia and foreign influence online); and hybrid warfare, 232–4; and MH17, 243;

Russia (*continued*)
proxies for cyber-terrorism, 164; and Ukraine, 233–4, 253. *See also* Soviet Union
Russia and foreign influence online: in Canada, 252, 253–6; and conspiracy theories, 241–2; COVID-19 disinformation, x; division and confusion, 242–4, 254–6, 258; meddling in 2016 U.S. election, 11, 188, 221, 244, 246–50; as mix of online and human work, 249, 250; online disinformation, 222, 227–8, 240–4, 245; past examples of elections meddling, 250–1; and social media, 222–3, 234, 240–1, 254–6; Ukraine disinformation, 233–4, 253
Russian Foreign Intelligence Service (Sluzhba Vneshney Razvedki or SVR), 102

Sagan, Scott D., 121, 122
Salisbury (UK) chemical weapon attack, 258
Sarai, Randeep Singh, 201
Saudi Arabia, 255
Scrivens, Ryan, 36
securitization, 15
security certificates, 81, 104
Security Council resolutions on financing, 71–2
Security of Information Act, 106
Security Review Program of CSE, 142
"the Service." *See* Canadian Security Intelligence Service
Shahnaz, Zoobia, 161–2
Shamoon virus, 155
Sharif, Abdulahi Hasan, 10, 61
Shultz, Richard H., 191
signals intelligence (SIGINT), 89

Sikh separatism, 21, 23–4
Sikhs in Canada, and foreign influence, 200–1
Singer, P.W., 155
single-issue extremism, 9–10, 36, 43, 44
"single narrative," 26, 29
skinhead movement, 37
Snowden leaks, 262
social engineering, and malware, 152
social media: and far-right extremism, 42–3; and foreign influence, 222–3, 234–5, 257–8; and foreign influence by Russia, 222–3, 234, 240–1, 254–6; and hybrid warfare, 231–2; laws, 269–70; and like-minded communities, 234–40; memes and GIFs, 237–8; and national security, 268–70; news and quality of content, 235, 236–7, 238, 240; and opinions and beliefs, 235–6, 238, 240. *See also* internet
social trends, and national security, 11
Soldatov, Andrei, 234
Soldiers of Odin (SOO), 39
Sons of Freedom, 21
Sony Pictures Entertainment, cyberattack, 156
Soufan Group, 69
South Asian community, and foreign influence, 255
South Asian extremism, 21, 23–4
Southern, Laura, 42
Soviet Union: "active measures," 190–1, 193; disinformation to discredit United States, 193–4; espionage in Canada, 94–7; foreign influence in Canada in Cold War, 190–5, 247, 248; legal

and illegal Soviet spies, 98–101, 102–4. *See also* Russia
Spavor, Michael, 128
spear-phishing, 152
"speech crime," 80–1
speech regulation, on internet, 268–9
Spencer, George Victor, 96
Sri Lanka conflict, 24–5
Standing Senate Committee on Banking, Trade and Commerce report, 171
state-owned enterprises (SOEs) in China: and corruption, 133–4; description and use of, 131–2, 135–7, 143; economic role, 133, 134–5, 137; and geoeconomics of China, 131–7, 143; history, 132–4; and investment in Canada, 135–6, 137, 138–9; and national security in Canada, 138–40, 143, 144
states: cyber-espionage, 164–5, 166; cyber-incidents and threats, 149, 155, 163; cybersecurity, 176–9; and digital technologies, 224–5, 227–8; and geoeconomics, 124; internet control, 225–7, 234; proxies for cyber-terrorism, 162–4; regulation of violent extremist content, 268–9. *See also specific states*
Stavropoulos, Alexander, 44
Stormfront, 41
"Strong, Secure, Engaged" defence strategy, 175–6
Stuxnet virus, 154–5
Su Bin, 121, 129
subversion: abuses in, 110–11; description as issue, 107, 109–10; suspects monitoring in Canada, 107–10, 111

supervisory control and data acquisition (SCADA) systems, cyberattacks, 154
Sweden, influence of far-right groups, 251
Syria, proxies for cyber-terrorism, 163
Syria conflict, and extremist travel, 64, 65, 66
Syrian Electronic Army (SEA), and cyber-terrorism, 160–1, 163

Tamil Tigers. *See* Liberation Tigers of Tamil Eelam (LTTE)
technology: forced transfers, 130; and national security, 264–6; and violent extremism, 84–5. *See also specific technologies*
telecommunications infrastructure and China, 141–3
terrorism: as charge, 48; and cyberattacks, 159–64; definition and use of term, 18–20, 53; forms and evolution, 9–10, 55, 84; "gamification," 46–7; international treaties and instruments, 19–20; as international trend, 9–10, 81, 86; listed terrorist entities, 38, 40; range of actions, 55–6; as source of violent extremism in Canada, 21–2; support for victims, 54. *See also* violent extremism
terrorism in Canada: charges, 10, 28, 52; facilitation, 70; history, 21–2, 25; law and legislation, 19–20, 52–3; legal definition, 20–1, 53; listed terrorist entities, 38, 53–4; terminology at CSIS, 48; as threat, 147; transnational terrorism, 22–5, 26. *See also* violent extremism in Canada

terrorist groups/organizations: Canadians joining in, 9, 63–6; definition in Canada, 20; as threat today, 9. *See also specific groups*
Texas fake annexation, 242
This Hour Has 88 Minutes podcast, 42
III% (Three Percenters), 39–40
Tibetans in China and Canada, 184, 204, 208
Tibet Association of Canada, 204
Toronto Eighteen, 28, 34, 59
Toronto van attack, 44, 238
trade policy, and geoeconomics of China, 125–7, 129
Translator Project, 247
transnational (or "spillover") terrorism: as concern, 28; definition and use of term, 22, 25; examples in Canada, 22–5, 26–8
transparency, 11–12, 272, 276–7
travel for extremist purposes, 63–8
treaties and international instruments, 19–20, 71–2
trojans, 151
trolls and troll farms, in Russia, 234
Trudeau, Justin, and government, 91, 92, 169–70, 175–6, 201
Trudeau, Pierre, and government, 3, 110, 111, 138
Trump, Donald, 37–8, 221, 246, 274–5
"Trumpism," 274–5
trust, 82, 271–3
Turdush, Rukiye, 183–4
TV5 (France) cyberattack, 156, 166
Twitter: cyber-terrorism, 160–1, 232; news, 236, 238; and Russian disinformation, 240, 247

Uighurs and Canada, 183–4, 208–9, 210, 216, 217, 267

Ukraine, 158, 170, 233–4, 243, 253
unauthorized access, as malware, 153
"United Cyber Caliphate," 161
United Front Work Department (UFW) of China, and foreign influence, 202, 203–4, 210, 212–13
United Nations Security Council resolutions on financing, 71–2
United States: COVID-19 and cyber-threats, ix; cultural influence in Canada, 190; cyber-espionage, 120, 121, 177; cyber-terrorism, 160–2; disinformation by Soviet Union, 193–4; election of 2016 (*see* election of 2016 in United States); espionage by Russia, 102–3; extremist threats, 48; far-right extremism rise, 37–8; far-right extremist content online, 269; infected hardware, 152–3; IP theft from China, 122–3; and Meng Wanzhou, 128; ransomware, 168–9; Red Scare, 107; terrorism finance charges, 74, 75
universities, 142, 184, 204, 209–11
University of Calgary, delisting by China, 127, 209, 218
USB flash drive infection, 152–3
U.S. State Department, listed terrorist entities, 40

Vavilov, Alex, and Tim, 103
Vavilova, Elena (aka Tracey Foley), 103–4
Via Rail plot (2013), 58, 59
Vigneault, David, 10, 147
Vincent, Patrice, 60
violent extremism: and COVID-19 pandemic, viii; and cyber-terrorism, 159–62; description and use of term, 18–19; and

emerging technologies, 84–5; evolving nature, 10, 54, 85, 263–4; intentions of extremists, 82–3; and mental health, 83–4; regulation of content, 268–9; support for victims, 54, 82. *See also* terrorism

violent extremism in Canada: Al Qaida and Islamic State, 29–33; attack planning, 56–63; border security, 81–2; Canada as target, 56–7, 63; charges, 52; facilitation, 70–1; and far-left extremism, 48–51; far-right and single-issue extremism, 36–48; finance and financing, 71–6; history, 21–2; homegrown, 62, 81; and hostile state actors, 33–6; inspiration for, 25–8; overview today, 28–9, 51–2, 55–6, 81–3, 86; radicalization, 76–81; range of actions, 55–6; sources, 21–8; terminology changes at CSIS, 48; travel for extremist purposes, 63–70. *See also* terrorism in Canada

violent insider, 122
virus on computers, 150, 154–5
"Voice of China," 206
vulnerabilities in software, 151

WannaCry ransomware, 169
War Memorial attack, 17
Wasaga Beach (ON), and ransomware, 169
Watkins, John, 109
Watts, Clint, 244, 247–8
WeChat messaging app, 183, 184, 214, 255
Weisburd, Andrew, 247–8
Weiss, Michael, 242, 243
West, Leah, 188
"Western Guard," 36

"whaling," 152
WhatsApp, 255–6
Whitaker, R., and colleagues, 97, 98–9, 108, 112
white supremacists, and internet, 41
Wikileaks, 248
Wilkie, Robert, 229
"Wimmins Fire Brigade," 50
Winter, Charlie, 162, 231
World Health Organization (WHO), cyber-threats and COVID-19, ix
World Peace Council, 192
World Tamil Movement (WTM), 24–5, 74, 196
"Worldwide Threat Assessment of the U.S. Intelligence Community," 120
worms on computers, 150–1

Xi Jinping: and foreign influence, 203; and Huawei, 128, 140; and innovation, 131; and SOEs, 134; vision for China, 125
Xinhua News Service, 205–6

Yahoo Mail, and cybercrime, 164, 171
"Yellow Vest" movement, 39
Yellow Vests in Canada, 39, 45
YouTube, and disinformation, 241
Yu, Wei Ling, 122
Yusufzai, Hasibullah, 69

al Zawahiri, Ayman, 31, 32
Zehaf-Bibeau, Michael, 17–18, 60–1, 68, 314n17
Zemenek, Ludek (aka Rudolf Adolf Herrmann), 100
"zero day" vulnerabilities and exploits, 151
ZeuS/Zbot Trojan, 151
Ziegler, Ingeborg, 100